Dynasty:
The Hereditary
Succession Politics
of North Korea

DYNASTY

The Hereditary

Succession Politics

of North Korea

by Kim Hakjoon

The Walter H. Shorenstein
Asia-Pacific Research Center
Stanford University

THE WALTER H. SHORENSTEIN ASIA-PACIFIC RESEARCH CENTER
(Shorenstein APARC) is a unique Stanford University institution focused on the
interdisciplinary study of contemporary Asia. Shorenstein APARC's mission is to
produce and publish outstanding interdisciplinary, Asia-Pacific–focused research;
to educate students, scholars, and corporate and governmental affiliates; to
promote constructive interaction to influence U.S. policy toward the Asia-Pacific;
and to guide Asian nations on key issues of societal transition, development,
U.S.-Asia relations, and regional cooperation.

The Walter H. Shorenstein Asia-Pacific Research Center
Freeman Spogli Institute for International Studies
Stanford University
Encina Hall
Stanford, CA 94305-6055
tel. 650-723-9741
fax 650-723-6530
http://aparc.stanford.edu

Dynasty: The Hereditary Succession Politics of North Korea
may be ordered from:
The Brookings Institution
c/o DFS, P.O. Box 50370, Baltimore, MD, USA
tel. 1-800-537-5487 or 410-516-6956
fax 410-516-6998
http://www.brookings.edu/about/press

Walter H. Shorenstein Asia-Pacific Research Center Books, 2015.
Copyright © 2015 by the Board of Trustees of the
Leland Stanford Junior University.

Library of Congress Cataloging-in-Publication Data
Kim, Hak-chun, 1943–
Dynasty : the hereditary succession politics of North Korea / by Kim Hakjoon.
    pages cm
Includes bibliographical references and index.
ISBN 978-1-931368-30-8 (alkaline paper)
1. Korea (North)—Politics and government—20th century. 2. Korea (North)—Politics and
government—21st century. 3. Kim, Il-song, 1912–1994. 4. Kim, Chong-il, 1942–2011.
5. Kim, Chong-un, 1984–6. Heads of state—Succession—Korea (North)—History.
7. Heads of state—Family relationships—Korea (North)—History. 8. Political culture—
Korea (North)—History. I. Title.
DS935.55.K488 2015
951.9305—dc23
                                                                        2015010175
First printing, 2015

Typeset by Classic Typography in 10.5/13 Sabon MT Pro

Dedicated to Dr. Irwin J. Schulman,
professor emeritus at the University of Pittsburgh,
under whom I studied Marxism and comparative communism.

Contents

Tables and Figure

Tables

Figure

Abbreviations

CC	Central Committee
CCP	Chinese Communist Party
CCPCC	Chinese Communist Party Central Committee
CDP	Chosŏn (Korea) Democratic Party
CMC	Central Military Committee (of the KWP)
CPC	Central People's Committee
CPKI	Committee for the Preparation of Korean Independence
CPSU	Communist Party of the Soviet Union
CPSUCC	Communist Party of the Soviet Union Central Committee
DPRK	Democratic People's Republic of Korea (North Korea)
GBCA	General Bureau for the Civilian Affairs (of the SOFHNK)
GPB	General Political Bureau (of the KPA)
IAEA	International Atomic Energy Agency
KCNA	Korean Central News Agency (of North Korea)
KCP	Korean Communist Party
KDP	Korean Democratic Party
KNDP	Korean New Democratic Party
KPA	Korean People's Army (of North Korea)
KPAGPB	Korean People's Army General Political Bureau
KPAGS	Korean People's Army General Staff
KPG	Korean Provisional Government
KPR	Korean People's Republic

KWP	Korean Workers' Party (of North Korea)
KWPCC	Korean Workers' Party Central Committee
KWPCCPC	Korean Workers' Party Central Committee Political Committee
KWPCMC	Korean Workers' Party Central Military Committee
KWPCCOGD	Korean Workers' Party Central Committee Organization and Guidance Department
MMDC	Maritime Military District Command
MPS	Ministry of People's Security
NDC	National Defense Commission (of North Korea)
NEUAJA	North-Eastern United Anti-Japanese Army
NIS	National Intelligence Service (of South Korea)
NKBKCP	North Korea Branch of the Korean Communist Party
NKCP	North Korean Communist party
NKCYFP	North Korean Ch'ŏndogyo Young Friends' Party
NKPA	North Korean People's Assembly
NKPC	North Korean People's Committee
NKPPC	North Korean Provisional People's Committee
NKWP	North Korean Worker's Party
NSP	Agency for National Security Planning (of South Korea)
OGD	Organization and Guidance Department
PAFM	People's Armed Forces Ministry (or People's Armed Forces Minister)
PRC	People's Republic of China
PSM	Public Security Ministry
ROK	Republic of Korea (South Korea)
ROK NIS	Republic of Korea National Intelligence Service
SFEA	Soviet Far Eastern Army
SIB	Special International Brigade (of the Soviet Far Eastern Army)
SKWP	South Korean Worker's Party
SOFHNK	Soviet Occupation Forces Headquarters in North Korea
SPA	Supreme People's Assembly (of North Korea)
SPASC	Supreme People's Assembly Standing Committee
SSM	State Security Ministry (or State Security Minister)
USAMGIK	United States Army Military Government in Korea
UNTCOK	United Nations Temporary Commission on Korea

Foreword and Acknowledgments

This book is an outgrowth of my paper, "The Hereditary Succession from Kim Jong Il to Kim Jong Un: Its Background, Present Situation and Prospect," presented at the Koret Conference "DPRK 2012" held on February 23–24, 2011, at Stanford University under the sponsorship of the Korean Program at the Walter H. Shorenstein Asia-Pacific Research Center (APARC). Gi-Wook Shin, director of Shorenstein APARC, and David Straub, associate director of the Korea Program, encouraged me to expand it to a book-length manuscript. In this sense, they are midwives of this book. George Krompacky, editor at Shorenstein APARC, has done an excellent job preparing the manuscript for publication.

The Central Library of DanKook (Tan'guk) University provided me with logistical support for my writing and Yim Young-jae (Im Yŏng-jae), endowed chaired professor of English language and literature at DanKook University, gave me stimulating comments. In particular, Lee Jong-seok (Yi Chong-sŏk), former Republic of Korea minister of unification and a leading scholar in the field of North Korean studies, and Cheong Seong-chang (Chŏng Sŏng-ch'ang), a senior research fellow at the Sejong Institute, led me in my efforts to find accurate data on Kim Il Sung and Kim Jong Il. At DanKook University, secretaries Cho Han Seok (Cho Han-sŏk), Kim Yoon-soo (Kim Yun-su), and Lee Il-bae (Yi Il-bae), along with Yoo Hyewon (Yu Hae-won) and Yun Ji Hoon (Yun Ji-hun) at the Northeast Asian History Foundation, searched for and collected materials. My thanks go to all of them, but all errors and misinterpretations, if any, are my own responsibility.

Since the early 1990s, I have published six books and more than twenty articles in English on North Korea. The most recent books are *North and South Korea: Internal Politics and External Relations since 1988* (The Society of Korean and Related Studies, 2006) and *The Domestic Politics of Korean Unification: Debates on the North in the South, 1948–2008* (Jimoondang, 2010). For this book, I borrowed some paragraphs, sentences, and phrases from my previous works with the permission of the publishers.

Throughout this book, I present East Asian names with the surname first. For transliteration of Korean names and words, I use the McCune-Reischauer romanization system except for personal conventions adopted by well-recognized individuals à la Western tradition (e.g., Syngman Rhee, whose surname was Rhee), established idiosyncratic romanization (e.g., Kim Il Sung, Kim Jong Il, and Kim Jong Nam), or commonly known place names (e.g., Seoul and Pyongyang). Kim Il Sung is said to have developed his own theory, one which translates as "self-reliance "or "self-determination." In many foreign publications, it has been written as *chuch'e* or *Chuch'e* following the McCune-Reischauer system, but since all North Korean official publications in English write it as *Juche*, I use that spelling.

I hope this work will help people outside of Korea understand the basic character of the North Korean regime and the problems it raises. I dedicate this work to Professor Irwin J. Schulman, my dissertation supervisor.

Kim Hakjoon
December 18, 2014
Seoul

Dynasty:
The Hereditary
Succession Politics
of North Korea

Kim Il Sung Family Tree

Legend:
- female
- male
- couple
- offspring

Kang Pan-sŏk (1892–1932)
Kim Hyŏng-jik (1894–1926)
Kim Il Sung (1912–1994)
Kim Ch'ŏl-ju (1916–1935)
Kim Yŏng-ju (1922–)
Kim Jong Suk (1917–1949)
Kim Sŏng-ae (1924–2014)

Kim Kyŏng-jin (1952–)
Kim Kwang-sŏp (1952–)
Kim P'yong-il (1954–)
Kim Sun-gŭm (1957–)
Kim Ŭn-song (1981–)
Kim In-gang (1983)
Kim Yŏng-il (1955–2000)
? (?–)
(three sons)

Chang Sŏng-t'aek (1946–2013)
Kim Kyŏng-hui (1946–)
Chang Kŭm-song (1977–2006)
Chang Su-kil (?–)
Kim Kŭm-sol (1997–)

Sin Chŏng-hui (?–)
Kim Sŏl-song (1974–)
Kim Ch'un-song (1975–)
Ri Sŏl-ju (1989–)
Kim Ju-ae (2013–)

Sung Hye-rim (1937–2002)
Kim Jong Nam (1971–)
Kim Yŏng-suk (1947–)
Ko Yong-hŭi (1952–2004)
Kim Jong Chul (1980–)
Kim Jong Un (1984–)
Kim Yŏ-jong (1988–)
Kim Ok (1964–)

Kim Jong Il (1942–2011)
Ri Hye-kyŏng (?–)
Kim Han-sol (1995–)
Kim Sol-hŭi (1999–)

Notes: Some offspring omitted due to space considerations; no distinction made between formal and informal marital relationships.

1 Introduction

The Democratic People's Republic of Korea (DPRK, or North Korea) has received much attention from the international community since the Korean War erupted with the North's invasion of the Republic of Korea (ROK, or South Korea) on June 25, 1950. In particular, since the DPRK's nuclear development project became widely known during the late 1980s and early 1990s, this Stalinist country has made not only its neighbors, but also the West, anxious over the potential for calamity its weapons program presents. After the "Jasmine Revolution," which toppled oppressive, corrupt, and dictatorial regimes in Northern African and Middle Eastern countries between late 2010 and early 2011, many in the international community pondered the fate of North Korea, another ruthlessly dictatorial and corrupt country. Might something similar happen in North Korea, a country notorious for its leaders' luxurious private lives, for drug trafficking, starvation, defections, and for the harsh suppression of human rights symbolized by its concentration camps?

Myanmar's about-face from years of repression was of special relevance to North Korea. The Myanmar government, notorious for its corrupt military rule since 1962, softened its hardliner stance and began conceding political freedoms. Democracy icon Aung San Suu Kyi and her party, the National League for Democracy, won by-elections held on April 1, 2012. Political developments there have also raised the question: can North Korea be like Myanmar?

Amid varied speculations on the future course of North Korea, its dictator Kim Jong Il (Kim Chŏng-il), the successor and eldest son of deceased "Great Leader" Kim Il Sung (Kim Il-sŏng), died on December 17, 2011, of a heart attack. During the state funeral, his son Kim Jong Un (Kim Chŏng-ŭn), who had been designated as his successor in October 2010, emerged as the undeniable leader of North Korea. The Kims were thus able to realize an unbroken hereditary succession over three generations. But the ascension of this third generation raised more than a few questions. Who is Kim Jong Un? Who are the people sustaining the succession regime? Will Kim pursue a reform policy and forego the nuclear project? What are the basic characteristics of this new regime of hereditary succession?

With this in mind, this book attempts to examine two interrelated questions. First, what is the nature of North Korea's succession politics? As we shall see in the following chapters, the succession processes from Kim Il Sung to Kim Jong Il and from Kim Jong Il to Kim Jong Un were full of dark, frightening, and bloody stories of the type seen in Solzhenitsyn's *Gulag Archipelago* as well as in Shakespeare's tragedies, *Macbeth*, *Othello*, *Hamlet*, and *King Lear*. In short, the succession transitions reveal that the regime is based partly on state violence and coercion. North Korean authorities have devised many "theories" to justify the hereditary succession. Those theories, wrapped in abstract, pseudo-philosophical concepts that sound bizarre to anyone outside the DPRK, testify that the regime is also based partly on myths and a personality cult of its top leaders. This analysis of North Korean succession politics rests on a narrative of the alpha and omega of North Korea as a polity and lays bare its reality.

The second question is, What are the implications of North Korean succession politics for the nation's external and internal policies, including the development of its nuclear weapons program? However, my primary emphasis will be on the first question, regarding the nature of DPRK succession politics.

Research Methods

Methodological Lessons from Soviet Studies

T. H. Rigby, a British diplomat-turned-scholar, once termed the domestic politics of the Soviet Union as "crypto-politics," shrouded in secrecy and communicated through words resembling cryptograms. He argued that by resorting to public and open materials alone, it was almost impossible to confirm what was actually happening inside the Kremlin; speeches by political leaders, questions and answers at the Supreme Soviet Congress, public releases by the party and the government, reports by newspapers, magazines, and other media did not give an accurate picture.[1] Under such

---

1   T. H. Rigby, "Crypto-Politics," in *Communist Studies and the Social Science*, ed. Frederic J. Fleron, Jr. (Chicago: Rand McNally and Co., 1969), 116–28.

conditions, the only technique or method to examine Soviet domestic politics was "Kremlinology." It meant a comprehensive examination of Soviet materials, reading between the lines, taking note of the appearance of new words as well as the disappearance of conventional words, calculating the frequency or infrequency of the use of specific words, and paying great attention to the protocol order among political leaders. Photographs were also important sources for the Kremlinological approach, since some photographs were found to be fabricated or doctored for political purposes.[2]

Let me recall some famous cases that are useful to our analysis of North Korean succession politics. Immediately after the official announcement of Joseph Stalin's death on March 5, 1953, the now-defunct Communist Party of the Soviet Union (CPSU) released a full list of members of its Central Committee's (CC's) Presidium (formerly known as the Politburo). But something was different from past lists: now their names were listed not in hierarchical order, but in *alphabetical* order. Western Kremlinologists interpreted this to mean that the Politburo had not reached an agreement on the hierarchical order at the top level and that a collective leadership was emerging.[3]

On the following day (March 6), the Soviet official media announced that Georgi M. Malenkov had resigned from the CPSUCC secretary position and was taking over the premiership that had been occupied by Stalin. A few weeks later, the Soviet official media released an old photograph purportedly taken three years earlier. On February 15, 1950, Stalin and Mao Zedong, chairman of the Chinese Communist Party (CCP) Central Committee, had concluded the Sino-Soviet Friendship and Alliance Treaty in the Kremlin. In the original photograph showing the signing, four men had been in the foreground: Stalin, Andrei Vyshinski (Soviet foreign minister), Mao, and Zhou Enlai (Chinese foreign minister). But in the newly released "old" photograph showing the same scene, Malenkov, then the CC secretary and incumbent premier, appeared next to Mao, thanks to the removal of three people who had separated them. Malenkov thus attempted to heighten his political stature by moving himself to the center and removing his rivals (e.g., Molotov, who was next to Stalin in the original).[4]

In early July 1953 the opera *The Decembrists* was presented at the Bolshoi Theatre in Moscow. When the Soviet official media released the list of

2 Erik P. Hoffmann, "Methodological Problems of Kremlinology," in *Communist Studies and the Social Science*, ed. Frederic J. Fleron, Jr. (Chicago: Rand McNally and Co., 1969), 129–49.

3 Darrell P. Hammer, *The U.S.S.R: The Politics of Oligarchy* (Boulder, CO: Westview Press, 1986), 193.

4 "Caesar-2 Death of Stalin," ESDN 0001408610, CIA Freedom of Information Act Electronic Reading Room, http://www.foia.cia.gov.

the CPSU leaders who attended, the name of Lavrentiy Beria, the feared interior minister who was regarded as the second-most powerful individual in the party, was absent. The *New York Post* reported that "Perhaps Beria doesn't like [it]." But a young Russia specialist at the American Embassy in Moscow, Robert C. Tucker, thought differently. Vladimir Lenin, the founder of the Soviet Union, held the anti-Czarist revolt by the Decembrists in 1825 in high regard as the first Bolshevik revolution, so viewing it was a *must* for the leaders and cadres of the CPSU. Tucker thus sensed that Beria's absence was abnormal. Tucker, the first American who was officially allowed by Soviet authorities to marry a Russian woman living in Soviet Russia, stressed to Ambassador Charles E. Bohlen the importance of confirming Beria's whereabouts. Soon the American embassy was able to secure intelligence that Beria, the head of both the regular and political police under the Interior Ministry, had been arrested and imprisoned.

Forty years later, Amy Knight, a Russia specialist at the U.S. Library of Congress, would reveal that drama in detail. In late June 1953 Nikita Khrushchev, the only secretary remaining in the CPSUCC, succeeded in persuading some of its Presidium members, including Prime Minister Malenkov and Defense Minister Nikolai Bulganin, to "purge" Beria. Khrushchev was then able to mobilize a small military unit under the direct influence of Marshal Georgy Zhukov to come to the Presidium meeting held inside the Kremlin on June 26, 1953. Zhukov, the "Liberator of Berlin"—a friend of Khrushchev and fellow Ukrainian—had that unit, whose members included Leonid Brezhnev, arrest Beria (who had once humiliated Zhukov publicly) and sent him to the Air Force prison. Beria would be executed by the end of the year, and eleven years later Brezhnev would become the top leader of the Soviet Union, ousting Khrushchev.[5]

On September 12, 1953, the official Soviet media reported that the CPSUCC had "elected" Khrushchev its "first secretary." Western Kremlinologists concluded that he was at the head of the Presidium. But, noting that his new title was lowercased, they also determined that his position as a front runner was not solid. Three years later, when the Soviet official media reported that the CPSUCC had re-elected him as its "First Secretary," Kremlinologists noted the change in capitalization and interpreted that to mean his position had been consolidated. But again recalling that Stalin's title had been "General Secretary," they also believed that his power must be far weaker than Stalin's.[6]

---

5 Amy Knight, *Beria: Stalin's First Lieutenant* (Princeton: Princeton University Press, 1993), 194–200.

6 Hammer, *U.S.S.R.*, 206.

On February 14, 1956, the historic Twentieth CPSU Congress was held in Moscow. At the opening ceremony, Khrushchev proposed a moment of silence for "Joseph Stalin, Klement Gottwald, and Tokuda Kyuichi, three leaders in the world communist movement, who had passed away recently." In the past, it would have been unthinkable to mention Stalin in the same breath as a Czechoslovakian communist leader and a Japanese communist leader. From this statement, as reported in the Soviet media, many Kremlinologists sensed that Khrushchev would initiate a de-Stalinization campaign. Indeed, on February 25, the last day of the Congress, Khruschev officially denounced his former boss as a merciless, lawless, one-man dictator who had murdered countless innocent people. Khrushchev revealed that he himself, despite being a member of the Presidium, did not know after attending dinners hosted by Stalin whether his next destination would be home or Stalin's prison.[7]

On October 16, 1964, the Soviet official media reported that the CPSUCC was relieving Khrushchev of all his responsibilities and electing Leonid Brezhnev, the ceremonial head of the Soviet Union, as "First Secretary." Two years later, the Soviet official media began to refer to Brezhnev not as "First Secretary" but as "General Secretary," indicating his expanded power. Ten years later, the Soviet official media began to call him *Vozhd* (leader) of the CPSU, a title that had been reserved for Stalin alone. Now, it seemed, there was no challenge to Brezhnev's authority.[8]

However, between February and March of 1982, *Pravda*, the CPSU's official daily newspaper, printed a series of unconventional articles, using metaphors and not revealing any real names or titles. Some of the writings were in the form of a novel or a letter. Ordinary readers had no way to understand their meaning. Only well-trained top Kremlinologists in the United States could discern that some of articles were attacking Brezhnev, while others were defending him. In addition, they could comprehend that with Brezhnev seriously ill and his death imminent, Yuri Andropov, the powerful KGB head, was manuvering to become his successor. They even predicted that Andropov would succeed Brezhnev on his death. About seven months later, their analysis and prediction proved accurate.[9] All of the above-mentioned cases show that Kremlinologists needed to be well-trained professional decipherers of cryptographic words and careful discerners of photographs.

7 Hammer, *U.S.S.R.*, 297.

8 Ibid.

9 Jerry F. Hough, "Soviet Succession: Issues and Personalities," *Problems of Communism* 31, no. 5 (September–October 1982): 28–38; Sidney I. Ploss, "Soviet Succession: Signs of Struggle," *Problems of Communism* 31, no. 5 (September–October 1982): 43–44.

Kremlinological Approach to North Korean "Crypto-Politics"

Rigby's "crypto-politics" is also a term applicable to North Korean domestic politics. Indeed, the DPRK official media have used many cryptic words—except when it comes to the clear litany of excessive praise given to Kim Il Sung and Kim Jong Il. One famous case was the phrase *tang chung'ang* (party center), which began to appear frequently in the official media after February 1974. Neither South Korean "Kremlinologists" nor ordinary North Korean party members could comprehend the exact meaning of this phrase. As we shall see in chapter 3, only in late 1979 or early 1980 did some of them come to understand that it referred to Kim Jong Il. He had coined the phrase to envelop himself in an air of mystique as he prepared to become the official successor in 1980.

Given that North Korean domestic politics may also be termed "crypto-politics," is the Kremlinological approach likewise applicable to North Korean domestic politics in general and in succession politics in particular? The answer proves to be yes: In the following chapters, we shall see how well-trained South Korean "Kremlinologists" have been able to explain events taking place inside the veiled North Korean power structure. For example, in the late 1970s and early 1980s, they predicted that Kim Jong Il would become Kim Il Sung's successor without facing any serious challenge. After the death of Kim Il Sung in July 1994, they proposed a "non-collapse" theory that asserted the Kim Jong Il leadership would continue for more than a decade. In other words, they persuasively argued that there would be no collapse of the existing North Korean regime. In March 2007 Kim Man-bok, director of the ROK National Intelligence Service (NIS), the main intelligence agency and successor of the Agency for National Security Planning (NSP), briefed the press that there was a high probability that Kim Jong Un would become Kim Jong Il's successor.[10] In 2009 Cheong Seong-chang (Chŏng Sŏng-ch'ang) of the Sejong Institute, a South Korean think tank focusing on international and North Korean affairs, even correctly predicted that Kim Jong Un would appear in public in October 2010 as Kim Jong Il's successor.[11]

Likewise, Robert Carlin, with more than twenty years' experience at the U.S. Department of State examining North Korean public communiqués and

10 Quoted in Yi Yŏng-jong, *Hugyeja Kim Chŏng-ŭn* [Kim Jong Un, the successor] (Seoul: Nŭlp'um Plus, 2010), 96.

11 This writer's telephone interview with Dr. Cheong on September 3, 2009, in Seoul. See also Cheong Seong-chang, "Kim Jong Il's Illness and Prospects for Post-Kim Leadership," *East Asian Review* 20, no. 4 (Winter 2008): 20–24; Cheong, "Kim Jong Un's Early Life and Personality," *Vantage Point* (2009): 8–12.

releases, has demonstrated his expertise in the Kremlinological approach. At the U.S.–North Korean talks held in Geneva from September 23, 1994, which were aimed at finding a solution to the nuclear crisis, DPRK delegation head first vice foreign minister Kang Sŏk-chu said to his American counterpart, "We cannot accept the inspection by the International Atomic Energy Agency." Noting that Kang changed the conventionally used "never" to "not," Carlin sensed a change in the North Korean context and policy conflicts between hardliners (represented by the military) and moderates (represented by diplomats). According to Carlin, Kang had been forced, under strong pressure from the hardliners, to use the emphatically negative word "never." To facilitate an agreement, however, Kang gave a delicate hint to his American counterpart that the North was willing to accept inspections by changing the wording to "not." In other words, while protecting himself against criticism from hardliners by using the word "not," Kang hoped that the American delegation would catch the subtle change in his position and not back out of negotiations. The American delegation accepted Carlin's judgment on the significance of Kang's use of the word "not." The North would indeed finally agree to inspections, paving the way to the conclusion of the Agreed Framework on October 21, 1994.[12] In sum, a few top "Kremlinologists" in the West have found many useful clues from the "system of cryptic, semi-esoteric communication"[13] used in North Korean remarks, releases, and the media.

But the Kremlinological approach is not the only method used in the analysis of North Korean "crypto-politics." There are many others, including psychological and psycho-pathological approaches to Kim Jong Il. As we shall see in chapters 2 and 4, many students of North Korean studies have explained Kim's relationships with his stepmother and his first common-law wife in terms of the loss of his biological mother in childhood.[14] And after his first cerebral hemorrhage, in August 2008, the medical approach prevailed. World-renowned medical doctors throughout the West appeared in the media, predicting his fate and the regime's future. For a while it seemed that medical scientists were replacing social scientists in the study of North Korean succession politics. But we should pay more serious attention to the following four points.

12 Don Oberdorfer, *The Two Koreas: A Contemporary History* (New York: Basic Books, 2014), 276–77.

13 Morgan E. Clippinger, "Kim Chong-il in the North Korean Mass Media: A Study of Semi-Esoteric Communication," *Asian Survey* 21, no. 3 (March 1981): 289.

14 The representative case was Paek Sang-ch'ang, "Salbu ŭisik i kŭ ŭi in'gyŏk ŭl p'agoe haetta" [His sub-conscious desire to kill his own father destroyed his humanity], *Wŏlgan Chosun*, August 1994, 126–37.

First, North Korea as a polity has always been ruled or governed by the Kim Il Sung–Kim Jong Il family. Historically, most dictators have depended primarily on their family members and relatives as trustworthy and loyal. The two Kims were no exception. Indeed, many aspects of North Korean succession politics may be explained not only by this nepotism, but by feuds or alignments among Kim family members. In this regard, it is thus essential to know the family background of Korean Workers' Party (KWP) and Korean People's Army (KPA) cadres. In the North, however, it has become taboo to publicly report details of marriages and blood relations of ruling officials. Because Kim Jong Il's marriages and his "wives" were never officially made public, researchers must get such data through diverse channels. For example, it was three photographs taken in one of Kim Jong Il's secret residences on August 19, 1981, that confirmed that Kim Jong Nam (Kim Chŏng-nam) was his son by his common-law wife, Sung Hye-rim (Sŏng Hye-rim). These were printed in memoirs published in 2000 by the same wife's sister, who had defected to the West in 1996.[15]

Second, it is essential to identify those who belonged to the "first generation of the revolution," i.e., those who were anti-Japanese guerrillas during the Japanese occupation of Korea led by Kim Il Sung, and their descendants. Kim Il Sung built and maintained his political system and power based on this group. Since all descendants of the "first generation of the revolution" studied at the prestigious Man'gyŏngdae Revolutionary School (established in 1947 in Pyongyang) and entered into the ruling elite group in the KWP, the KPA, and other organizations, it is important for researchers to trace their careers and the relations among them. They usually have been called the "second generation of the revolution." It is also necessary to know whether someone is a graduate of the Fourth People's School (an elementary school), the First Basic Middle School, Namsan (South Mountain) Higher Middle School, or Kim Il Sung Comprehensive University, all of which are in Pyongyang and are Kim Jong Il's alma maters. The academic cliques centered on Kim Jong Il can be very useful in understanding succession politics in the North.

Third, North Korean succession politics has depended heavily upon two political instruments. One is extensive and exhaustive political indoctrination, by propaganda, agitation, and state rituals.[16] The other is the unlimited use of surveillance, coercion, and violence, as exemplified by arbitrary imprisonment

---

15 Sung Hye-rang (Sŏng Hye-rang), *Tŭngnamu chip* [The wisteria house] (Seoul: Chisik Nara, 2000), plates 256–57.

16 As for the political importance of state rituals in North Korea, see Gavan McCormack, "Kim Country: Hard Times in North Korea," *New Left Review*, no. 198 (March–April 1993): 21–48.

without any sort of indictment or trial, public executions, imprisonment for political reasons, and the existence of concentration camps. To borrow Harold D. Lasswell's concepts, the succession politics of the North has always and necessarily demanded both symbol-manipulators and coercion-violence specialists.[17]

In this context, it is a *must* for researchers to examine specific institutions related to political indoctrination on the one hand, and surveillance-coercion-violence on the other. Regarding the former, the KWP's Propaganda and Agitation Department is most important; as for the latter, the most important institutions are the Organization and Guidance Department (OGD); the KWP Central Military Committee (CMC); the People's Armed Forces Ministry (PAFM); the Public Security Ministry (PSM); the Ministry of People's Security (MPS); the State Security Ministry (SSM); the General Political Bureau (GPB) of the Korean People's Army (KPA); and the National Defense Commission (NDC). Without understanding the character, duties, and cadres of these state institutions, any study of succession politics would miss its essential elements.

Fourth, succession politics in North Korea has been influenced by the policies of its neighboring countries, and especially the People's Republic of China (PRC). As long as the PRC does not want a change in the status quo on the Korean Peninsula—for fear that drastic change in the North would risk turmoil, disorder, or even anarchy—it will tend to support, or at least not oppose, hereditary succession. As we shall see in the following chapters, Kim Il Sung met Deng Xiaoping, the then most powerful leader in the PRC, to persuade him to recognize the succession to Kim Jong Il, and Kim Jong Il met Hu Jintao to encourage the CCP head to receive Kim Jong Un as his successor. Researchers need to pay great attention to Chinese stances on succession issues.

Research Materials

From the beginning, it should be admitted that an examination of North Korean cases is much more difficult than an examination of Soviet Russian cases because reliable data are extremely limited. Andrei N. Lankov, a Russian specialist on North Korea who studied Korean in Pyongyang during 1984–85, wrote that "the Soviet Union under Stalin may be said to have been an open society in comparison with North Korea," and that "to the students of North Korean politics, the condition for the research of the North is worse than that of the Soviet Union." Calling the North "an absolute secret country," he

---

17 Harold D. Lasswell and Daniel Lerner, eds., *World Revolutionary Elites: Studies in Coercive Ideological Movements* (Cambridge: The M.I.T. Press, 1965), ch. 1.

lamented the "chronic paucity of reliable data" on this closed country. He added that in the North, he could not even find Soviet materials that would have been easily accessible by average citizens in Moscow.[18]

The paucity of primary data is a hallmark of North Korean studies. Moreover, as far as "palace politics" involves "succession politics" with Kim Jong Il as its major actor, it is impossible to find raw data. Human intelligence (HUMINT), in particular, is extremely limited. However, that does not mean that research is hopeless. There are many types of materials that are worth careful scrutiny. Most of the remainder of this chapter details those sources, followed by a brief discussion of this book's organization and a summary of each of its chapters.

Official Publications on Kim Il Sung and Kim Jong Il

First, there are official publications related to Kim Il Sung, Kim Jong Il, and their families. These include Kim Il Sung's autobiography, biographies of both Kim Il Sung and Kim Jong Il,[19] and speeches and writings by the two Kims.[20] These publications are replete with stories, theories, and even myths that glorify the two Kims, many which sound implausible to people outside of North Korea. In the case of Kim Il Sung's speeches and writings, there have been so many revisions, deletions, and additions after the fact that their credibility has suffered.[21] When Kim Jong Il had de facto power over his father and also after his father's death,[22] he seems retroactively to have inserted remarks favorable to himself (purportedly made by Kim Il Sung) into an eight-volume autobiography of Kim Il Sung published during the elder Kim's final years. By repeatedly examining these

18 Andrei N. Lankov, *Severnaia Koreia: Vchera I Segodnia* , trans. Kim Kwang-rin, *Soryŏn ŭi charyo ro pon Pukhan hyŏndae chŏngch'i sa* [North Korea's contemporary political history seen through Soviet materials] (Seoul: Orŭm, 1995), 6.

19 For example, see Paek Pong, *Minjok ŭi t'aeyang Kim Il-sŏng Changgun* [General Kim Il Sung, the sun of the nation] (Pyongyang: Inmun kwahaksa), vol. 1 (1968), vol. 2 (1969), vol. 3 (1971). Its English version, *Kim Il Sung: Biography*, was published in 1969 by Guardian Associates in New York City.

20 Chosŏn rodongdang [The Korean Workers' Party] ed., *Kim Il-sŏng Sŏnjip* [Selected works of Kim Il Sung] (Pyongyang, 1992–99), 28 vols. See also *Juche! The Speeches and Writings of Kim Il Sung* (New York: Grossman Publishers, 1972).

21 This subject was extensively discussed in Suh Dae-sook, Yi Wan-bŏm, Chŏn Hyŏn-su, and Kang Kwang-sik, *Pukhan hyŏndaesa munhŏn yŏn'gu* [A study of the literature in contemporary North Korean history] (Seoul, 2001). For a comparative analysis of Kim Il Sung's works, Suh Dae-sook, *Korean Communism, 1945–1980: A Reference Guide to the Political System* (Honolulu: University of Hawaii Press, 1981).

22 Kim Il-sŏng (Kim Il Sung), *Segi wa tŏburŏ* [With the century] (Pyongyang: Chosŏn rodong-dang ch'ulp'ansa), vols. 1–6 (1992–95) and vols. 7–8 (1996–98).

materials, admittedly a tedious task, one can find clues to understanding the political situation of the time. Official biographies of Kim Jong Il also give many examples of his expertise as a symbol manipulator through the creation of myths. [23]

The Official Media

A second source of useful materials is the official media. Among the most important are *Rodong Sinmun* (Labor Newspaper), the KWP's official daily, and *Kŭlloja* (Workers), the KWP's official monthly publication. *Minju Chosŏn* (Democratic Chosŏn), [24] the official daily jointly published by the cabinet and the Standing Committee (or Presidium) of the Supreme People's Assembly (SPA), is somewhat less significant. *Chosŏn Inmin'gun* (The [North] Korean People's Army), an official daily jointly published by the PAFM and the KPAGPB, and *Chosŏn Ch'ŏngnyŏn Chŏnwi* (Chosun Youth Vanguard), an organ of the Kim Il Sung Socialist Youth League, deserve regular perusal by researchers. The daily *Chosŏn Sinbo* (Korea Newspaper) in Korean, and its English weekly *People's Korea*, both published by the General Federation of Koreans in Japan, have consistently represented North Korean positions. The sole DPRK state news agency, Chosŏn Chungang T'ongsinsa (Korean Central News Agency, KCNA), usually has its reports and commentaries reprinted in *Rodong Sinmun* and *Minju Chosŏn*.

The North has opened a total of about four radio stations and television stations in Pyongyang. Since they usually repeat news, articles, and commentaries by the above-mentioned publications, most North Korea watchers abroad tend to underestimate them as information sources, but they can be useful. For example, on November 18, 1986, the Central Television Station in Pyongyang, together with the KCNA, decisively cleared up a murky rumor circulating abroad for at least three days that Kim Il Sung had recently been killed. The broadcaster showed Kim Il Sung appearing at the Pyongyang airport to receive the Mongolian head of state, Jambyn Batmonh.

Finally, the U.S. Foreign Broadcast Information Service (FBIS) used to publish the *Daily Report*, including English translations of North Korean broadcasts. Researchers who depend primarily on English sources will wish

---

23 For example, see Choe In-su, *Kim Jung Il: The People's Leader* (Pyongyang: Foreign Languages Publishing House), vol. 1 (1983) and vol. 2 (1991). See also *Kim Jong Il: Short Biography* (Pyongyang: Foreign Languages Publishing House, 2001).

24 Broadly speaking, there are two names representing Korea. One is Han'guk, which may be translated as the "country of the Han people." The other is Chosŏn, which has been translated as "morning freshness." Nowadays, it is usual that the North calls itself Chosŏn while the South calls itself Han'guk.

to consult it. An archive of the *Daily Report* through 1996 is available online. In recent years, North Korea has established websites making KCNA and other official news and propaganda available in the original Korean and also in English and other languages.

"Internal Confidential Documents"

Confidential documents distributed within the party, administrative agencies, and the military are a third type of valuable materials. The North Koreans call them *naebu pimil mun'gŏn* (internal confidential documents). The scope of their distribution varies in accordance with their aims and importance. ROK intelligence agencies have occasionally secured those materials through espionage activities, captured North Korean agents, and North Korean defectors. These materials have provided useful information that could not be gained through the above-mentioned official publications. As we shall see in chapter 5, one such "internal confidential document" distributed among the KPA in 2002 helped keen-eyed "Kremlinologists" in the South conclude that Kim Jong Il was preparing to designate his successor from among his two sons by Ko Yong-hŭi. A later "internal confidential document," distributed among the KPA in 2009, clearly showed that Kim Jong Un was being groomed as the successor.

Mobile Phones and Email

Fourth, ROK intelligence services have at times been able to wiretap telephone conversations of North Koreans, including high-level party and military leaders. For example, as we shall see in the following chapters, the South Korean NSP was able to wiretap a telephone conversation between Kim Il Sung and his daughter in May 1982.[25] Also, a few hours after Kim Jong Il's hospitalization due to a cerebral hemorrhage in August 2008, the ROK NIS wiretapped an interesting telephone conversation between Kim Jong Il's close aide at the hospital and a powerful North Korean army general. When the general asked "whether His Excellency General is sleeping," the aide hesitated, but when the general asked "whether His Excellency General is sleeping for good," he replied, "No."[26] From such conversations, the NIS concluded that Kim Jong Il had not died. More dramatically, when a North Korean medical team scanned Kim Jong Il's damaged brain immediately after his hospitalization and emailed the images to a French

25 Kim Yŏn-gwang, "Taebuk chŏppo chŏnsŏn ŭi pisang" [An alarm on the intelligence front towards North Korea], *Wŏlgan Chosun* (August 1994): 207–20.
26 Yi, *Hugyeja Kim Chŏng-ŭn*, 100–101.

medical team in Paris, the NIS succeeded in intercepting about five of the images.[27]

Active and regular exchanges of intelligence on the North among South Korean, Japanese, and American intelligence institutions have enhanced those governments' understanding of North Korea. In recent years, a PRC information agency has become cooperative with its South Korean counterpart. Information provided by a Russian official agency has also proved helpful, albeit in a limited way.

It has become easier for many North Korean defectors living in the South to occasionally contact their family members and relatives in the North by using mobile phones. North Korean defectors regularly send money from their earnings in the South to relatives in the North via well-organized underground networks based in South Korea, China, and probably also in North Korea. In recent years, their relatives in the North can buy and use mobile phones.

Although conversations must be short and both sides are careful in selecting topics of conversation, cell phone conversations have provided useful current information about the North. To note one remarkable example, during February 5–7, 2007, Kim Jong Il was conducting field inspections in North Hamgyŏng Province. This trip—typical of Kim's trips around North Korea—was kept secret and not disclosed in advance. However, Chu Sŏngha, a *Dong-A Ilbo* (*Tonga Ilbo*, East Asia Daily) reporter in Seoul, was able to confirm that Kim was visiting Ch'ŏngjin, the largest harbor city of the province. He learned of the trip through a regular telephone conversation with a source in that region. Chu was born and reared in that province and he graduated from Kim Il Sung Comprehensive University in Pyongyang before defecting to the South in 1998; he still has a good number of "friends" there. About ten hours after Chu's exclusive report, which was widely broadcast by Seoul radio and television, the North's Central Television Station in Pyongyang hurriedly reported that Kim had returned from a field guidance tour of North Hamgyŏng. Such a same-day report on Kim Jong Il's movements was indeed exceptional, not only in the South but also in the North.

The North Korean authorities, beginning in about 2008, are known to confiscate mobile phones owned by people not affiliated with either the party or the military, as well as those owned by low-level officials and officers. The regime has even prohibited some from buying cell phones, regarding them as

27 Kim Yŏn-gwang, "Han'guk chŏngbo tangguk Kim Chŏng-il noesajin hwakpŏ noe choljung hwagin" [The ROK intelligence agency secured Kim Jong Il's brain images and confirmed his cerebral hemorrhage], *Wŏlgan Chosun* (December 2008): 62–69.

unwanted tools that might result in the opening of the closed society. However, Voice of America (VOA)—quoting an annual report from Orascom Telecom, which had finalized a special contract with North Korea in 2008—broadcasted that as of June 30, 2011, about 666,500 North Koreans had mobile phones.[28] By 2014 that figure had reportedly increased to more than two million, although phones on the Orascom network could not make international calls.[29]

Also in this general category should be added the number of defectors now in the South who are engaged in publishing weekly and monthly reports on the North, the most representative of which is the monthly *Keys*. Some, such as the *Daily NK*, are operating online dailies. These publications are sources on the daily lives of ordinary North Koreans. Occasionally they report on "disturbances" and even "riots" in particular regions, perhaps in the hope that these reports will lead to a nationwide uprising against the regime itself. Since there are elements of such wishful thinking and agitation expressed in these publications, researchers must carefully scrutinize them and compare them with other sources.

Foreign Residents and Visitors to North Korea

A fifth source of information is reports by foreign diplomats[30] and officials, journalists, writers, international aid organization officials, and medical doctors who have visited or resided in Pyongyang. Except for Luise Rinser, a (West) German novelist who had talks with Kim Il Sung in Pyongyang five or six times before his death,[31] and Julie Moon (Mun Myŏng-ja), a Korean-American living in Washington, D.C., who had talks with both Kim Il Sung and Kim Jong Il,[32] few foreigners have positively assessed the North Korean political, economic, and social situation. Madeleine Albright, who as U.S. secretary of state had talks with Kim Jong Il in October 2000 in Pyongyang, did comment positively on him, while also pointing out his country's dictatorial

28 Details of the VOA report were printed in *Munhwa Ilbo*, August 11, 2011, 2.

29 Yonho Kim, *Cell Phones in North Korea: Has North Korea Entered the Telecommunications Revolution?* A US-Korea Institute at SAIS & Voice of America Report (United States: US-Korea Institute at SAIS, 2014). There is some controversy concerning the number of Koryolink subscribers versus the real number of mobile phone users.

30 For example, see Hans Maretzki, *Kim-ismus in Nordkorea* (n.p.: Anita Tykve Verlag, 1991). The writer was East Germany's last ambassador to Pyongyang. His observations were limited to the latter part of the 1980s.

31 Luise Rinser, *Nordkoreanisches reisetagebuch* (Frankfurt am Main: Fischer Verlag, 1981).

32 For Julie Moon's exclusive interview with Kim Il Sung in April 1994, see *Mal* (June 1994): 36–44.

character.[33] In sharp contrast, Norbert Vollertsen, a German physician who had been engaged in medical assistance activities to North Koreans in 1999–2000, severely criticized the North Korean regime for its harsh oppression of its people and their "wretched" living conditions.[34] But none of them was in a position to comprehend the secretive palace politics in Pyongyang.

Some South Koreans, including government officials, lawmakers, businessmen, scholars, journalists, and athletes, have visited the North. Only a few of them, however, were able to meet Kim Il Sung or Kim Jong Il, even briefly. A very exceptional case was the secret talks with both leaders in Pyongyang held by Sŏ Tong-gwŏn, then director of the ROKNSP, in October 1991. As we shall see in chapter 3, after his return to Seoul, he assured then ROK president Roh Tae-woo (No T'ae-u) that Kim Jong Il's successor status was undeniably solid and that even Kim Il Sung frequently asked for his opinions and judgment. Sŏ added that, contrary to some outside reports, Kim Jong Il seemed to have been healthy.[35] After the first-ever summit talks between then ROK president Kim Dae Jung (Kim Tae-jung) and Kim Jong Il, then the chairman of the NDC, in June 2000 in Pyongyang, the number of South Korean politicians, officials, and journalists who met and talked with Kim Jong Il increased somewhat. Park Geun-hye (Pak Kŭn-hye), the daughter of former ROK president Park Chung Hee (Pak Chŏng-hŭi), and current president of South Korea, had talks with Kim Jong Il in Pyongyang in May 2002. Roh Moo-hyun (No Mu-hyŏn) as well had talks as ROK president with Kim in Pyongyang in October 2007 in the second and, so far, last inter-Korean summit. These leaders did not, however, write any articles giving their assessment of Kim.

Photographs

Sixth, photographs are a significant source of information. For example, for a long time, North Korean historians printed in their official publications a photograph showing Kim Il Sung at his public debut, a mass rally in Pyongyang on October 14, 1945, held after his return to North Korea from the Soviet Far East. The picture showed Kim Il Sung standing alone on the stage, as if from the beginning he was the country's leader. However, the

33 Madeleine Albright (with Bill Woodward), *Madam Secretary* (New York: Miramax Book, The Easton Press, 2003), 459–71.

34 See his *Mitch'in kot esŏ ssŭn ilgi* [Dairy of a mad place], trans. Kim Chu-il (Seoul: Wŏlgan Chosunsa, 2001) and *Inside North Korea* (New York: Encounter Books, 2006).

35 Kim Yong-sam, "Chŏn kukka anjŏn kihoek pujang Sŏ Tong-gwŏn ŭi pisa wa kyŏnggo" [Former National Security Planning Agency Director Sŏ Tong-gwŏn's secret stories and warnings], *Wŏlgan Chosun* (May 2000): 150–67.

original picture of the same scene, which was found in U.S. archives in the early 1970s, showed him wearing a Soviet medal and standing before four Soviet generals under the Soviet flag.[36] North Korean historians had doctored the photograph to hide the fact that Kim was chosen for the North Korean leadership by the Soviet Union. A much more recent case of fabrication involved a photograph provided by the KCNA to the Pyongyang branch office of the Associated Press (AP) on July 16, 2011. The photograph, which AP distributed worldwide, showed serious flooding in a Pyongyang neighborhood. The photo was reprinted across South Korea as well as in the international press, evoking sympathy for the North Korean people. Some international relief organizations started a campaign to send food and medicine to the North. But—to arouse such a response—the North had in fact doctored the photograph to show the floods as more dire than they in fact were. Two days later, AP officially retracted the picture, explaining that it had been altered.[37]

Another case pertains to a notoriously incorrect report about a close assistant to Kim Jong Il. On May 17, 2003, a Seoul news agency created a sensation in the South by reporting that Kil Chae-gyŏng, vice chief of Kim Jong Il's secretariat, had recently taken refuge in the United States. But one South Korean daily repudiated the report with a photograph of Kil's tombstone in Pyongyang, whose epitaph clearly showed that he had died on June 7, 2000, almost two years before his "defection." This newspaper company fortunately had on file about two hundred photographs of the tombstones of North Korean VIPs in a Pyongyang national cemetery reserved for "revolutionaries" and "patriots" and thus was able to find Kil's.[38]

DPRK Novels

Seventh, novels published in the North can be a source of information. As is well known, North Korean authorities do not allow freedom of expression, including the written word. Novels may not deviate from the official party line and guidance. But Sŏ Chae-jin, a South Korean sociologist who focuses on North Korea, has proposed that a careful and thorough reading of North Korean novels reveals "another society in North Korea."[39] For example, some short stories describe the aspirations of ordinary people for higher status. They reveal that while PhDs and professors are envied,

36 Robert A. Scalapino and Lee Chong-sik, *Communism in Korea* (Berkeley: University of California Press, 1972), (*The Movement*), plates between 332 and 333.

37 *JoongAng Ilbo*, July 19, 2003, 1.

38 *JoongAng Ilbo*, May 19, 2003, 6.

39 Suh Jae-jean (Sŏ Chae-jin), *Tto hana ŭi Pukhan sahoe: Sahoe kujo wa sahoe ŭisik ŭi ijungsŏng yŏn'gu* [Another society in North Korea: A study on the duality between social structure and social consciousness] (Seoul: Nanam, 1995), 6.

low-level workers are despised.[40] Unfortunately, such sources cannot give any clue to the understanding of palace politics.

Defectors' Memoirs

Eighth, memoirs by North Korean defectors can be useful. Despite the tightening of border control, merciless repatriation of defectors to the North by Chinese public security officials, and subsequent heavy punishment by the North, the number of North Korean defectors is sharply increasing. Some are still roaming in China and other Asian countries, seeking a country to offer them asylum. A few defectors have been successful in settling down in the West, including the United States. But a significant portion of them, whose number reached 27,500 as of August 31, 2014, are living in the South.

How Should Researchers Read Memoirs by North Korean Defectors?   It is useful to divide "defectors" into at least four groups based on the causes of their defection. The first group represents the small number of "reluctant" defectors who had to leave, not because of political beliefs, but because of interpersonal strife. After defecting, they did not criticize Kim Il Sung and Kim Jong Il; in fact, in media interviews they tended to protect the images of the two Kims. A prime example is Kim Chŏng-min, who defected in June 1988 during a visit to African countries as president of the Ocean Trading Company, operated directly by the KWPCC Organization and Guidance Department (OGD). He never published his memoirs. Only after Kim Il Sung's death in July 1994 did he allow an influential Seoul monthly to interview him. Positioning himself as one of Kim Jong Il's friends from childhood, he recalled only positive things about Kim Jong Il and expressed confidence that his leadership would not collapse.[41] In the 1990s, the defection of a high-ranking North Korean diplomat and his family was prompted by a love affair between his son and the daughter of a Western diplomat. In this case, too, the defecting diplomat neither published his memoirs nor agreed to interviews with the media.

The second category of defectors consists mainly of those who, due to crimes they committed in the North, such as embezzlement and adultery, had no choice except to defect. In contrast with the first group, they have tended to publish their memoirs for money or for security clearance by ROK public security authorities. None of them, however, had ever met Kim Il Sung, Kim Jong Il, or key members of the KWP and KPA.

40 Suh, *Tto hana ŭi Pukhan sahoe*, 250–57.

41 Yi Chong-hwan, "Hyŏngnim Kim Chŏng Il, aitte put'ŏ 'chewang' iŏtta" [Elder brother Kim Jong Il was an "emperor" from childhood], *Sindonga* no. 8 (August 1994): 332–44.

Most defectors are in the third group: ordinary people trying to meet basic survival needs, like food, who chose to defect to China, other Asian countries, or South Korea. Since their defections are motivated by starvation, a few of them actually return home to the DPRK via China after earning enough money to bribe North Korean officials and to be able to live in the North.

In stark contrast, the fourth category of defectors chose to flee to the South based on their ideological beliefs—these defectors often do publish their memoirs.[42]

On the whole, most defectors have not published memoirs in order to avoid hurting their families who remain in the North. In cases where they did publish memoirs, some prudent or compromising defectors refrained from criticizing Kim Il Sung, Kim Jong Il, or other members of the "royal family," so as not to further offend North Korean authorities. It is common knowledge that as long as a defector only criticizes such aspects of North Korea as the economy and society, avoiding openly mentioning the "holy family," the North Korean authorities will not execute the defector's family members still in the North. As long as the defectors live relatively silently in the South, their family members remaining in the North may not be seriously persecuted, although they certainly may suffer unfavorable conditions. A small number of defectors seem to have published their memoirs for financial gain, or to secure the confidence of ROK public security institutions. On the other hand, some others have crossed the line by criticizing the "royal family" directly, with the firm conviction that their exposure of its tyranny and corruption would stir up public indignation abroad and invite strong pressure upon the North.

Excluding those who published memoirs before the 1990s, as of December 2011 about twenty defectors have published their memoirs. These memoirs can be classified in terms of the author's status in the North.

Memoirs by Members of the "Royal Family"   These are people who had been close to Kim Jong Il and his first son, Kim Jong Nam. Two memoirs in this group deserve special mention: one by Yi Il-nam (whose pseudonym was Yi Han-yŏng) and another by his mother, Sung Hye-rang (Sŏng Hye-rang).[43] As

---

42 For example, see Kim Kye-ch'ŏl, "Konghwaguk t'alch'ul, sa-sip-sa-nyŏn manŭi kwihyang" [My defection from North Korea and return home after forty-four years], *Wŏlgan Chosun*, July 1994, 657–720.

43 Yi Han-yŏng, *Taedong-gang royal p'aemilli Sŏul chamhaeng sip-sa-nyŏn* [Fourteen years of secret lives in Seoul by a North Korean royal family"] (Seoul: Dong-A Ilbosa, 1996). This book was revised as follows. Yi Han-yŏng, *Kim Jong Il royal p'aemilli* [The Kim Jong Il royal family] (Seoul: Sidae Chŏngsin, 2004). See also Sŏng, *Tŭngnamu chip*.

we will see in detail in chapter 3, in the 1970s Kim Jong Il lived with Sung Hye-rim, Sung Hye-rang's younger sister, without being married, and his son Kim Jong Nam was the child produced by this unofficial union. As Kim Jong Nam's aunt and de facto governess, Sung Hye-rang was able to closely observe Kim Jong Il and Kim Jong Nam. And her son, Yi Il-nam, as Kim Jong Nam's first cousin and sole friend, was able to infrequently see Kim Jong Il, but spent a good amount of time with Kim Jong Nam. Yi Il-nam's younger sister, Yi Nam-ok, also saw Kim Jong Il and Kim Jong Nam in person. But neither Il-nam nor his sister Yi Nam-ok ever saw Kim Il Sung in person. When Kim Jong Il allowed Kim Jong Nam to study in Geneva with his aunt and his two first cousins, the cousins defected to the West.

In perspective and detail, Sung Hye-rang's autobiography is much more valuable than her son's memoirs or her daughter's interviews with the media. It includes much raw material worthy of serious consideration in analyzing both Kim Jong Il and Kim Jong Nam, although it tends to protect the images of both. But since she defected in 1996, her observations ended at that point. She never saw Kim Il Sung, nor did she see Kim Jong Il's new "wife" Ko Yong-hŭi and their children. While Sung Hye-rim herself died in Moscow on May 18, 2002, without leaving behind any sort of memoirs or interviews, her son Kim Jong Nam has given a number of interviews with Japanese and other foreign journalists in Hong Kong, Macao, and Tokyo.

Now let us turn to the two memoirs by the pseudonymous Fujimoto Kenji, who as a Japanese chef to Kim Jong Il and his family for thirteen years became a de facto member of the royal family.[44] Before his escape to Japan in 2001, he was able to closely observe Kim Jong Il, the new "wife" Ko Yong-hŭi, their two sons, Jong Chul (Chŏng-ch'ŏl) and Jong Un, and one daughter, Yŏ-jŏng. He was one of an extremely limited number of people who was able to observe—all together in one place—Kim Jong Il, Ko Yong-hŭi, their three children, Kim Jong Il's sister and her husband (Kim Kyŏng-hŭi and Chang Sŏng-t'aek), as well as two or three cardinal cadres of the KWP and the KPA. Fujimoto Kenji even saw Kim Ok, who became Kim Jong Il's new "wife" after the death of Ko Yong-hŭi on May 26, 2004. Thus, in examining the palace politics of the North and the succession process from Kim Jong Il to his second son, Fujimoto's memoirs and interviews are much more valuable than any others. He has emphasized that apart from what he personally witnessed, he did not add anything. A lifelong sushi chef

44 Fujimoto Kenji, *Kim Chŏng Il ŭi yorisa* [Kim Jong Il's chef] (published in 2003 in Japanese), trans. Sin Hyŏn-ho (Seoul: Wŏlgan Chosunsa, 2003) and Fujimoto Kenji, *Pukhan ŭi Hugyeja, oe Kim Chŏng Ŭn in'ga?* [Why was Kim Jong Un selected as the North Korean successor?], trans. Han Yu-hŭi (Seoul: Max Media, 2010).

who had never been interested in Marxism-Leninism, any other ideologies, or indeed any subject in the humanities or social sciences, Fujimoto made no pretense of knowing more than he actually did. Moreover, his prediction in 2003 that neither Kim Jong Nam nor Kim Jong Chul, but rather Kim Jong Un would become the successor, a prediction based on his eyewitness observations, proved to be correct in 2010.

Defector Memoirs by Top-Level KWP Officials   This category of defector's memoirs is a very limited one. It includes two, almost identical, recollections by Hwang Chang-yŏp, who defected to the South in February 1997 as secretary for international affairs of the KWPCC.[45] He had been president of Kim Il Sung Comprehensive University and chairman of the SPA. Moreover, he was the core theoretician who developed *Juche*, the North's trademark ideology. He had met Kim Il Sung, his younger brother Kim Yŏng-ju, the Kim Jong Il–Ko Yong-hŭi couple, the Kim Kyŏng-hŭi–Chang Sŏng-t'aek couple, and a significant portion of important cadres of the KWP and the KPA. But he never mentioned Ko Yong-hŭi and their children in his books.

Memoirs by Lower-Level Officials   This category includes memoirs by mid-level or low-level diplomats and officials of state administrative agencies, governmental business firms, the KWP, and the KPA.[46] Most of them never had the chance to visit the exclusive residence area reserved for North Korean ruling elites for the purpose of seeing Kim Il Sung, Kim Jong Il, and their family members in person. Therefore, although they could convey the political, economic, and social environments of the North in general, they could not speak on palace politics in general or succession politics in particular. Certain memoirs, such as the memoirs of Kang Myŏng-do, who claimed to be the son-in-law of North Korean premier Kang Sŏng-san, have

45 Hwang Chang-yŏp, *Nanŭn yŏksa ŭi chilli rŭl po'atta: Hwang Chang-yŏp hoengonok* [I saw the truth in history: Memoirs by Hwang Chang-yŏp] (Seoul: Han'ul Publishing Co., 1999). Its revised edition was published in 2006 by Sidae chŏngsin. See also Hwang Chang-yŏp, *Pukhan ŭi chinsil kwa hŏwi* [North Korea's truth and falsehood] (Seoul: Sidae Chŏngsin, 1999; rev. ed., 2006).

46 For example, see Ko Yŏng-hwan, *P'yŏngyang i-sip-o si* [Twenty-five hours in Pyongyang] (Seoul: Koryŏwŏn, 1992). Ko was a low-level diplomat working at the North Korean Embassy in the Democratic Republic of Congo before his defection to Seoul in 1991. See also Yŏ Man-ch'ŏl, Kim Yong, and Kim Yŏng-sŏng, *Hŭin kŏt to kŏmta* [Even white is said to be black] (Seoul: Tana, 1996). See also Ch'oe Chu-hwal, *Puk Chosŏn ipku* [The door into North Korea], *Pukhan ŭi sijang, chip, kyot'ong, saŏp munhwa* [North Korea's market, housing, transportation, and business culture] (Seoul: Chisik kongjakso, 2000). The author was director of the Joint Venture Bureau, Ryongsŏng Trade Company under the auspices of the PAFM with the rank of colonel. He defected to the South via China in October 1995.

little value as far as this issue is concerned.[47] The North has officially denied that he was Kang Sŏng-san's son-in-law, denouncing him as the "dirty dregs of humanity."[48]

How should we evaluate the four books published in Seoul based on oral statements by Pak Pyŏng-yŏp (pseudonyms Sin Kyŏng-wan, Sŏ Yong-kyu, or Hwang Il-ho), former vice director of the KWP Propaganda and Agitation Department?[49] As we shall see in chapters 2 and 3 in detail, while some parts of his recollections deserve serious consideration, other areas flatly contradict proven facts. He tends to defend both the DPRK and the KWP and protect the images of the two Kims. Since he defected (or possibly was kidnapped) to the South in the 1980s, he never knew Ko Yong-hŭi and her children with Kim Jong Il. Naturally he would not have anything useful to say about the succession from Kim Jong Il to Kim Jong Un.

Memoirs by Captured DPRK Terrorists and Spies   The fourth category of memoirs is those by former North Korean terrorists and spies captured by South Korean authorities. The representative example was written by Kim Hyŏn-hŭi, a woman who had been involved in the bombing of Korean Air Flight 858 in November 1987.[50] Such individuals never encountered Kim Il Sung, Kim Jong Il, or other important cadres of the KWP or the KPA, so their recollections have definite limits for our study.

Memoirs by Escapees   The fifth category includes memoirs by those who successfully escaped the North after experiencing the notorious jails for political prisoners or concentration camps. There are two sorts of famous memoirs that merit serious consideration. One are those written by South Koreans, e.g., Sin Sang-ok, a top South Korean movie director, and his wife Chŏe Ŭn-hŭi, a famous South Korean movie actress. The couple was

47 Kang Myŏng-do, *Pyongyang ŭn mangmyŏng ŭl kkum kkunda* [Dreaming of defection in Pyongyang] (Seoul: JoongAng Ilbosa, 1995).

48 As for the North Korean allegation, see Kim Min-hŭi, "Kwisunja tul ŭi chŭngŏn midŭlman han'ga?" [Are the defectors' testimonies reliable?], *Mal* (September 1994): 155–61. The remarks by Pyongyang Radio Broadcasting Station were quoted on p. 156. Some said that Kang Myŏng-do's wife was not a biological daughter but a foster daughter of Kang Sŏng-san.

49 For example, see Chŏng Ch'ang-hyŏn, *Kyŏt'esŏ pon Kim Chŏng Il* [Kim Jong Il as seen by an entourage], (Seoul: T'oji, 1999). The revised edition was published in 2000 by the Kimyŏngsa Publishing House.

50 Kim Hyŏn-hŭi, *Ije yŏja ka toego sip'ŏyo* [Now I want to be a woman] (Seoul: Koryŏwŏn, 1991), *Sarang ŭl nŭkkil ttaemyŏn nunmul ŭl hŭllimnida* [When I feel love, I shed bitter tears] (Seoul: Koryŏwŏn, 1992). See also her attorney An Tong-il's observations on her, *Nanŭn Kim Hyŏn-hŭi ŭi silch'e rŭl poatta* [I saw the real side of Kim Hyŏn-hŭi"] (Seoul: Dong-A Ilbosa, 2004).

kidnapped by Kim Jong Il in 1978 but succeeded in escaping to the West in 1986. During this time Sin was incarcerated in a jail for political prisoners. The couple later met and had talks with both Kim Il Sung and Kim Jong Il.[51] They even secretly recorded their discussions with Kim Jong Il, which would be released to the public after their escape. The other sort of memoirs are those written by North Korean defectors themselves. A famous one was written by Kang Chol-hwan (Kang Ch'ŏl-hwan), whom then U.S. president George W. Bush met in the White House in June 2005.[52] While the first category of memoirs written by "royal family" members reveals the exceedingly luxurious lives in the North, this last category of memoirs exposes the dark side of the North.

In sum, for students of North Korean succession politics, there are a good number of memoirs by those who experienced life in North Korea. But researchers should approach them with caution. Even Khrushchev's famous recollections, established as authentic, include some incorrect English translations, edited phrases, and even errors in historical facts.[53] As for defectors' memoirs, usually prepared by ghost writers, researchers should heed the advice of Wada Haruki, a renowned historian at the University of Tokyo, who suggested that researchers may find clues from memoirs for further research, but should not depend too heavily upon them.

How This Study Is Organized

This book consists of this introduction and seven more chapters, organized in chronological order. Chapter 2 examines the rise of Kim Il Sung from an anti-Japanese guerrilla leader in 1931 to his emergence as the "Great Leader" of the North Korean unitary system in 1967. The family background of Kim Il Sung and Kim Jong Il, Kim Il Sung's career as an anti-Japanese guerrilla leader in Manchuria and the Soviet Far East during the period of Japanese occupation of Korea, his capture of political power in

51 For example, see Sin Sang-ok and Ch'oe Ŭn-hŭi, *Nere Kim Chŏng Il imnaeda* [I am Kim Jong Il] (Seoul: Haengnim ch'ulp'ansa, 1994) and *Uri ŭi t'alch'ul ŭn kkŭtnaji anatta* [Our escape is not over] (Seoul: Wŏlgan Chosunsa, 2001).

52 Kang Chol-hwan and Pierre Rigoulot, *Les Aquariums de Pyongyang* (Paris: Editions Robert Laffont, 2000), trans. by Yair Reiners with a new preface by the author, *The Aquariums of Pyongyang: Ten Years in the North Korean Gulag* (New York: Basic Books, 2001). See also Lee Soon-ok, *Eyes of the Tailless Animals: Prison Memories of a North Korean Woman* (New York: Living Sacrifice Book Co., 1999); Kim Yong, *Long Road Home: Testimony of a North Korean Camp Survivor* (New York: Columbia University Press, 2009).

53 John Merrill, "Review of *Khrushchev Remembers*, Vol. 1 and Vol. 2," *Journal of Korean Studies* 3 (1981): 181–91.

post-liberation North Korean politics under Soviet military occupation, and his establishment of a "unitary system" with himself as the center in 1967, will be discussed in this chapter.

Chapter 3 examines succession politics from Kim Il Sung to Kim Jong Il from 1967 to 1980. I first explain the succession struggles inside the KWP leadership and the advent of Kim Jong Il as the "terminator." Next, I look at Kim Jong Il's role in the establishment of the "unitary thoughts system." The third part explains the process leading to the Fifth KWP Congress in 1970. Finally, I review the process leading to Kim Jong Il's final capture of the successorship at the Sixth KWP Congress in 1980.

Chapter 4 details the process leading to Kim Jong Il's full-scale assumption of power during 1981–94. I explain the process in which, by 1983, the Kim Jong Il successorship was consolidated. Next, I deal with the emergence of the joint regime of Kim Il Sung and Kim Jong Il. Then, I discuss the subtle, yet important change from the joint regime of Kim Il Sung and Kim Jong Il to the joint regime of Kim Jong Il and Kim Il Sung. Finally, I cover Kim Jong Il's private life with Sung Hye-rim, his common-law wife, and their son, Kim Jong Nam.

Chapter 5 looks at North Korean politics under Kim Jong Il from July 1994 to February 2002, when Kim Jong Il began to prepare the succession to one of his two sons by Ko Yong-hŭi—Kim Jong Chul and Kim Jong Un. First, I deal with the period from 1994 to 1997, when Kim Jong Il ruled or governed North Korea without having assumed the title of KWP general secretary and by using the "dying injunctions of Kim Il Sung" as his major moral duty and justification. Next, I will look at the period beginning in 1997 when Kim Jong Il finally assumed the official title of KWP general secretary. The constitutional revision that expanded the role as well as the authority of the National Defense Commission and the introduction of the doctrine of "military-first politics," both in 1998, are also discussed. I next examine the rampant personality cult surrounding Kim Jong Il, one designed to boost his leadership. Finally, I deal with his private life with Ko Yong-hŭi, his other common-law wife, and their two sons, Kim Jong Chul and Kim Jong Un. The two sons' studies in their teens in Switzerland are discussed in detail.

Chapter 6 covers the process leading to Kim Jong Il's final decision in 2008 to select Kim Jong Un as his successor and Kim Jong Un's public debut as successor in October 2010. Kim Jong Il's stroke in August 2008 was the dividing line in the period discussed in this chapter. Following medical treatment, he hastened the succession process. As a result, the process was shortened and compressed. The power struggle among the few top-level cadres of the KWP and the KPA over the succession is also discussed. The final section of this chapter reviews North Korean politics since October 2010. The personnel change in the North Korean power structure and a series of military provocations against the South in 2010 are examined in this context.

Chapter 7 deals with the period after Kim Jong Il's death in late December 2011. Since the succession had been well prepared for prior to his death, Kim Jong Un's ascension to the top leadership position was crystal clear, as early as the state funeral. However, the personnel lineup that Kim Jong Il prepared for his successor was gradually dismembered, grimly exemplified by the execution of Chang Sŏng-t'aek, Kim Jong Un's uncle, in December 2013. A generational change was signaled by the replacement of Kim Jong Il–era old guards with Kim Jong Un's own people. This chapter traces that process.

Chapter 8 attempts to foresee the future of the succession regime. As a whole, this chapter argues that, although the North Korean situation may seem unstable, the regime may well continue, due to its peculiarities and the lack of an organized opposition.

2 The Rise of Kim Il Sung, 1931–67

FROM GUERRILLA LEADER TO THE DPRK'S "UNITARY LEADER"

Kim Il Sung's Family Background and Its Political Implications for Succession Politics

To comprehend the seventy-year history of North Korea from August 1945—when the Korean Peninsula was divided into north and south—and the particulars of succession politics from Kim Il Sung to Kim Jong Il, and from Kim Jong Il to Kim Jong Un, it is essential to understand the background of the Kim family. Needless to say, hereditary rule over North Korea for seven decades has made the history of the country synchronous with the history of the Kim Il Sung family itself.

Kim Il Sung was born into a hereditary line of of people who attended to the tombs of the elite *yangban* class. The *yangban* were landowning aristocrats holding civil or military office who stood at the top of the four classes in the Chosŏn dynasty's strict social structure.[1] A tomb manager was usually given a thatched-roofed house with two rooms and a kitchen, as well as small plots of land to cultivate for his own livelihood, in return for taking care of his *yangban* landlord's ancestral tombs. Tomb managers belonged to the third social class, and their income was very low. In traditional Korea and even in contemporary South Korea, it is common to identify oneself by one's clan seat (*pon'gwan*) because Koreans believe that it indicates one's family

---

1 Kim Il Sung's family background is detailed in his autobiography, *Segi wa tŏburŏ* [With the century] (Pyongyang: Chosŏn rodongdang ch'ulp'ansa), vol. 1 (1992), 1–25. See also Lee Chong-sik, "Kim Il Sung of North Korea," *Asian Survey* 7, no. 6 (June 1967): 374–82 ; Suh Dae-sook, *Kim Il Sung: The North Korean Leader* (New York: Columbia University Press, 1988); and Bradley K. Martin, *Under the Loving Care of the Fatherly Leader: North Korea and the Kim Dynasty* (New York: Thomas Dunne Books, 2004). I relied upon these works for basic data about Kim Il Sung presented here.

origins. North Korean authorities abolished the clan-seat system, arguing that it was a remnant of feudalism. In 1992, however, two years before his death, Kim Il Sung revealed that his family belonged to the Chŏnju Kim clan of North Chŏlla Province in the south.

Kim Il Sung's ancestors lived for a long time on the outskirts of Chŏnju. The tomb of the founder of the Chŏnju Kim clan is still well preserved on Moak Mountain between Chŏnju and Wanju. At the first summit talks between Kim Dae Jung, then president of the ROK, and Kim Jong Il, chairman of the DPRKNDC, held on June 13–15, 2000, in Pyongyang, the tomb became a topic of discussion between the two leaders. According to a South Korean aide who recorded their conversations, when Kim Dae Jung mentioned the founder's tomb, Kim Jong Il was appreciative.[2]

Kim Il Sung's Parents

Between 1810 and 1820, the Kim family moved to a farming region called Man'gyŏngdae ("ten thousand scenic views") in Taedong County, South P'yŏng'an Province, whose capital is Pyongyang. As their job was essentially the same as before, they remained poor. In the 1890s, Kim Po-hyŏn and Ri Po-ik had three biological sons: Hyŏng-jik, Hyŏng-nok, and Hyŏng-gwŏn. Kim Hyŏng-jik was the biological father of Kim Il Sung. After the founding of the DPRK in 1948, Hyŏng-nok's son would become first director of political affairs at the Man'gyŏngdae Revolutionary School, and then vice director of the Propaganda and Agitation Department at the KPAGPB with the rank of lieutenant general; Hyŏng-gwŏn's son would become vice-premier of the DPRK cabinet. The couple also had three daughters. It is assumed that one or two died before reaching adulthood. At any rate, two sons-in-law of a daughter, i.e., Kim Il Sung's aunt, would enter into the core of the KWP and DPRK cabinet: Yang Hyŏng-sŏp, presently vice-chairman of the SPA Presidium and a member of the KWPCC Politburo, and the late Hŏ Tam, former foreign minister, vice-premier, and KWPCC Politburo member.[3]

Kim Hyŏng-jik was born in 1894 at Man'gyŏngdae and received a traditional education in a humble primary school in the same village. In 1908, he married Kang Pan-sŏk, who had been born in 1892 in Ch'ilgol, a farming village near Man'gyŏngdae. Her family and close relatives had formed the small village of Ch'ilgol; they owned much land in Ch'ilgol and even factories in Pyongyang. Her father, Kang Ton-uk, was a revered Christian elder at

---

2 I interviewed the aide on condition of anonymity on August 11, 2011, in Seoul.

3 Hwang Chang-yŏp, *Na nŭn yŏksa ŭi chilli rŭl poatta: Hwang Chang-yŏp hoengnok* [I saw the truth in history: Memoirs by Hwang Chang-yŏp] (Seoul: Han'ul Publishing Co., 1999), 151.

Ch'ilgol Church, as well as vice-principal at the Ch'angdŏk School attached to the church. He taught the Chinese classics as well as the Bible. His daughter's name, Pan-sŏk, might be translated as "grand rock" or "foundation stone," indicating his firm belief in Christianity.[4] Not surprisingly, the Kang clan in Ch'ilgol produced many Christians, including pastors, elders, and deacons. For example, Kang Yang-uk, Kang Ton-uk's second cousin, became a Presbyterian pastor, and Kang Pan-sŏk herself became a deaconess. The Kang clan also produced many anti-Japanese activists, including Kang Ton-uk and his son. Because of his anti-Japanese activities, Kang Pan-sŏk's elder brother was imprisoned in 1924, dying immediately after his provisional release in 1941. Today, Ch'ilgol has been designated a historical site by the North.[5] The North has only designated places related to the Kim Il Sung family as "historical sites."

Since the founding of the DPRK in September 1948, many members of the Kang clan in Ch'ilgol have held significant positions in North Korea's power structure. One example was the Reverend Kang Yang-uk, who was elected vice-chairman of the DPRK four times before his death in 1983. His son became ambassador to Romania, and his son-in-law was appointed ambassador to the Soviet Union and then vice-chairman of the SPA. Other members of this family—Kang Hŭi-wŏn, Kang Hyŏn-su, Kang Chu-il, and Kang Kwan-ju—became chairman of the Pyongyang People's Committee, first secretary of the KWP Pyongyang Committee, director of the KWP United Front Department, and vice director of the KWP United Front Department, respectively. Even today, the Kang clan is still called the "Ch'ilgol Kang" clan, connoting its strength.[6]

Probably under his father-in-law's influence, Kim Hyŏng-jik also accepted Christianity and entered the middle-school section of Sungsil School, which was established in Pyongyang in 1897 by the Northern Presbyterian mission of the United States. But, according to official North Korean publications, "he fought against the American pastors and teachers—who . . . were pro-Japanese imperialists—and left the school voluntarily" in winter 1912.[7] Soon after, he briefly became a teacher at a small Christian school. It is ironic that his son, Kim Il Sung, born into a Christian family, would become a

4 In the New Testament, Jesus compared his first disciple Peter to the rock or "foundation stone" on which he would build his church.

5 *Rodong Sinmun*, January 21, 1975, 2.

6 Kang Myŏng-do, *Pyongyang ŭn mangmyŏng ŭl kkumkkunda* [Dreaming of defection in Pyongyang] (Seoul: JoongAng Ilbosa, 1995), 56–59. As I wrote earlier, Kang Myŏng-do's memoirs should be examined with caution, but his explanation of the Ch'ilgol Kang clan is credible.

7 For example, see *Rodong Sinmun*, March 23, 1977, 4.

staunch anti-Christian leader.[8] On April 15, 1912, when Kim Hyŏng-jik was a student at Sungsil, his first child was born at Man'gyŏngdae. This son was named Sŏng-ju and would later be called Il Sung. Since the founding of the DPRK, Man'gyŏngdae, as Kim Il Sung's birthplace, has become the most revered place in the North—the sanctified house and surrounding area have become important elements of the personality cult around Kim Il Sung.

In the autumn of 1917, Japanese authorities jailed Kim Hyŏng-jik at Pyongyang Prison for ten months on charges he was a member of the recently exposed Korean National Association, an underground anti-Japanese organization in Pyongyang. While North Korean official publications have proudly emphasized this story, South Korean authorities have rejected it, alleging that there was no official record to substantiate the claims. But in the ensuing debates, reliable testimony has been found: the diary of the Reverend Pae Min-su, who had been one year junior to Kim Hyŏng-jik at Sungsil.[9] Pae wrote in his diary that under Kim's guidance, he joined the Korean National Association for the liberation of Korea and that he was imprisoned with Kim and other comrades at Pyongyang Prison. Later Pae studied at Princeton Theological Seminary in the United States and became a Presbyterian pastor in Pyongyang. Immediately after Soviet occupation of the north, he fled to the south to fight against Soviet Russia and North Korean communists. In 1946 he came to realize that Kim Il Sung was the very son of Kim Hyŏng-jik, whom he had greatly respected throughout his life. Pae lamented that "the most noble Christian patriot's son has become the worst enemy of the Christian Church."[10]

Kim Il Sung's Early Studies in Manchuria

According to Kim Il Sung's autobiography, in 1918, when he was six years old, his mother brought him along to Pyongyang Prison. The boy saw how his father suffered in the aftermath of being interrogated under torture. Kim Il Sung recalled, "The fact that I saw my father at prison was a major turning point in my life. I felt the true face of evil Japanese imperialism from head to toe. I never forgot this scene during the whole period of my anti-Japanese guerrilla movement."[11] In light of Reverend Pae's recollections on torture, Kim Il Sung's recollections of this time seem credible.

8 Choe Young-ho, "Christian Background in Early Life of Kim Il Sung," *Asian Survey* 26, no.10 (October 1986): 1082–91. See also *Rodong Sinmun*, March 23, 1997, 4.

9 Pae Min-su, *Who Shall Enter the Kingdom of Heaven?*, an autobiography typewritten in 1951, quoted in Pang Ki-jung, *Pae Min-su ŭi nongch'on undong kwa kidokkyo sasang* [Pae Min-su's rural reconstruction movement and Christian thoughts] (Seoul: Yonsei University Press, 1999), 62–67.

10 Ibid., 211.

11 Kim, *Segi wa tŏburŏ*, vol. 1, 32–33.

About a year after his release, Kim Hyŏng-jik emigrated to southeastern Manchuria with his wife and two sons, Sŏng-ju and Ch'ŏl-ju, and opened a traditional herbal medicine clinic. It is unclear where he had studied herbal medicine, and official North Korean publications and Kim Il Sung's autobiography do not clarify the point. We only know that "through his friend at home, he borrowed a diploma which certified him as a graduate of Severance Medical School in Seoul."[12] This medical school—presently the medical school of Yonsei (Yŏnse) University—has no record of Kim Hyŏng-jik. In 1925, the Japanese consulate in Chientao reported to the foreign ministry that his income was very high among the Korean immigrants living in his town, adding that he still maintained a stance of "non-cooperation" towards Japan.[13] Around this time, his third biological son, Yŏng-ju, was born.

As for Kim Il Sung's new life in Manchuria, we can point out two facts. First, he began studying Chinese from the age of seven and gained an understanding of Chinese culture. Even after his father's sudden death in 1926 at the age of thirty-two, his mother made him attend Wiwŏn Middle School, an expensive private school for Chinese in Jilin, Manchuria. His fluent command of Chinese would later help him in his common struggle with the Chinese against the Japanese in Manchuria in the 1930s. After the founding of the DPRK, he would have talks with Chinese counterparts, including Mao Zedong, Liu Shaoqi, Zhou Enlai, and Deng Xiaoping, in Chinese without depending upon interpreters. Second, as a student at Wiwŏn, he learned about Marxism-Leninism from his Chinese teacher, Xiang Wei. As a member of the CCP, Xiang introduced Maxim Gorky's revolutionary novel *Mother* and Lenin's "On Imperialism" to the young Kim.[14] Under Xiang's direct influence, Kim entered the Korean Communist Youth Association in Jilin in 1929 and became involved in anti-Japanese demonstrations.

Kim Il Sung was incarcerated in Jilin Prison by pro-Japanese Chinese military authorities but released in 1930. During this imprisonment, the Reverend Son Chŏng-do, a classmate of Kim's deceased father at Sungsil School and a fervent anti-Japanese activist in Jilin, helped Kim.[15] Kim Il

12 For example, see Kim, *Segi wa tŏburŭŏ*, vol. 1, 59–60.

13 Quoted in Yi Myŏng-yŏng, *Kwŏllyŏk ŭi yŏksa: Chosŏn rodongdang kwa kŭndaesa* [A history of power: The Korean Workers' Party and modern history"], 2nd ed. (Seoul: Chongno Sŏjŏk, 1989), 232–33.

14 As for Xiang's recollections, see Wada Haruki, *Kita Chōsen* (Tokyo: Iwanami Shoten, 1998), trans. by Sŏ Tong-man and Nam Ki-jŏng, *Pukchosŏn* [North Korea] (Seoul: Tolbegae, 2002), 41.

15 Rev. Son's other son, who became a medical doctor in Omaha, Nebraska, published his memoirs on his relationship with Kim. See Sohn Won-tai, *Kim Il Sung and Korea's Struggle: An Unconventional Firsthand History* (Jefferson, MO: McFarland and Co., 2003).

Sung recollected emphatically that throughout his life he never forgot how Reverend Son looked after him with "fatherly care." Ironically, Reverend Son's eldest son would become the ROK chief of naval operations, minister of national defense, and ambassador to West Germany during the Syngman Rhee administration in 1948–60.

Kim Il Sung's Guerrilla Activities with Kim Jong Suk in Manchuria and the Soviet Far East

After his release from prison at the age of eighteen, Kim Il Sung left school and roamed through four towns in southeastern Manchuria, meeting many Koreans who were attempting to organize an anti-Japanese movement with the Chinese. At one point, he joined the Down with Imperialism Alliance led by the Korean Ri Chong-rak, and became friends with members of the General Alliance of Korean Youth in southern Manchuria. It was at this time that he changed his given name from Sŏng-ju to Il Sung. According to his memoirs, his Korean comrades urged him to do so to reflect their common wish that he should "become the sun (in Chinese, *richeng* 日成) of the Korean nation."[16]

Kim Il Sung's Relationship with the CCP

The September 18 Incident of 1931 (also known as the Mukden Incident or the Manchurian Incident), which signaled the full-scale Japanese invasion of Manchuria, was a turning point in Kim Il Sung's career. One month later, at the age of nineteen, he joined the CCP's Manchurian Provincial Committee, in which Liu Shaoqi served as secretary. In February 1932 Kim also joined an anti-Japanese guerrilla unit under the leadership of a Chinese military officer. Two months later, he established a separate small Korean group within that unit.[17] Since the 1970s the KWP has claimed that Kim Il Sung established the anti-Japanese guerrilla unit on April 25, 1932, and developed it into the Korean People's Revolutionary Army in February 1934.[18] Historians have not found any documentation to substantiate this claim.

16 Kim, *Segi wa tŏburŏ*, vol. 2, 107.

17 Wada Haruki, *Kim Il Sung and the Anti-Japanese War in Manchuria* (in Japanese) (Tokyo: Heibonsha, 1992), trans. by Yi Chong-sŏk (Seoul: Ch'angjak kwa Pip'yŏngsa, 1992), 84–91.

18 For North Korean claims, see Paek, *Minjok ŭi t'aeyang Kim Il-sŏng Changgun*, vol. 1, 100. For critical comments see, Suh Dae-sook (Sŏ Tae-suk), *Hyŏndae Pukhan ŭi chidoja Kim Il Sŏng kwa Kim Chŏng-il* [Contemporary North Korean leaders, Kim Il Sung and Kim Jong Il] (Seoul: Ŭryu Munhwasa, 2000), 40.

Kim Il Sung thus began his communist career as a CCP member. A few North Korean official publications, up to around 1960, recorded that fact correctly, although they did not explain it in detail.[19] Beginning in 1961, however, official sources concealed the truth, writing merely that he had entered the "communist party" in 1931, while stressing that Kim had devoted his life entirely to Korean independence and revolution. It was not until 1992, two years before his death, that Kim Il Sung acknowledged he had been a member of the CCP.[20]

While Kim Il Sung was expanding his Korean guerrilla unit, other Koreans established similar units in four nearby regions, with a total membership of about 360.[21] According to official North Korean publications, they were united into the Eastern Manchurian Anti-Japanese Guerrilla Unit.[22] Many of them suffered from witch hunts conducted by the Eastern Manchurian Special Committee, part of the CCP's Manchurian Provincial Committee. Alleging that many Korean communist guerrillas within the CCP were actually Japanese spies, the special committee started a campaign to identify and purge them. In 1933 alone, 431 innocent Koreans were executed.[23] Kim Il Sung was imprisoned on similar charges but, thanks to strong support from Zhou Baozhong, a Manchurian Provincial Committee cadre, he was released. When the Manchurian Provincial Committee inaugurated the Second Corps of the Northeastern People's Revolutionary Army in 1934 (in addition to the First Corps organized in 1933), Kim was appointed political commissar of its third band. In the midst of witch hunts that continued until 1936, Kim seemed to have played a major role in defending innocent Koreans; according to official North Korean publications, one of the Korean guerrilla fighters saved from being purged by him was Kim Il. After the founding of the DPRK, Kim Il would be appointed the DPRK's prime minister and elected as a KWPCCPC member.[24]

Reliable research has concluded that Kim Il Sung's "courageous" role contributed to the heightening of his prestige and trust among Korean

19 For example, see Rim Ch'un-ch'u, *Hangil mujang t'ujaeng sigi rŭl hoesang hayŏ* [Recollecting the period of anti-Japanese armed struggle] (Pyongyang: Chosŏn rodongdang ch'ulp'ansa, 1960), 69.

20 Kim, *Segi wa tŏburŏ*, vol. 2, 67–68.

21 Wada, *Kim Il Sung*, 90–91.

22 For example, see Paek, *Minjok ŭi t'aeyang*, vol. 1, 104.

23 Chang Se-yun, *Chungguk tongbuk chiyŏk minjok undong kwa Han'guk hyŏndaesa* [The nationalist movement in the Chinese northeastern region and Korea's contemporary history] (Seoul: Myŏngjisa, 2005), 279.

24 *Rodong Sinmun*, March 9, 1984, 3.

revolutionaries in southeastern Manchuria.[25] During this period of Japanese resistance, his mother died of cancer at the age of forty in Manchuria in 1932; his younger brother, Ch'ŏl-ju, was killed during an anti-Japanese battle in Manchuria in 1935, leaving no offspring; and his father's youngest brother, Hyŏng-gwŏn, who had shot a Japanese policeman, died in a Seoul prison in 1936.

In 1936 the Northeastern People's Revolutionary Army reorganized itself into the Northeastern United Anti-Japanese Army (NEUAJA). Kim Il Sung was promoted to commander of the Third Division of the Second Corps of the First Route Army. The Third Division numbered around six hundred soldiers, half of whom were Korean. Since Kim's division fought together with the Fifth Corps of the Second Route Army under the commander of Zhou Baozhong, he sometimes received instructions from Zhou. Apart from Kim Il Sung, other Korean guerrilla leaders within the NEUAJA included Ch'oe Yong-gŏn, Kim Ch'aek, Ch'oe Hyŏn, Kang Kŏn, and Rim Ch'un-ch'u, all of whom would later become core leaders of the KWP and DPRK. Ch'oe Yong-gŏn would become the head of state, and Kim Ch'aek, Ch'oe Hyŏn, Rim Ch'un-ch'u, and Kang Kŏn would become vice-premier, national defense minister, foreign minister, and army chief of staff, respectively.

Kim Il Sung's activities expanded and he continued to receive promotions. In the same year, he was appointed political commissar of the First Route Army and was allowed to simultaneously command his own separate unit of about one hundred soldiers—the "Kim Il Sung Battalion." As his name began to be known in Korea proper, young Koreans, including about twenty orphans, joined his battalion. These included Chu To-il, Ch'ŏn Mun-sŏp, Paek Hak-rim, Ri Ŭl-sŏl, and Ryu Kyŏng-su. All of them would become cardinal cadres of the KWP and KPA.[26] Kim Il Sung soon inaugurated a special unit whose primary purpose was the protection of Kim himself and his headquarters; its members also served as messengers within his battalion. Members of the battalion and Kim's team became key cadres in the KWP and KPA. An example is O Paek-ryong, who would become the KWP director of the Military Affairs Department with the rank of general and a member of the KWPCCPC. As a group, Koreans who fought against the Japanese with Kim Il Sung as their leader in Manchuria in the 1930s would later be called the "Manchurian faction" in post-liberation North Korean politics.

25 Han Hong-koo, "Wounded Nationalism: The Minsaengdan Incident and Kim Il Sung in Eastern Manchuria" (PhD diss., University of Washington, 1999), 341–45.
26 Kim, *Segi wa tōburŏ*, vol. 6, 224 and 263; vol. 8, 129–33, and 283.

The most significant achievement in Kim Il Sung's career as a resistance fighter against the Japanese was the victory at the Battle of Poch'ŏnbo. In June 1937 Kim Il Sung's guerrilla unit succeeded in crossing the Yalu River and invading Poch'ŏnbo, a small inland village in Kapsan County, South Hamgyŏng Province. After destroying the police station, post office, and administrative office, they returned to their base camp. This battle became so widely known through a series of reports in the *Dong-A Ilbo*, a leading Korean nationalist daily published in Seoul, that Kim Il Sung became famous in his homeland.[27] The battle would become one of his political assets in the post-liberation politics of North Korea.

It should be noted that at the Battle of Poch'ŏnbo the Kim Il Sung Battalion received decisive assistance from domestic Korean communists in Kapsan County, who had organized the underground Association for the Restoration of the Fatherland. They included Pak Kŭm-ch'ŏl, Pak Mun-sang (pseudonym Pak Tal), Ri Che-sun, Kwŏn Yŏng-byŏk, Ma Tong-hŭi, and Ri Song-un. Unlike the guerrillas belonging to the Kim Il Sung Battalion, all of them were arrested. Some were executed or died in prison, while others would be released from prison after the liberation of Korea. As members of the so-called Kapsan faction, they would also enter into high-level KWP and DPRK posts.

In the wake of the Battle of Poch'ŏnbo, Japanese authorities were able to confirm the real identity of Kim Il Sung through harsh interrogations involving torture. Soon the Japanese attempted to win him over, capitalizing on the fact that Ri Chong-rak, Kim's leader in the Down with Imperialism Alliance, had himself gone over to the Japanese side. In 1938 Ri succeeded in locating Kim Il Sung's secret camp, only to be executed by Kim's lieutenant.[28] The Japanese authorities responded by creating a special military battalion consisting of Japanese officers along with Korean officers belonging to the army of Manchukuo, the puppet state established by Japan in 1932. This special battalion, with superior weapons and equipment, vigorously pursued the Kim Il Sung Battalion. Lacking sufficient food, Kim and his four hundred men were forced to retreat on foot to a wooded area near the Sino-Korean border from December 1938 to March 1939, a mid-winter march that lasted about one hundred days. Official North Korean publications have called this retreat the "March in Distress" or the "Arduous March," the same term North Korean leaders would use for the starvation and other economic hardships that their country suffered in the 1990s.

27 For example, see the extra edition of *Dong-A Ilbo*, June 5, 1937.

28 Paek Pong, *Minjok ŭi t'aeyang Kim Il Sŏng changgun* [General Kim Il Sung, the sun of the nation] (Pyongyang: Inmun Kwahaksa), vol. 1, 289–93.

After the August 1948 founding of the ROK, those Korean Manchukuo officers who had pursued Kim's battalion would end up forming an important part of the South Korean officer corps. For example, Paek Sŏn-yŏp, Yim Ch'ung-sik, Sin Hyŏn-jun, and Kim Sŏk-bŏm would become army chief of staff, national defense minister, marine corps commander, and naval defense commander, respectively. Kim Paeg-il and others would become corps or division commanders.[29] Chŏng Il-gwŏn, who would become army chief of staff during the Korean War of 1950–53, was also a Manchukuo military officer at this time, although he was not a member of the special military battalion. Thus, in a sense, the present military confrontation between the two Koreas had already started in Manchuria by the late 1930s.

Kim Il Sung and the Communist Party of the Soviet Union

In May 1939 Kim Il Sung and his soldiers succeeded in safely settling down in a village in Manchuria. But five months later, the Japanese Kwantung Army in Manchukuo initiated full-scale operations against the NEUAJA, including the Kim Il Sung Battalion. The NEUAJA collapsed as a unified organization in 1940, by which time most of its officers and soldiers had been killed or captured or had surrendered. With the Kim Il Sung Battalion suffering the same fate, Kim decided to escape to the Soviet Far East. In August 1940, before his escape, he married his guerrilla comrade, Kim Jong Suk (Kim Chŏng-suk), in the Manchurian mountainside. Born five years after Kim in 1917 and from an extremely poor farming family in Hoeryŏng, North Hamgyŏng Province, she had once saved Kim Il Sung's life in battle.[30]

On October 23, 1940, Kim Il Sung and Kim Jong Suk arrived at the Russian border near Khabarovsk with four comrades. The Soviet border army took them in custody, suspecting that they might be Japanese spies. At that critical moment, Zhou Baozhong, who had barely managed to escape to the Soviet Far East, appeared. Thanks to his persuasive advocacy, they were released and posted to a field operation school in an area located between Vladivostok and Voroshilov (now known as Ussuriysk), where Kim Il Sung received training in parachute and intelligence operations.[31] Around this time, five other Koreans—Ch'oe Yong-gŏn, Ch'oe Hyŏn, Kim Ch'aek, Rim

---

29 Paek Sŏng-yŏp, *Kun kwa na* [The army and I] (Seoul: Taeryuk Yŏn'guso, 1989), 111.

30 As for Kim Jong Suk, see Jasper Becker, *Rogue Regime: Kim Jong Il and the Looming Threat of North Korea* (Oxford: Oxford University Press, 2005), 48, and Martin, *Under the Loving Care*, 43.

31 Yi Chong-sŏk, *Pukhan-Chungguk kwan'gye, 1945–2000* [Relations between North Korea and China, 1945–2000] (Seoul: Chungsim, 2000), 21.

Ch'un-ch'u, and O Chin-u—also arrived in the Soviet Far East. According to an official Soviet document, all of them, including Kim Il Sung, joined the Soviet Red Army in June 1942.[32] Two months later, the Soviet Far Eastern Army (SFEA) inaugurated the Special International Brigade (SIB) or the Eighty-Eighth Brigade at Vyatskoye, near Khavarovsk, with a combination of Chinese, Korean, and Soviet-Korean guerrillas. Zhou Baozhong was appointed its commander; Ch'oe Yong-gŏn its vice chief of staff; and Kim Il Sung was appointed its first battalion commander, with the Soviet rank of captain.[33] Ch'oe Yong-gŏn, Kang Kŏn, and Kim Ch'aek also received the Soviet rank of captain, while Ch'oe Hyŏn and Kim Il received the Soviet rank of first lieutenant.

The SIB belonged not to the Soviet Defense Ministry but to the Soviet Interior Ministry, which was responsible for the defense of the frontier and had its own military forces. However, its de facto supervisor was Major General Andrei Romanenko, director of the General Political Bureau, First Independent Army, SFEA, in Voroshilov. He had Lieutenant Colonel Grigory Mekler, his adjutant responsible for propaganda, regularly inspect the SIB's teaching and training. In February 1944 Mekler met Kim Il Sung through Zhou Baozhong, who gave Kim high praise. Mekler seems to have reported this to Romanenko.[34] As we will see later, Romanenko and Mekler would play major roles in the post-liberation politics of North Korea under Soviet military occupation. More importantly, Romanenko's immediate superior was Colonel General Terenti Shtykov, chief political commissar of the SFEA, who regularly reported on activities of the SIB to Interior Minister Lavrentiy Beria in Moscow. Shtykov would supervise all North Korean affairs during the Soviet military occupation, and become the first Soviet ambassador to the DPRK.

According to the same Soviet document, all SIB members received preliminary education in a special program arranged by the Soviet army infantry school in Khavarovsk. After that short course, according to this document, Kim Il Sung received further preliminary education in Marxism-Leninism at the "central organization of the party."[35] What does the "central organization of the party" mean? Does it mean an organization belonging to the central party of the CPSU in Moscow? The Soviet document in question does not clarify that point.

32 Quoted in Gavril Korotkov, *Stalin and Kim Il Sung* (in Russian), trans. by Ŏ Kŏn-ju, 2 vols. (Seoul: Dong-A Ilbosa, 1992), vol. 1, 163–64. The name of the original publisher was not recorded.

33 Kim, *Segi wa tŏburŏ*, vol. 8, 81–82 and 144.

34 Wada, *Kim Il Sung*, 247 and 282, quoting from the diary of Zhou Baozhong.

35 Gavril Korotkov, *Stalin and Kim Il Sung*, vol. 1, 75.

However, there are some clues. Immediately after his return to Pyongyang following the liberation of Korea, Kim Il Sung was reported to have said that "some months after the Soviet entry into the war against Nazi Germany in 1941, the Soviet Union invited me to Moscow and made me take a rest."[36] In 1991, Yu Sŏng-ch'ŏl, a Korean-Russian member of the SIB, testified that in September 1943 he was Kim Il Sung's translator during Kim's visit to Moscow.[37] In 1992, recalling Rim Ch'un-ch'u's explanation given in 1961 in Pyongyang, Sin Kyŏng-wan, a former mid-level cadre of the KWP, testified that Kim had visited Moscow with Zhou Baozhong in 1943 and 1944.[38] In 1998, four years after Kim's death, his posthumous memoirs confirmed that he had visited Moscow.[39] If those recollections are true, we would be interested in the allegation by Gavril Korotkov, a Russian military historian who dug up many classified Soviet documents, that Kim Il Sung had a daughter born during the Second World War to a Russian woman whom Kim had met casually, and that the daughter was living in St. Petersburg without knowing the truth about her father.[40] In sum, those recollections strongly suggest that the "central party" indicated in the Soviet document was CPSU headquarters in Moscow.

In July 1945, one month before the Soviet entry into the Pacific War against Japan, the SFEA allowed the Korean guerrillas to organize their own committee—the Korean Operational Committee. Kim Il Sung and Ch'oe Yong-gŏn were assigned to its military-political affairs and its party affairs, respectively, and Kim Ch'aek was assigned to assist the two men. They agreed that, after the liberation of Korea, they would inaugurate a Korean communist party separate from the CCP, with Kim Il Sung as its leader.[41] About ten days after the Japanese surrender on August 15, 1945, the SFEA awarded the Soviet national flag decoration to ten SIB members, including Kim Il Sung and three other Koreans. At the same time, according to the above-mentioned Soviet document, General Maxim Purkayev, commander of the

36 Quoted in O Yŏng-jin, *Hana ŭi chŭngŏn: Sogun chŏngha ŭi Pukhan* [A testimony: North Korea under the Soviet military government] (Seoul: Chungang Munhwasa, 1952). This book was reprinted by the National Territorial Unification Board of the ROK in 1983. The quoted part is on p. 109 in the reprinted version.

37 Martin, *Under the Loving Care*, 49.

38 JoongAng Ilbo T'ŭkpyŏl ch'uwi chaeban, ed. *Pirok: Chosŏn minju ŭi inmin konghwaguk* [Secret records: The Democratic People's Republic of Korea] (Seoul: Joong-Ang Ilbosa, 1992), 70. Hereafter cited as *Secret Records*.

39 Kim, *Segi wa tŏbulrŏ*, vol. 8, 448–55.

40 Korotkov, *Stalin and Kim Il Sung*, vol. 1, 75.

41 Sin Chu-baek, *Manju chiyŏk Hanin ŭi minjok undongsa, 1920–1945* [A history of the Korean nationalist movement in the Manchurian region, 1920–1945] (Seoul: Asea Munhwasa, 1999), 489–92.

SFEA Second Field Army, had an interview with Kim. General Iosif Shikin, a military committee member of that army, also participated in the interview. When Purkayev asked Kim whether he would go to North Korea if ordered by the Soviet army, Kim replied that he would do his best to be helpful to world revolutionary objectives. Purkayev concluded that Kim's answers were excellent. In consultation with Shtykov and Purkayev, SFEA commander marshal Aleksandr Vasilevsky sent a report to Beria, recommending Kim's return to Pyongyang as the leader of the Korean Operational Committee. When Beria reported it to Stalin, adding his favorable assessment, Stalin signed it and ordered Marshal Vasilevsky to fully support Kim.[42]

The Birth of Kim Jong Il

Kim Jong Suk gave birth to Kim Il Sung's first child and son, Kim Jong Il (Kim Chŏng-il), or Yuri Irsenovich Kim in Russian. According to official North Korean publications, Kim Jong Il was born on February 16, 1942, at "a bloody battlefield of a decisive anti-Japanese battle,"[43] although the specific name of his birthplace was not mentioned. Yi Chong-sŏk, a leading South Korean scholar on Kim Il Sung and Kim Jong Il, speculated that his birthplace might be a military camp at Voroshilov near Vladivostok, or a hospital in Vladivostok.[44] Kim Tan, son of a former North Korean vice justice minister and Kim Jong Il's classmate in junior high and high school in Pyongyang, remembered that Jong Il used to say that his birthplace was a military camp in Khabarovsk.[45] However, as we shall see in chapter 3, North Korean authorities began to claim in 1984 that Kim Jong Il was born in a secret Korean communist guerrilla camp located at Mount Paektu (Whitehead Mountain).

A number of researchers have asserted that Kim Jong Suk gave birth to Kim Il Sung's second child, a son named Shura, in Russia in 1944. They add that in 1948, three years after the Kim family's return to Pyongyang, Shura (or Man-il, his Korean name) drowned in a pond at the family's residence.[46] However, Purkayev wrote in his above-mentioned report that as

42 Korotkov, *Stalin and Kim Il Sung*, vol. 1, 180–85.

43 *Inmin ŭi chidoja* [The people's leader] (Pyongyang: Chosŏn rodongdang ch'ulp'ansa, 1982), vol. 1, 3.

44 For example, see Yi Chong-sŏk, *Saero ssŭn hyŏndae Pukhanŭi ihae* [An understanding of contemporary North Korea: A newly written edition] (Seoul: Yŏksa Pip'yŏngsa, 2000), 491.

45 JoongAng Ilbosa, ed. *Kim Chŏng-il: Hanbando chŏlban ŭi sangsogin* [Kim Jong Il: An heir to half of the Korean Peninsula] (Seoul: JoongAng Ilbosa, 1994), 53

46 For example, see Yi Chong-sŏk, "Chusokkung chŏpsuhan o-sip-i-se hwangt'aeja" [The fifty-two-year-old crown prince who received the palace of the chairman], *Sindonga* (August 1994), 243.

of September 1945 Kim Il Sung had one son, Yuri.[47] In 2002, Augusta Sergeyevna, a lifelong resident of Vyatskoye, recalled the birth of Kim Jong Il in detail. Asserting that Kim Jong Il was born in 1941 with his twin brother, Shura, in Vyatskoye, where the Soviet military camp was located, she said that Shura drowned in a village well at the age of three or four. She even pointed out his tomb to an interviewer.[48]

For a long time, Kim Il Sung concealed from the North Korean people his escape to the Soviet Far East and his assignment with the SIB, just as he hid the fact that he had started his communist career as a CCP member. It was not until 1998, four years after his death, that his posthumous memoirs acknowledged his time in Russia, although even then the term "escape" was not used. The memoirs merely note that he accepted a Comintern instruction to continue anti-Japanese guerrilla activities in the Soviet Far East.[49] This is one example of how facts were covered up, either by Kim Il Sung himself, or by the regime.

To be fair, his fourteen-year fight, whether he was affiliated with the Chinese or the Soviets, *is* worthy of praise. But the facts reveal that "by 1945 [the Korean communist movement, and by extension, Kim Il Sung] had been exposed to only one practical model of governance: the Stalinist mobilization state."[50] To elaborate, what he learned through guerrilla activities under communist auspices was how to maintain power through illegal and unjust Stalinist tactics—deceit, intrigue, threat, imprisonment, torture, violence, murder, and even massacre. Unfortunately, such harsh power tactics would also become ingredients of the Kim Il Sung–Kim Jong Il leadership.

Kim Il Sung's Struggles to Launch the KWP and DPRK, 1945–49

The Opening of Soviet Occupation Forces Headquarters in Pyongyang

Two days after the American dropping of the atomic bomb on Hiroshima, on August 6, 1945, the Soviet Union declared war against Japan and started military operations against Japanese forces in Manchuria. Between August 9 and 18, the SFEA Twenty-Fifth Army occupied major cities in Manchuria and the northern part of what is presently North Korea. On August 15, Japan officially announced its surrender to the Allied Powers, who immediately decided to divide the Korean Peninsula into north and

---

47 Quoted in Korotkov, *Stalin and Kim Il Sung*, vol. 1, 180.

48 *Choson Ilbo*, August 23, 2002, A13.

49 Kim, *Segi wa tŏburŏ*, vol. 8, 51–81.

50 Adrian Buzo, *The Guerrilla Dynasty: Politics and Leadership in North Korea* (Boulder, CO: Westview Press, 1999), 11.

south at the 38th parallel, with Soviet troops occupying the north and U.S. troops the south. On August 25–26, the Soviet army entered Pyongyang, the key city in the north as well as the capital of South P'yŏng'an Province, and opened the Soviet Occupation Forces Headquarters in North Korea (SOF-HNK). Although its commander was Colonel General Ivan Chistiakov, a career solider, Major General Nikolai Lebedev, its chief political commissar, was more influential. Lebedev received instructions directly and regularly from Colonel General Shtykov, the chief political commissar of the Maritime Military District Command (MMDC) in Voroshilov, which had been reorganized from the SFEA First Field Army on September 2, 1945. Since the MMDC was empowered to supervise the north, Shtykov was called the Soviet governor-general in North Korea.[51]

As occupiers of Pyongyang, the Soviets came to recognize the existence of two domestic Korean political forces: anti-communist (or simply non-communist) nationalists, and communists. Immediately after liberation and before the Soviet occupation, the former inaugurated the Committee for the Preparation of Korean Independence (CPKI) in South P'yŏng'an Province, with Cho Man-sik, an anti-Japanese Christian elder, as chairman. While recognizing his leadership, the SOFHNK made Cho reorganize the committee as a coalition body with domestic communists. Hyŏn Chun-hyŏk, a leader of the domestic communists in the north, was assassinated in Pyongyang by members of the anti-communist White Robe Society, who then fled to the south. This was the first in a series of assassinations on both sides.

51 Erik Van Ree, *Socialism in One Zone: Stalin's Policy in Korea, 1945–1947* (New York: Berg Publishers, 1989), 101–103. There are a number of major works dealing with the period from August 15, 1945, to September 9, 1948, with emphasis upon Kim Il Sung's capture of political power in the north, including Robert A. Scalapino and Lee Chong-sik, *Communism in Korea*, 2 parts (Berkeley: University of California Press, 1972), 1 (*The Movement*), 236–55; Kim Il-p'yŏng, ed. *Pukhan ch'eche ŭi surip kwachŏng* [The process of the establishment of the North Korean regime] (Seoul: The Far Eastern Affairs Institute, Kyŏngnam University, 1991); Paik Hak-soon, "North Korean State Formation, 1945–1950," unpub. PhD diss. (Philadelphia: University of Pennsylvania Press, 1993); Yi Chong-sŏk, *Saero ssŭn hyŏndae Pukhan ŭi ihae* [An understanding of contemporary North Korea: A newly written edition] (Seoul: Yŏksa pip'yŏngsa, 2000); Andrei Lankov, *From Stalin to Kim Il Sung: The Formation of North Korea, 1943–1960* (London: Hurst and Co., 2002); Charles K. Armstrong, *The North Korean Revolution, 1945–1950* (Ithaca: Cornell University Press, 2003); and Sŏ Tong-man, *Pukchosŏn sahoe chuŭi ch'eje sŏngnipsa, 1945–1961* [A history of the establishment of the Socialist regime in North Korea, 1945–1961] (Seoul: Sŏnin, 2005). I myself have also published a two-volume book on the process leading to the birth of the DPRK and the Korean War. On account of space considerations, I will omit footnotes for the most part in this section, as far as facts and interpretations are already well known through the above-mentioned works.

The political situation in the south was different from that in the north. On August 16, a day after the Japanese surrender, leftists and some rightists jointly inaugurated the CPKI in Seoul under the leadership of Yŏ Un-hyŏng, a left-leaning anti-Japanese activist. Japanese authorities gave Yŏ authority to maintain order. At the same time, Pak Hŏn-yŏng, a leading anti-Japanese communist, resurrected the Korean Communist Party (KCP)—which had become defunct under harsh persecution by Japanese authorities—in Seoul with himself as first secretary. On September 6, two days before the arrival of American occupation forces, Yŏ upgraded the CPKI to the Korean People's Republic (KPR) in cooperation with Pak. They expected that the Americans would recognize the KPR as the lawful government in the south.

However, the Americans refused to recognize the KPR and instead established the United States Army Military Government in Korea (USAMGIK). They also refused to acknowledge the authority of the Korean Provisional Government (KPG) in Chungking, China, which was preparing its return home. Accordingly, Syngman Rhee, the first president of the KPG, Kim Ku, then chairman of the KPG, and other KPG leaders had to return in private capacities. While refusing to recognize the KPR and KPG, to the chagrin of both, the USAMGIK aligned with the newly organized Korean Democratic Party (KDP), made up of domestic rightists, including "collaborators" in the Japanese occupation period. This decision was read as a clear message that the United States would not tolerate a leftist revolutionary movement in the south.

Observing the political trends in the south, the Soviet Union took a series of significant steps. On September 20, Stalin sent a confidential telegram to the MMDC and SOFHNK, which included important instructions that might be interpreted as a Soviet plan to establish a separate regime in the north.[52] Almost at the same time, Stalin sent Major General Andrei Romanenko of the MMDC to Pyongyang. Under the SOFHNK, the Soviet political soldier opened the General Bureau for the Civilian Affairs (GBCA) in Pyongyang. With ten bureaus, each led by a high-ranking Soviet officer, the GBCA would play the role of de facto Soviet military government in the north.

As Chistiakov had brought some Soviet-Koreans to the SOFHNK, Romanenko also brought other Soviet-Koreans to the GBCA. Who were these Soviet-Koreans? They were mainly from Kazakhstan and Uzbekistan, countries that were part of the Soviet Union. The Soviet-Koreans had been

52 Chŏn Hyŏn-su, "Soryŏn kun ŭi Pukhan jinju wa tae-Pukhan e chŏngch'aek" [The Soviet military occupation and its policy towards North Korea], *Han'guk tongnip undongsa yŏn'gu* [Studies on the Korean independence movement], no. 9 (1995): 355.

forced to immigrate to Central Asia from the Far East in 1937 by Stalin and were educated in one of the high-level schools in the region. Among them, Hŏ Kai was so eminent in the CPSU that he would play a major role in North Korean politics. By September 1946, the two Soviet officials brought in more Soviet-Koreans, bringing their total number to about 250. As a whole, they are said to have formed the Soviet-Korean faction. But they were for the most part administrative assistants and translators, lacking power and cohesiveness among them.

Kim Il Sung's Return to North Korea and Creation of the NKBKCP

Simultaneous with the arrival of Romanenko, Stalin allowed Kim Il Sung and about fifty partisans to return to North Korea. It was on September 19 that they arrived at Wŏnsan Harbor in the East Sea (Sea of Japan) on board the Soviet battleship *Pugachev*. Two days later, Kim reached Pyongyang. Soon Kim met with Lebedev and his lieutenant, Mekler, and asked them to announce publicly that he had also joined the Soviet battle against Japan in Manchuria and North Korea. Although they rejected his demand, they promoted him from captain to major. The two advised Kim to use an alias and to not show himself to the public in order to make his future public debut more dramatic. At Mekler's arrangement, Kim met with Cho Man-sik to seek his support. Recognizing Kim's anti-Japanese guerrilla credentials, Cho was sympathetic. But Kim felt that Cho's cooperation was not sufficient, Mekler recalled, and Kim planned to physically intimidate him. Only Mekler's intervention prevented this. Kim also met with important Korean communists in the north to persuade them to inaugurate a separate communist party there, but they rejected Kim's move. Expressing their support of the KCP in Seoul as the center of the Korean communist movement throughout the Korean Peninsula, they warned that Kim's attempt would split the party. With Soviet intervention and subsequent secret talks between Kim and Pak Hŏn-yŏng, however, a compromise was reached to organize the North Korean Branch of the KCP (NKBKCP) in Pyongyang. In all of these operations, Lebedev and Mekler recollected, Kim cleverly used the strategy of staging meetings in extravagant restaurants, where patrons were waited upon by geisha, to reach accords supporting his political aims.[53]

As a result, the NKBKCP was formally inaugurated on October 10. However, it was controlled by the Korean communist faction; around eleven of the seventeen members of its executive committee belonged to this faction. Moreover, the faction's leaders, Kim Yong-bŏm and O Ki-sŏp, were chosen as

53 *Secret Records*, vol. I, 55–56; 105–18.

the NKBKCP's first secretary and second secretary, respectively. Among the partisans, in addition to Kim Il Sung, only Kim Ch'aek and Kim Il managed to get chosen as members. The inauguration ceremony ended with cheers given only to Pak Hŏn-yŏng, who was staying in Seoul. Nevertheless, the formal founding of the NKBKCP was an important step for Kim Il Sung: after his absence from Korea for about twenty years, in three weeks he had succeeded in overcoming strong opposition from the domestic communist faction.

While thus inaugurating a single communist party organization, the SOFHNK also established a unitary administrative organization in the north. On October 11, the SOFHNK started operating under its direct command the North Korean Administrative Bureau, consisting of ten bureaus, including for finance, industry, education, and public security. Clearly this body was the "embryonic government of North Korea" and "represented the first step toward the establishment of a separate state of North Korea."[54] Most directors were technocrats trained and experienced in each of their fields in Korea proper. Kim Il Sung did not assume any post in this body, but his close partisan comrade, Ch'oe Yong-gŏn, served as director of the public security bureau, which controlled the police. As a guerilla fighter from the age of nineteen to thirty-three, Kim Il Sung always stressed the primacy of the armed forces and police. This was a distinctive characteristic of Kim Il Sung and his partisan comrades. They formed the Manchurian faction in North Korean politics—with "faction" the appropriate term, in the sense that its members were strongly cohesive and recognized Kim Il Sung as their sole leader.

On October 14, 1945, just a few days after the inauguration of the unified communist party organization and the unified administrative body, the SOFHNK held a mass rally in Pyongyang to introduce Kim Il Sung to the northern Korean people for the first time since his return home. At the age of thirty-three, he was praised as "General Kim Il Sung, the national hero." In consultation with Lebedev, Kim soon inaugurated two institutions, albeit without publicly announcing their creation. One was the Pyongyang School, whose aim was to train future politico-military cadres; Kim Ch'aek, a representative partisan comrade of Kim Il Sung, was named principal while other guerrilla comrades of Kim Il Sung became instructors. The school only accepted students related either to the Kim Il Sung family or to Kim's guerrilla comrades. It would eventually develop into the Central Party School and the party's Central Military School. The other institution was

54 Scalapino and Lee, *Communism in Korea*, vol. 1, 334–33.

the Korean Aviation Association, which aimed to train airplane technicians; Kim Il Sung was its first president. Unlike his political rivals, Kim Il Sung, from the very outset, paid great attention to the training of party, military, and military-related cadres.

The SOFHNK's next goal was the formation of non-communist parties who would be "friendly" to the communist party. The SOFHNK observed that the majority of northern Korean people were anti-communist and even anti-Soviet. To oversee them more easily, it persuaded Cho Man-sik to organize a party with nationalists as the main focus. Most non-communist nationalists, including landlords, factory owners, businessmen, and Christians, also urged him to organize a party that would represent them. Accordingly, on November 3, Cho launched the Chosŏn Democratic Party (CDP) with himself as chairman.

The hitherto dormant conflict between communists and nationalists erupted in late November, with civilian revolts occurring at Yong'amp'o and Sinŭiju, major cities in North P'yŏngan Province. In Sinŭiju, the communists were only able to suppress revolts by resorting to the use of armed forces. Kim Il Sung himself had to appear before citizens to try to assuage them. These incidents resulted in the beginning of a large exodus to the south by nationalists in general and Christians in particular, which weakened the CDP's power base. Meanwhile, some important domestic communists, including First Secretary Kim Yong-bŏm and his wife, Pak Chŏng-ae, became supporters of Kim Il Sung. Ri Chu-ha, a veteran domestic communist, went to Seoul to help Pak Hŏn-yŏng there.

In early December 1945 new communist leaders appeared in Pyongyang; they were returnees from Yan'an, China, where they had fought against the Japanese under CCP auspices. Kim Tu-bong and Kim Mu-jŏng led this group. Although they are said to have formed the Yan'an faction in north Korean politics, they were not actually united. Mu-jŏng, a leading guerrilla fighter who had participated in the CCP's Long March to Yan'an under Peng Dehuai, was so confident of his career that he acted solo. Known to the Korean public as "General Mu-jŏng," he used to say that, unlike Kim Il Sung, he was "a real general." A number of the Yan'an returnees—notably Hŏ Chŏng-suk, an influential woman cadre—became Kim Il Sung supporters. However, Mu-jŏng and the others were forced by the SOFHNK to abandon their own military units that had been formed in China.

The NKBKCP convened its third extended executive committee meeting on December 17–18, 1945, in Pyongyang. A group of SOFHNK officers were conspicuous as observers. The organization's most significant decision was the election of Kim Il Sung as first secretary. Former first secretary Kim

Yong-bŏm and second secretary O Ki-sŏp were demoted to second secretary and organizational affairs director, respectively. Hŏ Kai, a leader of Soviet-Koreans, was elected labor affairs director, while Mu-jŏng, the Yan'an returnee, was elected cadre department director. Pak Chŏng-ae, now loyal to Kim Il Sung, was elected women's affairs director. As a whole, Kim Il Sung's leadership became solidified at this meeting. At the time, NKBKCP membership numbered around seven thousand.

On December 21, 1945, the NKBKCP, through its organ *Chŏngno* (The right line), published Kim Il Sung's official biography. The work emphasized Kim's leadership of the anti-Japanese guerrilla struggles while omitting reference to his training in the SIB, apparently since the Soviet army was unpopular due to its initial misdeeds in North Korea. Around this time, Kim Il Sung's wife, Kim Jong Suk, and son, Jong Il, arrived from the Soviet Far East under the watch of two partisans, Chŏn Mun-sŏp and Cho Myŏng-rok. They came to Pyongyang via Unggi (now Sŏnbong), a port located at the Russo-Korean border. The two minders, formerly Kim Il Sung's bodyguards in Manchuria and the Soviet Far East, would later play major roles in North Korean politics.[55]

A few days later, the Allied powers reached an important agreement on the future of Korea. The United States, Soviet Union, and Great Britain (and Kuomintang China in absentia) concluded the "Protocol on Korea" in Moscow, and on December 28, 1945, released its full text, which consisted of four clauses. The agreement pledged the establishment of an all-Korean provisional government based on U.S.-Soviet negotiations, on the one hand, and a right-left coalition among Koreans, on the other hand. The agreement also pledged that a new Korea would be built on the basis of purging pro-Japanese collaborators from all governmental positions. The most controversial clause in the agreement was that a Korean provisional government might remain under a four-power trusteeship for as long as five years. In both the north and south, most anti-communist nationalists rejected the agreement. They argued that the trusteeship clause offended the pride of the Korean nation and would hinder Korean independence. In contrast, both in the north and the south, most communists and leftists accepted it, arguing that the provisional government clause was conducive to Korea's independence.

The SOFHNK demanded that CDP chairman Cho Man-sik support the Moscow agreement. When Cho refused due to the controversial trusteeship clause, the SOFHNK placed him in custody and removed him as CDP chairman. Soon many of his followers and fellow Christians fled to the south.

---

55 Chŏng Ch'ang-hyŏn, *Kyŏt'esŏ pon Kim Chŏng-il* [Kim Jong Il as seen by an entourage] (Seoul: T'oji, 1999), 26.

Until the middle of 1946, the SOFHNK allowed their escape to the south, reasoning that it would facilitate its control over the north. According to American government statistics, about five hundred thousand northern Koreans had fled to the south by the end of 1945.[56] When the SOFHNK removed Cho, it instructed Kim Il Sung (in the north) and Pak Hŏn-yŏng (in the south) to mobilize support for the Moscow agreement. In the virtual absence of anti-trusteeship forces, Kim was able to mobilize a broad base of northern Korean mass support for the agreement. But in the ensuing debates and conflicts surrounding the Moscow agreement in the south, accompanied by the assassination of KDP chairman Song Chin-u, most anti-communist nationalist media depicted Pak and the KCP as "pro-Soviet national traitors." Accordingly, Pak encountered formidable obstacles in the effort to mobilize the southern Korean masses in support of the Moscow agreement. Political analysts at the time commented that the Moscow agreement politically killed Pak but boosted Kim Il Sung.

Inauguration of the NKPPC and Kim Il Sung

In 1946 the political situation in the north turned more favorable for Kim Il Sung. On February 8 the SOFHNK helped the North Korean Administrative Bureau expand and upgrade itself to the North Korean Provisional People's Committee (NKPPC), with Kim Il Sung as its chairman. Kim Tu-bong, the leader of the Yan'an returnees, and the Reverend Kang Yang-uk, a leader of the CDP and the second cousin of Kim Il Sung's maternal grandfather, became its vice-chairman and secretary general, respectively. While O Ki-sŏp, the major domestic communist challenging Kim Il Sung's leadership, assumed the directorship of the organizational affairs bureau, Ch'oe Yong-kŏn, a partisan comrade supporting Kim Il Sung's leadership, became director of the public security bureau. The NKPPC was established without due process or elections—it was the result of a prearranged plan between the SOFHNK and Kim Il Sung. The start of the Cold War between the United States and the Soviet Union around late 1945 and early 1946 may well have encouraged Stalin to pursue his original plan of September 20, 1945, to establish a separate regime in the north.

A new organization and reorganization of parties followed. By the end of February, Kim Il Sung changed the name of the NKBKCP to the North Korean Communist Party (NKCP), without going through any official

---

56 Kathryn Weathersby, "Soviet Aims in Korea and the Origin of the Korean War, 1945–1950: New Evidence from Russian Archives," *Working Paper* (Washington, DC: Cold War International History Project, Woodrow Wilson International Center for Scholars), no. 8 (November 1993), 13.

procedure. The CDP elected Ch'oe Yong-kŏn as its chairman; the Yan'an returnees inaugurated the Korean New Democratic Party (KNDP) with Kim Tu-bong as its chairman; and the adherents of Ch'ŏndogyo (The Religion of the Heavenly Way) inaugurated the North Korean Ch'ŏndogyo Young Friends Party (NKCYFP) with Kim Tal-hyŏn as its chairman. These three parties were satellite parties, common in communist states.

At a ceremony in Pyongyang to commemorate the twenty-seventh anniversary of the March 1 Independence Movement, young anti-Communist activists dispatched by the White Robe Society in the south failed in an attempt to assassinate Kim Il Sung, Ch'oe Yong-gŏn, and Kim Ch'aek. Unscathed, Kim Il Sung initiated a series of socialist reform measures, including land reform in March and an eight-hour work day in June. In particular, land reform, which was associated with fierce class struggles in the countryside, evoked extensive support for Kim from the peasantry, while decisively weakening the financial base of anti-communist nationalists and Christians. Again, many of the latter fled to the south, where they would constitute staunch anti–Kim Il Sung forces.

By this time, the U.S.-Soviet conference as stipulated in the Moscow agreement ended without any result. As the failure dissipated unification euphoria in the south, the rightists, led by Syngman Rhee, began a campaign to establish a single governing body in the south by Koreans against the NKPPC. But Yŏ Un-hyŏng, chairman of the Korean People's Party—the reincarnation of his original KPR—opposed Rhee's campaign. Recalling the right-left negotiation clause in the Moscow agreement, he started a Right-Left Coalition Committee with Kim Kyu-sik, the former KPG vice-chairman and center-right leader.

The NKWP and the NKPC

At this juncture, Stalin secretly invited Kim Il Sung and Pak Hŏn-yŏng to Moscow. In early July 1946 Stalin urged Kim to merge his NKCP with the KNDP, and Pak to merge all leftist parties into a single communist party. Shtykov, Lebedev, and other Soviet officers who were present at this meeting sensed that Stalin had finally decided to designate Kim as the leader in the north.[57] During August 28–30, about seven weeks after his return to Pyongyang, Kim finalized the merger of the NKCP and KNDP into the North Korean Workers' Party (NKWP), whose total membership reached approximately 366,000. To soothe KNDP members, Kim Il Sung tactically yielded the NKWP chairmanship to KNDP chairman Kim Tu-bong, while Kim himself

---

57 Korotkov, *Stalin and Kim Il Sung*, vol. 1, 243–45.

settled for the vice-chairmanship. But it should be recalled that at the congress Kim Tu-bong praised Kim Il Sung as "our leader" and cheered him.[58] Apart from Stalin, Kim Il Sung was the only person who was cheered at this congress.

In the meantime, Kim Il Sung founded a central school to train cadres in the field of public security and created a central battalion of public security cadres, a paramilitary organization, both under the NKPPC. He also began promoting the cult of personality surrounding him. At Kim Jong Suk's strong urging, the NKPPC disseminated throughout the north the "Song of General Kim Il Sung," a paean to Kim's anti-Japanese guerrilla activities. The North Korean General Federation of Artists published the book *Our Sun: The Special Edition of General Kim Il Sung*. Contributors to the book portrayed Kim as "our nation's sun," "our country's great sun," and "our hero with miraculous abilities." This was the first time Kim Il Sung was called "our nation's sun." A few literary figures called him *Suryŏng*, i.e., "head commander" or "leader," equivalent to *Führer* in German or *Vozhd'* in Russian.[59] On October 1, the NKPPC officially opened Kim Il Sung Comprehensive University.

About this time, Kim Il Sung's wife, Kim Jong Suk, gave birth to a daughter, Kyŏng-hŭi. Years later, Kim Kyŏng-hŭi and her husband would play important roles in the succession from Kim Jong Il to Kim Jong Un.

In contrast to Kim Il Sung's rise, Pak Hŏn-yŏng's road was thorny. In late May 1946 the USAMGIK began to suppress the KCP on the grounds that it was involved in counterfeiting. The USAMGIK declared martial law during September and October and suppressed a "people's resistance" led by leftists in North Kyŏngsang Province. While Pak Sang-hŭi, an elder brother of Park Chung Hee (Pak Chŏng-hŭi, future ROK president) and father-in-law of Kim Jong Pil (Kim Chong-p'il, future ROK prime minister), led one of these "riots" and was executed under martial law, some of his comrades fled to the north. In October, Pak Hŏn-yŏng also had to flee to the north; he hid in a coffin, pretending to be a corpse, to avoid capture. Still, southern Korean leftists were able to inaugurate the South Korean Workers' Party (SKWP) in November in Seoul with Hŏ Hŏn, an anti-Japanese lawyer, as chairman. Pak Hŏn-yŏng was elected in absentia as one of the three vice-chairmen.

While the south was plagued by "leftist revolts," the north consolidated the NKPPC without serious resistance. Under a prearranged plan by the MMDC and SOFHNK, on November 3 the NKPPC administered nationwide

---

58 Kuksa P'yŏnch'an Wiwŏnhoe, ed., *Pukhan kwan'gye saryo chip* [Compilation of historical records related to North Korea] (Kwach'ŏn: Kuksa P'yŏnch'an Wiwŏnhoe, 1982–2005), vol. 1, 126. Hereafter cited as *Historical Records Related to North Korea*.

59 Ibid., vol. 12 (1995), 124.

local elections for the inauguration of people's committees at the provincial, municipal, and county levels in the north. The elections were held using a white-black box system, common in the Soviet bloc in Eastern Europe but without precedent in Korea. After the elections, the MMDC and SOFHNK planned to hold another election to inaugurate the North Korean People's Assembly (NKPA). When Stalin agreed to this plan, Shtykov convened a meeting with Chistiakov, Romanenko, and Kim Il Sung on January 3–4, 1947, at his MMDC office. In accordance with their agreement, a conference of provincial, municipal, and county people's committees was held during February 17–20, 1947, in Pyongyang. On the last day, the conference inaugurated the NKPA, the members of which in turn created a standing committee. Kim Tu-bong was elected its chairman, with NKCYFP chairman Kim Tal-hyŏn and CDP chairman Ch'oe Yong-gŏn elected as vice-chairmen.

On February 22 the NKPA replaced the existing NKPPC with the North Korean People's Committee (NKPC), thereby solidifying its organizational structure. The NKPA elected Kim Il Sung as its chairman and delegated all authority to him to create its leadership. Kim's appointment of his partisan comrade Kim Ch'aek as vice-chairman was noteworthy. As Kim Il Sung would later recall, Kim Ch'aek supervised all cadres of the NKPC and NKWP so sternly that even Pak Hŏn-yŏng and Kim Tu-bong feared him.[60] Kim Ch'aek would, for example, threaten to send O Ki-sŏp without trial into the "people's revolutionary prison," where conditions were harsher than those of past Japanese prisons in Korea. It is significant that the establishment of the NKPA and the NKPC correlated with the intensification of the Cold War between the United States and the Soviet Union. Stalin may have sensed that the establishment of a separate regime in the north was inevitable.

With the consolidation of power, Kim Il Sung strengthened the function of the internal affairs bureau of the NKPC. As the successor to the public security bureau of the NKPPC, the new bureau was empowered to supervise all of the regular police, secret police, and border defense corps. It was an exact copy of the Soviet Union's People's Commissariat of Internal Affairs (NKVD) under Beria. Its power in general and the secret police's power in particular were extensive. Some declassified documents of February 1947 and June 1947 showed activities by secret agents who not only monitored the daily movements of Christians, schoolteachers, and leaders of "friendly" parties, but also encouraged students to inform the police about other students and even their teachers. In November 1947 Kim Il Sung unilaterally issued an official order to the internal bureau "to extensively infiltrate

60 Kim, *Segi wa tŏburŏ*, vol. 8, 150.

informants among the people and to form a web of informants throughout the nation."[61] The NKCP likewise instructed all media that reports and comments opposing or criticizing its leaders, decisions, and activities were prohibited.

Kim Il Sung also purged oppositionists, some Christian pastors, and student leaders. The NKWP introduced the Soviet literary theory of "noble realism" under which all artists, poets, and novelists should portray only "noble" aspects of "real" societies. Some followed this line; others fled to the south. Most artistic figures were forced to praise the Soviet Union, Stalin, and Kim Il Sung to a higher degree. For example, composer Kim Tong-jin became famous for his rendition of the song, "The Song of General Kim Il Sung," which was publicly sung at official events. The writer Han Sŏr-ya portrayed Kim as "the sun, parents, and mentor of thirty million Korean people throughout the peninsula," and Han Chae-tŏk called Kim "the head commander of the people, the hero of the nation, and our sun."[62] Ironically enough, Kim Tong-jin and Han Chae-tŏk would defect to the South in the 1950s, and Han Sŏr-ya, refusing to continue to praise the "fat bourgeois" (Kim Il Sung), was purged in 1962.

Kim Il Sung and Birth of the KPA

The period between early March and late November 1947 was another turning point in North Korea's course. In March, U.S. president Harry S. Truman announced the "Truman doctrine," the gist of which was his administration's firm determination to resist Soviet aggression in Europe and Asia. This was followed in June by the European Recovery Program, proposed by U.S secretary of state George C. Marshall. Rejecting the Marshall Plan, the Soviet Union in September inaugurated the Cominform, an international communist organization including all Eastern European countries except Yugoslavia, with the Soviet Union as its leader. Against this backdrop, U.S.-Soviet negotiations and right-left negotiations for the establishment of a Korean Provisional Government, as stipulated in the Moscow agreement, had no chance to succeed. Yo Un-hyŏng, who attempted to realize the right-left coalition, was assassinated by the White Robe Society; Chang Tŏk-su, a KDP strategist who worked hard for the establishment of a separate government in the south, was assassinated by anti-separatist government forces in the south. In light of these events, Ri Sŭng-yŏp, Pak Hŏn-yŏng's first lieutenant in the SKWP, and his comrades fled to the north. They formed the SKWP faction, with Pak Hŏn-yŏng as its leader.

61 *Historical Records Related to North Korea*, vol. 10, 198–234.
62 Ibid., vol. 30, 162–66; vol. 12, 290–93.

Naturally, both the United States and Soviet Union accelerated their plans to establish their respective separate regimes on the Korean Peninsula. When the United States, which enjoyed majority support in the United Nations, referred the Korean independence issue to that body, the Soviet Union opposed it. Finally, in November, the UN decided to deal with the Korean case through the United Nations Temporary Commission on Korea (UNTCOK), under which a general election for the establishment of a unified national government on the peninsula was to be held in 1948. The SOFHNK and NKPC charged that the UN decision violated the principle of national self-determination and refused UNTCOK access to the northern half of the peninsula.

At this point, Ch'ŏndogyo central headquarters in Seoul dispatched emissaries to its Pyongyang branch with instructions that its adherents in the north should organize a movement in support of UNTCOK access to the north. But NKCYFP chairman Kim Tal-hyŏn reported this to Kim Il Sung, resulting in the arrest of about ten thousand Ch'ŏndogyo followers.

Soon, the SOFHNK and the NKPC launched a North Korean army, even before the inauguration of the North Korean regime per se. On February 8, 1948, the NKPC declared the Korean People's Army (KPA) formally established; Ch'oe Yong-gŏn was named general commander and Kim Il Sung the supreme commander. Most strategic posts were occupied by Kim Il Sung's partisan comrades. For example, Kim Il and Kang Kŏn were appointed vice commander and chief of staff, respectively. Ch'oe Kwang, Ch'oe Yong-jin, Kim Kwang-hyŏp, Ri Yŏng-ho, Ryu Kyŏng-su and O Chin-u were appointed chiefs of staff at the division or brigade level, or as regimental commanders. They would go on to play major roles in North Korean politics.

While holding actual power over the military, Kim Il Sung strengthened his leadership of the party. At the Second NKWP Congress held March 27–30, 1948, he not only openly and harshly criticized the domestic communists, including O Ki-sŏp, but even forced them to engage in self-criticism in front of the delegates. Hŏ Kai's intervention was noteworthy: he accused the domestic communists of continuing to hold on to wrong thoughts and pressed them to deepen their self-criticism.[63] They then admitted that one of their errors had been not properly criticizing Mu-jŏng—who was regarded a probable contender to Kim Il Sung—and so they proceeded to criticize Mu-jŏng's "heroism." On the final day, most delegates praised Kim Il Sung with the highest compliments and gave him a thunderous round of applause. Hŏ Kai was an exception. In his concluding report to the congress, he never even mentioned Kim Il Sung's name. However, thanks to the SOFNHK's strong support, Hŏ

---

63 Ibid., vol. 1, 397–418.

would be elected one of two NKWP vice-chairmen, together with Kim Il Sung. Kim Tu-bong, who praised Kim Il Sung seven times in his closing speech, was allowed to maintain his position as NKWP chairman.

About this time, the UNTCOK decided to hold a general election in the south only on May 10, 1948. At this juncture, Kim Ku and Kim Kyu-sik, former chairman and vice-chairman of the KPG, respectively, and other nationalists and leftists in the south participated in the North-South Joint Conference of political parties and social organizations held April 19–26, 1948, in Pyongyang. Their professed purpose was to avoid the perpetuation of national division by establishing a single unified government throughout the peninsula. But when the conference began, it became clear that everything had been prearranged by the northern side, leaving the southern participants as "invited guests." That is why they refused to participate in the second North-South Joint Conference held in June 1948 in Pyongyang.

On May 10 general elections were held in the south, on the basis of which a Constituent Assembly was convened in Seoul. The Constituent Assembly elected Syngman Rhee as the president of the Republic of Korea, whose establishment was officially proclaimed on August 15, 1948. However, the political situation in the South was gloomy. On Cheju Island, located south of South Chŏlla Province, bloody conflict between rightists and leftists had claimed the lives of many civilians. In South Chŏlla Province, a mutiny inspired by the SKWP was barely suppressed under martial law. One of the court-martialed defendants was ROK army major (and future ROK president) Park Chung Hee, who was severely tortured and was expected to receive the death penalty. Through intervention by Park's seniors at the former Manchukuo Imperial Army Academy, the penalty was commuted to life imprisonment, and he was eventually pardoned. About six months later, Kim Ku, who became President Rhee's key political rival, was assassinated by an ROK army second lieutenant. The assassin, pardoned by the Rhee administration, would be killed by a South Korean youth in 1996.

Kim Il Sung and the Birth of the DPRK and the KWP

Political development in the north proceeded much more smoothly. Fifteen days after the establishment of the ROK, the NKPC administered general elections in the north and inaugurated the Supreme People's Assembly (SPA) with Hŏ Hŏn, who had fled to the north in early 1948, as its speaker. Kim Ch'aek welcomed Hŏ wholeheartedly. As an attorney-at-law, Hŏ had defended Kim in court *pro bono* during the Japanese colonial period and had helped Kim escape to Manchuria. Although Hŏ was SKWP chairman, he did not side with Pak Hŏn-yŏng. Rather, like his daughter, Hŏ

Chŏng-suk, he became a faithful supporter of Kim Il Sung. Kim Tu-bong, the leader of the Yan'an returnees and NKWP chairman, was chosen as the SPA's Standing Committee chairman, a post that was regarded as the titular head of state. CDP chairman Ch'oe Yong-gŏn and NKCYFP chairman Kim Tal-hyŏn were chosen as SPA vice-chairmen, and the Reverend Kang Yang-uk of the CDP was appointed SPA secretary general.

The SPA adopted a constitution for the Democratic People's Republic of Korea (DPRK) and elected Kim Il Sung as premier of the cabinet. Pak Hŏn-yŏng, leader of the SKWP faction, was appointed first vice-premier and foreign minister. Pak's first lieutenant, Ri Sŭng-yŏp, was appointed justice minister. Kim Il Sung's faithful partisan comrades, Ch'oe Yong-gŏn and Kim Ch'aek, were appointed national defense minister, and vice-premier as well as industrial minister, respectively. Pak Il-u, a Yan'an returnee, was appointed internal minister. About seven Soviet-Koreans were appointed as vice ministers in internal, defense, education, and other ministries. On September 9, 1948, the establishment of the DPRK was proclaimed. An examination of the leadership of the KWP and the DPRK at this time leads us to the conclusion that the North Korean regime started as a coalition body among four groups (the Manchurian faction, the SKWP, Yan'an returnees, and Soviet-Koreans), although Kim Il Sung maintained hegemony.

By the end of December 1948 the Soviet Union had withdrawn its occupation forces from the North and sent Shtykov as ambassador to the DPRK. The North reciprocated by sending Chu Yŏng-ha, who had switched allegiance from Pak Hŏn-yŏng to Kim Il Sung, as ambassador to Moscow. During March 5–17, 1949, Kim Il Sung and Pak Hŏn-yŏng held two talks with Stalin in Moscow. When Kim proposed an invasion of the South to unify the peninsula, Stalin dissuaded him, pointing out the presence of U.S. forces there. Pak attempted to persuade Stalin by stressing that SKWP members in the underground would rise up when the North initiated an armed attack against the South. But Stalin held firm. On the last day, a Soviet Union–DPRK agreement on economic and cultural cooperation was signed.

Three months after returning to Pyongyang, Kim Il Sung succeeded in secretly integrating the NKWP and the SKWP into the KWP. Kim Il Sung was elected its CC chairman and Pak Hŏn-yŏng of the SKWP and Hŏ Kai of the Soviet-Russians were elected first vice-chairman and second vice-chairman, respectively. Under them, three secretaries were elected: First Secretary Hŏ Kai, Second Secretary Ri Sŭng-yŏp of the SKWP, and Third Secretary Kim Sam-ryong, who was leading the underground SKWP organization in Seoul. The Political Committee (PC), with nine members, was created within the KWPCC as the KWP's highest decision-making body. Kim Il Sung, Pak Hŏn-yŏng, Hŏ Kai, Ri Sŭng-yŏp, and Kim Sam-ryong were automatically elected. In addition to the five, Kim Tu-bong (SPASC chairman), Hŏ Hŏn (SPA speaker), Kim Ch'aek (vice-premier and industrial minister), and Pak Il-u (internal minister) were elected. In sum, this lineup superficially demonstrated that the KWPCCPC represented a coalition among the Manchurian faction, the SKWP faction, the Soviet-Koreans, and the Yan'an returnees— but the real power belonged to Kim Il Sung and his Manchurian faction. Now, at the age of thirty-seven, Kim Il Sung assumed the reins of the North Korean regime as both KWPCC chairman and the DPRK premier.

From Coalition Regime to Unitary Regime, 1949–67

The Death of Kim Jong Suk

By the end of June 1949 Kim Il Sung had succeeded in becoming the indisputable leader of the newly formed DPRK. But three months later, on September 22, 1949, he experienced a personal tragedy that would affect both the domestic and succession politics of North Korea. It was the death of his wife, Kim Jong Suk, at the age of thirty-two. There are two versions of the cause of her death. The conventional version, based mainly on Sin Kyŏng-wan's recollections, was that during the delivery of her fourth child in the special ward of Pyongyang's Namsan Hospital she lost too much blood and died. According to this version, she left behind a will for her partisan comrades, including Ch'oe Yong-gŏn, Kim Il, and Kim Ch'aek, to the effect that they should rear Kim Jong Il as successor and be faithful to his father. At the funeral, they are said to have pledged that they would observe her dying wish.[64]

In contrast, Kang Myŏng-do, a North Korean defector who belongs to the "royal" Ch'ilgol Kang clan to which Kim Il Sung's mother belonged, alleged that Kim Jong Suk's death was related to Kim Il Sung's extramarital relationship with Kim Sŏng-ae. Born on December 29, 1924, in a farmhouse in Kangsŏ County, South P'yŏng'an Province, Kim Sŏng-ae attended school through junior high. Around 1947 she entered the KPA as a soldier and became a telephone operator in Kim Il Sung's official residence in Pyongyang. According to Kang, Kim Il Sung began an illicit relationship with the pretty and intelligent Kim Sŏng-ae. Kang noted that in comparison Kim Jong Suk was neither smart nor—with her dusky face and small eyes— pretty. Aware of the relationship, Kim Jong Suk was said to have demanded Kim Il Sung's presence at her delivery, during which she hemorrhaged. When Kim did not appear, she rejected medical treatment and finally passed out.[65] It is impossible to judge which version of her death is true. But as we shall

64 Chŏng, *Kyŏt'esŏ pon Kim Chŏng-il*, 30.
65 Kang, *Pyongyang ŭn mangmyŏng ŭl kkumkkunda*, 60–61.

see later, the premature death of their biological mother would affect the lives and the formation of Jong Il's and Kyŏng-hŭi's personalities.

Kim Il Sung's Purge of Rivals during the Korean War

Let us return to Kim Il Sung's activities after his return to Pyongyang. Recall that Stalin had not heeded Kim Il Sung and Pak Hŏn-yŏng's exhortations to recognize their plans to invade the south. Nonetheless, Kim Il Sung continued to do his best to persuade Stalin through Shtykov, the Soviet ambassador to the North. After the establishment of the PRC in Beijing on October 1, 1949, Kim became more intent than ever on his plan, to which Stalin at last consented in January 1950. Accordingly, in April 1950 Kim Il Sung and Pak Hŏn-yŏng secretly met Stalin and secured final approval. A month later, they secretly met with Mao Zedong in Beijing and gained his approval as well. After this behind-the-scenes maneuvering, Kim launched the war on June 25, 1950.

Northern forces' occupation of Seoul during the first days of the war and their continued advance southward for two months encouraged both Kim Il Sung and Pak Hŏn-yŏng. Pak and his SKWP faction had expectations that their power base might be restored under communist occupation. But there was no popular uprising as Pak had repeatedly predicted, for the ROK public security agencies had already executed underground SKWP leaders, including Kim Sam-ryong and Ri Chu-ha, and some former leftists had switched their loyalties to the ROK. In addition, Kang Kŏn, chief of staff at the KPA supreme command and a member of the Manchurian faction, was killed by ROK forces. On September 15, 1950, the course of the war was changed by General Douglas MacArthur's successful landing of U.S. forces under the UN flag at Inch'ŏn, the gateway to Seoul. With the KPA forced to retreat, Kim Il Sung had his younger brother Kim Yŏng-ju take refuge along with his children Jong Il and Kyŏng-hŭi in Jilin, Manchuria.

During this crisis, Kim Il Sung sent Pak Hŏn-yŏng to Mao to mobilize military support. However, according to one Chinese scholar who was able to read classified documents at the PRC Foreign Ministry archives, Pak asked Mao to support his planned coup d'état to overthrow the Kim Il Sung regime and establish a pro-PRC regime with Pak as its head. Mao was said to have rejected Pak's proposal, arguing that it was dangerous to put the proposal into effect during the course of war. The scholar added that Kim later learned about this betrayal and decided to execute Pak.[66] At any rate, it was only thanks to Chinese military intervention from late October 1950 that North Korea was saved. Kim Il Sung, who narrowly escaped the total

---

66 Correspondent Hong Sun-do's article from Beijing printed in *Munhwa Ilbo*, April 26, 2005, 20.

collapse of his state, convened the Third Plenum of the KWP Central Committee on December 21 in Pyŏrori, Kanggye County, North P'yŏng'an Province, located at the Sino-Korean border. Kim punished many cadres at the meeting, irrespective of their factional affiliations, but within a few weeks he rehabilitated all of them—except Mu-jŏng. Only through the intervention of Peng Dehuai, who came to Korea as Chinese People's Volunteers Commander, was Mu-jŏng barely able to return to China. In the meantime, the Kim Il Sung loyalist Kim Ch'aek, who was a KWPCCPC member and a vice-premier, died of heavy drinking in a dugout.

Kim Il Sung's purges would continue. In December 1952 he convened the Fifth Plenum of the KWPCC in Pyongyang and denounced former SKWP leaders, including Pak Hŏn-yŏng, Ri Sŭng-yŏp, Ri Kang-guk, and Rim Hwa, who now occupied important posts in the KWP and DPRK. At this session it was decided to eradicate all "factionalists" related to the former SKWP. With the conclusion of the Korean armistice agreement on July 27, 1953, the drama of purges against Kim Il Sung's political rivals became public. On August 4, the suicide of Hŏ Kai, the leader of the Soviet-Koreans, was officially announced. Lankov supports the widely circulated speculation that Hŏ might have been murdered.[67]

Three days later, the arrest of twelve high-ranking KWP officials, including Ri Sŭng-yŏp and other former SKWP charter members, was also officially announced. They were charged as "American spies who had penetrated into the KWP." They were also accused of having organized an anti-DPRK and anti-KWP coup d'état. If the coup had been successful, we are told, Pak would have become DPRK premier and Ri would have become KWPCC chairman. It is noteworthy that they were all were indicted in a special military court established at the Supreme Court by Prosecutor General Ri Song-un, a member of the Kapsan faction, which had helped Kim Il Sung and his partisan comrades attack Poch'ŏnbo in 1937. Even more significant is that Kim Yŏng-ju, Kim Il Sung's only living biological brother, was appointed secretary of the court to oversee the trial. All defendants were harshly tortured, and Rim Hwa, the poet who had written the lyrics of the militant "Song of People's Resistance," attempted to commit suicide out of desperation. Through a single-trial system that took only four days, most defendants were sentenced to death and immediately executed.

In December 1955, by the decision of the Sixth Plenum of the KWPCC, Pak Hŏn-yŏng was indicted by a special trial of the Supreme Court. Like his former SKWP comrades, Pak was also severely tortured. The SPASC appointed Ch'oe Yong-gŏn its chief and presiding judge. In its one-day

67 Lankov, *From Stalin to Kim Il Sung*, 152.

review of the case, the court sentenced Pak to death. It is still unclear pre-
cisely when he was executed, but a high-ranking KWP official who defected
to Moscow testified that Pak was executed around the summer of 1956,
immediately after the CPSU leadership sent a letter to Kim Il Sung expressing its regrets over Pak's death sentence.[68] His execution meant the end of
the domestic communist faction, including the SKWP faction as a whole.

Shortly after the initial trial of the SKWP faction ended, probably in
August 1953, Kim Il Sung allowed Jong Il (age eleven) and Kyŏng-hŭi (seven)
to return home from Jilin, Manchuria. The children would learn that their
father had married Kim Sŏng-ae and that the two had had their first child in
1952, a daughter named Kyŏng-jin. According to Kang Myŏng-do's recollections, Jong Il and Kyŏng-hŭi heard through their nurse, Kang Po-bi of the
Ch'ilgol clan, that their new stepmother had had something to do with their
biological mother's death, and so (according to Kang) they came to hate her.
Kim Jong Il would later reward Kang Po-bi with a fancy house and car.[69]

It is hard to judge the veracity of Kang's allegation. Jong Il and Kyŏng-
hŭi grew up without a mother from a young age. Particularly after Kim Il
Sung and Kim Sŏng-ae had their first son, P'yŏng-il (1954), and second son,
Yŏng-il (1955), Jong Il would frequently visit his uncle Kim Yŏng-ju, the
only living biological brother of Kim Il Sung, and O Chin-u, a partisan comrade who had been close to Kim Jong Suk. Sometimes Kim Ok-sun, a female
partisan comrade who had also been close to Kim Jong Suk, took care of
them both. Sin Kyŏng-wan—who only ever had positive things to say about
Kim Jong Il—recalled: "Whenever Jong Il went to school and returned home
on foot, he accompanied Kyŏng-hŭi as her guardian. When Kyŏng-hŭi wept,
yearning for her mother in the street, he attempted to placate her. Jong Il
used to say that in order not to make their father sad, they should not weep.
Seeing that scene, Pyongyang citizens also shed tears."[70]

Accordingly, Jong Il and Kyŏng-hŭi never called Kim Sŏng-ae "mother"
or "mom." They just called her *ajumi*, a northern euphemism for a house-
maid. But Jong Il altered his attitude to some extent to please his father. In
contrast, Kyŏng-hŭi did not hesitate to point out that while her biological
mother had been a glorious anti-Japanese guerrilla fighter, her stepmother
was a mere telephone operator in her father's residence. Kyŏng-hŭi even
refused meals prepared by her stepmother, instead preparing meals for herself.[71] In chapter 3, we shall see how relationships among the members of the
Kim Il Sung family evolved.

68 Yi, *Saero ssŭn hyŏndae Pukhan ŭi ihae*, 418.
69 Kang, *P'yŏngyang ŭn mangmyŏng ŭl kkumkkunda*, 60–61.
70 Quoted in Chŏng, *Kyŏ'tesŏ pon Kim Chŏng-il*, 31–32.
71 Kang, *Pyongyang ŭn mangmyŏng ŭl kkumkkunda*, 60–61.

The August 1956 Factionalist Incident

With Khrushchev's rise, the Soviet Union began in late 1953 to stress the necessity of détente between East and West, which created unfavorable conditions for Kim Il Sung's leadership. Kim's response was the *Juche* ideology, introduced in a speech in December 1955. *Juche* can be translated as "self-reliance" or "self-determination" in regard to one's judgment and actions. By introducing this expression—which has a patriotic and nationalistic flavor—Kim made it clear that he would not follow the line suggested by the CPSU or CCP but adopt methods he felt appropriate to the Korean situation. Based on this theory, he purged Pak Il-u and Pang Ho-san, Yan'an returnees, and harshly criticized the Soviet-Russians Pak Ch'ang-ok, Ki Sŏk-bok, and Pak Yŏng-bin.

In 1956, a more serious challenge to Kim Il Sung's leadership came from Moscow. At the Twentieth Congress of the CPSU (February 14–25), First Secretary Khrushchev initiated a de-Stalinization campaign, attacking Stalin's personality cult and proposing a collective leadership. Khrushchev also stressed the principle of coexistence between the capitalist and socialist camps. Kim responded positively, as shown by steps he took to dismantle the cult of personality surrounding himself. In a speech to KWP cadres on April 7, 1956, Kim stressed the importance of "collective leadership." He argued that the KWP should decide its policies and programs based on debates in which all its members participated, not just on the will of one individual or leader. He also openly instructed KWP members not to use the term "Suryŏng" or "Dear Leader," and he fiercely criticized Malenkov, Kaganovich, Molotov, and Bulganin, whom Khrushchev expelled from the CPSU. In addition, he did not purge any of those remaining among the Soviet-Koreans, Yan'an returnees, or SKWP. But in the composition of the KWPCC and its PC, he doubled the membership of his Manchurian comrades. While maintaining the KWPCC chairmanship himself, Kim coopted Ch'oe Yonggŏn, his Manchurian comrade and incumbent CDP head, by naming him to the KWPCC vice-chairmanship.

Kim Il Sung soon toured nine countries, including the Soviet Union and Eastern European socialist countries, to obtain economic aid. Seven weeks after his return to Pyongyang, the August Plenum of the KWPCC was held on August 30–31, 1956. When Kim finished his report on the foreign trip and the First Five-Year Plan, which would start in January 1957, the Yan'an returnees, in cooperation with the Soviet-Koreans, initiated criticism of him. There were two common themes to their criticism. One was targeted at Kim's economic policy, which put priority on heavy industry. They proposed instead placing more emphasis on agriculture and light industry to relieve the hardships of the masses. The second criticism attacked the Kim Il Sung personality cult and his one-man dictatorship; they proposed the adoption of a collective leadership and to end the excesses of the personality cult. Officials of the Soviet embassy in Pyongyang definitely played a role in the background—they implied to the anti–Kim Il Sung leaders in the KWP that Ch'oe Ch'ang-ik, then-KWPCCPC member, vice-premier, and finance minister, might lead the KWP on condition that Kim Il Sung would maintain the premiership.[72]

Kim Il Sung, however, retained majority control of the KWPCC. In addition, "Kim's position also gave him opportunities to bribe and blackmail high-level cadres individually."[73] Accordingly, he could expel them from party posts or the party itself. When Kim Il Sung's forces threatened the oppositionists with arrest and imprisonment, some Yan'an returnees, including Sŏ Hŭi and Yun Kong-hŭm, fled to China, while a few Soviet-Koreans hurriedly returned to Russia.

In September the CCP and the CPSU dispatched a joint delegation to Pyongyang, represented by Peng Dehuai, CCPCC politburo member and defense minister, and Anastas Mikoyan, CPSUCC politburo member and vice-premier. The delegation demanded that those who had been purged be rehabilitated and that there be no future purges. In the draft of his speech to be delivered to the KWP, Mikoyan even recommended Kim's resignation from the KWP chairmanship. For the time being, Kim Il Sung pretended to meet many of these humiliating demands.

Meanwhile, Soviet armed suppression of the anti-Moscow popular uprising in Hungary in October 1956 and Chinese persecution of anti-CCP intellectuals in the nationwide rectification campaigns of 1957 created a new situation allowing Kim Il Sung to reverse the trend against him in the North. Terming what had happened at the August Plenum as the "August Factionalist Incident," Kim resumed a series of purges against his political "enemies." He deprived Ch'oe Ch'ang-ik, second-in-charge among the Yan'an returnees, of the vice-premiership and KWPCCPC membership and Pak Ch'ang-ok, the head of the Soviet-Koreans, of a vice-premiership and KWPCC membership, and had them both imprisoned. Soon he expelled Kim Tu-bong from the SPASC chairmanship, and sent him along with other minor opponents to a local reeducation camp. Yun Kong-hŭm's wife and two sons, as well as Sŏ Hŭi's wife and daughter, who had not been able to escape from the North, were executed. In addition, through a nationwide project to exchange KWP membership cards, many "factionalists" were purged. As Lankov writes, "The attempt to change the North Korean political line and replace the

---

72 Quoted in Chŏng, *Kyŏt'esŏ pon Kim Chŏng-il*, 421.

73 Andrei Lankov, *Crisis in North Korea: The Failure of De-Stalinization, 1956* (Honolulu: University of Hawaii Press, 2005), 129.

country's leadership through legal means, as permitted by the North Korean constitution and party statutes, ended in complete failure."[74]

In March 1958 Kim Il Sung held two important conferences. One was the First Conference of KWP Representatives, although the KWP constitution and regulations of the time had no clause providing for such a meeting. At the conference Kim Il Sung publicly humiliated Kim Tu-bong and his followers. Kim Tu-bong and the remnants of the Yan'an returnees are known to have died on a rural farm between 1960 and 1963. Kim Il Sung also purged Pak Ŭi-wan and other Soviet-Koreans. The other conference was a plenary meeting of KPA cadres. Reiterating that the KPA should only follow the tradition of his anti-Japanese guerrilla movement in Manchuria, Kim eradicated many officers related to the Yan'an returnees and Soviet-Koreans. Kim Yŏng-ju, the only living biological brother of Kim Il Sung, was appointed chief of a section within the powerful KWPCCOGD in 1959, where he assisted his brother.

Kim Il Sung's anti-revolutionary factionalist campaigns continued in 1960. According to an account by a North Korean defector to China who had commanded a campaign as political commissar of a KPA division, about ten thousand people were executed, murdered, or forced to work in coal mines between 1958 and 1959.[75] Renowned South Korean researcher Yi Chong-sŏk concluded, "The period between late 1956 and 1960 in North Korea was a time of raging winds, which eliminated all dissidents. Since then, the North moved with Kim Il Sung as its centripetal force."[76] Similarly, Andrei Lankov wrote,

> The period of 1956–1960 must be considered a major turning point in North Korean history, the years of the definitive establishment of the Kim Il Sung regime as we know it. During 1945–1956, North Korea had merely represented a second-rate "people's democracy," indistinguishable in many ways from the various Communist states of Eastern Europe. During 1956–1960, however, North Korea formed some of its own unique features.[77]

While mercilessly eradicating those who bore "thoughts of different colors," Kim Il Sung announced that agricultural collectivization had been accomplished by August 1958 and the First Five-Year Plan, based on the *Ch'ŏllima* Movement,[78] was achieved by 1960. He also publicly stated that

74 Ibid., 103–31.
75 Ryŏ Chŏng, *Pulk'e muldŭn Taedong kang: Chŏn inmin kun sadan chŏngch'l wiwŏn ŭi sugi* [The Taedong River has been dyed red: Manuscripts by a former political commissar of a KPA Division] (Seoul: Dong-A Ilbosa, 1991), 80–85.
76 Yi, *Saero ssŭn hyŏndae Pukhan ŭi ihae*, 424.
77 Lankov, *Crisis*, 223.
78 The Ch'ŏllima is a mythical winged horse that flies with great speed; the movement was based on intensive labor exploitation.

the socialization of commerce and industry was complete. In official words, North Korea had become a completely communist society.

In late April 1960 the Syngman Rhee administration in the South collapsed as a result of a nationwide student uprising. With the fall of Rhee, a strong symbol of the Korean independence movement, and the subsequent rise of Rhee's successors, who had had little experience in the Korean independence movement, Kim Il Sung could now portray himself as Korea's only legitimate revolutionary. At first, the North viewed with interest the military coup d'état staged by Major General Park Chung Hee and retired Lieutenant Colonel Kim Jong Pil on May 16, 1961, and the subsequent establishment of a military regime in the South. As noted earlier, Park's immediate elder brother and Kim Jong Pil's father-in-law was Pak Sang-hŭi, the very man who had joined the leftist revolt in North Kyŏngsang Province and who had been executed in October 1946. And Park himself had been an SKWP member, although he later switched his allegiance to the ROK government.

North Korea immediately sent Hwang T'ae-sŏng, a close friend of the late Pak Sang-hŭi, as an emissary to the South to meet Kim Jong Pil, the then powerful director of the newly established Korean Central Intelligence Agency (KCIA). Hwang had fled north in October 1946, where he became vice-minister of trade. Hwang's mission was to sound out the military junta's attitude about opening inter-Korean dialogue. In consultation with Park, Kim Jong Pil had Hwang executed in order to erase U.S. suspicions that the newly inaugurated military junta was pro-North or communist.

North Korea responded by defaming Park Chung Hee personally. Noting that Park had graduated from the Manchukuo Imperial Army Academy as well as the Japanese Army Staff College and had eventually become a Manchukuo military officer, the North branded him a pro-Japanese element. In addition, the major forces that formed or sustained the political leadership of the military junta were former Manchukuo military officers, and had graduated from the Manchukuo Imperial Army Academy. In the South Korean military establishment, they were said to have formed a Manchurian faction. In the eyes of the North Korean leadership—with its own Manchurian faction as its center and core—the Manchurian faction of the South Korean military was their erstwhile enemy. From the inauguration of the Park Chung Hee regime until its end in 1979, inter-Korean relations can be characterized as the resurgence of a military confrontation between the Manchurian factions of the North and the South.

Perceiving the military coup in the South as the American CIA's scheme to prepare a military attack on the North by strengthening anti-communist forces in the South, Kim Il Sung visited Moscow and Beijing to bolster the North's military ties with those two giants of international communism. Kim would conclude a de facto military treaty with the Soviet Union on July 6, and another with the PRC on July 11. Two months after his return to Pyong-yang, during September 11–18, 1961, Kim Il Sung convened the Fourth KWP Congress. The composition of the new CC and its PC reflected the conspicu-ous control of the KWP by the Manchurian faction, which occupied about 80 percent of the CC. The congress elected Kim Il Sung as CC chairman, and Ch'oe Yong-gŏn, Kim Il, Pak Kŭm-ch'ŏl, and others as CC vice-chairmen. While announcing the seven-year economic plan (1961–67) and envisaging rapid progress for North Korean industry, the KWP congress also installed a new clause, one that stipulated that decisions made by the KWP representa-tive congress should be ratified by a plenary meeting of the KWPCC. In late October 1962, the SPA elected Ch'oe Yong-gŏn as its SC chairman, the titular head of state, and Kim Il Sung as premier of the cabinet.

About this time, Sino-Soviet conflict bubbled to the surface. The Soviet "capitulation" in the Cuban missile crisis in late October 1962 was disturb-ing to the North Korean leadership. Criticizing Khrushchev's "revisionism," the North began to promote *Juche* ideology through its media and adopted a line calling for the militarization of the whole country. It became clear that the North was turning itself into a garrison state. The establishment of diplomatic relations between the ROK and Japan, and the ROK's mili-tary intervention in the Vietnam War, which further consolidated the U.S.-ROK military alliance amidst the Sino-Soviet rift, seem to have hardened the North's stance even more. In April 1965, at the Ali Archam Academy of Social Sciences of Indonesia, Kim Il Sung elaborated his theory of Korean revolution and strategy of triple revolution—revolution in the North, the South, and the world at large.[79] At the same time, North Korea intensified its overall posture against the United States and the ROK. The CCP fully sup-ported Kim, while the CPSU criticized him.

The military coup against the Sukarno leadership and the subsequent inauguration of a pro-U.S., anti-PRC regime in Indonesia and the intensi-fication of the Cultural Revolution in the PRC between late 1965 and early 1966, a movement that attacked the old generation of the Chinese commu-nist revolution, seem to have made Kim Il Sung reconsider his former pro-PRC stance. On August 12, 1966, *Rodong Sinmun* (Labor news) published an editorial, "Let's Support the Independent Line," signalling the North's superficial neutrality between Moscow and Beijing but actually marking the beginning of a transition to a pro-Moscow stance. Two months later, dur-ing October 5–12, 1966, the Second Conference of KWP Representatives

---

79 For the full text of Kim's speech, see Li Yuk-sa (Ri Yuk-sa), ed. *Juche!: The Speeches and Writings of Kim Il Sung* (New York: Grossman Publishers, 1972), 21–64.

was convened. On the final day, the newly constituted CC (the fourth CC) adopted a new leadership structure. The chairmanship and vice-chairmanship were abolished, the post of general secretary was introduced, and a secretariat was created within the Central Committee. The structure clearly resembled that of the CPSU.

Since the secretariat was empowered to execute the policies and resolutions of the Central Committee Political Committee (CCPC, i.e., the former Politburo) and review whether they were being correctly executed by the party and government agencies at lower levels, it was regarded as the KWP's most powerful organ. Kim Il Sung was chosen as general secretary and empowered to lead the secretariat on a daily basis. The ten newly elected secretaries included Ch'oe Yong-gŏn, Kim Il, Pak Kŭm-ch'ŏl, Ri Hyo-sun, Kim Kwang-hyŏp, Hŏ Pong-hak, and Kim Yŏng-ju. All of them were from either the Manchurian or Kapsan factions. By this time, to ordinary observers there was no dividing line between these two factions, since they had fought together in the Battle of Poch'ŏnbo in 1937. These two factions also occupied the majority of the CCPC. They included Pak Sŏng-ch'ŏl, Ch'oe Hyŏn, Ri Yŏng-ho, Hŏ Pong-hak, Ch'oe Kwang, O Chin-u, Rim Ch'un-ch'u, and Kim Tong-gyu. The composition of the presidium of the CCPC also showed the same trend. Among its six members, four (Kim Il Sung, Ch'oe Yong-gŏn, Kim Il, and Kim Kwang-hyŏp) were from the Manchurian faction, and two (Pak Kŭm-ch'ŏl and Ri Hyo-sun) were from the Kapsan faction. In the composition of the secretariat, there were some exceptions. These were Pak Yong-guk and Kim To-man, who had studied at Moscow together with Kim Yŏng-ju. This showed the rise of pro-Soviet elements in accordance with the North's tilt from Beijing toward Moscow, also evidenced by the ousting of the remnants of the Yan'an returnees, Kim Ch'ang-man and Ha Ang-ch'ŏn, from high-ranking KWP posts. While economy-oriented figures such as Ri Chong-ok and Ri Chu-yŏn were demoted, key military figures including Ch'oe Kwang and O Chin-u were promoted.[80]

At the beginning of 1967, the Red Guard in China began to attack Kim Il Sung, denouncing him as "a millionaire, aristocrat, and fat revisionist." Red Guard posters appeared in Beijing accusing the KWP leadership of living in luxury while the people suffered.[81] They even alleged that Kim had been arrested by Ch'oe Yong-gŏn. The North responded that the Red Guard was fabricating lies. At least one Red Guard allegation was certainly incorrect: Kim Il Sung's position as the North's one-man dictator was, in fact, solid.

80 Scalapino and Lee, *Communism in Korea*, vol. 1, 609.
81 Ibid., 641

3   Kim Jong Il's Rise to Succession, 1967–80

Succession Struggles Inside the KWP Leadership and the Advent of Kim Jong Il, 1967–70

Initial Stage: Manchurian Faction vs. Kapsan Faction

As would become known later, a few KWPCC leaders had already started to quietly debate the succession issue among themselves as early as the late 1950s. The decisive moment was provided by Khrushchev's de-Stalinization campaign, initiated in February 1956, and the August Factionalist Incident it helped inspire. Kim Il Sung, Ch'oe Yong-gŏn, Kim Il, and other former anti-Japanese partisan leaders concluded that the CPSU leadership's "erroneous" choice of Stalin's successor might cause a Sino-Soviet dispute and a weakening of the monolithic international communist movement. Anti-Soviet movements in Poland and Hungary in 1956, as well as similar movements in other Eastern European countries and China in 1956–57, were seen as inevitable repercussions of the CPSU's "incorrect" decision on Stalin's successor. The Cultural Revolution in China in the late 1960s would also be read in a similar context. Since Mao Zedong seemed to have transferred the CCP leadership to the Gang of Four, the Red Guard under them dared to attack the first generation of the revolution and, accordingly, China fell into chaos. Based on this line of reasoning, a limited number of KWPCCPC members unofficially pushed for an earlier resolution of the succession issue in the North.[1]

---

1 JoongAng Ilbosa, ed., *Kim Chŏng-il: Hanbando chŏlban ŭi sangsogin* [Kim Jong Il: An heir of half of the Korean Peninsula] (Seoul: JoongAng Ilbosa, 1994), 71–75. For sources, I primarily depend on recollections by former KWP functionaries, including Sin Kyŏng-wan, who had worked at the KWPCC but later defected to the West.

Since 1966 the first generation of the revolution—led by Ch'oe Yong-gŏn and Kim Il, who along with Kim Il Sung constituted a triumvirate—had tacitly regarded Kim Yŏng-ju as Kim Il Sung's successor. Born in 1920 or 1922, Kim Yŏng-ju was Kim Il Sung's only living biological brother. He had studied at Moscow State University and the CPSU central party school for higher-level cadres sometime around 1946–47, and he held the real power over the KWP as its strong first vice director and then as director of the OGD since the early 1960s. In October 1966 he was also elected a CC secretary and one of the CCPC's alternate members. The triumvirate had also tacitly agreed that Kim Yŏng-ju himself should be succeeded by a member of the second generation of the revolution.

Leaders of the Kapsan faction, however, resisted this implicit agreement. Pak Kŭm-ch'ŏl (former KWPCC vice-chairman and incumbent KWPCC secretary as well as KWPCCPC member) and Ri Hyo-sun (incumbent KWPCC secretary and KWPCCPC member) both opposed the scheme, arguing that Kim Yŏng-ju's anti-Japanese career was suspect. Indeed, there were allegations that he had been an assistant to, or a translator for, the Japanese army in Manchuria. Since Pak was a renowned anti-Japanese activist who had been sentenced to life imprisonment in 1937 and released from prison only after Korean liberation, and Ri was not only a famed anti-Japanese activist himself but the elder brother of Ri Che-sun, a leading anti-Japanese activist who had been executed in prison just a few months before liberation, their opposition could not be disregarded. Pak and Ri were aiming for Pak himself to be considered as the successor.[2]

Power struggles surfaced as policy debates. While the Kapsan faction advocated an economy-first policy, the Manchurian faction in general and its hardliners in particular supported a military-first policy. From March 1967 Kim Il Sung began to side openly with the Manchurian faction. Two months later, instead of Kim Il Sung, it was Kim Jong Il who initiated and led the anti-Kapsan faction campaign in earnest.

The Advent of Kim Jong Il

Let us first trace the path that Kim Jong Il followed after his return to Pyongyang from Jilin, Manchuria, in August 1953. According to his official biography, he graduated from the Fourth People's School in 1954 and Basic Middle School in 1957. A couple of months before graduation, he joined a school group called the Korean Democratic Youth League. In September

2 Yi T'ae-sŏp, *Kim Il-sŏng ridŏswip yŏn'gu: Suryŏngch'ek ŭi sŏngnip paegyŏng ŭl chungsim ŭro* [A study of the Kim Il Sung leadership: With emphasis on the background of the establishment of the leadership system] (Seoul: Tulnyŏk, 2001), 428–36.

1957 he entered Namsan Higher Middle School, which was reserved exclusively for children of KWP and KPA members and DPRK cabinet cadres with the rank of at least vice minister.

As a student, Kim Jong Il twice accompanied his father on visits to Moscow, once in October 1957 for the fortieth anniversary of the Russian Revolution, and again in January 1959, for the Twenty-first CPSU Congress.[3] Hwang Chang-yŏp, who as a KWP secretariat functionary was a member of Kim Il Sung's delegation in 1959, recalled Kim Jong Il's activities in Moscow. According to Hwang, Kim Jong Il held daily meetings with Kim Il Sung's attendants—including medical doctors and nurses—during which he received reports and issued instructions. In Hwang's eyes, Kim Jong Il's actions made no sense, as he was only seventeen years old and had no official party or government title. As Hwang describes it,

> Kim Jong Il used to drop his father's name whenever he asked a question of the attendants. To me, he usually said that his father wanted to know this or that. Moreover, he attempted to take care of his father in earnest. Although his father was only forty-seven years old, the son used to help his father by holding his arms and putting on his shoes. Kim Il Sung seemed to have been pleased with his son's actions.

Hwang's observations reveal he already sensed that the boy entertained political ambitions and that Kim Jong Il, rather than his uncle Yŏng-ju, might succeed his father.[4]

In April 1960, when student uprisings toppled the Syngman Rhee administration in the South, Kim Jong Il initiated an anti-U.S. demonstration, asserting that "we should fight for the withdrawal of the U.S. imperialists who are backing control of the Rhee puppet regime." Some of Kim's former classmates at Namsan Higher Middle School, later living in Russia, recollected that this demonstration became a model that would be followed throughout the North. Some Soviet diplomats and correspondents assigned to Pyongyang at that time noted that Kim Jong Il's initiation of the anti-U.S. demonstration in 1960 should be seen as the product of his close and unique observation of the North Korean political and international situation as Kim Il Sung's son.[5]

3 *Inmin ŭi chidoja* [The people's leader] vol. 1 (Pyongyang: The Korean Workers' Party Publishing Company, 1982), 102–262. For a biography of Kim Jong Il by a Western journalist, see Michael Breen, *Kim Jong Il: North Korea's Dear Leader* (New York: John Wiley and Sons, 2004).

4 Hwang Chang-yŏp, *Na nŭn yŏksa ŭi chilli rŭl po'atta: Hwang Chang-yŏp hoegorok* [I saw the truth in history: Memoirs by Hwang Chang-yŏp], rev. ed. (Seoul: Sidae Chŏngsin, 2006), 149–51.

5 JoongAng Ilbosa, ed., *Kim Chŏng-il*, 61–62.

During the 1959 Moscow visit, Kim Jung Il asked Hwang Chang-yŏp, who was a Moscow State University graduate, to give him a tour of that university. At the campus, a CPSU functionary in charge of North Korea encouraged Kim Jong Il to choose Moscow State University after his graduation from high school. According to Hwang, Kim Jong Il's response was resolute: "Never. We have an outstanding university called Kim Il Sung Comprehensive University. I will study at Kim Il Sung University."[6] As he had pledged, Kim Jong Il indeed entered the Faculty of Political Economy at Kim Il Sung Comprehensive University in September 1960. This might be regarded as a decision against the prevailing trend among youth from North Korean elite society, who preferred universities in the Soviet Union and Eastern Europe. Kim's official biography praised his decision: "It was the manifestation of the great *Juche* thought. He attempted to study the sciences based on the realities of the fatherland. To him, the real sciences and textbooks were located not in foreign countries but in Korea's realities."[7] But we should recall that as Khrushchev's attack upon the cult of personality was heightening, it might not have been desirable for Kim to choose a Soviet university. In addition, he may have feared that a long absence from North Korea could weaken his political position.

During his college days from September 1960 to April 1964, according to his official biography, Kim Jong Il not only attended regular courses but received special instruction on Korean revolutionary history centered on Kim Il Sung, KWP history, politico-economic theories, and linguistics. A noted North Korea watcher observed, "His uncle, Kim Yŏng-ju, then first [vice] director of the Organization and Guidance Department of the KWP, organized an advisory group made up of Kim Il Sung's staff and experts. The advisory group often gave Kim Jong Il the special task of writing on party affairs and policy issues."[8]

In October 1960, according to Kim's official biography, he presented an essay entitled "On Re-examining the Issue of the Unification of the Three Kingdoms in Korean History." Contrary to the conventional thesis that the kingdom of Silla had unified the three kingdoms by conquering Paekje and Koguryŏ in the seventh century, Kim argued that Silla's unification of the Three Kingdoms was so incomplete that it could not be called unification. Also according to his official biography, in January 1962 he published

6 Hwang, *Na nŭn yŏksa ŭi chinrlli rŭl po'atta*, 50.

7 *Widaehan ryŏngdoja Kim Chŏng-il changgun ryangryŏk* [Short biography of General Kim Jong Il, Great Leader] (Pyongyang: Pyongyangch'ulp'ansa, 1996), 21.

8 Kim Sung Chull (Kim Sŏng-ch'ŏl), *North Korea under Kim Jong Il: From Consolidation to Systemic Dissonance* (Albany: State University of New York Press, 2006), 37.

another essay, "Characteristics of Modern Imperialism and its Aggressive Nature." While attacking "the modern revisionists who were giving up the anti-imperialist struggle and revolution halfway," Kim suggested that the KWP continue the anti-imperialist struggle and revolution. In March 1964 he completed his graduation thesis, "The Place and Role of the County in the Building of Socialism."[9]

While in college, Kim Jong Il initiated a campaign to read ten thousand pages per year centering on Kim Il Sung's works. It is widely accepted that Kim Jong Il was an avid reader. Vadim Tkachenko, a former Soviet diplomat assigned to Pyongyang and CPSUCC functionary in charge of Korean affairs, recalled his meetings with Kim Jong Il in Pyongyang in the 1980s. Tkachenko said Kim Jong Il's study was filled with books and materials he had collected, and the breadth of his reading in many fields was evident.[10] In contrast to this scholarly aspect, however, Kim allegedly was already abusing power for personal ends while at college. A Russian professor who studied at Kim Il Sung University in the 1960s recollected that when a Korean classmate openly criticized Kim's arrogant and rude manner, Kim made the university authorities expel the classmate. The Russian professor, who refused to identify himself, added: "It was said that the student in question was banished to an unknown place. After that, whenever Kim Jong Il appeared on campus, most students would stop talking."[11]

While these recollections are unverifiable, the following three facts are more important. First, Kim Jong Il became a KWP member on July 22, 1961. Second, he frequently accompanied Kim Il Sung on field guidance visits to various parts of the country, widening his intellectual vision and enriching his "understanding of the real economy and effective modes of guidance and instruction."[12] In addition, he occasionally observed various meetings of the KWPCC, SPA, and the DPRK cabinet. Not only did he become personally acquainted with many significant figures, on occasion he would even criticize the remarks and stances of the members of these organizations. Third, according to some former Soviet diplomats and correspondents assigned to Pyongyang, he began to refer to Kim Il Sung's wife as "Lady Kim Sŏng-ae," implying that he did not recognize her as his stepmother. He also invented a new word, *kyŏtkaji* ("side branch"). On unofficial occasions, it was said that he referred to his stepmother, two half brothers, and half sister collectively

9 Foreign Languages Publishing House, *Kim Jong Il: Short Biography* (Pyongyang: Foreign Languages Publishing House, 2001), 21–34.

10 Quoted in JoongAng Ilbosa, ed., *Kim Chŏng-il*, 25–26.

11 Ibid., 64–65.

12 Kim, *North Korea under Kim Jong Il*, 38.

as a *kyŏtkaji muri*, i.e., "cluster of side branches."[13] Implicit in this name-calling was the notion that only Kim Jong Il himself and his biological younger sister, Kim Kyŏng-hŭi, formed the main trunk of the Kim Il Sung–Kim Jong Suk family tree. Nevertheless, such language never appeared in official publications.

What spurred Kim Jong Il to invent this terminology? Although we can only guess, there may be a clue in the story of his half brother, P'yŏng-il. Many North Korean defectors and foreign diplomats who resided in Pyongyang recalled that P'yŏng-il closely resembled his father. Public pictures taken in his adulthood confirm this. In contrast, Kim Jong Il's outward appearance was unimpressive. He himself reportedly confessed to Ch'oe Ŭn-hŭi, a South Korean movie actress abducted to the North, "I am so short and fat that I look like a dwarf and a bag full of foul garbage."[14] From the beginning, Kim Jong Il might have entertained an inferiority complex toward his half brother. Without regard for Jong Il's feelings, Kim Il Sung would proudly point out P'yŏng-il and say that "in my family, a true general was born."[15] Kim Il Sung's remarks might have further caused Jong Il to fear that his father might make his half brother the successor. Sin Kyŏng-wan—the KWP mid-level cadre—rejected such concerns. He argued that, from boyhood, P'yong-il dared not even to speak to Jong Il, who was ten years older.[16]

In any event, Kim Jong Il continued his efforts to please his father and secure his confidence. One example was his development of the theory on the role of the *Suryŏng* ("head leader") in Korea's process of revolution. The gist of Kim Jong Il's theory was that "since Suryŏng is not an individual but the brain of the masses, the term 'personality cult' does not stand to reason." He added, "As a living organism protects its own brain, the communists and people must defend their leader from the attack and slander of class enemies of all hues."[17] He presented this theory before the public in 1960 and 1963. It was in the first half of the 1960s that Kim Jong Il seems to have begun his ceaseless efforts to win Kim Il Sung's favor within the family.

13 JoongAng Ilbosa, ed., *Kim Chŏng-il*, 62.

14 Ch'oe Ŭn-hŭi, *Ch'oe Ŭn-hŭi ŭi kobaek* [Ch'oe Ŭn-hŭi's confessions] (Seoul: Random House Korea, 2007), 212.

15 Quoted in Kang Myŏng-do, *Pyongyang ŭn mangmyon gŭl kkumkkunda* [Pyongyang is dreaming of a flight of the north] (Seoul: JoongAng Ilbosa, 1995), 63.

16 Chŏng Ch'ang-hyŏn, *Kyŏt'esŏ pon Kim Chŏng-il* [Kim Jong Il as seen by an entourage], rev. ed. (Seoul: Kimyŏngsa, 2000), 38.

17 Quoted from his June 12, 1963, talk, "The Working-Class Leader Plays a Decisive Role in the Revolutionary Struggle." Foreign Languages Publishing House, *Kim Jong Il*, 27.

On April 1, 1964, around the time of his graduation from Kim Il Sung University, Kim Jong Il was posted to the KWPCC's powerful OGD with Kim Yŏng-ju as its director. He actually started working on June 19, 1964, with the official title, "guidance instructor at the central section for the guidance of the cabinet." According to Kim's official biography, he delivered an inaugural speech that stressed that "the KWP was founded and is led by Comrade Kim Il Sung. Its Central Committee is its General Staff that realizes Comrade Kim Il Sung's thoughts and leadership over the entire Party and society."[18] This speech may have pleased his father.

Soon Kim Jong Il was transferred to the comprehensive guidance section within the same organization's guidance department. The section was in charge of the PAFM and its GPB, and the National Railroad Ministry and its GPB. Through his posts in the central guidance department and the comprehensive guidance department, Kim could grasp the whole picture of governance in the North.[19] In September 1964 he was appointed to a guidance personnel position in the central guidance section. "Guidance personnel" refers to professional party cadres who, by themselves, organize certain tasks and who sometimes supervise lower party units. Kim Sung-chull (Kim Sŏng-ch'ŏl), a renowned scholar on North Korea, elaborates:

> With this position, Kim was now able to utilize the party's power and conduct his own duties independently. His major duty was the dissemination of Kim Il Sung's instructions and the party's documents to the general public. For this purpose, he handled literature and arts, publications, and broadcasting, all of which were not only his favorite fields but also significant subjects for the personality cult of his father and for his own image building.[20]

In 1966, Kim Jong Il was promoted from "guidance instructor" to "senior guidance instructor" at the central guidance section. Simultaneously, he was assigned to the guidance of the team responsible for the physical protection of Kim Il Sung, the supreme responsibility in the North. With that assignment, he could observe and even supervise all aspects of the KWPCC, SPA, and DPRK cabinet. According to North Korean official statistics, from 1964 to 1966 he also accompanied his father on thirty-one field guidance tours in two years. Accordingly, he was able to build up a political status that could not be easily challenged by others, and his influence became extensive. For example, Hwang Chang-yŏp recalled that he

18 Ibid., 37.
19 Chŏng, *Kyŏt'esŏ pon Kim Chŏng-il*, 98–99.
20 Kim, *North Korea under Kim Jong Il*, 39.

was appointed president of Kim Il Sung University in April 1965, thanks to Kim's recommendation.[21]

Kim Jong Il's activities expanded to include international affairs. In April 1965, he accompanied Kim Il Sung to a conference commemorating the tenth anniversary of the inauguration of the Non-Aligned Movement in Bandung, Indonesia, where he also joined his father's talks with Indonesian president Sukarno. His official biography claimed that Kim Il Sung introduced his son to Sukarno, remarking that "he is my chief aide-de-camp in charge of my personal safety. Without his assent, I don't move an inch." If this statement is true, it means that Kim Jong Il had already fully secured his father's confidence. At the banquet for Sukarno, Kim Jong Il made a speech to the effect that the first and foremost objective in the development of the Non-Aligned Movement was to strengthen unity. His official biography adds, "During his stay in Indonesia, Kim Jong Il met many political and social figures. His analysis of the world situation and emphasis on the validity and invincibility of the Non-Aligned Movement moved them greatly."[22]

Kim Jong Il's Active Role in the Establishment of the Unitary Thoughts System, 1967–70

The Purge of the Kapsan Faction

Kim Jong Il made his political debut before the KWP at the secret Fifteenth Plenum of the Fourth KWPCC, held May 4–8, 1967. There, Kim Jong Il openly criticized the Kapsan faction and led the effort to purge its leaders, Pak Kŭm-ch'ŏl and Ri Hyo-sun. Kim made three major accusations. First, Pak and Ri had obstructed the Ch'ŏllima Movement. This project to mobilize workers called for their voluntary and enthusiastic devotion without consideration of any kind of reward, but Pak and Ri had argued that the party should adopt Soviet economist Yevsei Liberman's "material incentive theory." Kim criticized the Liberman model as a product of Soviet revisionism. Second, Pak and Ri had opposed the party's policy of increasing the industrial growth rate, arguing that the party should pursue balanced growth between industry and agriculture. Third and most seriously, Pak and Ri had downplayed the relative importance of the anti-Japanese guerrilla movement in Manchuria, arguing that the domestic anti-Japanese movement that they themselves had led in South Hamgyŏng Province also deserved high appreciation.

21 Hwang, *Na nŭn yŏksa ŭi chilli rŭl po'atta*, 170.
22 Foreign Languages Publishing House, *Kim Jong Il*, 43–44.

Criticizing Pak and Ri as factionalists, revisionists, and feudalists who had committed numerous crimes, Kim Jong Il succeeded in ousting not only them but also their followers—Vice-Premier Ko Hyŏk and science education minister Hŏ Sŏk-sŏn—from the KWP. Initially, Kim Jong Il assigned them to low-level positions in farming regions; ultimately, they were sent to reeducation camps, never to be heard from again.

There are three noteworthy points in Kim Jong Il's initiation of the anti-Kapsan campaign. The first is that he became strongly aligned with O Chin-u, KWPCCPC alternate member and KPAGPB director. This alignment, of which other KWPCCPC members were not aware, would continue until O's death from natural causes in 1995. Second, Kim also ousted Kim Yŏng-ju protégés Kim To-man and Pak Yong-guk from the KWPCC secretariat.[23] In hindsight, one may argue that Kim Jong Il's efforts to become his father's successor and exclude his uncle began at this meeting. Third, the alignment between the Manchurian and Kapsan factions, which had begun in 1937, finally ended. Now the Manchurian faction remained the only faction in North Korean politics.

Escalation of the Kim Il Sung Personality Cult

On May 25, about two weeks after the the Fifteenth Plenum ended, Kim Jong Il began a movement to establish a "unitary thought system." Kim Il Sung's philosophy would be at its core, and the movement itself was called the "May 25 instruction." At Kim's strong urging, the Sixteenth Plenum of the Fourth KWP Central Committee, held from late June to early July 1967, officially approved a ten-point program to implement the Kim Il Sung unitary thought system. Henceforth, only Kim Il Sung's thought was to be regarded as orthodox. It had to be observed strictly and without vacillation; all other thought was heretical and had to be thoroughly eradicated.

According to the memoirs of Sung Hye-rang, elder sister of Kim Jong Il's common-law wife, all North Koreans, irrespective of age, were required to memorize the ten-point program. All books in libraries, offices, and even homes were subject to censorship by the authorities. Many books—judged as containing revisionist or bourgeois thought—were confiscated and even vandalized and burnt. All Western paintings and sculptures were destroyed and all Western musical recordings and scores were burnt. Even the introduction of foreign technology was banned. All painters, musicians, literary

23 Yi Chong-sŏk, *Saero ssŭn hyŏndae Pukhan ŭi ihae* [An understanding of contemporary North Korea: A newly written edition] (Seoul: Yŏksa Pip'yŏngsa, 2000), 428–30.

figures, and technicians suspected of having entertained revisionist or bourgeois thought were sent to local reeducation camps, farms, and mines. It was the North Korean version of the Chinese Cultural Revolution.[24]

As many students of North Korean politics have agreed, the role played by Kim Jong Il in the purge of the Kapsan faction and the establishment of the Kim Il Sung unitary thought system not only heightened his authority, but also further increased Kim Il Sung's confidence in him.[25] A few months later, in November 1967, the SPA elected Ch'oe Yong-gŏn as SC chairman and also named a new cabinet with Kim Il Sung as its premier. Kim Il, Ri Chong-ok, Kim Kwang-hyŏp, Nam Il, and others were appointed vice-premiers, while Kim Ch'ang-bong and Pak Sŏng-ch'ŏl were appointed vice-premiers and chosen to serve concurrently as defense minister and foreign minister, respectively.

At the beginning of 1968, North Korean actions shocked the international community. On January 21, 1968, North Korean commandos approached the ROK presidential mansion intent on assassinating President Park Chung Hee, although the mission ended in complete failure. Two days later, the North seized an American surveillance vessel, the USS *Pueblo,* and its crew off the coast of North Korea. The United States had to open a series of tedious negotiations with the North for the crew's release, which was finally obtained in December.

It was in this atmosphere that the Seventeenth Plenum of the Fourth KWP Central Committee, held in April 1968, declared the thought of Kim Il Sung as its unitary thought. The ramifications were extensive. Henceforth, the thought of Kim Il Sung, i.e., *Juche* ideology, was elevated to the level of quasi-religious scripture. This provided further impetus to the Kim Il Sung personality cult. By the end of 1969, more than one million books were printed that praised not only him but also his parents and grandparents as anti-imperialistic revolutionaries and independence activists. On September 7, 1968, two days before the twentieth anniversary of the DPRK's founding, senior KWPCC cadres visited the tombs of Kim's parents and grandparents to pay homage.

Kim Il Sung was also elevated from being the leader of only the Korean nation to being the leader of the entire world's working class. Typically, when referring to Kim, up to fifteen adjectives—such as "unequaled," "iron-willed," "ever-victorious," and "gifted"—would be prefixed to his

24 Sung Hye-rang, *Tŭngnamu chip* [The wisteria house] (Seoul: Chisik Nara, 2000), 312–15.

25 Yi Chu-ch'ŏl, *Kim Chŏng-il'ŭi saenggak ilgi* [A reading of Kim Jong Il's thoughts] (Seoul: Chisik Kongjakso, 2000), 24.

name.[26] In April 1969 the North held the National Social Scientists Seminar in Pyongyang. It adopted the Suryŏng theory, under which Suryŏng Kim Il Sung was compared to the brain of the human body. It also defined Kim Il Sung as "the unitary supreme Suryŏng."[27] The Kim Il Sung personality cult had indeed entered an entirely new phase.

The dramatic intensification of his personality cult provided Kim Jong Il with many more opportunities to widen his sphere of action. The arts in general, and drama, film, and music in particular, were promising for Kim, since he was proclaimed as a talented expert in these fields. According to his official biography:

> From childhood, Kim Jong Il demonstrated an extraordinary awareness of the beauty and power of imagination with which he approached the things and phenomena around him in an artistic way. . . . He was sensitive to the world of music, having a high level of skill of playing musical instruments and an exceptional sense of acoustics.[28]

Such claims appear to have at least some substance. Sin Sang-ok, an acclaimed movie director in South Korea, and his wife, Ch'oe Ŭn-hŭi, a famous movie actress, concluded that Kim was very talented not only in drama and film but also in music. They based their assessment on the numerous talks they had with Kim after he had them kidnapped from Hong Kong to the North in 1978. They recounted their experiences in memoirs published after their dramatic escape to the West via Vienna in 1986.[29]

With the personality cult in full swing, Kim was appointed culture-arts guidance section chief in the KWP propaganda-agitation department sometime between late 1967 and early 1968. The department's director was Kim Kuk-t'ae, son of the late Kim Ch'aek; thus Kim Kuk-t'ae, like Kim Jong Il, belonged to the second generation of the revolution. However, Kim Kuk-t'ae was ill and so delegated most of his duties to Kim Jong Il. Moreover, the culture-arts department, which worked together with the propaganda-agitation

---

26 For the personality cult surrounding Kim Il Sung at this time, see Hyŏn Sŭng-il, *Pukhan i ch'irun munhwa sohyŏngmyŏng: Sanŏp chŏngch'aek myŏn esŏ ŭi kŭkjwa nosŏn ŭl chungsimŭro* [The cultural revolution North Korea underwent: With emphasis on the extreme leftist line in industrial policies]; and In'gok Hwang Sŏng-mo paksa hwan'gap kinyŏm nonmun chip kanhaeng wiwŏnhoe, ed., *Sahoe kujo wa sahoe sasang* [Social structure and social thoughts] (Seoul: Simsŏldang, 1986), 263–87.

27 Yi, *Saero ssŭn hyŏndae Pukhan ŭi ihae*, 430–32.

28 Foreign Languages Publishing House, *Kim Jong Il*, 44–45.

29 Sin Sang-ok and Ch'oe Ŭn-hŭi, *Uri ŭi t'alch'ul ŭn kkŭtnaji anatta* [Our escape is not over] (Seoul: Wolgan Chosŏnsa, 2001), 288–89.

department, was led by an economist, Ri Kŭm-mo. Kim Il Sung appears to have appointed Ri, a typical technocrat in economy and industry, to this position because he was unlikely to interfere with Kim Jong Il's work.

Thus enjoying a free hand, Kim Jong Il used his new position to publicly identify himself with his father. Among other things, he produced the documentary film *Man'gyŏngdae*, named for Kim Il Sung's birthplace. While it focused on Kim Il Sung, it included detailed stories about Kim Jong Il. To give the identification of father and son further prominence, the *Rodong Sinmun* published a lengthy article on the documentary on February 16, 1968, Kim Jong Il's twenty-sixth birthday.[30]

About this time Kim Jong Il put forward the "speed war thesis" for the production of artistic works. Kim argued that all poets, novelists, painters, sculptors, musicians, and filmmakers should, within the shortest period of time, produce the highest-quality work in accordance with the unitary thought of Kim Il Sung. He coined the catchphrase, "à la anti-Japanese guerrilla," meaning that all artistic work should reflect the spirit and deeds of Kim Il Sung's anti-Japanese guerrilla activities in Manchuria in the 1930s. In the same vein, Kim Jong Il founded the April 15 Creation Company. Taking its name from the date of Kim Il Sung's birth, the company was tasked with producing scenarios praising Kim Il Sung's anti-Japanese partisan activities.[31]

A year later, Kim Jong Il was promoted to vice director of the propaganda-agitation department. Between 1969 and 1970, writers and artists began to refer to him as "Dear Comrade Leader" and even "Dear Brilliant Leader." In September 1970, Kim was assigned as vice director of the culture-arts department.[32]

Road to the Fifth KWP Congress, and the Prominence of Kim Yŏng-Ju, 1968–70

As Kim Il Sung's cult of personality and related propaganda activities expanded, the North's military stepped up its provocations against the South and the United States. In November 1968 it dispatched commando units to agricultural areas in the South near the East Sea (Sea of Japan), and in April 1969 it shot down a U.S. naval reconnaissance plane over the East Sea. Later it became known that Cho Myŏng-rok, a senior North Korean Air Force officer trained as a MIG fighter pilot in the Soviet Union, initiated

---

30 Yi, *Saero ssŭn hyŏndae Pukhan ŭi ihae*, 499.
31 Chŏng, *Kyŏ'yesŏ pon Kim Chŏng-il*, 105.
32 Yi, *Saero ssŭn hyŏndae Pukhan ŭi ihae*, 499.

TABLE 3.1
Some of the hardliners purged December 1968–January 1969

Name	Position
Kim Kwang-hyŏp	KWPCCPC member, KWPCC secretary, and vice-premier
Kim Ch'ang-bong	KWPCCPC member and defense minister
Ri Yŏng-ho	KWPCCPC member and KPA marine corps commander
Sŏk San	KWPCCPC member and public security minister
Hŏ Pong-hak	KWPCCPC alternate member and KWP chief of southern operations

and engineered the shoot-down. Even the Soviet Union, however, warned against the North's bellicosity.[33] About this time, the North's military seems to have begun to apply pressure on Kim Il Sung not to reduce the defense budget in favor of bolstering agriculture and industry. CCP materials alleged that hardliners in the North's military were seeking to limit Kim's absolute power. Although this cannot be verified, it is clear that between 1968 and 1969 the military was becoming more influential politically.[34]

At this critical juncture, Kim Il Sung decided to purge a number of "warmongering ultra-leftists" (see table 3.1). Ch'oe Kwang, a KWPCCPC member, was also purged on the charge that, as KPA chief of general staff, he had been negligent in supervising these cadres. In reality, they had been the main figures behind the planning and execution of the bold but risky operations against the South. They may have calculated that if their ventures proved successful, their influence would expand sharply within the KWP, allowing them to challenge Kim Yŏng-ju in the succession struggle.

Kim Il Sung, however, was much shrewder than they. Between late December 1968 and January 1969, he succeeded in purging hardliners in both the KWP and the KPA. This time, too, the close-knit team of Kim Jong Il and O Chin-u played a key role behind the scenes. As noted earlier, O had been close to Kim's mother, Kim Jong Suk, during the anti-Japanese guerrilla movement in Manchuria, and Kim Jong Suk had arranged O's marriage to Chŏn Kŭm-sŏn, Kim Jong Il's former teacher. As a boy, Jong Il had frequently visited O's residence after his mother's death. O was now rewarded with an immediate promotion to KPA chief of general staff.

33 As for the Soviet position, see the public speech of N. V. Podgorny, Soviet head of state, made upon his arrival in Pyongyang on May 16, 1969. *Pravda*, May 17, 1969, *Current Digest of the Soviet Press* 21, no. 20 (June 4, 1969): 7.

34 This was examined in my book, *Pukhan o-sip-nyŏn sa* [A fifty-year history of North Korea] (Seoul: Dusan Dong-A, 1996), 254.

Among those purged, only Ch'oe Kwang would be rehabilitated, five years later and after having worked in a coal mine. This was due both to his own achievements and to his wife's link to Kim Jong Il. As explained previously, his wife, Kim Ok-sun, had taken care of Kim Jong Il and Kim Kyŏng-hŭi after their mother's death. It now became evident that the Manchurian faction, the only faction in North Korean politics after the purge of the Kapsan faction, had undergone its own schism.[35]

About twenty months after the purge of these audacious military leaders, the Fifth KWP Congress was held November 2–13, 1970, the first party congress since the Fourth KWP Congress in September 1961. In those intervening nine years, the North had experienced many changes. One was generational: about 70 percent of the North's total population was under thirty years of age and had thus been educated and trained under the DPRK. A second change was that a number of anti-Japanese revolutionaries had died. Kim Il Sung thus began the Fifth Congress with an address memorializing the "thirty-six revolutionary comrades" who had died since the last congress.

The generational change was also reflected in the composition of the new KWP leadership. More young cadres and technocrats were recruited for the newly composed CC, including for its secretariat and political committee (PC). Typical technocrats who advanced into the secretariat or the PC were Ri Kŭm-mo, Kim Chung-rin, Yang Hyŏng-sŏp, and Chŏng Chun-t'aek. In contrast, with the exception of the triumvirate of Kim Il Sung, Ch'oe Yong-kŏn, and Kim Il, plus O Chin-u and Ch'oe Hyŏn, aged partisans were removed from the secretariat and the PC. Kim Yŏng-ju's re-election to the secretariat and his promotion to full membership in the PC were conspicuous; while relatively young, perhaps about fifty, he now ranked sixth in the PC. He was regarded as the most powerful man in North Korea after only Kim Il Sung, who was again chosen as secretary general.[36]

Formalization of Kim Jong Il's Succession at the Sixth KWP Congress, 1971–80

The Nebulous, Byzantine Relationships among Kim Jong Il, Kim Yŏng-ju, and Kim Sŏng-ae

While Kim Yŏng-ju was viewed as Kim Il Sung's heir-apparent at the Fifth KWP Congress, Kim Jong Il's status remained undefined. According to Sin Kyŏng-wan's testimony and other materials, old partisan leaders—including

---

35 Yi, *Saero ssŭn hyŏndae Pukhan ŭi ihae*, 484; See also Scalapino and Lee, *Communism in Korea*, 614–15.

36 Scalapino and Lee, *Communism in Korea*, 662.

Ch'oe Yong-gŏn, Kim Il, and Ch'oe Hyŏn—suggested to Kim Il Sung that Kim Jong Il should be included in the CC as at least an alternate member. As vice director of the propaganda-agitation department, Kim Jong Il held a position that made him eligible to become a CC alternate member. But Kim Il Sung was said to have rejected the proposal, arguing that Kim Jong Il's youth might make him vulnerable to criticism.[37]

Instead of allowing his son to enter the Central Committee, Kim Il Sung took a measured step. Under Kim Il Sung's influence, the congress reached an important agreement that would help Kim Jong Il exercise his influence upon the KWP through the CC secretariat. On November 12, 1970, the congress expanded the CC's authority by allowing the secretariat to "debate and decide about cadre issues, foreign issues, and immediate issues regularly."[38] As Yi Chong-sŏk has pointed out, this was seen as a provision allowing Kim Jong Il to intervene in the secretariat's decisions for his political purposes behind the scenes of this powerful organization.[39]

During this period, a number of events took place that proved fortuitous for Kim Jong Il. The most important one was the deterioration of Kim Yŏng-ju's health—he was diagnosed with serious problems of the autonomic or peripheral nervous system. The chronic disease forced him to frequently vacate his office as KWPCCOGD director to visit a clinic at Mount Myohyang in Yŏngbyŏn, South P'yŏng'an Province, or even clinics in the Soviet Union or Eastern Europe. He was said to have returned hurriedly to Pyongyang from a Romanian clinic just one month before the opening of the Fifth Party Congress; Kim Jong Il filled in for him during preparations for the congress.[40] Privately, PC members also criticized Kim Yŏng-ju for his failure, as the powerful director of the OGD, to prevent the party from having tilted toward ultra-leftists in the late 1960s.[41]

Even after the Fifth Korean Workers' Party Congress, Kim Jong Il seems to have continued to fill in for his ailing uncle. Since the first vice director of the OGD was Pak Su-dong, a Kim Il Sung University classmate, Kim Jong Il could easily hold the reins of this powerful organization. It meant that Kim Jong Il could control the party's two core departments—propaganda-agitation and organization and guidance. Using both, Kim Jong Il led a new campaign to compel the cadres of the KWP, SPA, and the DPRK cabinet to memorize all of Kim Il Sung's published works. He held a series of national

37 Quoted in JoongAng Ilbosa, ed., *Kim Chŏng-il*, 88–89.
38 Yi, *Saero ssŭn hyŏndae Pukhan ŭi ihae*, 500.
39 Ibid.
40 JoongAng Ilbosa, ed., *Kim Chŏng-il*, 79.
41 Ibid., 78–79.

contests where participants recited the works from memory. It was said that Kim Jong Il himself used his ability to recite Kim Il Sung's works from memory before cabinet members and party cadres as a means of exercising control over them.[42] In July 1971 he founded the *P'ibada* (Sea of blood) opera group to prepare revolutionary operas commemorating Kim Il Sung's armed struggles against Japanese forces in Manchuria in the 1930s. Yet while Kim Jong Il was expanding his influence with Kim Il Sung's blessing, Kim Yŏng-ju was known not to have abandoned his aspirations to become the successor.

Meanwhile, Kim Sŏng-ae, Kim Il Sung's legitimate wife, was also emerging as a power contender. At the Fifth KWP Congress in November 1970 she was elected as a CC member. When Kim Il Sung made remarks in January 1971 to the effect that Kim Sŏng-ae's words were tantamount to his own, most KPA and cabinet cadres began to treat her as Kim Il Sung's representative. Even cabinet ministers and KPA central department directors were said to have treated her as second only to Kim Il Sung. In October 1971 she was elected chairperson of the Korean Democratic Women's League, replacing Kim Ok-sun, a partisan comrade who had been close to Kim Jong Suk and who had taken care of Kim Jong Il and Kim Kyŏng-hŭi after their mother's death. In December 1972 she was also elected to the SPA and its Standing Council, which replaced the Standing Committee. During this time, Kim Sŏng-ae flaunted her influence. Sung Hye-rang recollected that Kim would even vehemently scold Kim Jong Il himself.[43] Sung also recalled that in 1970 Kim Sŏng-ae used her influence in ousting Pak Chŏng-ae—a woman whom Kim Il Sung had appointed to key posts since his return to Korea in 1945—from KWPCCPC membership. Some months later, Pak was said to have been demoted to the level of a local farming-area functionary.[44] A former SSM functionary testified after his defection to the South that Pak died in a political prison camp,[45] but the allegation has not been verified.

Kim Sŏng-ae continued to wield influence. While posting her biological brothers—Kim Sŏng-gap and Kim Sŏng-ho—and other close relatives to key offices, she attempted to erase Kim Il Sung's first wife, Kim Jong Suk, from North Korean history. A former KWPCC functionary recollected that some literary figures who had praised Kim Jong Suk were demoted or even sent to coal mines. In addition, she attempted to abolish the distribution

42 Ibid., 86–87.

43 Sung, *Tŭngnamu chip*, 323 and 368.

44 Ibid., 323.

45 Paek Myŏng-gyu, "Kukka'anjŏn powibu" [The State Security Ministry], http://pscore.org/xe/episode/11509 (October 5, 2011).

system that gave privileges to the old partisans. She also promoted a sort of Kim Sŏng-ae personality cult within the Democratic Women's League. To shrewd observers, she was seen as North Korea's Jiang Qing—the parallel to Mao's wife, who had ousted Liu Shaoqi and Deng Xiaoping during the Cultural Revolution in China.[46]

In contrast to Kim Sŏng-ae, who attempted to reduce privileges to the old partisans, Kim Jong Il doggedly took care of them, always reiterating, "We should respect the first generation of the revolution." He is said to have assigned exclusive physicians and nurses to them, distributed foodstuffs to them before any others, and even arranged their sons' and daughters' marriages. According to a Beijing University professor who studied at Kim Il Sung University in the early 1970s, it was widely rumored that Kim Jong Il visited old partisans with gifts on the first day of the new year. As a result, he was said to have secured their absolute support.[47]

Kim Il Sung's Final Decision

Amid this jockeying by Kim Yŏng-ju, Kim Jong Il, and Kim Sŏng-ae, Sin Kyŏng-wan reports that elders of the first generation of the revolution pushed for Kim Jong Il to be chosen as the successor. There was a tumor growing conspicuously on Kim Il Sung's neck. The fear that the leader might be seriously ill spurred them to think the succession issue should be resolved before Kim Il Sung's *hwan'gap*—the sixtieth anniversary of his birth, traditionally regarded in Korea as marking the completion of one life cycle and the beginning of another. Following the elders' recommendation in late April 1971, the plenary meeting of the PC continued its discussion with Kim Jong Il as the central theme. On June 24, Kim Il Sung made a significant speech before the Sixth Korean Socialist Labor Youth League Congress. He publicly declared that the youth should carry on the revolution; that the revolution continued generation by generation; and that by new generations continuing the revolution, the revolution would be sustained. In this speech, he termed the youth as the successors of the revolution.[48]

In hindsight, one might conclude that when Kim Il Sung delivered that speech, using terms such as "generation by generation" and "the successors," he had already decided to designate his first son, Jong Il, as his successor. Later, news of the failed coup d'état against Mao Zedong by Lin Biao, who had been

46 Chŏng, *Kyŏt'esŏ pon Kim Chŏng-il*, 114.
47 Quoted in JoongAng Ilbosa, ed., *Kim Chŏng-il*, 42–43.
48 Chosŏn chung'ang t'onginsa, ed., *Chosŏn chung'ang nyŏn'gam 1972* [The Korean central yearbook 1972] (Pyongyang: Chosŏn chungang t'ongsinsa, 1972), 285–86.

designated as Mao's successor, and of Lin's futile effort to escape to the Soviet Union in September 1971 may have reinforced Kim Il Sung's determination. But Kim Il Sung seems to have deferred a final decision because, in the wake of the post-1971 Sino-American détente, Kim was focused on switching from a stance of confrontation to one of dialogue with South Korea.

Kim Jong Il's efforts to secure the succession continued in 1972. In February and March, a few months before the sixtieth anniversary of Kim Il Sung's birth on April 15, 1972, he presented—before Kim Il Sung and his old partisan comrades—a number of revolutionary operas, including *The Sea of Blood*, *The Flower Girl*, and *Tell the Story, Forest*. These were all works that Kim Il Sung had had created during the anti-Japanese guerrilla struggles to encourage and delight his guerrilla soldiers and people living in "liberated areas." It was said that the operas—*The Sea of Blood* in particular—were impeccable works of art that brought the audience to tears as they recalled the old days in Manchuria. Kim Il Sung lavishly praised his son for his efforts.[49]

A politically more meaningful event occurred during Kim Il Sung's *hwan'gap* celebration. In the middle of a feast, Kim Kyŏng-hŭi, Kim Jong Il's sister, began to weep loudly as she recalled their deceased mother, Kim Jong Suk. According to Sin Kyŏng-wan, a guest at the feast, she even openly said something to the effect that the First Lady's seat should have been occupied by her deceased mother, a glorious anti-Japanese guerrilla fighter, but was instead occupied now by a woman without such a storied background. If true, Kyŏng-hŭi's remarks would have been seen as a public humiliation of Kim Sŏng-ae. According to Sin, many old partisans were moved by her tears and also wept loudly, repeatedly calling out "Oh! Jong Suk."[50] A few months later, Kim Jong Il "guided" an event commemorating the thirty-fifth anniversary of Kim Il Sung and his guerrilla fighters' victory at the Battle of Poch'ŏnbo. The fact that he "guided" this event was significant—it was a tacit declaration that he had become the successor to the anti-Japanese revolutionary tradition.[51]

Between late 1971 and early 1972, negotiations between the two Koreas proceeded rapidly. Kim Yŏng-ju emerged from the process as if he were the successor to Kim Il Sung, at least as portrayed in the Western press. In the historic North-South Joint Communiqué released on July 4, 1972, KWPCCOGD director Kim Yŏng-ju and his southern counterpart, KCIA

49 JoongAng Ilbosa, ed., *Kim Chŏng-il*, 90.
50 Quoted in Chŏng, *Kyŏt'esŏ pon Kim Chŏng-il*, 80–81.
51 Ibid., 91

director Yi Hu-rak, pledged to pursue Korean unification based on a spirit of national autonomy, peace, and grand harmony, "upholding the will of the[ir] respective superiors." This famous phrase left the strong impression on outsiders that Kim Yŏng-ju would eventually succeed his elder brother as the North's leader.

On October 17, 1972, about one hundred days after the adoption of the North-South Joint Communiqué, ROK president Park Chung Hee declared martial law. He inaugurated the *Yushin* (revitalization) regime, based on a secretly drafted constitution allowing him to be re-elected president without term limits. Two months later, on December 27, the North also revised the DPRK constitution to be the "DPRK Socialist Constitution." It declared the *Juche* ideology to be the DPRK's guiding line, although it did not officially abandon Marxism-Leninism.

Under the North's new constitution, Kim Il Sung became DPRK president. In that capacity, he also automatically became the supreme commander of the KPA and the chairman of the DPRK National Defense Commission. The new constitution also inaugurated the Standing Council, replacing the Standing Committee, within the SPA. Hwang Chang-yŏp was elected its chairman. Ch'oe Yong-gŏn, who had been chairman of the SPA Standing Committee since 1957, became one of the DPRK's two vice-chairmen;. the other was the Reverend Kang Yang-uk, Kim Il Sung's maternal grandfather's third cousin. The new constitution also inaugurated the Central People's Committee (CPC) with twenty-five members, including the DPRK president, vice presidents, KWPCCPC members, and alternate members. The CPC, with the DPRK president as its "head," was empowered to guide the executive, legislative, and judiciary branches of government. Under the CPC, an Administrative Affairs Board was inaugurated with Kim Il as its premier. The former cabinet was abolished.[52]

Immediately after the constitutional revision, the KWPCC held its PC plenum. Sin Kyŏng-wan recalled that at this meeting—held on December 29, 1972—most PC members proposed to Kim Il Sung that he designate Kim Jong Il as his successor. But Kim Il Sung persuaded them to postpone the final decision.[53] At the same time, under the direction of Kim Jong Il, the KWP changed its membership identification card and issued the new one only to those who passed a new security clearance. Kim Jong Il's enhanced political status was confirmed again in December 1972, when Kim Il Sung registered his candidacy for the SPA in the 216th constituency in Hŭich'ŏn

---

52 Suh Dae-sook, *Kim Il Sung: The North Korean Leader* (New York: Columbia University Press, 1988), 270–76.

53 Chŏng, *Kyŏt'esŏ pon Kim Chŏng-il*, 116.

County, Chakang Province. As keen observers quickly realized, 216 represented Kim Jong Il's birthday of February 16. In a similar vein, in February 1973 the February 16 Arts Technical College was established at Kanggye City, Chakang Province, located at the Sino-North Korean border.[54]

While thus steadily moving to have Kim Jong Il become his successor, Kim Il Sung in May 1973 established the powerful Ministry to Safeguard State Politics, commonly called the State Safeguard Ministry. It was an outgrowth of the Bureau to Safeguard State Politics, part of the Ministry of Social Safety. The new ministry, whose main duty was to monitor and control the thoughts and activities of the North Korean people, was put under the direct supervision of the DPRK president, Kim Il Sung. At the same time, the North expanded the existing Special Area for the Dictatorial Control of Anti-Social Elements to all provinces and put all of them under the jurisdiction of the State Safeguard Ministry. Concentration camps instituted within this area resembled those within Auschwitz during the Nazi Germany's occupation of Poland. Kim Pyŏng-ha, whose career had been spent in the agency responsible for Kim Il Sung's security and in the national police, was appointed its minister.[55] Control of the people through concentration camps was one of the crucial components of the Kim Il Sung regime; the number of such camps would increase sharply under Kim Jong Il's regime.

In early August 1973, Western media reported the sensational news that Kim Dae Jung, the main opposition candidate in the 1971 ROK presidential election, had been kidnapped. He had been taken from a hotel in Tokyo by the KCIA, which was still led by Yi Hu-rak, and had eventually resurfaced, shaken but not seriously harmed, in Seoul. On August 28, Yi's DPRK counterpart, Kim Yŏng-ju, released an official announcement that the North would not continue inter-Korean dialogue with a kidnapper. Ironically, this would be Kim Yŏng-ju's last public appearance. His health deteriorating, he went to a local clinic in Kangwŏn Province to recuperate. In September 1973, at the Seventh Plenum of the Fifth KWP Central Committee, Kim Jong Il was elected as the newest full member and appointed as CC secretary for organization and ideology. This automatically made him in charge of propaganda and agitation. It was now clear that Kim Jong Il was to be his father's successor.

There is circumstantial evidence that the North Korean regime may have been sensitive to criticism that it was implementing a hereditary succession. In the 1970 *Political Terminologies Dictionary*, published by the DPRK Academy of Social Sciences, the entry on "hereditary succession" clearly criticized it as a reactionary custom practiced in slave states, feudalistic states, and modern

54 Yi, *Saero ssŭn hyŏndae Pukhan ŭi ihae*, 42.
55 For more information, see Kim Hakjoon, *Pukhan o-sip-nyŏn sa*, 300–01.

capitalist states that exploit the working class. However, in the *Political Dictionary*, published in December 1973 by the same institute as a replacement for the *Political Terminologies Dictionary*, there was no entry on hereditary succession.[56]

In February 1974 Kim Jong Il was promoted to KWPCCPC membership and became a KWPCC secretary for the party, cabinet, and military. In addition, he was given the title "Hero of the Republic." Although these events were not made public at the time, it was clear that Kim had finally clinched the succession; in 2001 his official biography revealed that he became "Kim Il Sung's successor" in February 1974.[57] Kim Sung Chull writes,

> According to Suzuki Masayuki, a Japanese expert on North Korea, . . . these appointments were historic political events in North Korean politics on the grounds that Kim could utilize the positions not only for extending his power base in the party and state apparatuses but also for launching ideological initiatives to idolize his father, Kim Il Sung.[58]

In fact, immediately after assuming these posts, Kim Jong Il declared that the KWP should realize the "transformation of the country in accordance with Kim Il Sung's thought." He coined the new term, "Kimilsungism," a reference to "Kim Il Sung thought" or "*Juche* thought."

At the same February 1974 meeting, Kim Yŏng-ju was removed from the KWPCCPC and the CC secretariat and demoted to the position of cabinet vice-premier. By 1975 he had completely disappeared from sight—not only from the media but also from any public meeting. He was known to have gone to a local clinic in the northwestern province of Chakang. Some North Korea experts saw Kim Yŏng-ju's decline as the inevitable result of his worsening health. However, Hwang Chang-yŏp has asserted that his demotion was directly influenced by Kim Jong Il, who was reluctant to let him remain in the PC and secretariat.

Also according to Hwang, Kim Il Sung would say that "Jong Il's strong point lies in his *tokham* (cruelty or venomousness), while Yŏng-ju's weak point lies in his lack of *tokham*."[59] Indeed, as we shall see, cruelty would constitute a crucial component of Kim Jong Il's leadership attributes. A series of kidnappings in the 1970s of Japanese and Koreans, including the actress Ch'oe Ŭn-hŭi, and the bombing of ROK cabinet members and diplomats visiting Rangoon in 1983 are examples that reflect this *tokham*.

56 Lee Dong-bok, "North Korea After Sixth KWP Congress," *Korea and World Affairs* 5, no. 3 (Fall 1981): 415–40.

57 Foreign Languages Publishing House, *Kim Jong Il*, 58.

58 Kim, *North Korea under Kim Jong Il*, 41.

59 Hwang, *Na nŭn yŏksa ŭi chilli rŭl po'atta*, 114.

The Advent of the "Party Center"

On April 25, 1974, two months after Kim Jong Il's entry into the KWPCCPC, the *Rodong Sinmun* published an editorial that introduced the mysterious term "party center." It stressed, "In the road to accomplish the instructions given by the Great Leader and the policies given by the party center, it is an honor no matter whether we live or die." At first, most North Korean people did not understand the exact meaning of the "party center." They simply understood it as indicating a central organization of the KWP. But as we shall see later, they would realize belatedly that it referred to Kim Jong Il, who had himself invented the phrase to imbue his persona with an aura of mystery. Indeed, Kim was an inveterate manipulator of symbols.

Soon the de facto demotion of Kim Sŏng-ae and the purge of her brothers Kim Sŏng-gap and Kim Sŏng-ho and their associates followed. By December 1973, Kim Jong Il and old partisans, including Chŏn Mun-sŏp, Paek Hak-rim, and Cho Myŏng-rok, had decided to investigate their wrongdoings. Kim Kyŏng-hŭi's husband, Chang Sŏng-t'aek, who was chief of the KWPCCOGD's central guidance section, joined the investigation. The powerful investigative team of course confirmed that the group was responsible for many misdeeds and crimes. After reading the investigation report, Kim Il Sung became enraged and ordered a plenary meeting of the KWP Pyongyang Special City Committee, whose first organizational department director and then chief secretary had been Kim Sŏng-gap. As a result of the meeting, held in June 1974, Kim Sŏng-gap, then the political commissar at naval operations headquarters, and Kim Sŏng-ho, secretary of the KWP Hwanghae provincial committee, were deprived of all of their positions, and most of their associates were imprisoned or banished to local reeducation camps.[60] Soon a similar meeting of the Korean Democratic Women's League was held. Kim Sŏng-ae was ordered to be prudent in speech and action, but she was allowed to remain its chair and an SPA member. Thereafter, the Korean media referred to her not as an independent personage—"Lady Kim Sŏng-ae" or "Chairwoman Kim Sŏng-ae"—but merely as Kim Il Sung's "wife."[61]

About this time, Kim Il Sung concluded the Three Revolution Team Movement that he had inaugurated in February 1973 to galvanize support for the stagnant Six-Year Plan (1971–76). The three revolutions, based on the notion of continuous revolution, were revolutions in ideology/thought, technology, and culture. In fall 1974, Kim Il Sung entrusted his son with the task of mobilizing the masses through the use of the Three Revolution

60 JoongAng Ilbosa, ed., *Kim Chŏng-il*, 100–101.
61 Yi, *Saero ssŭn hyŏndae Pukhan ŭi ihae*, 55.

Team Movement, which maintained between forty and fifty thousand youth, both party and non-party members. Through this movement, Kim Jong Il attempted to streamline and strengthen his political base.[62]

The following year, North Korean official publications began to use the term "party center" more conspicuously. Suh Dae-sook notes:

> It was common to find such references as "our great *Suryŏng* and the *party center,*" "the father *Suryŏng* and the *party center,*" and "the new, creative, and independent direction of the *party center.*" In many articles and reports, the term "*party center*" was used to refer not to the inanimate object of the party's central organization but to the third-person singular, such as "the affection of the *party center*" and "the appeal of the *party center.*"[63]

Most North Koreans thus began to identify the term with Kim Jong Il.

Kim Jong Il's thirty-fourth birthday in 1976 was another turning point in solidifying his successor status:

> In 1976 the young Kim's birthday, February 16, was declared a public holiday and his portraits appeared in public buildings and schools together with his father's. Furthermore, his birthday was made the starting day of the "loyalty festival period" which was to reach its climax on April 15, the birthday . . . of the aged Kim Il Sung. [64]

More importantly, a campaign promoting Kim Jong Il's late mother, Kim Jong Suk, was suddenly launched. Even Kim Sŏng-ae, who had once attempted to erase her from history, joined the campaign. From mid-1976, Kim Jong Il began to filter all reports meant for Kim Il Sung, including submitting only summaries of some, at his own discretion.[65] Kim Jong Il was thus now wielding real power, while his father reigned.

In February 1977 the North published a booklet explaining that Kim Jong Il had been designated as Kim Il Sung's successor. At the same time, "the term 'party center' disappeared abruptly."[66] This was interpreted as a sign that some party cadres were expressing dissatisfaction with the father-to-son succession. Between late 1976 and early 1977, KWP Control Commission chairman Chi Kyŏng-su and PAFM vice minister Chi Pyŏng-hak died after harsh "ideological examinations."

62 Shinn Rinn-sup, "North Korean in 1982: Continuing Revolution under Kim Jong Il," *Asian Survey* 22, no. 1 (January 1982): 102–103.

63 Suh, *Kim Il Sung*, 279.

64 "Analysis: Kim Jong Il Cult to Be Escalated," *Vantage Point: Developments in North Korea* 7, no. 2 (February 1984): 13–14.

65 JoongAng Ilbosa, ed., *Kim Chŏng-il*, 108.

66 Suh, *Kim Il Sung*, 279–81.

In October 1977, DPRK vice-chairman Kim Tong-gyu, a renowned anti-Japanese fighter during the colonial period and the third-highest member of the KWP behind Kim Il Sung and Kim Il, was sent to a local political prison camp and died there around 1984. (The KWP's second-highest member, Ch'oe Yong-gŏn, had died in 1976.) Ryu Chang-sik, a KWPCCPC alternate member who had assisted with Kim Il Sung's state visits to Romania, Algeria, Mauritania, and Bulgaria in 1975, was also sent to a political prison camp.[67]

Kim Jong Il is known to have initiated a 1979 investigation of his younger half brother, P'yong-il, whom he had termed one of the "cluster of side-branches." When a special team exposed his wrongdoings, including much indiscreet womanizing, Kim Il Sung allegedly sent him to East Germany to study. It seemed that he was thus excluded from the candidates for succession.[68] Since the mid-1980s, he has roamed, first as a military attaché at the North Korean embassy in Belgrade, Yugoslavia, then successively as ambassador to Hungary, Bulgaria, Finland, Poland, and, as of December 2014, the Czech Republic. Others who belonged to the "cluster of side-branches" experienced a similar fate. Yŏng-il, a physicist by training, was sent first to Malta, then to Germany as a councilor in charge of science and culture at the North Korean interests section in Berlin,[69] where he died of cancer in 2000. Kyŏng-jin was sent first to Prague, then to Vienna, as the wife of North Korean ambassador Kim Kwang-sŏp.

The Sixth KWP Congress and the Formalization of Kim Jong Il as Successor

On October 26, 1979, ROK president Park Chung Hee was assassinated by his own KCIA director, Kim Chae-kyu. In the subsequent political turmoil in the South the members of a new military junta captured political power by mutinying against their superiors on December 12, 1979, and in May 1980 they massacred activists of the democratization movement in Kwangju, South Chŏlla Province, Kim Dae Jung's stronghold. Openly scorning the turbulence in the South, Kim Il Sung proudly presented Kim Jong Il as his

67 Suzuki Masayuki, *Kita Chosen: Shakai shugi to teno no kyomei* [North Korea: Resonance between socialism and tradition] (Tokyo: University of Tokyo Press, 1992), 112.

68 Kang, *Pyŏngyang ŭn mangmyŏng ŭl kkumkkunda*, 73–76.

69 "Following German reunification, . . . the former North Korean Embassy in East Berlin was turned into an Office for the Protection of the Interests of the Democratic People's Republic of Korea, with the People's Republic of China acting as protecting power." *Federal Foreign Office* website, http://www.auswaertiges-amt.de/EN/Aussenpolitik/Laender/Laenderinfos/01-Nodes/KoreaDemokratischeVolksrepublik_node.html

chosen heir to the North Korean people at the Sixth KWP Congress, held October 10–14, 1980. The younger Kim, he said, would assure the continuation of the revolutionary task "generation after generation." (For South Korean unification activists, this congress is still remembered as the occasion when the North proposed to the South the Democratic Confederated Republic of Koryŏ [DCRK] formula for unification.)

At this congress, Kim Jong Il's name was listed fourth in the five-member Presidium of the CC Politburo,[70] second on the ten-member CC Secretariat, and third in the ten-member CC Military Commission. More importantly, he was the only member of the KWP other than his father to hold concurrent membership in all three leading KWP organs. In retrospect, Kim Il Sung's decision to designate his first son as successor was "a carefully planned and executed act [that had been] in the making for a long time before" this official presentation at the Sixth Party Congress.[71] Marxism's first monarchy[72] had been established in North Korea.

70 It was at this congress that the CC Political Committee had its name changed to the CC Politburo.

71 Kihl Young-whan, "North Korea: A Reevaluation," *Current History* 81, no. 474 (April 1982): 155.

72 Anthony Paul, "Inside North Korea, Marxism's First 'Monarchy,'" *Reader's Digest* (February 1982): 73–77.

4 Joint Regime of the Two Kims, 1981–94

Consolidation of Kim Jong Il as Successor, 1981–84

Following Kim Jong Il's debut in October 1980, there were a series of signals that indicated the consolidation of his status as the de facto successor. In 1981 "numerous public references to [his] 'leadership'—a term previously reserved only for Kim Il Sung—reinforced the impression that Kim Jong Il's succession was all but complete. . . ."[1] On April 14, 1982, one day before Kim Il Sung's seventieth birthday, Kim Jong Il became the third-ranking member of the Presidium of the KWPCC Politburo, behind only his father and the ailing and aged Kim Il, and the second-ranking member of the KWPCC Military Commission, again, just below his father, and just above the aged PAFM minister O Chin-u. Moreover, the PAFM and PSM, two core instruments of intelligence, state violence, and coercion, were removed from the Administrative Affairs Board and placed under Kim Jong Il's direct control.

Two months later, an even more important decision was made in Kim Jong Il's favor. At a KWPCC Military Commission meeting in June 1982, Kim Il Sung ordered that "Kim Jong Il, who is guiding the armed forces through the KWPCC Military Commission in the capacity of the KWPCC secretary in charge of organization, should guide the armed forces directly by himself." He added that "all military works of the armed forces should be concentrated in Kim Jong Il, who will induce the unitary conclusion." The KWPCC Military Commission was renamed the KWP Central Military Commission, indicating that it was independent of and equal in status to the KWPCC. Hence a new administrative system supporting Kim Jong Il's

---

1 Shin Rinn-sup, "North Korea in 1981: First Year for *De Facto* Successor Kim Jong Il," *Asian Survey* 22, no. 1 (January 1982): 100.

"unitary conclusion" was institutionalized. This change meant that Kim Jong Il had become the de facto supreme leader of the North Korean armed forces.[2] This in turn indicated that the son was ready to take the father's place in the event of his death or incapacitation.

Around this time, a campaign to promote Kim Jong Il's personality cult was launched. The North Korean media called him "an outstanding philosopher-theoretician, wise leader of the Party, and prominent organizer." On May 19–20, 1982, the KCNA even called him the "Beloved Leader," a term previously reserved for his father. It referred to "the Great Leader Comrade Kim Il Sung and Beloved Leader Comrade Kim Jong Il."[3] North Korean periodicals carried articles on political and ideological guidance given by Kim Jong Il. Two of the most conspicuous were the theses "On the Idea of *Juche*," which was read at the "National Forum on the Idea of *Juche*" on March 31, 1982, and "Revolutionary View of the Leader," published in October 1982. A (North) Korean Central Broadcasting Station commentary on November 30, 1982, disclosed another of Kim Jong Il's theses, "The KWP Is a *Juche*-Oriented Revolutionary Party Succeeding the Glorious Tradition of the Down-with-Imperialism Alliance." These last two theses sought to demonstrate that the KWP's roots could be traced to 1926 when "young communists of the new generation," led by Kim Il Sung, had launched a true revolutionary struggle, and that this was now inherited by the successor generation.[4] The North Korean media stressed that Kim Jong Il was presenting his own theory for further developing Kim Il Sung's idea of *Juche* and that his guidance in the political and ideological fields was comparable to that of his father.[5]

Kim Jong Il began to receive official messages from foreign government leaders. Among the first were from Mauritanian president Mohamed Khouna Ould Haidala, a special envoy of Chad's president, and the Ugandan vice president. The Central African Republic's Andre Kolingba became the first foreign head of state to praise North Korea's successor-designate. At a farewell banquet in November 1982 ending a five-day visit to North Korea, he declared that "beloved leader Kim Jong Il's guidance has been energetic and distinguished."[6]

2 Cheong Seong-chang (Chŏng Sŏng-ch'ang), *Chungguk kwa Pukhan ŭi tang chungang kunsa wiwŏnhoe pigyo yŏn'gu* [A comparative study of the Party Central Commission of China and North Korea] (Sŏngnam: Sejong Institute, 2011), 28–31.

3 Kihl Young-whan, "North Korea: A Reevaluation," *Current History* 81, no. 474 (April 1982): 156.

4 "Analysis: Kim Jong Il Cult to Be Escalated," *Vantage Point: Developments in North Korea* 7, no. 2 (February 1984): 13–14.

5 Ch'oe In-su, *Kim Jong Il: The People's Leader* (Pyongyang: Foreign Languages Publishing House, 1983), 1.

6 *Rodong Sinmun*, November 13, 1982, 1.

On the domestic front, Kim Jong Il began his own "on-the-spot guidance" and inspection tours. He made his first such tour in 1981, and two more by the end of the year, another two in 1982, and three in 1983. During such tours as well as on other occasions, Kim was accompanied by prominent figures, including PAFM minister O Chin-u, Premier Ri Chong-ok, and foreign minister Hŏ Tam. To commemorate his father's seventieth birthday, Kim Jong Il oversaw the completion of Pyongyang's reconstruction in April 1982. Highlights included the construction of the Grand People's Study Hall, Kim Il Sung Stadium, the sixty-meter-high Arch of Triumph in honor of Kim Il Sung's "triumphant" return to Korea after the Japanese surrender, and the 170-meter-high *Juche* Idea Tower, which the North Korean media proudly proclaimed was the world's tallest stone tower.[7]

The year 1983 was important to Kim Jong Il's consolidation of his de facto status as successor. At the invitation of Deng Xiaoping, the real center of power of the CCP as the advisor to its Central Military Commission's Advisory Council, and Hu Yaobang, CCPCC general secretary, he visited China on June 2–12 and received the CCP's official recognition as North Korea's successor-designate.[8] This marked a reversal of the stance of the CCP leadership, which had been critical of hereditary succession. After Kim's return to Pyongyang, the North Korean regime began to propagate a new story, not in Korean but in Kim's English biography, that Kim Jong Il had been born "on the field of battle against the Japanese imperialists" at Mount Paektu, the highest and most revered peak in Korea, and that he grew up there.[9]

This period saw a number of bloody purges. The Economist Intelligence Unit, a London-based intelligence research institute, reported that there was "a purge of over a thousand opponents of the succession idea, between January and April, 1983," mainly among the military hierarchy.[10] But the purge of Kim Pyŏng-ha was particularly serious. As discussed above, in May 1973 he was appointed state safeguard minister, a position in control of the regular police, the political police, and the military police. From the time of his appointment he wielded and even abused his power so extensively that he came to be called "a villain worse than Beria," the notorious head of the Soviet Union's secret police appointed by Stalin. Around 1980, Kim Jong Il realized that Kim Pyŏng-ha, who answered only to Kim Il Sung, had

7 Foreign Languages Publishing House, ed., *Kim Jong Il*, 101–103.

8 Kihl Young-whan, "North Korea in 1983: Transforming the Hermit Kingdom?" *Asian Survey* 24, no. 1 (January 1984): 102.

9 Ch'oe, *Kim Jong Il*, 1.

10 Economist Intelligence Unit, *Quarterly Economic Review*, *China and North Korea*, no. 3 (1983): 18.

reported about Kim Jong Il to Kim Il Sung. Kim Jong Il immediately initiated a secret investigation into Kim Pyŏng-ha's wrongdoings. In March 1981 or 1982, following a series of harsh interrogations involving torture, Kim Pyŏng-ha killed himself, in his office with his own pistol, on orders from Kim Jong Il conveyed through O Chin-u.[11] Kim Ch'i-gu, who conducted Kim Pyŏng-ha's torture sessions, would himself die of a reputed car accident in the mid-1980s.

Kim Jong Il appointed Ri Chin-su, public security minister in charge of the regular police, to the vacant post. As a faithful public security professional who had risen from the ranks of the police and prosecution, Ri was credited with the effective control of the Sino–North Korean border and the tight management of all political prison camps. Under his new leadership, most of Kim Pyŏng-ha's lieutenants were eradicated, and the resulting vacancies were filled entirely by those faithful to Kim Jong Il. Kim Jong Il thus assumed control over one of the most important instruments of state violence and coercion. When Ri died in his sleep in October 1987 of carbon monoxide poisoning while on a field inspection tour, Kim Jong Il did not fill the vacancy. Instead, he had the vice minister lead the ministry under Kim's direct supervision.

In 1991 Kim Jong Il appointed Kim Yŏng-ryong, a Kim Il Sung University classmate who had built up his career mainly in the police, as the State Safeguard Ministry first vice director, and through him Kim Jong Il himself controlled the ministry. As the communist regimes in Eastern Europe and the Soviet Union collapsed, Kim Jong Il renamed the ministry as the State Security Ministry (SSM) in November 1992. As in the past, this ministry's officials were empowered to arrest anyone suspected of being an anti-state element—without a court warrant. Immediately after the renaming, Kim Jong Il visited the ministry. Stressing the primacy of state security, Kim Jong Il warned its cadres and functionaries, "You should not relax your surveillance of the people even for a moment. If the thing that has recently occurred in former socialist countries were to occur in our country, it would be you, state security safeguard ministry men, who are first killed by the people."[12]

11 Kang, *Pyongyang ŭn mangmyŏng ŭl kkumkkunda*, 70–73. See also the press interview of Kim Chŏng-min, a KWPCC cadre who defected to Seoul, printed in *Kyŏnghyang Sinmun*, June 8, 1998, 14. See also articles by Alain Jacob, a correspondent to Beijing, written after his brief visit to Pyongyang published in *Le Monde* on March 17, 18, 19, 1984. Jacob reported that Kim Pyŏng-ha had been removed from the post two years earlier.

12 Quoted in Paek Myŏng-gyu, "Kukka anjŏn powibu" [The State Security Safeguard Ministry], http://www.pscore.org/xe/episode/11509. Paek was an SSM functionary before his defection to the South in the early 2000s. He contended that Kim Pyŏng-ha committed suicide in February 1984.

The Joint Regime of Kim Il Sung and Kim Jong Il, 1984–86

The year 1984 represented a decisive point in Kim Jong Il's full-scale assumption of power. On February 16, his forty-second birthday, national poets praised him as the "greatest man" and the "lodestar, the star which is guiding our nation." The North Korean media extensively propagated the story that he was born in a secret camp on Mount Paektu, thus inheriting the "holy revolutionary spirit."[13] On his forty-fifth birthday, one of the "secret camps" allegedly built within Mount Paektu's dense forest during the anti-Japanese guerrilla struggle would be claimed as his birthplace. Since the restoration of that "secret camp" and its subsequent sanctification, it has been a required pilgrimage site for the North Korean people. Apart from Kim's birthplace, the numbers representing his birthdate—2/16—were also given an air of sanctity and mystery. For example, license plate numbers beginning with "216" were reserved for vehicles allocated to a small number of Kim's loyal retainers. Likewise, belonging to schools or military units whose name begins with "216" was and still is highly valued among North Koreans.[14]

In March 1984, with the death of the aged Kim Il, who was the second-ranking member of the KWPCC Politburo's Presidium but lacked real power, Kim Jong Il automatically became the second-ranking member, after his father.[15] This prompted the North Korean media to intensify its propaganda drive; Kim Jong Il was proclaimed as the "great theoretician who has expounded the theories and principles of the *Juche* ideology for world revolution into a complete system and has given perfect proof of its greatness." In April 1984 Pyongyang's Foreign Languages Publishing House published Kim's little red book, translated into English as *On Some Questions in Understanding the Juche Philosophy: Workers of the Whole World, Unite!* This book and his other works in Korean were translated into French and Spanish as well. By then, Kim Jong Il's personality cult had surpassed those of Stalin and Mao.

At this time, Kim Il Sung embarked on an exceptionally long visit to the Soviet Union and seven Eastern European countries. It lasted from May 17 to July 1, 1984, and in some ways resembled a retiree's leisure tour. Following his return to Pyongyang, the *Rodong Sinmun* from July 17 began to print photographs of Kim Il Sung in Western-style suits instead of his usual Mao suit, giving a strong impression that he had withdrawn from public life. It

13 For example, see poems published in *Choson Yesul* [Korean arts], February 1984 and April 1984.

14 Son Kwang-ju, *Kim Chŏng-il haebu* [An anatomy of Kim Jong Il] (Seoul: Sidae Chŏngsin, 2006), 18.

15 *The Pyongyang Times*, March 14, 1984, 1.

was thus not a great surprise when *Radio Pyongyang* finally announced on August 6 that Kim Jong Il was indeed Kim Il Sung's successor. Stressing Kim Jong Il's ability and "loftiness," the report contended that the Soviet Union and Eastern European countries had acknowledged during Kim Il Sung's visit the leadership of both Kim Il Sung and Kim Jong Il.[16] Beginning on September 7, the *Rodong Sinmun* actually began to treat Kim Jong Il as more important than Kim Il Sung. For example, its headline articles, which had always been devoted to Kim Il Sung, were now exclusively about Kim Jong Il. On October 10, *Radio Pyongyang* confirmed that Kim Jong Il, as the sole successor to Kim Il Sung, was in full charge of all affairs of the KWP and DPRK and was directing the party and the state under his unitary leadership. We may therefore conclude that from 1984 the North was governed or ruled by a joint regime of Kim Il Sung and Kim Jong Il.

This joint regime began to put priority on the reconstruction of its stagnant, even sinking, economy. The Second Seven-Year Plan (1978–84) had not succeeded in attaining any of its original goals. In March 1984, "Kim Jong Il called for a stricter implementation of the 'independent accounting system of enterprises,'" under which "the managerial autonomy of state enterprises" was to be strengthened and "the use of economic criteria in decision-making and material incentives" for workers was to be encouraged.[17] On August 3, 1984, he initiated a "consumer products campaign" aimed at increasing consumer goods production. A month later, he went one step further; on September 8, 1984, the Standing Council of the Seventh Supreme People's Assembly enacted the Joint Venture Management Law, which allowed the introduction of capital, including loans from the West. This development meant the North's basic developmental strategy could no longer be characterized as autarkic, the rhetoric of *Juche* notwithstanding. However, the new policy's results would prove to be negligible; although the North started the Third Seven-Year Plan in January 1987, only eight months later it would become "the first country to be declared formally in default of international loans."[18] In November 1988 the North would establish the Ministry of Joint Venture Industry, but it would make "little headway . . . in attracting foreign capital."[19]

16 Yi To-hyŏng, "Pyongyang Pangsong" [Radio Pyongyang], *Chosun Ilbo*, August 7, 1984, 1.

17 B. C. Koh, "North Korea in 1987: Launching a New Seven-Year Plan," *Asian Survey* 28, no. 1 (January 1988): 63.

18 Ibid., 64.

19 Kong Dan Oh, "North Korea in 1989: Touched by Winds of Change?" *Asian Survey* 30, no. 1 (January 1990): 76.

In 1985—the fortieth anniversary of Korean liberation—Kim Il Sung began using a new term. In June, speaking before a Japanese journalist, he said that the task of Korean unification should be realized in the "Kim Jong Il era," if it could not be in his own.[20] We can see in retrospect that this phrase reflected a generational change in the KWP leadership. Between the Sixth KWP Congress of 1980 and then, a number of Kim Il Sung's remaining partisan comrades and colleagues had died, including Ch'oe Hyŏn, Kim Il, O Paek-ryong, and Kang Yang-uk. In 1988 Rim Ch'un-ch'u would die, too. In contrast, a group of technocrats in their forties and fifties, who might be termed the "Kim Jong Il generation," had advanced into the higher echelons of power. Sons of old partisans had also been appointed to key posts. For example, Kang Sŏng-san, O Kŭk-ryŏl, and Kim Kuk-t'ae became premier, KPA chief of general staff, and director of the KWP cadres department, respectively.[21]

With this opening of his own era—even though it had actually begun in 1984—Kim Jong Il renewed a peace offensive toward the South and the United States. In January 1984 the North proposed a tripartite conference of the two Koreas and the United States to President Ronald Reagan via Chinese premier Zhao Ziyang. Although this proposal was not realized, another Kim initiative bore fruit. When the North offered relief supplies to flood victims in South Korea in September 1984, the South accepted and the aid's delivery was coordinated by the two Koreas' Red Cross societies. This paved the way for inter-Korean economic and Red Cross talks. In March 1985 the North also proposed a joint meeting of parliamentarians from the two Koreas, which the South again accepted, opening a third channel of inter-Korean talks. In this newly improved environment, there were exchanges of art troupes and visitors between the North and South in September 1985, marking the first time that members of separated families were able to travel to the other side for direct meetings with their relatives.

At this time the two Koreas opened secret discussions for an inter-Korean summit meeting. In October Chang Se-dong, director of the Agency for National Security Planning (NSP, the successor to the KCIA), secretly visited Pyongyang as an emissary of President Chun Doo-hwan (Chŏn Tu-hwan) and met Kim Il Sung in person. Chang noted later that Kim had to rely on a specially devised hearing aid because his hearing was so poor. Due to the

20 Dae-sook Suh, "North Korea in 1985: A New Era After Forty Years," *Asian Survey* 26, no. 1 (January 1986): 81.

21 *Dong-A yŏn'gam* [The Dong-A yearbook] (Seoul: Dong-A Ilbsosa, 1986), 261–63.

complicated situation on the Korean Peninsula, the series of secret talks did not reach an agreement.[22]

On July 15, 1986, Kim Jong Il proposed a new theory on the "revolutionary Suryŏng" in a confidential speech to KWP cadres and functionaries in charge of propaganda and agitation, entitled "On a Number of Questions in Educating *Juche* Thought." Since the Suryŏng, an absolute ruler and equivalent to the brain in a human body, was leading the anti-imperialist, socialist revolution at the global level, Kim stressed that the people should follow his teachings faithfully and unconditionally. But he went one step further. He noted that while human beings owe their biological lives to their parents, they owe their socio-political lives to the Suryŏng and should thus devote and, if need be, even sacrifice their lives to him.[23] With this, Kim solidified his position as the sole interpreter of *Juche* thought. He also advanced the thesis that the "Korean nation is the best," suggesting that it need not emulate or even listen to other nations.

The results of the elections for the Eighth Supreme Peoples' Assembly in November 1986 and the subsequent reshuffling of the Administrative Affairs Board bolstered Kim Jong Il's position even more. Most deputies to the SPA and members of the cabinet were close to Kim Jong Il and belonged to the so-called Kim Jong Il generation. In general, they were technocrats well versed in their respective fields. One example was the new premier minister, Ri Kŭn-mo. When Kim Jong Il was vice director of the KWPCC's culture and arts department in the late 1960s, Ri was its director. When Kim Jong Il led the construction of the Namp'o (later renamed West Sea) Barrage in the Yellow Sea in the early 1980s, Ri was the Namp'o city party secretary.[24] As Hwang Chang-yŏp recalled, "By 1986, Kim Jong Il held real power more firmly."[25]

There is another Hwang Chang-yŏp recollection that deserves discussion at this point. According to Hwang, Kim Jong Il had been dispatching a number of young and attractive women to Kim Il Sung to serve as his nurses since the early 1980s.[26] Some have suggested that his goal was to distract his father from domestic politics—and from Kim Sŏng-ae. In December 1987,

22 Ch'oe Po-sik, "Chang Se-dong kwa Kim Il-sŏng ŭi saengsaenghan pimil taehwa rok" [Records of vivid dialogues at secret talks between Chang Se-dong and Kim Il Sung], *Wŏlgan Chosun*, September 1988, 180–224.

23 The full text of this speech was published in the *Rodong Sinmun*, July 15, 1987, 1–2, a year after it was delivered. See also Kim Jong Il, *Juche ch'ŏlhak e taehayŏ* [On Juche philosophy] (Pyongyang: Chosun rodongdang ch'ulp'ansa, 2000), 70–74.

24 Koh, "North Korea in 1987," 66, fn. 6.

25 Hwang, *Na nŭn yŏksa ŭi chillirŭl po'atta*, 276.

26 Ibid., 254.

the *Berliner Morgen Post* reported that a North Korean woman, accompanied by a North Korean physician and three nurses, had given birth in a hospital in Vienna, hinting that the baby's father might be Kim Il Sung.[27] More information was provided on August 9, 1992, by the *Sankei Shimbun*, a Tokyo-based daily critical of the North. Its correspondent reported from Stockholm, Sweden, to the effect that Kim Song-juk, a former North Korean dancer and at that time Kim Il Sung's mistress, and daughter, Kim Paek-yŏn, had been spotted shopping at the Sheraton Hotel in Stockholm. The report added that Kim Paek-yŏn was born in May 1987 in a hospital in Vienna. South Korea's NSP unofficially confirmed the report, based on its wiretapping of telephone conversations between Stockholm and Pyongyang.[28]

There were rumors that Kim Il Sung had had another girl and a boy by other nurses. Yi Il-nam and Fujimoto Kenji have said that the boy's name was Hyŏn and the girl's name was Kŭm-song. They even contended that both were registered as the legitimate children of Chang Sŏng-t'aek and Kim Kyŏng-hŭi.[29] Recently, South Korean intelligence sources unofficially confirmed that Chang Hyŏn is the illegitimate son of Kim Il Sung and Chekal Ok-hwa, while Chang Su-gil—who has been registered in official records as the son of Chang Sŏng-t'aek and Kim Kyŏng-hŭi—is in actuality the son of Kim Kyŏng-hŭi and Kim Sŏng-ho, a top North Korean violinist known to have been executed.

The year 1988 marked the fortieth anniversary of the DPRK's founding, but some major developemts muted the celebratory mood. The North Korean leadership's pride was seriously wounded by the participation of the Soviet Union and Eastern European countries—the DPRK's traditional allies—in the Seoul Summer Olympics in September and October. The momentum provided by that participation led Hungary to establish diplomatic relations with the South in December, a breakthrough in Seoul's relations with communist states. To counter the Seoul Olympics, the North hosted the Thirteenth World Youth Festival in July 1989 in Pyongyang. During this period, the North escalated Kim Jong Il's personality cult. Mount

27 Quoted in an article written by O Chun-dong, a correspondent of South Korea's Yŏnhap News Agency to Tokyo, on August 9, 1992.

28 Yi Nak-yŏn, "Kim Il Sung, sumkyŏjin dal itta" [Kim Il Sung has a hidden daughter], *Dong-A Ilbo*, August 10, 1992, 8; see also "Kim Il Sung Has 5-year-old Daughter," *Korea Times*, August 11, 1992, 2.

29 Yi Il-nam, (alias Yi Han-yŏng), *Taedong kang royal p'aemilli Sŏul chamhaeng sip-sa-nyŏn* [Fourteen years of secret lives in Seoul by a North Korean royal family] (Seoul: Dong-A Ilbosa, 1996), 98; For Fujimoto's remarks, see O Tong-ryong, "Fujimoto Kenji hoegyŏn" [Interview with Fujimoto Kenji], *Wŏlgan Chosun*, no. 368, November 2010, 80.

Paektu was designated as "Jong Il Peak" and "special greenhouses were constructed at each provincial capital for the purposes of cultivating the 'Kim Jong Il flower.'"[30] In a move even more pregnant with meaning, the royal tomb of the legendary King Tan'gun was rebuilt. Tan'gun was said to have founded Old Chosŏn, the first Korean kingdom, in Pyongyang in 2333 BCE. Observing the retreat of socialism in Europe, the North looked to the founder of the Korean nation for spiritual support.

Kim Jong Il and Kim Il Sung's Joint Regime, 1986–94

The continuing existence of closed and oppressive communist regimes, such as that of the North, was running counter to international trends. In November 1989 East Germans demolished the Berlin Wall, a symbol of communist oppression and national division. A month later, the Romanian people toppled down their communist regime, executed dictator Nicolae Ceauşescu and his wife, and established a democratic government. By the end of 1990, all of the communist countries in Eastern Europe had been reborn as Western-style democracies. In September 1990, despite the North's strong opposition, the Soviet Union established diplomatic relations with the South. At the same time, the PRC agreed with the ROK to open reciprocal trade offices. Despite these precursors, North Korean leaders would be shocked and enraged in 1992 when the PRC finally established full diplomatic relations with the ROK.

On October 3, 1990, East Germany was absorbed into the West German state, the Federal Republic of Germany, as part of a Western-style democracy with a market economy. East Germany's leader until 1989, Erich Honecker, asked Kim Jong Il to grant him asylum. According to an official North Korean publication, when the North's Foreign Ministry officials were hesitant to make a decision, Kim Jong Il decided to accept Honecker's request after consulting with Kim Il Sung. Kim Jong Il was said to have instructed his foreign ministry to send an airplane to Germany to bring Honecker to Pyongyang. But at the last moment, Honecker fled to Russia.[31] With international winds blowing against its allies, the North in 1990 responded with new slogans to encourage its people, such as "Let Us Live in Our Own Way," "Our Way Socialism," and "Korean-Style Socialism."[32]

---

30 Oh, "North Korea in 1989," 77.

31 Kang Sŏk-chu, *Kim Chŏng-il yŏlp'ung* [A hot wind by Kim Jong Il], quoted in Kim Ch'ang-hui, *Kim ChŏngIl ŭi tillemma* [Kim Jong Il's dilemma] (Seoul: Inmul kwa Sasangsa, 2004), 139.

32 Foreign Languages Publishing House, ed., *Kim Jong Il*, 150.

The DPRK was forced to do more to adjust to the changing environment than just devise new slogans. Accepting a proposal from the South, the first-ever inter-Korean prime ministerial conference was held in September 1990 in Seoul. A month later, a second conference was held in Pyongyang. When the South Korean delegates met Kim Il Sung, they observed that his health was failing. During dinner, Kim Il Sung occasionally drooled; he also had to have an aide loudly relay the South Korean delegation's statements to him. Kim was also unable to firmly grasp his beer mug, and again his aide had to assist him.[33] Kim Jong Il capitalized on Kim Il Sung's failing health for his own political purposes. Reliable North Korean defectors recall that from the late 1980s, due to Kim Il Sung's declining health, Kim Jong Il instructed his lieutenants to report to Kim Il Sung not in writing but through carefully edited videotapes.[34]

The North's economic situation was also worsening year by year. Poor economic performance in general and shortages of energy, raw materials, and food in particular emerged as the most threatening factors for the socialist system. Against this backdrop, the North "beefed up its 'work-harder campaign'" in 1990. But that year the North's economic growth still registered negative 3.7 percent, and succeeding years would be even worse: −5.2 percent in 1991, −7.6 percent in 1992, and −4.3 percent in 1993. This quandary led the North to open its doors to the outside and to inaugurate Free Economic and Trade Zones based at the ports of Rajin and Sŏnbong, near the Tuman River, and Ch'ŏngjin, the key seaport in the northeast.[35] The results, however, would prove to be meager and, in 2001, the regime executed Vice Minister of Trade Kim Mun-sŏng on charges of failing to induce foreign investment.[36]

Later in 1990, presidents Roh Tae-woo and Kim Il Sung exchanged emissaries. In late September Roh secretly sent NSP director Sŏ Tong-gwŏn to Pyongyang, where he met both with Kim Jong Il and Kim Il Sung on October 1 and delivered Roh's proposal to hold inter-Korean summit talks. The North insisted that the South accept the Democratic Confederal Republic of Koryŏ formula for Korean unification at the proposed summit; as this was unacceptable to the South, the summit did not take place. Sŏ thus became the first South Korean official to meet Kim Jong Il, and he reported some interesting observations to Roh. Kim Jong Il appeared to be healthy and rational and to have consolidated his status as his father's successor. Kim Il

33 At the time, I was chief assistant for policy research to the ROK president, and was able to read the reports by the ROK delegation to the president.

34 Yi, *Taedong kang royal p'aemilli Sŏul chamhaeng sip-sa-nyŏn*, 58.

35 Rhee Sang-woo, "North Korea in 1990: Lonesome Struggle to Keep Juche," *Asian Survey* 31, no. 1 (January 1991): 73.

36 Yi Yong-su, "Puk" [The North], *Chosun Ilbo*, October 6, 2011, A4.

Sung referred to Kim Jong Il frequently when asked about delicate matters, and the two Kims seemed to have listened carefully to arguments and suggestions advanced by KWPCC secretaries in the meeting. In early November, Kim Il Sung sent his own emissary to Roh, Yun Ki-bok, the KWPCC secretary in charge of Southern affairs. Virtually the same arguments were exchanged and no agreement was reached.[37]

In 1991 both the North's foreign and domestic circumstances continued to worsen. In an April 19, 1991, interview with the Japanese daily *Mainichi Shimbun*, Kim Il Sung used a Korean proverb in referring to the dangers facing his country: "Even when the sky collapses, there is a hole through which to escape." Of course, the North Korean news media never reported on these dangers, but the North sought an "escape hole" in three ways. First, it entered the UN together with the South on September 17, 1991. UN acceptance of the North as a member meant that the international community recognized it as an independent country. Second, on December 13, 1991, the North and the South signed a Basic Agreement on Reconciliation, Non-aggression, Exchanges, and Cooperation. On January 20, 1992, the two sides also signed the North-South Joint Declaration on Denuclearization of the Korean Peninsula. Underlying these two documents were the principles that the two Koreas recognized each other and would seek to co-exist. Third, notwithstanding these two inter-Korean agreements, the North continued its nuclear development project as an insurance policy.[38]

Internally the North continued to take steps that would bring Kim Jong Il's succession nearer to realization. In May 1990 he was acclaimed as the first vice-chairman of the NDC, and in June 1991 he was named the "Head of the Revolutionary Armed Forces." On December 24, 1991, the Nineteenth Plenum of the Sixth KWPCC elected him as KPA supreme commander.[39] In April 1992, when Kim Il Sung was elevated to "Grand Marshal" in celebration of his eightieth birthday, Kim Jong Il was given "his first military rank [of marshal]. To mute any criticism, [PAFM minister] O Chin-u was promoted to marshal and eight other generals elevated to vice marshal at the same time, [and shortly after] 664 generals [also] received stars."[40]

37 Kim Yong-sam, "Chŏn kukka anjŏn kihoek pujang Sŏ Tong-gwŏn ŭi pisa wa kyŏnggo" [Former National Security Planning Agency Director Sŏ Tong-gwŏn's secret stories and warnings], *Wŏlgan Chosun*, May 2000, 150–67.

38 For detailed information, see Kim Hakjoon, *The Domestic Politics of Korean Unification: Debates on the North in the South, 1948–2008* (Seoul and Edison, NJ: Jimoondang, 2010), 359–74.

39 Foreign Languages Publishing House, ed., *Kim Jong Il*, 160.

40 John Merrill, "North Korea in 1992: Steering Away from the Shoals," *Asian Survey* 33, no. 1 (January 1993): 43.

As John Merrill of the U.S. State Department points out:

Kim Jong Il's appointment to military posts permitted him to share in his father's status without actually displacing him. . . . With the son clearly in charge, President Kim Il Sung signaled that the responsibilities of office no longer weighed so heavily—penning a poem for his son's fiftieth birthday [on February 16, 1992] and publishing the initial volumes of his memoirs, *With the Century* [*Segi wa tŏburŏ*].[41]

In April 1992 Kim Il Sung even told the *Washington Times* that Kim Jong Il was now "fully responsible" for running the country.[42] It was Kim Jong Il who acknowledged the congratulations of all the officers and soldiers of the KPA at the military parade held in Kim Il Sung Square in Pyongyang on April 25 in celebration of the sixtieth anniversary of the KPA's founding. On this occasion, he famously remarked, in his first-ever known public utterance, "Glory to the heroic officers and soldiers of the KPA."[43] Although the dividing line is not clear, it seems that beginning in 1990, when he was acclaimed as the NDC's first vice-chairman, the "joint regime of Kim Il Sung and Kim Jong Il" was transposed into the "joint regime of Kim Jong Il and Kim Il Sung."[44]

The third session of the Ninth Supreme People's Assembly was held on April 9, 1992, and the constitution was revised in favor of Kim Jong Il—it now allowed the SPA to elect the NDC chairman, a post which had been automatically occupied by the DPRK president. The revised constitution opened the way for Kim Jong Il to take over the NDC chairmanship through the SPA. In actuality, on April 9, 1993, the SPA elected Kim Jong Il as NDC chairman. Now that he had assumed complete power over the military—in addition to his power over the party—Kim Jong Il allowed Kim Yŏng-ju, his seventy-one-year-old uncle, to return to Pyongyang. At the Twenty-First Plenum of the KWP Central Commitee on December 9, 1993, Kim Yŏng-ju was elected as a Politburo member. Two days later, the sixth session of the Ninth SPA also elected him as one of five DPRK vice-chairmen.

The year 1993 began with a massive purge of military officers. The director of the KPA's Safeguard Bureau, Lieutenant General Wŏn Ŭng-hŭi, arrested eleven military officers who had studied in the Soviet Union, and

41 Ibid.

42 *Washington Times*, April 15, 1992; see also "NK's Kim Ready to Bury the Hatchet with U.S.," *Korea Times*, April 16, 1992, 1.

43 Foreign Languages Publishing House, ed., *Kim Jong Il*, 162–63.

44 Kim Jong Il's official North Korean biography divides the period from the Sixth KWP Congress to the death of Kim Il Sung into two periods; the first period covers October 1980 to December 1989, the second January 1990 to July 1994.

soon after arrested more officers with similar academic backgrounds. Most of them were stigmatized as "foreign spies" who had been poised to stage a coup d'état; they were executed or sent to political prison camps. Due to its "anti-espionage activities," the Safeguard Bureau was upgraded to the Safeguard Headquarters and Wŏn was promoted to general.[45]

In early 1993, as tensions escalated between the North and the International Atomic Energy Agency (IAEA) on the issue of IAEA inspections of the North's nuclear facilities, the United States and the ROK declared that they would resume their annual "Team Spirit" joint military exercise. On March 8, 1993, Kim Jong Il, in his capacity as KPA supreme commander, declared that the Korean Peninsula was in a "quasi" or virtual state of war. Four days later, the North announced its withdrawal from the Nuclear Non-Proliferation Treaty (NPT). After talks between Kim Il Sung and former U.S. president Jimmy Carter in Pyongyang on June 16, 1994, however, the North and the United States resumed talks in Geneva to defuse the nuclear crisis. On this occasion, Kim Sŏng-ae, who had never revealed herself during the previous twenty years, appeared before the public as the North's First Lady and conversed with Rosalyn Carter. At one point during the Kim Il Sung–Carter talks, Kim Jong Il relied upon Kim Sŏng-ae to hurriedly convey a short message to Kim Il Sung.[46] Thanks to Carter's mediation, Kim Il Sung also agreed to hold summit talks with ROK president Kim Young Sam (Kim Yŏng-sam) in Pyongyang in late July 1994.

Kim Jong Il's Five "Wives" and Three Sons and Their Significance in Succession Politics Since 1969–70

While expanding his political power and influence step by step on his way to full-scale capture of political leadership, Kim Jong Il was cultivating a private relationship with Sung Hye-rim, a married woman six years his senior who would give birth to the couple's sole child, son Kim Jong Nam. Sung Hye-rim's family history itself reveals a condensed history of Korea since the Japanese occupation of Korea, while her private life with Kim Jong Il tells us a brief history of North Korea since the late 1960s. Moreover, the birth of Kim Jong Nam has influenced succession politics in the North. For these reasons, tracing Sung Hye-rim's family background and her relationship with Kim Jong Il is informative. The task is made easier because her elder sister and her nephew both published memoirs after defecting to the

---

45 Paek Myŏng-gyu, "Kukka'anjŏn powibu" [The State Security Safeguard Ministry], http://pscore.org/xe/episode/11509.

46 Breen, *Kim Jong Il*, 75.

West and her niece conducted a series of interviews with the Western press.[47]
Their recollections reveal the true features of the "socialist paradise" pro-
pagandized by the North Korean regime and in particular the problematic
nature of the succession issue.

Sung Hye-rim's father was Sung Yu-gyŏng, born in 1905, the year that
Chosŏn dynasty Korea became a Japanese protectorate. Sung was from a
rich gentry-landlord family in Ch'angnyŏng County, South Kyŏngnam Province. Reared and educated in typical Confucian tradition, he was well versed
in the Chinese classics. At the age of fourteen, he married a rural girl in
a match arranged by his grandfather—an early marriage was customary
in that era in Korea. As the "new, modern sciences" began to be taught in
Korea under Japanese colonial rule (which began in 1910), the boy expressed
a desire to study in a Seoul school. When his father did not grant his request,
he appropriated a large amount of money from his family's safe and succeeded in entering Posŏng Middle School in Seoul in 1922. There he met
Rim Hwa and Ri Kang-guk, who would become the first KCP cadres in 1945
and then SKWP cadres in 1946. Around 1926, without having graduated
from middle school, Sung Yu-gyŏng again took a large amount of cash from
the family safe and went to Tokyo. As an older-than-usual middle-school
student in Japan, he studied Marxism as a theoretical weapon for Korean
independence and joined the New Korea Society (Sin'ganhoe), an influential
Korean independence movement organization. His membership resulted in
his being jailed twice, and he was set free thanks only to his father's bribery
of high-ranking Japanese officials. Sometime during 1931–32 he returned to
his hometown, but ultimately he went to Seoul, abandoning his arranged
marriage.

In 1933 in Seoul, Sung Yu-gyŏng met Kim Wŏn-ju, a reporter at a Seoul
daily. She was born in 1905 to an extremely poor farming family in Namp'o
County, South P'yŏng'an Province. Her father, an uneducated and unskilled
day laborer, was a drunk who regularly beat his wife and children. When her
elder brother died after being assaulted, she left home and was reared by a
benefactor whose name has been lost. She graduated from a famous girls'

47 Sung (Sŏng) Hye-rang, *Tŭngnamu chip* [The wisteria house] (Seoul: Chisik Nara,
2000); Yi Il-nam (alias Yi Han-yŏng), *Taedong kang royal p'aemilli Sŏul chamhaeng sip-
sa-nyŏn* [Fourteen years of secret lives in Seoul by a North Korean royal family] (Seoul:
Dong-A Ilbosa, 1996); Yi Nam-ok's interview with the *Daily Telegraph* (London) on
September 30, 1997. The romanization of the Yi family name can be confusing. Yi is
interchangeable with both Ri and Li. Usually, the North Koreans use Ri or Li and the
South Koreans use Yi; in more Anglicized versions of this surname, many South Koreans
use Lee or Rhee.

junior high school in Pyongyang and then from a sericulture technical college in Tokyo. Such an academic career was rare for Korean women then, even for women from rich families. Upon returning to Seoul, she became a reporter. Sung Yu-gyŏng proposed to her, pledging to divorce his first wife. The couple had their first child, a son named Il-gi, in 1933; their second, a daughter named Hye-rang, in 1935; and a third child, daughter Hye-rim, on January 24, 1937.

In December 1945, four months after the liberation of Korea, the couple joined the KCP, led by Pak Hŏn-yŏng. At that time, many progressive intellectuals in Korea were joining the leftist movement under the belief (or illusion) that socialism was the wave of the future. Moreover, a good number of the KCP leaders were also alumni of Sung Yu-gyŏng's schools in Seoul and Tokyo; some of them had even been his prison mates in Japan. To Kim Wŏn-ju, socialism represented first and foremost the antithesis of feudalism and male chauvinism, under which she and her mother had suffered in the past. In 1947, after liberating all of the tenants on his lands, husband Sung Yu-gyŏng went to the North for the sole purpose of meeting Kim Il Sung in person, bearing dozens of copies of a Russo-Korean dictionary, which was regarded as very valuable in the North. Kim Il Sung praised his patriotism, terming him a "progressive landlord and intellectual." Upon his return to Seoul, Sung Yu-gyŏng was immediately imprisoned by USAMGSIK authorities.

With her husband in prison, Kim Wŏn-ju traveled alone to Pyongyang in late April 1948, participated in the North-South Korean conference discussed above, and took charge of the foreign news desk at the *Rodong Sinmun*. In 1949, her son Il-gi went to Pyongyang just to taste the air of the "new world of socialism." The Korean War, which started on June 25, 1950, would enable their separated family to reunite in Pyongyang. Kim Wŏn-ju, who travelled to Seoul as an influential war correspondent with the advancing North Korean army, was able to return to Pyongyang in August 1950 with her husband Sung Yu-gyŏng, whom North Korean authorities released from prison, and their two daughters. At this time, Hye-rang was a student at Ewha (Ihwa) Girls' High School and Hye-rim attended P'ungmun Girls' Junior High School, both in Seoul.

The family did not enjoy a happy life in the North. Already in the early 1950s they were suffering because of their class origin (*sŏngbun*), even though their only son had joined the KPA and was reported to have been killed during the "war for the liberation of the fatherland." The KWPCC's decision in December 1952 to eradicate the SKWP "factionalists" was a heavy blow to them. As with others who had come to the North determined to devote their lives to the development of their socialist fatherland, the Sung family was forced to stand frequently before the rostrum for public self-criticism. The fact that Ri Sŭng-yŏp and Ri Kang-guk, former KCP and SKWP leaders, had been guarantors for the admission of Sung Yu-Gyŏng and Kim Wŏn-ju to the KCP would cause the whole family to be constantly harassed. As explained earlier, the two Ris were executed in 1953–55 as "American imperialists' spies and factionalists." The August Factionalist Incident of 1956 also haunted them. They were sent to a reeducation camp and forced to "confess" their ties with "factionalists," although they actually had no such connections. In addition, like other North Koreans, they struggled in extreme poverty with limited food and rags for clothing.

In 1959 elder daughter Sung Hye-rang married Ri T'ae-sun, a graduate of Moscow State University's mechanics department. He was from an extremely poor farming family and was the son of an anti-Japanese activist who had died in prison—thus his *sŏngbun* was outstanding. Their poverty was such that even paying for a wedding photograph was out of the question, and during their nine years of marriage, they never had a family photograph taken, went to a theater, or had a holiday. In 1968, when Ri T'ae-sun was a professor at the National Defense Research Institute at Hamhŭng, Hye-rang was informed of his sudden death. By the time she arrived at Hamhŭng, the funeral was already being held. The couple had two children between them, son Ri Il-nam (b. 1961—he would later change his given name to Han-yong) and daughter Ri Nam-ok (b. 1966). Sung Hye-rang never found out her husband's cause of death. Around the same time, her father was sent to a local farm to work as a cart-drawer while her mother was demoted to a local newspaper organization, then expelled from it, and finally forced to manage as a casual worker. One day, as her father was boiling forage for cows, Hye-rang wept before him and lamented, "Why did you come to the North? In order to feed cattle?"[48]

Hye-rang's younger sister, Hye-rim, had graduated from a girls' junior-high school in 1951 and was admitted to Kim Il Sung University. But she transferred to the newly founded School of Arts in Pyongyang solely to have "good meals" in the dormitory. From her youth, Sung Hye-rim was renowned for her beauty, and so it was that Ri Ki-yŏng, a novelist respected throughout the North and South for his anti-Japanese activism and proletarian literary works, asked Hye-rim to become his eldest son's bride. Not only was Ri president of the influential Korea–Soviet Union Culture Association and the Korean Literary Men's Association, but even Kim Il Sung praised him as "Korea's Maxim Gorky." The marriage thus had the potential to be helpful to the Sung family. In 1955, after graduation from the School of Arts in Pyongyang, Sung Hye-rim married the eldest son, Ri P'yŏng, and the couple had a daughter, Ok-dol, in 1956.

48 Sung, *Tŭngnamu chip*, 306.

Although a married woman with a child, Sung Hye-rim was allowed to enter the newly established College of Drama and Film in Pyongyang thanks to her mother's repeated appeals to the Ministry of Culture and Propaganda. She had a leading role in the 1962 film *In a Village near the Demarcation Line*, a project that fulfilled one of her graduation requirements. The film told the tale of a woman who, despite having to suffer under difficult conditions because of her husband's defection to the South, led her life courageously with a firm conviction in the Korean Workers' Party. Kim Il Sung openly praised it and awarded it the first-ever People's Prize for film; before long, Sung Hye-rim would become a movie star in the North.

In the case of Sung Hye-rim, there is truth in the Korean saying, "A beautiful woman's life is not long and her fortune is not good." Kim Jong Il, from his teenage years in high school, felt an attraction to the star. From his first glimpse of her, it is said that he had found the image of his mother, whom he had lost in his childhood. Kim Jong Il, however, was said to have married Hong Il-ch'on, a Kim Il Sung University classmate, one year after their graduation in 1965, and she gave birth to their daughter Hye-gyŏng in 1968. Sin Kyŏng-wan recalled that they divorced around 1968 or 1969, but North Korean authorities have denied Sin's statement about a Kim-Hong marriage.[49] Hwang Chang-yŏp later noted that until he defected from the North he had never heard about Kim Jong Il being married to Hong Il-ch'ŏn.

Kim Jong Il, who was in charge of films in the KWP department of culture and arts, frequently came to see the actress and began to date her. Sung Hye-rim, who in the past had suffered on account of her "bourgeois class origin," soon began to receive special treatment from the KWP, under strong pressure from Kim Jong Il. The KWP—which had originally ordered that her mother, Kim Wŏn-ju, be sent to the South as a secret agent to work for the revolution—cancelled the directive. The authorities promoted Sung Hye-rim to an honorable "actress with distinguished service," allowed her entry into the KWP, and in 1968 sent her to a film festival held in Phnom Penh, Cambodia. In Cambodia, she met with Prince Norodom Sihanouk and his wife. Upon returning to Pyongyang, she was praised by Kim Il Sung.

Back in Pyongyang, Sung Hye-rim divorced her husband, Ri P'yŏng. Although there were persistent allegations that Kim Jong Il forced the couple to divorce, her elder sister's son claimed, after his defection to Seoul, that when she fell out of love with her husband, Kim Jong Il seduced her so fervently that she finally decided to seek a divorce.[50] There are two versions of Ri's life after the divorce, one that he committed suicide and another that he remarried. It is

49 Quoted in Chŏng, *Kyŏt'esŏ pon Kim Chŏng-il*, 31.
50 Yi, *Taedong kang royal p'aemilli Sŏul chamhaeng sip-sa-nyŏn*, 17.

not possible to determine which version is correct, but his father, Ri Ki-yŏng, stopped writing after the 1970s, perhaps due to the distress he experienced from the incident. Ri P'yŏng's younger brother, Ri Chong-hyŏk, who was Kim Jong Il's classmate at Kim Il Sung University, has had a successful career path. He was chief of the DPRK Representative Mission to UNESCO in Paris, and chief of the DPRK Representative Mission to the Food and Agriculture Organization of the United Nations in Rome, with the rank of ambassador. Presently, he is a delegate to the SPA and vice-chairman of the [North] Korean Asia-Pacific Peace Committee, one of the DPRK's main channels to the West.

Between late 1969 and early 1970, Kim Jong Il and Sung Hye-rim began to live together in secret, without marrying. At the time, Kim was chief of the culture-arts guidance section at the KWP culture-arts department. Because he aspired to be Kim Il Sung's successor, Kim Jong Il had to conceal his illicit life with Sung Hye-rim, whom his father believed to still be Ri Ki-yŏng's daughter-in-law. Accordingly, Kim Jong Il hid everything related to Hye-rim. In Hye-rang's words, their relationship was *the* top secret in the North.

Since Hye-rim was a movie star, however, her sudden disappearance became a favorite subject of speculation among average citizens and especially among artists. While it beggars belief, anyone who spoke about her disappearance was subject to imprisonment or even to being executed without due process. Kim Yŏng-sun, one of Hye-rim's close friends in Pyongyang, adamantly testified as much in regards to her own case, after her escape to South Korea via China. Both she and her husband devoted their lives to their country, firmly convinced that Kim Il Sung was leading the anti-imperialistic struggle for the realization of socialism. Yet in 1970, they suddenly found themselves banished to a notorious concentration camp located in Yodŏk, a backcountry region surrounded by mountains. Soon their sons and daughter were also sent to the camp. It would be some months after their arrival at the concentration camp that they would learn why they were there: Kim Yŏng-sun simply knew Sung Hye-rim too well. The family's existence at Yodŏk was too miserable for words. Their only food was small quantities of corn and grasses; their clothes were rags; and they were forced to engage in hard labor from dawn to nightfall. The daughter died of starvation and a son was killed. Nine years later, Kim Yŏng-sun was released with the surviving son, and in 2001 she succeeded in escaping to China and finally to South Korea.[51]

Sung Hye-rim gave birth to Kim Jong Nam in a secret residence on May 10, 1971, and Hye-rim's mother, Kim Wŏn-ju, was allowed to live with them.

---

51 Kim Yŏng-sun, *Nanŭn Sŏng Hye-rim ŭi ch'in'gu yŏtta: Inmin ŭi sich'e ro irun changgun ŭi konghwaguk* [I was one of Sung Hye-rim's friends: The republic of the general built on people's corpses] (Seoul: Sŏul Munhak Ch'ulpa'anbu, 2009).

According to sister Sung Hye-rang's recollections, Kim Jong Il genuinely loved the boy. Nonetheless, Kim Jong Il was compelled to conceal Kim Jong Nam's existence. For example, whenever Jong Nam went to the Ponghwa Clinic—reserved only for the Kim Il Sung family and the top-level cadres of the KWP and KPA—Hye-rim's mother would use a car whose windows were opaque from the outside. Once when a four-month-old Kim Jong Nam was hospitalized in the clinic, Kim Sŏng-ae—DPRK First Lady and Kim Il Sung's wife—happened unexpectedly to visit the clinic. Hye-rang recollected, "My mother hurriedly embraced Jong Nam and the two hid themselves in the garden, in a heap of fallen leaves."[52]

While Hye-rim and her son Kim Jong Nam had the misfortune of having to lead concealed lives, there was no comparison to the painful wanderings of Ok-dol, Sung Hye-rim's daughter by her former husband. Ok-dol, who had not seen her mother for many years, would visit Sung Hye-rang's house in the slim hope that she might hear something about her mother. But even Ok-dol, Sung Hye-rim's own daughter, was not allowed to know where her mother lived. Ok-dol would graduate from Pyongyang Foreign Languages College's French department and, in 1977, marry Yun Song-rim (not Wang Song-rim, as written in some places), a diplomat assigned to the DPRK mission to Vienna. Since then, Ri Ok-dol has lived under an assumed name, Kim Ok-sun. Although they were once said to have defected to the West in the 1990s,[53] South Korean intelligence sources have confirmed that they are actually living in Vienna as North Korean diplomats.

Kim Il Sung, unaware of his son's secret life, urged Kim Jong Il to marry, reiterating that he wanted to see a grandson before his *hwan'gap* (sixtieth birthday). Hye-rim advised Kim Jong Il to marry a woman whom his father had designated; with Kim Jong Il securely married, Hye-rim thought she would be able to keep her son Jong Nam safe under her own protection. In October 1973, three months after he became KWPCC secretary for organization and ideology, Kim Jong Il officially married Kim Yŏng-suk, although the marriage was not publically announced. She was the daughter of a vice dean of Ch'ŏngjin Engineering College in North Hamgyŏng Province and a low-level functionary of the KWP central organization. She was known to be two or three years junior to Kim Jong Il. Hye-rang recollected Jong Il's behavior on his wedding day: "His younger sister Kyŏng-hŭi came to the secret residence to get Jong Il, who was enjoying a nap. When he was awakened, he seemed to be impudent."[54] Kim Yŏng-suk would give birth to

---

52 Sung, *Tŭngnamu chip*, 373–74.

53 Yi, *Taedong kang royal p'aemilli Sŏul chamhaeng sip-sa-nyŏn*, 132–36.

54 The implication is that Kim Jong Il was not happy about getting married. Sung, *Tŭngnamu chip*, 374.

two daughters, Sŏl-song and Ch'un-song. However, she was never shown in the North Korean media and to this day, South Korean intelligence has been unable to secure a photograph of her.

While Kim Il Sung expressed his love towards Kim Yŏng-suk and his granddaughters, he did not know about his son's secret life or the existence of Jong Nam. Moreover, Kyŏng-hŭi demanded that Hye-rim part with Kim Jong Il, suggesting that she herself would take care of the child Jong Nam. Hye-rim was enraged. According to Yi Il-nam, who frequently visited the residence (he was Jong Nam's cousin/Hye-rang's son/Hye-rim's nephew), Hye-rim demanded that Jong Il tell the truth to his father, shouting that she would appear with Jong Nam before Kim Il Sung in person. Il-nam alleged after his defection to Seoul in 1982 that Kim Jong Il warned Hye-rim—with a pistol—not to do so. Il-nam recalled that Kim Jong Il seemed to have told his father the truth around 1975 and that Kim Il Sung accepted Jong Il's relationship with Sung Hye-rim and the birth of Kim Jong Nam as *faits accomplis*. But Hye-rang asserted, to the contrary, that Kim Il Sung died without knowing about Jong Nam and that only a very few members of the Kim family knew him. According to Hye-rang, Jong Il, fearing that his illicit affair and the existence of an illegitimate son might infuriate his father and cost him his successor status, concealed the truth forever.[55] Since Jong Nam could not attend a regular school, he had to be tutored; beginning in March 1976 Hye-rang became Jong Nam's tutor and governess at the secret residence.

Sung Hye-rim suffered from insomnia, had a nervous breakdown, and developed heart disease in 1974; in 1975 Kim Jong Il sent her to a hospital in Moscow. Three years later, Kim Jong Il sent Kim Jong Nam to study at a Soviet elementary school in Moscow. Hye-rang, with her son Yi Il-nam and daughter Yi Nam-ok, was sent to Moscow to supervise Jong Nam's studies. But Jong Nam, who grew up in the finest of residences in Pyongyang, lavishly furnished, could not adapt to the abysmal facilities and toilets of the ordinary elementary school in his neighborhood. One day he returned home from school with his pants frozen hard after he had urinated in his pants rather than use the toilet.

In March 1980 Kim Jong Il allowed Kim Jong Nam to relocate to Geneva and study at an international school there. Hye-rang became his mentor, and Nam-ok and Il-nam were his companions in Geneva. Two years later, supposedly sensing that South Korean agents were active in their neighborhood

55 Yi, *Taedong kang royal p'aemilli Sŏul chamhaeng sip-sa-nyŏn*, 27, 84; Kim Hyŏn-sik and Son Kwang-ju, *Dok'yument'ari Kim Chŏng-il* [The documentary Kim Jong Il] (Seoul: Chonji Media, 1997), 232. See Sung Hye-rang's interview with *Time* published in Hong Kong on June 23, 2003, quoted in *Kungmin Ilbo*, June 24, 2003, 11.

and planning to "kidnap" them, they returned to Moscow. (Both North and South Korea maintained diplomatic missions in Geneva, including many intelligence officers, but Seoul did not have an embassy in Moscow until it established diplomatic relations with the Soviet Union in 1990.) Jong Nam, Nam-ok, and Il-nam enrolled at a French school in Moscow. In September 1982 Kim Jong Il allowed them again to study in Geneva with Hye-rang as their supervisor. Only a week later, however, Il-nam presented himself in Seoul as a political refugee; Hye-rang claimed that he had been kidnapped by South Korean agents.[56]

As a result of Il-nam's defection, Kim Jong Nam and his entourage had to return to Moscow. When in 1986 CPSUCC general secretary Mikhail Gorbachev began advancing his reform-oriented policy of *perestroika* in earnest, Kim Jong Il allowed Kim Jong Nam to leave the Soviet Union—declaring it to be "not our ally but a dirty country sold on U.S. dollars"—and study instead in Switzerland, "a neutral country maintaining high morality."[57] He studied fine arts in Geneva and showed some talent in portraiture. But soon he began to frequent bars at night and became involved with Western women. Enraged, Kim Jong Il recalled him, along with Hye-rang and Nam-ok, to Pyongyang and banished them to a local village. On one occasion, Kim Jong Il told his son to be prepared to go to a coal mine; while that never happened, and he was in fact allowed to return to Pyongyang, for two months he received only a limited quantity of daily necessities. Hye-rang recollected, "At that time, Kim Jong Il never visited our home. We were completely forgotten. Our house was a high-level prison, and we were lifers."[58]

Before long Kim Jong Il allowed Hye-rang and Nam-ok to stay with Hye-rim in Moscow. Surprisingly, they could meet Sung Il-gi, the elder brother of the Sung sisters who was thought to have died during the Korean War. He had taken refuge in Moscow but ultimately would return to Seoul.[59] In May 1992 Nam-ok took refuge in the West via Geneva, leaving a letter for Kim Jong Il asking for his understanding. In the letter, she told Kim Jong Il, who used to call her his "foster daughter," "Dad, please don't get angry with me. From my childhood, you repeatedly told me you would send me to Oxford or Cambridge, if I wanted. Now I want to study at Oxford. Just think that your daughter is acting in accordance with your promise. Please don't punish my mother. Instead, I will live in silence."[60] About ten months later, Kim Jong

56 Sung, *Tŭngnamu chip*, 306.
57 Ibid., 464.
58 Ibid., 484–85.
59 For an interview with him, see *Munhwa Ilbo*, December 20, 2011, 3.
60 Sung, *Tŭngnamu chip*, 494–95.

Nam would fire a gun blindly in the Koryŏ Hotel nightclub for foreign guests in Pyongyang.[61] The incident may have reflected the frustration, even wrath, that had built up in him. In the meantime, the Sung sisters' father had died in 1982 without seeing Hye-rim for twelve years while she was secretly living with Jong Il, and their mother died in 1994. In February 1996, Hye-rang took refuge in the West from Moscow via Geneva, where Nam-ok prearranged for her mother's defection. It is believed that Hye-rang and Nam-ok now live in France. Nam-ok is said to have married a Western diplomat.

Kim Jong Il's marriage with Kim Yŏng-suk did not last long, although he did not legally divorce her. Around the mid-1970s, he fell in love with Ko Yong-hŭi (alias Chŏng Il-sŏn). She was born in 1952 in Osaka, Japan, to Ko Kyŏng-t'aek, whose background has never been revealed.[62] Since Kim Jong Il occasionally called her "Ayumi," that presumably was her Japanese name.[63]

Ko Yong-hŭi followed her father to Pyongyang in the 1960s and was raised as a dancer in the national ballet troupe (Pyongyang Mansudae Art Troupe), which Kim Jong Il inaugurated in 1969. According to the memoirs of Fujimoto Kenji— Kim Jong Il's Japanese chef during 1988–2001—she was "indeed beautiful," reminding him of the Japanese movie stars Hara Setsuko or Yoshinaga Sayuri. Kim Jong Il lived with her from 1976 without being legally married. Two sons, Jong Chul (Chŏng-ch'ŏl, b. September 25, 1980) and Jong Un (Chŏng-ŭn, b. January 8, 1984), were born to the couple, plus a daughter, Yŏ-jŏng (b. September 26, 1988).[64]

As in the case of Sung Hye-rim, Kim Jong Il's life with Ko Yong-hŭi was kept hidden from Kim Il Sung. How could he keep these secrets for so long?

61 Ch'oe Yŏng-jae, "Kim Chŏng-nam Mist'eri" [The Kim Jong Nam mystery], *Sindonga*, no. 502 (July 2001): 132.

62 It is commonly said that Ko Yong-hŭi's father was the late Ko T'ae-mun, who had smuggled himself to Japan from South Korea. He grew up in Japan and became a judo expert. In 1961, he went to Pyongyang and became the supervisor of the judo team at the national athletes corps in Pyongyang. He died in 1979. But recently the South Korean intelligence agency confirmed that he was not Ko Yong-hŭi's father. Ko Yong-hŭi's birth year had been unclear. While Fujimoto Kenji recalled it as being 1950, Cheong Seong-chang is certain she was born in 1952, and the ROK NIS has unofficially confirmed 1952 as her birth year. Fujimoto Kenji, *Pukhan ŭi hugyeja, oe Kim Chŏng-ŭn in'ga?* [Why was Kim Jong Un chosen as North Korea's successor?], trans. Han Yu-hee (Seoul: Maxmedia, 2010), 59. See Cheong Seong-chang (Chŏng Sŏng-ch'ang), "Pukhan hugye munje wa kwŏllyŏk ch'ekt'ae mit pawŏ ellit'ŭ pyŏndong" [The North Korean succession issue, the power system, and the change in power elite], a paper presented at the Japanese Research Association of World Politics and Economy, July 22, 2011, 5.

63 Ibid., 70.

64 Fujimoto, *Pukhan*, 59.

Two anecdotes suggest that the answer was the abject fear that Kim Jong Il's ruthlessness and brutality engendered in those around him. The first story was retold by Sung Hye-rim's nephew. He said that one day around 1979, Kim Jong Il intercepted an anonymous letter to Kim Il Sung that accused Kim Jong Il of frequently holding wild parties. Through a secret and harsh investigation, Kim Jong Il identified the writer as a Kim Il Sung University professor and wife of Yi Myŏng-jae, vice director of the propaganda-agitation department of the KWPCC. When Kim Jong Il ordered his bodyguards to execute her, Yi Myŏng-jae himself volunteered to kill his own wife. When Kim Jong Il consented, Yi Myŏng-jae shot her to death before him, his bodyguards, and KWPCC core cadres.[65]

The second episode had to do with Ri Tong-ho, vice director of the KWPCC's United Front Department. During an evening banquet on February 16, 1982, to celebrate Kim Jong Il's fortieth birthday, Ri allegedly volunteered the toast, "Now your era is open, the Suryŏng's days are limited." Heavily intoxicated, Ri was said to have spat out that "the Suryŏng is already seventy years old. Can he live more than ten years or twenty years?" According to Kang Myŏng-do, Kim Jong Il exclaimed, "How dare you talk about the Suryŏng in such a way? Before the Suryŏng, I am also a mere soldier." [66] Kim ordered his bodyguards to shoot Ri, and with the sound of Ri's last scream, the party was over.

In the late 1980s one of Kim Jong Il's bodyguards, drunk, attempted to kill him while he was getting some fresh air after dinner at his exclusive villa in Hamhŭng, South Hamgyŏng Province. Fujimoto recalled that Ko Yong-hŭi shielded Kim by pushing him down while another guard killed the would-be assassin. Kim Jong Il confessed, "I thought it was my last," and expressed his deepest appreciation to her.[67] Fujimoto speculated that the bodyguard's relatives were sent to coal mines or political prisoners' camps.

65 Yi, *Taedong kang royal p'aemilli Sŏul chamhaeng sip-sa-nyŏn*, 170–72. This episode was discussed in Breen, *Kim Jong Il*, 67.

66 Kang, *Pyongyang ŭn mangmyŏng ŭl kkumkkunda*, 77–81. This episode was discussed in Breen, *Kim Jong Il*, 66–67.

67 Fujimoto, *Pukhan ŭi hugyeja, oe Kim Chŏng Ŭn in'ga*, 69.

5 Kim Jong Il's Unitary Leadership from His Father's Death to the Initial Decision to Designate a Successor, 1994–2002

The Period of Governance According to Kim Il Sung's Testament, 1994–97

The Death of Kim Il Sung

At noon on July 9, 1994, the North officially announced the unexpected news that Kim Il Sung had died of a heart attack the previous day at the age of eighty-two, "owing to heavy mental strains." As early as 1985 there had been reports of Kim Il Sung showing symptoms of declining health, such as those noted earlier by the South Korean delegates to inter-Korean talks. In April 1990 the Prague weekly *Svet v Obrazech* (World in photos) printed an intriguing photograph showing Kim Il Sung propped up by two young men at a meeting in Pyongyang. Paek Sang-ch'ang, a noted Seoul psychiatrist, contended that the photo suggested that Kim was susceptible to a cerebral hemorrhage.[1] Not long after, there was an intelligence report from Switzerland to Seoul that a renowned Swiss cardiac team had secretly visited Pyongyang and installed a pacemaker in Kim Il Sung.[2] Hwang Chang-yŏp recalled that in early 1994 Kim Il Sung's hearing and vision were sharply declining, and that in May he had secretly undergone eye surgery.[3] Considering Kim's age and probable medical conditions, the North Korean official announcement of a natural death is not difficult to accept as true.

1 Quoted in *Segye Ilbo*, July 8, 1990, 2.

2 I was chief assistant for policy research to the ROK president and in the summer of 1990 personally read this NSP report to the South Korean presidential office.

3 Hwang Chang-yŏp, *Na nŭn yŏksa ŭi chilli rŭl po'atta: Hwang Chang-yŏp hoegorok* [I saw the truth in history: Memoirs by Hwang Chang-yŏp], rev. ed. (Seoul: Sidae Chŏngsin, 2006), 312.

But there was other speculation that suggested that Kim's death was a consequence of tension or even conflict between himself and Kim Jong Il. After defecting to the South in the early 2000s, a high-ranking North Korean officer who had worked for Kim Il Sung at the powerful General Bureau of Security Forces recalled:

> Between July 3 and 6, in Kim Il Sung's resort offices at Mount Myohyang, not far from Pyongyang, there was serious debate between the father and son on ROK president Kim Young Sam's impending visit to Pyongyang. . . . While the father was enthusiastic about the meeting on the assumption that the meeting would pave the way to Korean unification under his leadership, the son expressed his concern that the opening of the possibility of unification would lead the North to its collapse.

Supposedly, it was during this discussion that Kim Il Sung first learned that most North Korean residents outside Pyongyang were suffering from a severe food shortage. The defector explained what happened when Kim discovered that fact:

> Abruptly, Kim Il Sung ordered his team of bodyguards to guide him to a local village, where he found that most people were starving. Kim angrily shouted that even during the period of anti-Japanese guerrilla struggles, he never starved the people under his control in the liberated area. Immediately all the provincial cadres who were in charge of that village prostrated themselves before Kim and cried that they deserved to be killed. Kim replied that they were not responsible; he returned to Pyongyang and harshly admonished his son that he should give up both the NDC chairmanship and the KWPCC secretaryship.[4]

The officer also recalled the actual moment of Kim's death:

> At one o'clock in the morning on July 8, Kim Il Sung's secretary found him lying unconscious in his study. The secretary immediately reported the situation to Kim Jong Il, who arranged a medical helicopter to be dispatched to Kim Il Sung's resort offices. However, the helicopter went down on the way to Mount Myohang in a heavy storm. At two o'clock in the morning, Kim Il Sung was declared dead by his North Korean medical staff.[5]

The defecting officer's claims have not been verified by reliable documents, but the part about Kim Il Sung's enthusiasm for the possibility of reunifica-

---

4 Hwang Il-do, "Chŏn Pukhan haeksim kwallyo ka chik'yŏ pon Kim Il-sŏng samang chikchŏn puja amt'u paek-i-sip sigan" [An undercover struggle of 120 hours between the father and son just before the death of Kim Il Sung as seen by a former core cadre of North Korea], *Sindonga* (August 2005): 143–64. See also Ŏm Sang-hyŏn, "P'yŏngyang pal koemunsŏ" [A mysterious document from Pyongyang], *Sindonga* (January 2005): 136–47.

5 Ŏm, "P'yŏngyang pal koemunsŏ," 142.

tion is supported by Hwang Chang-yŏp's own recollections. According to Hwang, "When physical rest was mandated by Kim Il Sung's eye operation, he was already excited about upcoming talks with former U.S. president Jimmy Carter. He became more excited about the scheduled summit talks with President Kim Young Sam, entertaining hopes that Korean unification would soon be realized."[6]

Pak Kap-dong, an anti-North Korean regime activist in Japan and a former SKWP cadre, alleged that Kim Jong Il, fearing that Kim Il Sung might deprive him of the successorship, might have killed his father.[7] However, Fujimoto Kenji's testimony gives us the strong impression that Kim Jong Il was overcome with grief upon his father's death, thereby indirectly refuting Pak's allegations. According to Fujimoto, immediately after Kim Il Sung's death, Kim Jong Il's wife Ko Yong-hŭi saw her husband in deep turmoil, staring at a pistol he was holding. Fujimoto recalled that she took away the pistol, shouting, "What are you thinking about?" Fujimoto added, "This made Kim Jong Il's trust in her even stronger."[8]

The Inauguration of Kim Jong Il's Regime and Its Power Base

More seriously discussed among outside observers was the issue of how power would transition from Kim Il Sung to Kim Jong Il, who at the time of his father's death was NDC chairman, KPA supreme commander, and KWPCC Politburo Standing Committee member. Some speculated that the succession would be smooth, since the junior Kim had already tamed—or eradicated—all probable challengers and opponents, and had solidified his successor status in the 1980s. There were already indications of a smooth transition. Kim Jong Il's name appeared first on the list of 273 national funeral committee members officially announced on July 9, the day after Kim Il Sung's death was officially made public. In addition, at the first public mourning before the body of Kim Il Sung on July 11, Kim Jong Il stood at the center of all the North Korean elite in attendance. The way that North Korean broadcasts referred to Kim Jong Il was also telling. On July 12 North Korean broadcasting called him the "highest supreme" and the "supreme leader of the party and the people," and on July 13 he was described as the "Great Leader" and "another Great Leader."[9] Further, on July 20, reporting on the official funeral service for Kim Il Sung, the North

6 Hwang, *Na nŭn yŏksa ŭi chilli rŭl po'atta*, 312–13.
7 Quoted in *Dong-A Ilbo*, July 12, 1994, 5.
8 Fujimoto Kenji, *Pukhan ŭi hugyeja, oe Kim Chŏng-ŭn in'ga?* [Why was Kim Jong Un chosen as North Korea's successor?], trans. Han Yu-hee (Seoul: Maxmedia, 2010), 69.
9 "Kim Jong Il Raised to Highest Positions," *Korea Times*, July 14, 1994, 1.

Korean media stressed that a "leadership system based on Dear Leader Kim Jong Il" should be firmly established.[10] This led North Korea watchers abroad to predict that Kim Jong Il's assumption of the posts vacated by his father's death—KWPCC general secretary and DPRK president—would be formalized in the near future.

However, in television footage of his father's state funeral, Kim Jong Il looked sickly and listless. This prompted speculation that he was either ill or caught up in a power struggle. On August 24 the South Korean media broadcast news of a special report from the ROK embassy in Bonn, Germany, to its foreign ministry. It was based on a report by German diplomats in Pyongyang, which claimed that "leaflets calling for the overthrow of Kim Jong Il were recently scattered in a diplomatic compound."[11] Three days later, the KCNA and other North Korean media confirmed that leaflets had been distributed in Pyongyang, but accused South Korean agents of distributing them: "The current clamor over leaflets is a smear campaign launched by the South Korean Agency for National Security Planning after it printed these disgusting leaflets and let them fly in the air."[12] The official media added that there was no confusion among the North Korean people following the death of Kim Il Sung and that the country was united around Kim Jong Il, the "destiny and future of our people."[13] Still, his long absence from public view fueled chronic speculation that he was either unwell or enmeshed in a power struggle. Some observers envisioned a power struggle within the Kim family and KWP leadership. A significant number even predicted North Korea's collapse in three stages: collapse of the Kim Jong Il regime, abandonment of the socialist system, and disintegration of the DPRK as a state.[14]

But on October 16 the reclusive Kim Jong Il finally reappeared in public for the first time since July 20; he attended a memorial service marking one hundred days since his father's death. Standing at the center of a rostrum flanked by Senior Vice President and People's Armed Forces Minister Marshal O Chin-u and Prime Minister Kang Sŏng-san, Kim seemed in much better health than at his last appearance. North Korea watchers abroad went so far as to interpret this to mean that top figures in the ruling KWP and military high command were using this occasion to pledge their loyalty to the younger Kim. Amid ongoing debates abroad about the stability—or instability—of his regime, Kim Jong Il contributed a lengthy essay

10 "Kim Jong Il Hailed as Leader," *Korea Times*, July 21, 1994.

11 "Anti-Kim Jong Il Fliers Scattered in Pyongyang," *Korea Times*, August 24, 1994.

12 "P'yang Radio Confirms Distribution of Leaflets," *Korea Times*, August 28, 1994.

13 Quoted in *Korea Times* over three days—August 25, 28, 29, 1994.

14 This point was summarized in Kim Hakjoon, "North Korea Falling Apart?" *Korea Observer* 24, no. 2 (Summer 1998): 259–85.

to *Rodong Sinmun*, "Socialism is a Science," on November 1. This first essay published by Kim Jong Il after the death of his father argued that socialism would win out eventually, despite its collapse in Eastern Europe.[15] Soon the North Korean media began to propagate the simplistic theme, "Kim Il Sung is Kim Jong Il and Kim Jong Il is Kim Il Sung." In the meantime, on October 21, with Kim Jong Il's final approval, the North had concluded an "Agreed Framework" in Geneva with the United States on the North Korean nuclear project. Concluding this agreement contributed, to some extent, to the improvement of the North's image in the international community.

While Kim Jong Il had clearly assumed leadership of North Korea, the prediction that he would assume the two highest posts in the North was wrong; likewise, predictions of a power struggle or DPRK collapse were both incorrect. As for power struggles within the Kim family, one incident deserves attention. In the initial broadcast coverage showing mourners, Kim Il Sung's widow, Kim Sŏng-ae, and her elder son, Kim P'yŏng-il, were both shown, but they were edited out of the rebroadcasts.[16] Kim Sŏng-ae's name appeared 104th on the state funeral service committee list, while Kim P'yŏng-il didn't make the list at all. This meant that Kim P'yŏng-il, then ambassador to Finland, was already out in the power succession. He left Pyongyang immediately after the funeral, and openly stated in Helsinki on August 31, 1994, that Kim Jong Il was his late father's only legitimate successor.[17] In light of Kim Jong Il's activities and North Korean media commentaries and reports, it is clear that the Kim Jong Il regime was inaugurated immediately after the death of Kim Il Sung.

The North Korean power elite who supported the Kim Jong Il regime at that time were, in short, a combination of generations: the old, those who directly participated in the North Korean revolution, including the anti-Japanese guerrilla movement; and the new, those who were born into the system. Almost all the first-generation revolutionaries were political or military officials (see table 5.1). The new generation may be divided into two groups. The first, consisting of sons, nephews, and cousins of the first generation, all graduated from Man'gyongdae Revolutionary School. Sharing a strong sense of solidarity with Kim, they held vital positions in the party, government, and military. This group was more familiar to those outside of North Korea. The second group did not have blood ties to the revolution but had expertise in diverse fields necessary for regime management. They

15 Kim Jong Il, "Sahoechuŭinŭn kwahakita" [Socialism is a science], *Rodong Sinmun*, November 4, 1994, 1–3.

16 Samuel S. Kim, "North Korea in 1994: Brinkmanship, Breakdown, and Breakthrough," *Asian Survey* 35, no.1 (January 1995): 14.

17 *Dong-A Ilbo*, September 2, 1994, A2.

TABLE 5.1

The Kim Jong Il regime power base

The old generation: revolutionaries and guerillas			
O Chin-u	*People's Armed Forces minister*	Ch'oe Kwang	*KPA chief of general staff*
Pak Sŏng-ch'ol	*State vice-chairman*	Kim Ch'ol-man	*NDC member*
Paek Hak-rim	*Public Security minister*	Chŏn Mun-sŏp	*State Control Committee chairman*
Ri Ŭl-sŏl	*NDC member*		

The new generation, first group: relatives of the old generation			
Kang Sŏng-san	*Prime minister*	Kim Kuk-t'ae	*KWPCC Politburo member*
O Yong-bang	*KWPCMC member*	Ri Pong-wŏn	
O Kŭk-ryŏl		Kim Kyŏng-hŭi	*Kim Jong Il's younger sister*
Chang Sŏng-t'aek	*Kim Kyŏng-hŭi's husband*	Kang Ch'ang-ju	*KPA Corps commander*
Rim Hyŏng-gu		Ri Kil-song	
Paek Pŏm-su		Kim Hwan	
Ch'oe Yong-hap		Ch'oe Mun-sun	

The new generation, second group: experts			
Name	*Field*	*Name*	*Field*
Kye Ŭng-t'ae	*Public security*	Chŏn Pyŏng-ho	*Military supply*
Han Sŏng-ryong	*Economics*	Ch'oe T'ae-bok	*Education*
Kim Chung-rin	*Workers' organization*	Kim Ki-nam	*Propaganda*
Sŏ Kwan-hŭi	*Agriculture*	Hwang Chang-yŏp	*Political thought and international affairs*
Kim Yong-sun	*South Korea*		

were specialists drawn from a wide variety of fields—politics, diplomacy, the military, economics, science, ideology, and the arts.[18]

The Beginning of Yuhun T'ongch'i

How was Kim Jong Il able to rule and govern the North without assuming official titles as head of the KWP and DPRK president? The answer was

18 Chŏng Yŏng-t'ae, *Kim Chŏng-ul ch'ejeha ŭi kunbu yŏkhal: Chisok kwa pyŏnhwa* [The role of the military under the Kim Jong Il regime: Continuity and change] (Seoul: Research Institute for National Unification, December 1995), 3–6. See also Chŏn Hyŏn-jun, *Kim Chŏng-il chŏngkwŏn ŭi kwŏllyŏk ellit'ŭ yŏn'gu* [A study on the power elite of the Kim Jong Il regime] (Seoul: Research Institute for National Unification, October 1995), 4–7. See also Lee Dong-bok, "Political Dynamics in North Korea: Implications of Kim Jong Il's Succession to Power," in *The Future of North Korea: Implications for the Korean Peninsula and Northeast Asia* (Seoul: Institute of Foreign Affairs and National Security, Ministry of Foreign Affairs, 1995), 67.

the so-called *Yuhun t'ongch'i*—governance based on teachings left behind by Kim Il Sung. Kim Jong Il apparently decided to wear his father's mantle of absolute command and incomparable charisma. As Samuel Kim notes,

> no state in our times has built so many monuments (over 30,000) or launched so many ideological campaigns in glorification of its political leader, with the paradoxical consequence that Kim Il Sung has been elevated to the status of an irreplaceable demigod.[19]

The desperate economic situation may have been another factor in Kim Jong Il's choice of strategy. On December 8, 1993, Prime Minister Kang Sŏng-san officially acknowledged before the Twenty-First Plenum of the Sixth KWPCC that the Third Seven-Year Plan (1987–93) had failed. Consequently, the regime established a three-year transition period from 1994 to 1996, demanding that the people respond with an "arduous march." Scapegoat Kim Tar-hyŏn, a typical technocrat and an ardent supporter of reform and opening up of the North Korean economy, was dismissed as both deputy premier and state planning committee chairman and sent to manage a local factory. In 2000, despondent, he reportedly committed suicide.[20]

In this situation, it was clever of Kim Jong Il to hide behind the curtain of the Great Leader, whom the North Korean media called "immortal." In countries outside of the DPRK, the concept of *Yuhun t'ongch'i* is almost without parallel. One North Korea watcher in Seoul, however, compared it to Stalin's "'great pledge' made before the body of his late predecessor, Lenin. [Stalin] vowed at the funeral service . . . to live up to [Lenin's] will to maintain the unity of the Communist Party and strengthen the proletarian dictatorship."[21] It should be stressed, however, that unlike Kim Il Sung's positions of KWPCC general secretary and DPRK president, Lenin's offices were not left unfilled on his death.

What were the distinctive aspects of this *Yuhun t'ongch'i*? First, North Koreans put the Kim Il Sung personality cult on an even higher plateau. As an initial step, North Korean officials announced that they would commemorate the first anniversary of Kim Il Sung's death by mummifying his body to permanently preserve it inside Pyongyang's Kŭmsusan Hall, which had served both as Kim's office and his residence. As the second anniversary of Kim Il Sung's death approached, Kŭmsusan Hall was lavishly rebuilt and renamed Kŭmsusan Memorial Palace.[22] With the dedication of Kŭmsusan

---

19 Kim, "North Korea in 1994," 14–15.

20 Yi Yong-su, "Pukhan" [The North], *Chosun Ilbo*, October 6, 2011, A4.

21 Kim Ch'ang-sun, "Junior Kim's *Yuhun* Rule May Weaken His Leadership Position," *Vantage Point: Developments in North Korea* 9, no. 9 (September 1996): 10.

22 ROK Ministry of National Unification, *Chugan Pukhan tonghyang* [Weekly trends in North Korea], no. 288 (July 6–12, 1996): 10–11.

Memorial Palace as a sanctuary, the North Korean authorities actively promoted "the immortality of Kim Il Sung."[23] The power elite called for the people's continued support, reminding North Koreans of Kim Il Sung's final instructions that everyone should unite around Kim Jong Il. From 1994, adoration of Kim Il Sung exceeded merely touting him as the "founder of socialist Korea and sun of the Korean nation" and entered a new dimension of rhetoric by asserting, "We Koreans are the Kim Il Sung nation." Even Stalin, perhaps the most ruthless dictator in modern history, did not make Russians call themselves the "Stalin nation." On September 9, 1996—the forty-eighth anniversary of the DPRK—the North Korean authorities began using yet another inflated expression: "Korea is the Comrade Kim Il Sung country." On that day the *Rodong Sinmun* editorial claimed, "Korea is the Comrade Kim Il Sung state. Accordingly, this republic should be named after him. . . . We should do everything in our power to develop our republic as a state befitting Comrade Kim Il Sung's name."[24]

Another distinctive aspect of *Yuhun t'ongch'i* was to feature Kim Jong Il as an extremely loyal and pious successor to Kim Il Sung. In an effort to identify the son with the father, the official media described Kim Jong Il as the "embodiment of loyalty and filial piety" and as the "possessor of sublime loyalty and loftiest morality." Touting Kim Jong Il as the "embodiment of loyalty and filial piety to Kim Il Sung," a June 8, 1996, *Rodong Sinmun* editorial asserted that Kim Jong Il's leadership played an instrumental role in upholding Kim Il Sung's revolutionary feats and accomplishments. The North Korean authorities emphasized, "As Comrade Kim Jong Il honors his father with loyalty and filial piety, the Korean people should devote their single mind of loyalty and filial piety to Comrade Kim Jong Il." And the message delivered in early June 1996 to the North Korean people through government-controlled media said, in short, that to realize Comrade Kim Il Sung's final instructions, North Koreans ought to become Comrade Kim Jong Il's loyal subjects and brave even the harshest of adversity to fulfill his will and ideology.[25]

The terms used by the North Korean media during this period focused on North Korea as a Confucian nation, not as a Marxist or socialist country. North Korean experts on propaganda and agitation knew that an appeal based on Confucianism would be most effective in a traditionally Confucian

23 For example, see the speech by Ch'oe Su-hŏn, DPRK vice foreign minister, before the UN on October 11, 1995, quoted in Samuel S. Kim, "North Korea in 1995: The Crucible of Our Style Socialism," *Asian Survey* 36, no.1 (January 1996): 63.

24 Quoted in *Choson Ilbo*, September 12, 1996, 3.

25 *Chugan Pukhan tonghyang*, no. 288, 17.

society such as North Korea. This practice would become more prevalent after Kim Jong Il's assumption of the KWP general secretaryship in 1997.

Yuhun t'ongch'i enabled Kim Jong Il to be placed on the same level as his father, as illustrated by the new slogan, "Kim Il Sung is Kim Jong Il and Kim Jong Il is Kim Il Sung." At a central memorial ceremony on July 7, 1996, on the second anniversary of Kim Il Sung's death, KWPCC secretary Ch'oe T'ae-bok proclaimed, "Comrade Kim Il Sung is Comrade Kim Jong Il and Comrade Kim Jong Il is the party."[26] The North Korean regime highlighted Kim Jong Il's leadership aptitude and ability in an effort to elevate the personality cult of Kim Jong Il to Kim Il Sung–sized dimensions. In a January 9, 1996, editorial, *Rodong Sinmun* hailed Kim Jong Il not as the "interpreter of *Juche* philosophy" but as the "originator of red-flag philosophy"; on February 6 the newspaper declared, "Comrade Kim Jong Il is the party and the party is Comrade Kim Jong Il"; and on July 12, the paper claimed that Kim Il Sung, the day before he died, told Kim Jong Il, "You realize everything I visualize." A week later, an editorial stressed that Kim Jong Il has the "ability to change adversity to prosperity, and misfortune to fortune."[27]

The glorification of Kim Jong Il reached a new level with claims that the son's "sterling leadership" had contributed to Kim Il Sung's revolutionary achievements. A *Rodong Sinmun* editorial of March 19, 1996—"Kim Il Sung, the Greatest Political Elder of this Country"—is a good example:

> No country in the world had a leader like Kim Il Sung, who led the country and people for fifty years. . . . The greatness of the Kim Il Sung administration lies in its longevity. The political life of a leader lacking ability, leadership, and authority is destined to be short. . . . The history of the Kim Il Sung administration during the past thirty years perfectly coincides with that of Kim Jong Il's revolutionary activities. The president (Kim Il Sung) and his successor (Kim Jong Il) are the two supreme pinnacles of the revolution as well as a political gem crystallized through Kim Jong Il's most laborious joint struggle. . . . Kim Jong Il is a statesman of Kim Il Sung's caliber and a great man with uncanny abilities. A Kim Il Sung-type statesman at the helm of the party's revolution, Kim Jong Il succeeded his father's political philosophy of cherishing the people as if they were divine. He is a capable and gifted man who rose to the top of the party structure, not through anyone's help, but through a series of revolutionary activities he accomplished with his extraordinary capabilities.

On June 9, 1996, the *Rodong Sinmun* repeated the same theme: "The history of Kim Il Sung's revolutionary activities is linked to the history of

---

26 *Chugan Pukhan tonghyang*, no. 287 (July 29–July 5, 1996): 8.
27 *Chugan Pukhan tonghyang*, no. 290 (July 20–26, 1996): 2–5.

Kim Jong Il's struggles and Kim Jong Il's achievements in leadership shine through Kim Il Sung's revolutionary feats."

In reality, Kim Jong Il's performance was very poor for a leader with the ability to change "misfortune to fortune." The North Korean economy was in serious decline. After consecutive years of flooding (1995–96), a drought followed in 1997. North Korea's agricultural sector was devastated by natural disasters. Numerous private and public reports by outsiders conveyed the prevailing malnutrition, starvation, and even massive number of deaths in the North. For example, Walter Russell Mead, an adviser to a New York–based international charity organization, wrote after a brief visit to North Korea in August 1996:

> The 1995 harvest was heavily damaged [by floods]; more than a million metric tons of food reserves, 335,000 tons of chemical fertilizer, and 480,000 animals disappeared in the surging waters. . . . I didn't see a chicken or a cat anywhere in North Korea. . . . I did not see a single pigeon in Pyongyang. . . .[28]

In sum, under *Yuhun t'ongch'i,* the North's economy recorded negative growth for four consecutive years, just as it had in the preceding four years (1990–93). The North's economy was compared to a "wrecked ship sinking deeper and deeper into the sea."[29]

With the country's outlook so dismal, a series of highly publicized defections began immediately after the death of Kim Il Sung. In late July 1994 Kang Myŏng-do, a company chief active in China under KWP auspices—and who claimed to be the son-in-law of Prime Minister Kang Sŏng-san—arrived in Seoul via Hong Kong.[30] Also appearing in Seoul around the same time was Cho Myŏng-ch'ŏl, a full-time instructor of economics at Kim Il Sung University who was the son of a former construction minister. In September 1995 Lieutenant Colonel Ch'oe Chu-hwal of the PAFM defected to the South. In December 1995 Ch'oe Se-ung, the son of a former finance management department director of the KWP, defected with his wife and children to Seoul from London, where he had worked as the North Korean representative to an international maritime organization.[31] In January 1996

---

28 Walter Russell Mead, "More Methods than Madness in North Korea," *New York Times Magazine,* September 15, 1996.

29 Namkoong Young, "Trends and Prospects of the North Korean Economy," *Korea and World Affairs* 20, no. 2 (Summer 1996): 219–35; *A Report on North Korea's Situation* co-authored by four research institutes (three American and one Russian) under a grant from the Rockefeller Foundation. For a synopsis, see *Segye Ilbo,* September 8, 1996, 3.

30 According to some defector sources, Kang Myŏng-do was once married to Prime Minister Kang Sŏng-san's daughter, but they had divorced.

31 His wife, Sin Yŏng-hŭi, formerly a dancer in the Mansudae Art Troupe, published her recollections; see Sin Yŏng-hŭi, *Chindallae kkot p'ilttae kkaji* [Until the azalea blossoms], 2 vols. (Seoul: Munyedang, 1996).

Hyŏn Sŏng-il, former Kim Il Sung University professor and incumbent third secretary at the North Korean embassy in Zambia, defected to Seoul with his wife—his father was Hyŏn Ch'ŏl-gyu, former director of the cadres department as well as first vice director of the KWPCCOGD, and his uncle was Hyŏn Ch'ŏl-hae, a KPA general as well as vice director for organizational affairs of the KPAGPB.[32] A month later, as noted earlier, Sung (Sŏng) Hye-rang, elder sister to Kim Jong Il's common-law wife, defected to Western Europe. In May 1996, pilot Ri Ch'ŏl-su dramatically defected to the South in a MiG-19 fighter jet. Seven months later, seventeen North Koreans, all from one extended family, defected to the South via China. At the same time, two North Korean intelligence agents based in China fled to Hong Kong, seeking asylum in South Korea. In January 1997 two families totaling eight people defected to the South via China.[33]

In February 1997 Hwang Chang-yŏp, former Kim Il Sung University president and incumbent KWPCC secretary, known as principal architect of *Juche* thought, took refuge in Seoul via China with his trusted associate, Kim Tŏk-hong. The news about Hwang—the highest-ranking North Korean ever to defect—was a media sensation. Six months later, Chang Sŏng-kil, ambassador to Egypt, his wife, and elder brother Chang Sŏng-ho, an economic counselor at the General Representative Mission in France, defected to the United States. The defection of North Korean diplomats would continue. In 1999, Kim Kyŏng-p'il, a second secretary of the North Korean interests section in Berlin, and his wife defected to the United States, and Hong Sun-gyŏng, a science and technology counselor at the embassy in Thailand, defected to the South.[34]

Defection was not the only response to the situation in North Korea. In June 1995 a number of KPA Sixth Corps military leaders, stationed in the northeast and headquartered in Ch'ŏngjin, prepared to stage a coup d'état. It is said that regional cadres of the KWP and state agencies also joined the plan. Kim Yŏng-ch'un, the Sixth Corps commander, learned of their plan and arrested all of them with the assistance of the KPA's Safeguard Headquarters. Kim would be promoted to KPA chief of general staff in October 1995; at least twenty-four (and perhaps as many as forty) cadres of the corps and state

32 Hyŏn Sŏng-il, *Pukhan ŭi kukka chŏllyak kwa p'awŏ ellit'ŭ: Kanbu chŏngch'aek ŭl chungsim ŭro* [North Korea's state strategy and power elite: Special reference to the cadre policy] (Seoul: Sŏnin, 2007), 5–6.

33 For example, see Satterwhite, North Korea in 1996," 14. See also Ahn, J. H., "14 North Korean 'Boat People' Reach South," Associated Press, May 12, 1997.

34 R. Jeffrey Smith, "North Korean May Bring Arms Data: Top Diplomat in Cairo Defects to U.S. with Members of Family," *Washington Post*, August 27, 1997, 8; *Korea Times*, January 21, 1999, 1.

agencies were executed. Fujimoto Kenji recalled the conversations between Kim Jong Il and seven generals on December 30, 1995, at Kim Jong Il's office. Kim Jong Il asked, "Did you shoot them?" A general replied, "Yes, sir. We shot them yesterday."[35] This case became known as the Sixth Corps Coup d'état Conspiracy Incident.[36] Two years later, in 1997, workers at an ironworks in Sinch'ŏn, Hwanghae Province, created a massive disturbance with an attempted labor strike. Again, it was the KPA Safeguard Headquarters that suppressed it.[37]

Kim Jong Il's Assumption of the KWP General Secretaryship, Constitutional Revision, and "Military-First Politics," 1997–98

Assumption of the KWP General Secretaryship

North Korea had been without an official leader of the ruling KWP—i.e., the general secretary of its Central Committee—for three years and three months following the death of Kim Il Sung in July 1994. Kim Jong Il, the KWP's de facto top leader, delayed taking the job title, apparently in part to adhere to the three-year mourning period traditionally observed on the death of a Korean monarch. Then, on September 27, 1997, the KWP's South P'yŏng'an provincial branch held a representative conference and unanimously passed a resolution that the party "*acclaim* Great Leader Kim Jong Il as its general secretary" [italics added].[38] The resolution did not use the term "elect," "appoint," or even "draft," but "acclaim." The Korean term used was *ch'udae*, which is difficult to translate into English. *Ch'udae* implies that the party members implored Kim Jong Il to assume the post of general secretary, although as a great or even semi-divine man who pays no heed to position or title, he had no interest in the post. North Korean official publications in fact claimed that he refused to accept their repeated pleadings.[39] We might go so far as to say that the term *ch'udae* per se reveals and encapsulates the unique character of the North Korean polity. At any rate, the passage of the resolution set the stage for Kim to officially become the party's top leader. Soon, all other branches at the KWP and the KPA followed suit. Finally, on October 8, two days before the fifty-second anniversary of the party's founding, both its Central Committee and Central Military Committee jointly declared that the party "acclaimed" Kim Jong Il as its general secretary.[40]

35 Fujimoto Kenji, *Kim Jong Il's Chef* (published in 2003 in Japanese), trans. Sin Hyŏn-ho, *Kim Chŏng-il ŭi yorisa* (Seoul: Wŏlgan Chosŏnsa, 2003), 154–55.
36 Paek, "Kukka anjŏn powibu," 4.
37 Ibid.
38 Foreign Languages Publishing House (ed.), *Kim Jong Il*, 191–92.
39 Ibid.
40 *Rodong Sinmun*, October 9, 1997, 1.

TABLE 5.2
Composition of the DPRK Politburo Presidium, 1980–1995

Date	Members	Notes
October 1980	Kim Il Sung, Kim Il, O Chin-u, Kim Jong Il, Ri Chong-ok	
July 1983	Kim Il Sung, Kim Il, O Chin-u, Kim Jong Il	*Ri Chong-ok dismissed*
March 1984	Kim Il Sung, O Chin-u, Kim Jong Il	*Kim Il dies*
July 1994	O Chin-u, Kim Jong Il	*Kim Il Sung dies*
February 1995	Kim Jong Il	*O Chin-u dies*

Three points should be noted here. First, according to the KWP's own stipulations, its general secretary was to be elected by congress, so in this sense the method by which Kim Jong Il ascended to be the official top leader of the KWP was not in accordance with party statutes. Second, Kim Jong Il was declared general secretary of the KWP, while according to party statutes, the party's highest post is *general secretary of the KWP's Central Committee*. Was Kim attempting to demonstrate that he was above party statutes? Third, as Samuel S. Kim details, "the most powerful organ in the North Korean political system, the Presidium [Standing Committee] of the Politburo," had by this time effectively become defunct. As table 5.2 shows, membership had "steadily declined from five in October 1980 (Kim Il Sung, Kim Il, O Chin-u, Kim Jong Il, and Ri Chong-ok)" to four in July 1983 with the dismissal of Ri Chong-ok; it dropped "to three in March 1984 with the death of Kim Il, to two in July 1994 with the death of Kim Il Sung," and in February 1995, "with the death of O Chin-u," only Kim Jong Il remained.[41] The Politburo Standing Committee vacancies were never filled.

Kim Jong Il's assumption of the post of KWPCC general secretary was soon accompanied by a series of purges, including executions. The most extensive and frightening case was the *simhwajo* (literally "depth investigation team") case led by Chang Sŏng-t'aek, first vice director of the KWPCCOGD, and Ch'ae Mun-dŏk, director of the Public Security Ministry Political Bureau (in charge of the regular police). During 1997–2000 this team, consisting mainly of functionaries working in the police, prosecutorial authorities, and SSM, "deepened" its investigation of the pasts of all North Korean citizens, including their activities during the 1950–53 Korean War. Consequently, around twenty-five thousand people were stigmatized as "spies of the South Korean intelligence agencies or U.S. imperialists." Most of them

41 Samuel S. Kim, "North Korea in 1999: Bringing the Grand *Ch'ollima* March Back In," *Asian Survey* 40, no. 1 (January–February, 2000): 153.

TABLE 5.3

Prominent victims of the 1997–2000 simhwajo *campaign*

Name	Post/title
Sŏ Kwan-hŭi	KWPCC secretary of agriculture
Kim Chŏng-u	Chairman of the Committee for the Promotion of External Economic Relations
Ch'oe Ryong-hae	Chairman of the Kim Il Sung Socialist Youth League
Kwŏn Hŭi-gyŏng	Director of information on foreign and southern affairs of the KWPCC and former ambassador to Moscow
Ch'oe Pong-man	KWP CC vice director of funds
Mun Sŏng-sul	KWP CC vice director of funds
Kim Yŏng-ryong	SSM first vice director
Sŏ Yun-sŏk	Responsible Secretary of the KWP South Pyongyang Province Committee
Sons of O Kŭk-ryŏl and Kye Ŭng-t'ae	Both KWPCC core cadres

were imprisoned, sent to a remote barren countryside, or even executed, while others committed suicide in prison.[42]

Victims of the *simhwajo* included a number of prominent names, and notably all of them were KWP cadres—not military leaders (see table 5.3).

We know when three of these victims met their fates. Sŏ Kwan-hŭi was accused of misguiding the state's agricultural policy by refusing to introduce new technology into agricultural production; he was publicly executed in September 1997 in Pyongyang. Kim Chŏng-u was executed in December 1997, and Mun Sŏng-sul, one of Kim Jong Il's few confidants, was executed in March 1999. When in 2001 Kim Jong Il sensed that the *simwhajo* case had gone so far as to alienate the people from the KWP, he instructed a review and investigation of its own activities. To assuage popular sentiment, he scapegoated and purged many *simwhajo* leaders, including Ch'ae Mun-dŏk. They were accused of abusing their power under the influence of "foreign, anti-DPRK forces," with the aim of driving a wedge between the people and the KWP. Kim Jong Il then restored the honor of a few of the *simwhajo* victims.[43] Mun Sŏng-sul was, postmortem, declared innocent;

42 Hwang Il-do, "Chŏn Pukhan haeksim kwallyo ka ssŏn Kim Chŏng-il kwŏllyŏk changak pihwa" [Secret stories written by a former core bureaucrat in North Korea], *Sindonga* (October 2005), 120–36. See also Hyŏn Sŏng-il, *Pukhan ŏi kukka chŏllyak kwa p'awŏ ellit'ŭ: Kanbu chŏngch'aek ŏl chungsim ŏro* [North Korea's state strategy and power elite: with reference to the cadre policy] (Seoul: Sŏnin, 2007), 391–94.

43 Hyŏu, *Pukhan ŏi kukka chŏllyak kwa p'awŏ ellit'ŭ*, 393.

Ch'oe Ryong-hae, who had been sent with his family to the mountainous backcountry, was allowed to return to Pyongyang in the mid-2000s. Ch'oe's family background—his father Ch'oe Hyŏn was one of Kim Il Sung's close guerrilla comrades and national defense minister under Prime Minister Kim Il Sung—was probably a point in his favor. Kim Jong Il later renamed the Public Security Ministry as the Ministry of People's Security (MPS).

Although Kim Jong Il had finally assumed the top official KWP leadership position, he could not solve the national calamities that continued during the three years following his father's death. He was forced to continue to ask for international food aid to provide his own people with sustenance and had to ask North Koreans to endure extreme difficulties when he declared 1998 the year of a "forced march" (*kanghaenggun*). It was the continuation of the 1994–97 "arduous march." Yet, with the military supporting him and the people following him, Kim Jong Il was able to navigate the crises and remain in power.[44]

Constitutional Revision

Elections for the Tenth Supreme People's Assembly were held on July 26, 1998, and the new SPA was convened on September 5 of that year. Just one day before the opening of the new SPA—seeking to highlight it and enhance Kim Jong Il's prestige—North Korea's official organs boasted that the country had successfully launched its first satellite on August 31. U.S. sources initially declared the event to have been a missile test launch, specifically of the Taepodong-1, a two-stage rocket with an estimated range of 1,200 miles. Later they determined the event was, in fact, a failed attempt to launch a small satellite. Still, an American analyst argued:

> At a minimum, this first launch of a two-stage missile with a range of well over 1,000 miles represented a major advance for North Korea. If deployed and combined with a nuclear, chemical, or biological warhead, this capability would represent a significant new and destabilizing threat in Northeast Asia.[45]

When the new SPA convened on September 5 it revised the DPRK constitution.[46] The new preamble codified the identity of North Korea as a theocratic Kim Il Sung state by declaring that "Kim Il Sung is the founder of the

44 Suh Dae-sook, "New Political Leadership," in *The North Korean System in the Post-Cold War Era,* ed. Samuel S. Kim (New York: Palgrave, 2001), 73.

45 David G. Brown, "North Korea in 1998: A Year of Foreboding Developments," *Asian Survey,* 39, no. 1 (January 1999): 129.

46 For the full text of the revised constitution, see *Rodong Sinmun,* September 6, 1998, 1–2.

Democratic People's Republic of Korea and socialist Korea" and the "sun of the nation." The post of *chusŏk*—chairman or president of the state, which had been occupied solely by Kim Il Sung—was abolished. According to the official media, Kim Jong Il said that no person could dare use the "sacred" title of *chusŏk* and that Kim Il Sung would be remembered as the eternal *chusŏk*. In fact, the revised constitution declared Kim Il Sung to be the "eternal *chusŏk* of the Republic." With the elimination of this position, four vice-chairman posts were also abolished.

Without the *chusŏk* position, who would play the role of head of state? For that purpose, the revised constitution established the new post of chairman of the Standing Committee within the SPA, and the SPA elected—inasmuch as anything can be called an "election" in the DPRK—Kim Yŏng-nam, a KWPCC Politburo member, as its chairman. A former foreign minister and vice-premier who had built his career within the party apparatus dealing mainly with foreign affairs, Kim was well prepared to receive foreign dignitaries and to participate in international conferences. The SPA also elected Kim Yŏng-dae and Yang Hyŏng-sŏp as vice-chairmen, and four elderly leaders of the Kim Il Sung era—Ri Chong-ok, Pak Sŏng-ch'ŏl, Kim Yŏng-ju, and Chŏn Mun-sop—as honorary vice-chairmen of its standing committee. Not long after, two of these men died—Chŏn in 1998 and Ri a year later—but the resulting vacancies were left unfilled.

The revised constitution reduced the organs and functions of the SPA, as elaborated by Suh Dae-sook:

> [Within the SPA] there was a Secretariat headed by a Chairman and eleven members who were heads of various social, labor, peasant, and women's organizations. This Secretariat performed functions similar to the Chinese Political Consultative Committee. In the past, the SPA had at least four to six standing committees, but they were reduced to a bare minimum of two, the Bills Committee and the Appropriations Committee. The Procurator-General was appointed and the President of the Central Court was elected. Compared to the government of Kim Il Sung, this is a simple, but peculiar form of government.[47]

The September 5 constitutional revision also strengthened the power of the NDC. The previous constitution had defined the NDC as the "highest military guidance organ of state sovereignty." However, the revision added that the NDC was also the "organ that manages overall national defense issues." Accordingly, the NDC chairman was empowered to "guide overall national defense tasks." The previous constitution had also stipulated that the NDC was empowered to declare a state of war and to issue mobilization

47 Suh, "New Political Leadership," 74.

orders "in an emergency." The revision, however, broadened the NDC's and its chairman's power by deleting the phrase "in an emergency."

Kim Yŏng-nam "politely" recommended to the SPA that the republic acclaim Kim Jong Il as the NDC's chairman; the SPA accepted his recommendation unanimously and "with thunderous applause." When Kim Jong Il accepted the offer, Kim Yŏng-nam publicly expressed "heartfelt thanks" and interpreted the post of NDC chairman as "the highest post of the state, which 1) controls and leads the totality of capacities (or, potentials) in politics, military, and the economy; 2) protects the destiny of the state and the people; and 3) symbolically represents the dignity of the people and the honor of the fatherland."[48] In this sense, the revised constitution was actually the Kim Jong Il Constitution, although it was officially designated the "Kim Il Sung Constitution."

The SPA elected three vice marshals as top officials of the NDC. KPAGPB director Cho Myŏng-rok became the NDC's first vice-chairman, while PAFM minister Kim Il-ch'ŏl and former KPAGPB director Ri Yong-mu became vice-chairmen. From that moment, Cho's status as the second man in the North Korean power hierarchy became crystal clear. As the regime's most influential military leader, he delivered the keynote address on the fifth anniversary of Kim Il Sung's death on July 8, 1999.[49] It was also Cho who visited the White House and met U.S. president Bill Clinton, Secretary of State Madeleine Albright, and Secretary of Defense William Cohen in October 2000.

The SPA elected as its members Kim Yŏng-ch'un (vice marshal and chief of general staff of the KPA), Yŏn Hyŏng-muk, Ri Ŭl-sŏl (marshal and Security Safeguard Forces commander), Paek Hak-rim (vice marshal and public security minister), Chŏn Pyŏng-ho, and Kim Ch'ol-man (vice marshal and military transportation minister). Except for Yŏn, a former premier who had built his career in the field of military supply within the party apparatus and was the Chakang provincial party chief, and Chŏn, a KWPCC Politburo member in charge of military supply, the rest were core KPA leaders. In sum, eight of the NDC ten members were professional military leaders on active duty, including two marshals and six vice marshals.

Another significant constitutional revision was the abolition of the Central People's Committee—the super-cabinet where most important policies of the state had been deliberated and decided—and the Administrative Affairs Board as the cabinet. A newly established cabinet organization (*naegak*) was charged with administering the government's economic and social

48 *Rodong Sinmun*, October 6, 1998, 1.
49 Samuel S. Kim, "North Korea in 1999," 154.

policies, but not military and security policies. The People's Armed Forces Ministry was excluded from the cabinet and put directly under the guidance of the NDC. The number of cabinet posts was reduced from forty-one to twenty-eight. The number of vice prime ministers was reduced from ten to two. It was not surprising that the SPA elected Hong Sŏng-nam, a typically colorless technocrat who rose up the ranks of the party and government apparatus, as premier to lead the cabinet. Paek Nam-sun, former ambassador to Poland, was appointed foreign minister.[50] In contrast to his "big shot" predecessors such as Pak Hŏn-yŏung, Nam Il, Hŏ Tam, Pak Sŏng-ch'ol, and Kim Yŏng-nam, all well known for their political weight, Paek was a career diplomat and negotiator faithful to the party line.

Military-First Policy

Kim Jong Il had thus reorganized the DPRK government to place the military in a commanding position.[51] His restructuring reflected his "military-first policy" (sŏn'gun chŏngch'i), which was proclaimed at the Tenth Supreme People's Assembly. With the NDC now the key decision-making organization of the state, the SPA Presidium and the cabinet were relegated to the status of secondary governmental organizations. Evaluating "the Kim Jong Il government under the leadership of the NDC" as being "a rather simple if not an abridged form of government," Suh Dae-sook concluded:

> The new government can hardly qualify as a regime of collective leadership because the center of real power in "military-first politics" is concentrated in the chairman of the NDC. The Standing Committee of the SPA seems to perform the perfunctory legislative function of giving the government legitimacy by passing the decisions of the NDC unanimously, and the cabinet seems to administer the policies decided by the NDC.[52]

As for the NDC, Professor Suh elaborated in detail:

> It is indeed the most powerful organization of the government of Kim Jong Il. His prescription for new government was the creation of what we might call a military government. It is not simply a government where active or former military officers participate in the state politics, but rather it is a government that has systematized the rule by the professional military. It is a government that upholds the Chairman of the National Defense Commission as the de facto head of the state, and his professional military officers on active duty constitute

50 *Rodong Sinmun*, September 6, 7, 8, 9, 1998.
51 Suh Dae-sook, "Military-First Politics of Kim Jong Il," *Asian Perspective* 26, no. 3 (2002): 154.
52 Ibid.

[an] absolute majority of the most important and powerful organization of the government, the National Defense Commission.[53]

Thus Selig S. Harrison was correct when he described the constitutional revision as "a bloodless coup."[54]

The ever-growing influence of the military was a subject of debate among North Korea watchers. Some interpreted it as indicating that Kim Jong Il's hold on power was tenuous and the political situation unstable.[55] Others, however, argued that he was in fact maintaining his control over the military by assigning military personnel to higher positions, adjusting the ranking of military officials to correspond to that of high officials in the KWP, and making frequent visits to military troops and military events.[56] A small number of observers believed this did not mean that the military outranked the party and insisted that the military was still under the party's control; their interpretation was that Kim Jong Il was utilizing the military rather than relying on it.[57] However, Professor Suh concluded:

> Kim Jong Il has replaced the party with the military to govern the country. Kim Jong Il has instituted a new politics called "military-first" politics. North Korea today simply pays lip service to the importance of the party, but the signs of the rise of the military are everywhere, and the military presence can be felt in all aspects of political and social life.[58]

Suh maintained that Kim Jong Il strengthened the position of the military authorities for crisis management and continued to maintain his influence upon the military. As a result, the military was playing a stronger role in maintaining national defense, foreign relations, management of the economy, and social order.

The KWP showed its loyalty to Kim Jong Il's military-first policy when it adopted the slogan, "The Military Is the Party, the People, and the Nation." In an editorial on June 15, 1999, *Rodong Sinmun* stated: "Our party's policy of giving priority to [the] army is invincible . . . [and] the perfect mode

53 Suh, "New Political Leadership," 76.

54 Selig S. Harrison, *Korean Endgame: A Strategy for Reunification and U.S. Disengagement* (Princeton: Princeton University Press, 2002), 60.

55 "Obsession with 'Socialism of Our Own Style' Stumbling Block to Solving Serious Economic Troubles," *Vantage Point: Developments in North Korea* (Seoul: The Naewoe Press) 21, no. 3 (March 1998): 2.

56 Park Young-ho, "North Korea under Kim Jong Il and South Korea's Policy towards North Korea," *Korea and World Affairs* 21, no. 4 (Winter 1997): 522.

57 Pak Jae-kyu, "It Will Be Convenient for Kim Jong Il to Deal With Foreign Countries in the Capacity of State President," *Vantage Point* 21, no. 6 (June 1998): 9–10.

58 Suh, "Military-First Politics," 146.

of politics in our times." The editorial continued, "Even if the people are not prepared politically and ideologically, socialism cannot collapse when the army stands true to it." It asserted that the necessity of a military-first policy for true independence "is a serious lesson drawn from the history of socialist politics in the twentieth century."[59] Wada Haruki, who had defined North Korea as the "guerrilla state," noted that with the military-first policy, North Korea had become a "regular army state."[60]

Rise of the Personality Cult, Extensive Use of Historical Legacies, Patriotism, and Mass Mobilization, 1997–2000

The Emergence of Neo-Confucianism

The consolidation of power in the hands of Kim Jong Il was first accompanied by the rise of the personality cult surrounding his parents, Kim Il Sung and Kim Jong Suk; along with Kim Jong Il himself, the three were glorified as the "Three Great Generals of Mount Paektu." The North Korean official mass media regularly published editorials, commentaries, and articles that praised them with absurd and fawning descriptions.[61] Statues of them and monuments to them were erected throughout the nation, one after another.

As of September 9, 1997, North Korea officially changed its year-numbering system (yŏnho) to begin with Kim Il Sung's birth. Thus, the year 1912 is called Juche year 1, 2012 is Juche 100, etc. (North Korea now uses both the Juche and the common, or Christian, era systems.) Furthermore, Kim Il Sung's birthday, April 15, was elevated to the status of "Anniversary of the Sun" (t'aeyang chŏl). The biography of his first wife, Kim Jong Suk, was newly published in December 1997. The rising Kim Jong Suk personality cult came at the expense of Kim Il Sung's second wife, Kim Sŏng-ae. On April 24, 1998, her political position as chair of the Central Committee of the Korean Democratic Women's League was transferred to Ch'on Yŏn-ok. In November 1998 her first son, Kim P'yŏng-il, was transferred to Poland from Finland as ambassador, thus continuing his ambassadorial life in exile

59 As detailed in Kim, "North Korea in 1999," 154, taken from KCNA reporting on the *Rodong Sinmun* editorial on June, 16, 1999, http://www.kcna.co.jp/item/1999/9906/news06/16.htm.

60 Wada Haruki, "The Establishment and Evolution of the Guerrilla State," *Sekai*, October 1993. See also Wada Haruki, *Puk Chosŏn: Yugyŏktae kukka esŏ chŏnggyu kun kukka ro* [North Korea: From a guerrilla state to a regular army state], trans. from Japanese by Sŏ Tong-man and Nam Ki-jŏng (Seoul: Tolbegye, 2003).

61 For example, see *Rodong Sinmun*, September 1–October 31, 1997.

in Europe that began in Hungary and proceeded to Bulgaria. He had a son (Kim In-gang) and a daughter (Kim Ŭn-song) by his wife, Kim Sun-gŭm. Kim Sŏng-ae's misfortunes continued when, in May 2000, her youngest son, Kim Yŏng-il, died of liver disease in Berlin. In November 2014, she herself died of Alzheimer's disease in Pyongyang at the age of ninety. The North Korean regime never released the news of her death.

Kim Jong Il propaganda continued apace. There were reports of "miracles" centering on his alleged birthplace on Mount Paektu. New songs and poems of praise were disseminated. Reciting the slogan, "We Will Sacrifice Our Lives Willingly For Our Great Leader General Kim Jong Il," became an important ritual in the daily lives of ordinary citizens. The North Korean regime started a new campaign in 1998: "Let Us Follow the Spirit of the Late Kim Kwang-ch'ŏl," based on the story of a soldier who fell on a grenade to save his superior in 1990. On February 16, 1998, Kim Jong Il's birthday, *Rodong Sinmun* editorialized that all North Koreans were engaged in "sacred struggles" to guarantee Kim's "absolute authority," safeguard the "command post of the revolution" headed by him, and keep the "socialism of our own style" intact in all political, economic, and military arenas. On June 12, 1998, the paper's editorial urged the North Korean people to live in accord with the spirit of "blowing oneself up" to save the Great Leader in case of an emergency.

Every success achieved by a North Korean citizen was attributed to the "wise, noble, and correct" leadership of Kim Jong Il, who was usually portrayed as the "all-knowing genius in all fields throughout the world." For example, when Chŏng Sŏng-ok won the gold medal in the women's marathon at the 1999 World Championships in Athletics in Seville, Spain, the North's official media hailed her success as the concrete result of the "Great Leader's benevolent care and wise teaching." She told the nation, "Because from start to finish I ran while thinking of Great Leader General Kim Jong Il's kind and correct teachings, I was able to win." She was immediately awarded the medal of Hero of the Republic. Soon *Rodong Sinmun* called her "Great Leader General Kim Jong Il's daughter" and initiated the "Let Us Live as Chŏng Sŏng-ok Lives" campaign, with the simple message that the North Korean people should live always thinking of Kim Jong Il's teachings.[62]

The practice of comparing North Korea to a single extended family (*tae kajok*) and Kim Jong Il to its head (*hoju*) became more frequent in the North's official media. Kim was usually portrayed as the master of a large family who "grants parental benevolence" to his sons and daughters—the

---

62 For example, see *Rodong Sinmun*, September 8, 15, 18, 1999.

North Korean people. To repay this "benevolent parental love," the North Korean people were incessantly urged to render endless "loyalty" (*ch'ung*) and "filial piety" (*hyo*) to their "mother as well as father Kim Jong Il."[63] Benevolence, loyalty, and filial piety are three fundamental concepts of Confucianism. Close examination of such editorials and commentaries published in North Korean official organs led readers to the inevitable conclusion that North Korea had become a neo-Confucian state, at least on the surface.

From the time of Kim Jong Il's assumption of the KWP general secretaryship, the North Korean official media began to put more emphasis on the historical legacies of the Korean nation rather than on *Juche* ideology. It became common to pay homage to Tan'gun—the legendary founder of the ancient Korean kingdom of Old Chosŏn, centered on Mount Paektu or Pyongyang—and King Tongmyong, who founded the Koguryŏ kingdom after the collapse of Old Chosŏn. Along these lines, North Korean archaeologists and historians proposed a new "theory" claiming that the basin of the Taedong River, including Pyongyang, was one of five cradles of ancient global civilization. Academic conferences supporting the "Taedong River Civilization" theory were held, and this was disseminated in the North's official publications.[64] The message was clear: the two Koreas should be unified under the leadership of the North, which is the inheritor of the historical legacies of ancient Korea and Koguryo. North Korea's ideologues emphasized that Pyongyang was the capital of both ancient Korea and Koguryŏ, implying that Pyongyang should and would be the capital of a unified Korea.

North Korean official organs also began to use the term "patriotism," which had hitherto typically been denounced as a bourgeois ideology. They now taught, "We Should Overcome All Difficulties and Pains with Strong Patriotism." Historical patriots from Korea's past were newly introduced to the North Korean people on a regular basis, with an emphasis on those heroes' willingness to sacrifice their lives for king and country. The message was obvious: everyone in North Korea should be prepared to devote their lives to safeguard Kim Jong Il, just as historical patriots sacrificed their lives to safeguard the fatherland and king. Even Chŏng Mong-ju—whose loyalty to the Koryŏ kingdom cost him his life—was hailed as a true patriot. In doing so, North Korea's official historians ignored the fact that earlier they had branded him a reactionary who had sought to preserve a corrupt and decaying dynasty.[65] Such extensive use of patriotism was reminiscent of

---

63 For example, see *Rodong Sinmun*, September 22, 1997
64 For example, see *Rodong Sinmun*, March 11 and October 3, 1998.
65 *Rodong Sinmun*, January 31, 1999.

Stalin, who appealed to the Russian people with similar terms during the "Great Patriotic War for the Defense of the Fatherland."

All of these examples indicated that the North Korean regime recognized the effectiveness of appealing to Confucian, nationalistic, and patriotic values at a time when socialist systems in most countries were collapsing. Speeches and articles by North Korean leaders were characterized by the frequent use of traditional terms drawn from Korean society rather than from socialist teachings. Kenneth Quinones, who had visited North Korea more than ten times after 1992, wrote: "North Koreans are Koreans [who regard] Confucius first, Marx last."[66] It may be reasonable to conclude that socialism was being replaced by traditional belief systems in modern North Korea.

There were, however, at least three themes that did not change. The first was excessive and frequent mass mobilization, based on various state rituals, for the purpose of cultivating the personality cults of Kim Il Sung, Kim Jung Suk, and Kim Jong Il. The most important of these were the birthdays of the latter two and the anniversary of the former's death. Military-related events tended to be commemorated the most. For example, North Korea celebrated the anniversaries of the appointment of Kim Jong Il as NDC chairman and KPA supreme commander. The founding date of the KPA became one of the three major commemorated dates in North Korea. (The other two are the birthdays of Kim Il Sung and Kim Jong Il.) On October 25, 2000, "even the fiftieth anniversary of the entry of the Chinese People's Volunteers into the Korean War was celebrated with a mass rally of military solidarity between the Chinese and Korean peoples."[67]

The second unchanging theme was that of anti-imperialism and anti-Americanism. The North Korean official media incessantly indoctrinated its people with the simple proposition that North Koreans should fight against the U.S.-led imperialists by rallying around the leadership of Kim Jong Il.

The third enduring theme was the comparison of North Korea's "benevolent and superior" system with the "wicked and inferior" capitalist system of foreign countries, including South Korea. In particular, the financial crisis that hit the South Korean economy in late 1997 and subsequent social problems, such as widespread joblessness in 1998, became major targets of the North's propaganda. In contrast, its official media portrayed North Korea as a country that guaranteed the basic livelihood of the people, thanks to the benevolent and noble leadership of Kim Jong Il.[68]

66 C. Kenneth Quinones, "North Korea Beyond the Illusion: An American's Personal Perspective," *Sin Asea* (New Asia) 4, no. 4 (Winter 1997): 43, 45.

67 Suh, "Military-First Politics," 147.

68 For example, see *Rodong Sinmun*, October 16, October 22, November 7, and December 4, 1997.

Goal of a "Strong and Prosperous Great State" and Budding "Pragmatism"

After North Korea recorded a poor harvest in 1997, the January 1 joint editorial of *Rodong Sinmun* and *Chosŏn Inmin'gun* (Korean People's Army) had to repeat that agricultural recovery would be a major national priority. However, meaningful economic or agricultural reforms did not follow in 1998 and the structural causes of the DPRK's food problem were not addressed. The leadership clung to the conventional method of initiating a new campaign to evoke the people's zeal for work. A good example was the "Campaign for Making a Revolution to Increase the Production of Potatoes." The campaign, which began in October 1998 in Taehongdan County, Ryanggang Province, did succeed in increasing potato production. From 1999 Kim Jong Il propagated the slogan, "The Potato Is the White Rice and the King of All Foodstuffs." Still, the regime was unable to feed its people and again had to depend on considerable food aid from the World Food Programme (with WFP aid coming mainly from the United States), China, South Korea, Europe, as well as from private-sector organizations.[69]

North Korea's industrial performance was also very poor, as summed up by an American analyst:

> The World Food Programme reports that the fertilizer industry, a regime priority, was operating at about 20 percent of capacity. Anecdotal information indicates that factory utilization rates remained similarly low and that transportation was out of service or decrepit. Basic services such as electricity and municipal water were not functioning reliably, even in Pyongyang. Published statistics from Japan, China, and South Korea indicate that North Korea's trade with those countries declined substantially. . . .[70]

In sum, 1998 was the eighth consecutive year that the North Korean economy contracted, although, at −1.1 percent, the rate of decline was the lowest during that period.

With the agricultural and industrial sectors in crisis, the North Korean regime declared the goal of rebuilding the DPRK as a "strong and prosperous great nation" (*kangsŏng taeguk*) simultaneous with the closing of the Tenth SPA's First Session. The meaning of that slogan was elaborated in a January 1, 1999, joint editorial of *Rodong Sinmun, Chosŏn Inmin'gun,* and *Ch'ŏngnyŏn chŏnwi* ("Youth Vanguard," a publication of the Kim Il Sung Socialist Youth

---

69 Brown, "North Korea in 1998," 128. See also *Rodong Sinmun*, October 3, 1998; January 3 and February 26, 2000.

70 Brown, "North Korea in 1998," 128.

League) under the headline of "Let this Year Mark a Turning Point in Building a *Kangsŏng Taeguk*." It explained that a *kangsŏng taeguk* was a state that is politically, ideologically, militarily, and economically strong.

To realize the goal, the joint editorial called for the Second *Ch'ŏllima* March. As a noted North Korea watcher aptly indicated, "Once again, the breakthrough mentality of the First *Ch'ŏllima* March of the late 1950s, which parroted Mao's Great Leap Forward, was brought back in a total mobilization campaign to rescue the sinking ship of the state."[71] The Second *Ch'ŏllima* March was a military mobilization campaign such that "almost all important infrastructure, including roads and bridges, [were] constructed by the military, and the military [was also] mobilized to support agriculture and mining."[72] Kim Jong Il, who had avoided committing himself to economic affairs, now became vigorously engaged in economic activities. "In the first ten months of 1999, he was reported to have made more than twenty-one on-the-spot inspection tours of nonmilitary units, compared to a handful in preceding years."[73] The trend continued to the end of his rule.

In addition to the Second *Ch'ŏllima* March, the regime continued the "Spirit of Kanggye" campaign.[74] On April 22, 2000, a joint editorial of *Rodong Sinmun* and *Kŭlloja* ("Worker," the monthly publication of the KWP) urged the North Korean people to devote their energy to increasing production in agriculture and other industries under the "Spirit of Kanggye." Similar articles appeared regularly in official North Korean publications.

By this time, the Mount Kŭmgang tourism program agreement, reached between the two Koreas in October 1998 in accordance with the Kim Dae Jung administration's Sunshine Policy, proved to be very helpful to the North. As explained by Samuel S. Kim in 1999:

> For Pyongyang, it is the easiest and safest way of earning hard currency (about $157 million a year). During the first year of operation . . . 146,148 tourists, including 61 foreigners, have visited the scenic mountain. The amount of hard currency (U.S. dollars) that Hyundai promised to pay in a six-year period . . . totals $942 million in exchange for exclusive rights to develop the tourist site until 2030.[75]

71 Kim, "North Korea in 1999," 152.
72 Ibid., 154.
73 Ibid.
74 Kanggye is the capital of Chakang Province. Its inhabitants suffered greatly under North Korea's "arduous march."
75 Kim, "North Korea in 1999," 161.

Kim continued to describe how the North Korean economy was improving:

> In 1999, inter-Korean trade rose 50 percent to an all-time record US$333 million, from $221.94 million in 1998. Inter-Korean processing-on-commission trade, first begun in 1992, is expected to hit a record $100 million in 1999. Such trade, mostly involving South Korean firms providing investment and equipment and North Korea supplying labor, totaled $82.7 million for the first ten months of the year, up from the previous high of $79 million in 1997. The number of manufactured products also grew from 98 in 1997 to 169 in 1999. Moreover, what started out as a relatively simple production line for fabrics and shoes now extends to color television sets, auto wiring, computer monitors, and audio cassettes.[76]

The South's economic assistance to the North became more active from 2000, when the first-ever inter-Korean summit was held on June 13–15; Kim Jong Il had talks with visiting ROK president Kim Dae Jung in Pyongyang and agreed to develop inter-Korean exchange and cooperation in many areas, including economic ones. Based on the spirit of the "Pyongyang declaration" agreement, the South supplied the North with three hundred thousand tons of Thai rice, two hundred thousand tons of Chinese corn, and one hundred thousand tons of fertilizer. The North concluded an agreement with the South's Hyundai Group "to build a multibillion-dollar industrial complex in the city of Kaesŏng, just north of the western DMZ. . . ." Samuel S. Kim called the development "a most promising potential opening for the North Korean economy."[77]

According to Stephen W. Linton's testimony to a Senate subcommittee, three factors contributed to an improvement, albeit modest, in the North Korean economy:

> Indubitably, foreign food assistance, particularly from the United States, deserves a major share of tribute for saving and improving the life of the average North Korean. . . . Foreign economic assistance and barter trade has also played a major—if unmeasured role [sic] in the modest gains in the quality of life in North Korea.

> The primary credit for North Korea's modest economic gains has been the informal economy. These so-called "informal coping mechanisms," including produce from private plots, farmer's markets, etc., adopted by North Korea's tough and resilient population, have halted North Korea's precipitous economic slide toward oblivion. Although the economic situation is

76 Ibid., 161–62.

77 Samuel S. Kim, "North Korea in 2000: Surviving through High Hopes of Summit Diplomacy," *Asian Survey* 41, no. 1 (January–February 2001): 17.

still precarious, improvement in the overall food supply has meant that some officials are beginning to refer to the "Arduous March" (North Korea's official euphemism for the famine) in the past tense.[78]

These factors, combined with the North's own efforts, allowed the country to record a positive growth rate (6.2 percent) in 1999, for the first time since 1990. The trend continued through the end of 2003. The economic growth rates for 2000, 2001, and 2002 were 1.3 percent, 3.7 percent, and 1.2 percent, respectively. The North's economy nevertheless remained far behind the South's. As of 2002, according to the Bank of Korea, the North's economy was 1/27 of the South's; the North's per capita income ($706) was 1/13 that of the South's ($8,900); and the North's foreign trade was 1/128.

Outside specialists advised that to revive the failed economy the North Korean regime must reform its autarkic national economy, operated according to the outmoded Stalinist model, and induce a large inflow of foreign capital. But the revised constitution rejected such prescriptions by stipulating that the nation must base itself on a self-sufficient economy. There was, however, a small loophole—Article 24 under Chapter 2, "Economy," allowed its citizens private property rights, declaring that the "state shall protect private property and guarantee its legal inheritance." In addition, Kim Jong Il relaxed some of the economic restrictions on DPRK citizens, such as allowing the individual acquisition of domestic animals and the purchase of small houses and commercial buildings. However, as Suh Dae-sook warned, "this [could] not be interpreted as a change in the [North's] basic economy policy."[79]

Suh's warning appeared to be borne out by regularly published editorials in *Rodong Sinmun* and the monthly *Kŭlloja* that stressed the primacy of a self-sufficient national economy. For example, on March 5, 1999, the paper cautioned against the "poison" contained in foreign aid extended in the name of economic cooperation. On September 7, 1999, a joint editorial of the paper and *Kŭlloja* repeated the theme that only a self-sufficient national economy was correct for the country and the people. The paper and the monthly repeatedly rejected the ideas of "globalization of the economy" and "open international economic community" proposed by Western scholars and bureaucrats.[80]

Nonetheless, new terms like *silli* (actual profit) began to appear one by one in *Rodong Sinmun*. On November 13, 1999, "The Guarantee of Actual

78 "Testimony of Stephen W. Linton, PhD, Chairman, Eugene Bell Foundation, Before the Senate Subcommittee on East Asian and Pacific Affairs," June 5, 2003.

79 Suh, "New Political Leadership," 77.

80 For example, see *Rodong Sinmun*, March 3 and September 1, 1998.

Profit in Economic Projects" stressed that "in economic projects, utilitarian (or, pragmatic) value (*silyong chŏk kach'i*) should be exhaustively calculated in order to guarantee economic interests." On January 1, 2000, a joint editorial of *Rodong Sinmun*, *Chosŏn Inmin'gun*, and *Ch'ongnyon chonwi* also repeated the same theme.

Around the same time, *Rodong Sinmun* began to discourage the "subjective desires" of party-state officials, workers, and peasants. Targets should be achieved not by "subjective desire," the paper stressed on November 12, 1999; instead, "advanced scientific technologies" should guide and control all economic projects. On July 24, 2000, a joint editorial of *Rodong Sinmun* and *Klloja* repeated the theme. In later years, the "thought that values science highly" (*kwahak chungsi sasang*) became a popular expression in speeches by Kim Jong Il and other leaders, as well as in articles appearing in North Korean official publications.

This new trend aligned with the regime's efforts to study the market economy, which began in 1997 when it first sent a "group of fifteen economic officials to Shanghai—the showcase of China's reform-minded opening-up policies of the previous two decades"—under the auspices of the United Nations Development Program. DPRK officials studying market economics overseas would number around four hundred through the period 1998 to June 2001, with field training undertaken in China, Australia, and Hungary.[81]

The North Korean regime's new emphasis on "actual profit" and "science and technology" led to Kim Jong Il's remarks on "new thinking and substantial change" during his January 2001 visit to China. Kim told his Chinese counterparts that he was greatly impressed by the "changes in Shanghai, which surpassed all imagination." He was reported to have chided his North Korean attendants: "What have you done until now? We should seek a substantial change."[82] From China, he went not to Pyongyang but to Sinŭiju, the harbor city in North Korea's Chagang Province. From January 21 to 23 he inspected factories there, stressing the need for *hyŏksin* (reform) and *saeroun chŏnhwan* (new transformation) based on "modern science and technology."[83]

Two months later, *Rodong Sinmun* announced the regime's launch of its

"new thinking campaign" to adjust ideological perspectives and working attitudes to advance the "state competitiveness" that was required in the new

81 *Vantage Point*, 25, no. 1 (January 2002): 34.
82 *Rodong Sinmun*, January 15, 2001.
83 *Rodong Sinmun*, January 22–24, 2001.

age. . . . [Pyongyang] called for reforms in all fields, even to the sphere of ideology, by emphasizing the "cultivation of capabilities needed in the twenty-first century."[84]

Surprisingly, the paper contended, on March 29, 2001, that "a self-sustaining economy should accommodate the principle of actual profit."

Kim Jong Il's "new thinking campaign" reached a climax on July 1, 2002, when the regime launched measures to overcome the crisis by improving its methods of economic management. Discussing the state of the DPRK in 2002, Ahn Yinhay (An In-hae) aptly noted that "the measures were aimed at improving, rather than reforming, management of the North Korean economy by adjusting prices drastically, rather than through a long-term policy." Ahn summarized the measures:

> The state-managed rationing system was abolished, the foreign exchange rate was adjusted to a realistic level, and currency exchange was freed to strengthen the consumption capacity of the people. The economy has been partially monetized. North Korea can be seen as preparing to adopt a market system because these changes are preconditions to a market-oriented economy. New management techniques such as incentives and accountability are being adopted to make people actively participate in the economy. Moreover, independent accounting at enterprises has been reinforced, product markets have been set up, wage incentives increased, organization principles in the agricultural sector improved, and the self-managed distribution system for agricultural products extended.[85]

In sum, the new program was a "policy of stabilization through intentional inflation." Some observers saw it as a step in the direction of a market-based economy in order to alleviate the country's desperate situation.[86] However, it would not succeed in improving economic management.

The fact that the North Korean regime took such measures reflected the severity of the nation's crisis. The chronic food shortage, breakdown of the public distribution of commodities including food rationing, and widespread disease were all too evident. Outside observers frequently reported on the miserable conditions of the North Korean people. In October 1997

84 *Rodong Sinmun*, March 6, 2001, as quoted in Ahn Yinhay, "North Korea in 2001: At a Crossroads," *Asian Survey* 42, no. 1 (January–February 2002): 47.

85 Yinhay Ahn, "North Korea in 2002: A Survival Game," *Asian Survey* 43, no. 1 (January–February 2003): 51–52.

86 Lee Jung-Chul, "The Implications of North Korea's Reform Program and Its Effects on State Capacity," *Korea and World Affairs* 26, no. 3 (Fall 2002): 357.

United States congressman Tony Hall, in a statement upon return from his third visit to North Korea, said:

> Each time I have seen clear signs of a famine's hidden horrors, and what I saw this week reinforced my sense that most of the Korean people there have slid even further into trouble. . . . People in the countryside continue to teeter on the brink of a massive disaster.[87]

Back home from a survey tour of North Korea in February 1998, a Swedish official said millions of North Koreans were on the verge of starvation. The U.S. Central Intelligence Agency estimated one million North Koreans starved to death during the period 1995–98. Quoting a deputy bureau chief in the North Korean Agricultural Commission, Ch'a In-dŏk, the Chinese news agency *Xinhua* reported on January 20, 1998, that many North Koreans had died as a result of natural disasters like typhoons and tsunamis, another indication of the emergency food situation in the North.[88] Andrew Natsios of World Vision evaluated the condition of North Korean children as comparable to what he had seen in Ethiopia during the famine of the mid-1980s. But not all experts were in agreement; after examining the available materials, one North Korean watcher argued, "the report that millions of people died from starvation seems to be an exaggeration." He suggested that "mass starvation mainly occurs among the lower classes of the population, and children in particular."[89]

A vivid observation was made by Elisabeth Rosenthal, a *New York Times* correspondent in Beijing and physician, who visited North Korea in early February 2001 with AmeriCares, a private United States–based relief organization:

> After nearly a decade of crisis, the human tragedy in North Korea continues to outpace and outwit relief efforts. North Koreans are less hungry than during the worst food shortages, in 1997, thanks in large part to international aid. . . . But the ongoing deterioration of the country's infrastructure—particularly its health and sanitation systems and its energy supply—has left many North Koreans in a continued downward spiral.[90]

87 *Congressman Tony Hall News*, October 17, 1997, 1.

88 Xinhua, "DPRK in Urgent Need of Foreign Food Aid: Official," January 20, 1998.

89 Kim Philo, "The Sociopolitical Impact of Food Crisis in North Korea," *Korea and World Affairs* 23, no. 2 (Summer 1999): 213–14. According to official figures, at least 220,000 people died of starvation between 1995 and 1998, but South Korea and the United States estimate that as many as two million may have died. See Ser Myo-ja, "North's Infant Death Rate Stays High," *JoongAng Daily*, December 20, 2003.

90 Elisabeth Rosenthal, "Collapse of Health System Adds to North Korea's Crisis," *New York Times*, February 20, 2001.

The Emergence and Education of Kim Jong Chul and Kim Jong Un

As detailed in chapter 4, Kim Jong Il had sent Sung Hye-rim to Moscow in 1975. From 1976 Kim lived with Ko Yong-hŭi as a couple, but without a formal marriage, producing two sons, Kim Jong Chul (Chŏng-ch'ŏl) and Kim Jong Un (Chŏng-ŭn), and one daughter, Kim Yu-jŏng. Kim Jong Il apparently had a happy life with Ko Yong-hŭi. Fujimoto has attested that Ko frequently aided Kim with thoughtful advice and, as noted earlier, once even saved his life. The relationship may have been tested when, in early May 1998, Ko Yong-hŭi's younger sister Ko Yong-suk, her brother-in-law Pak Kŏn, a senior diplomat active in Geneva, and the couple's sons exiled themselves to the United States from Geneva with a huge amount of U.S. dollars that had been deposited in a Swiss bank for Kim Jong Il. According to sources that included South Korean intelligence officers, "Ko and her husband defected because they knew so many secrets of the internal goings-on in Pyongyang and were scared . . . the U.S. authorities gave the couple new identities and 'through plastic surgery made them into completely different people.'"[91] Despite this family betrayal, however, Kim Jong Il took no action against Ko Yong-hŭi, recalling that "a couple of times, she saved my life."[92]

What was known about brothers Kim Jong Chul and Kim Jong Un? It should be stressed that information about both is still limited. It was only after 2007 that Jong Chul and Jong Un made regular public appearances, albeit still without being identified in the media. Fujimoto Kenji might be the only outsider who was able to closely observe them in the North. In January 1990, at his exclusive villa in Sinch'ŏn County, South Hwanghae Province, Kim Jong Il had a meeting with top secretaries of the KWPCC, including Hŏ Tam (international affairs), Chang Sŏng-t'aek (organization and guidance), Kim Yong-sun (inter-Korean affairs), Kim Ki-nam (propaganda and agitation), and Kwŏn Hŭi-kyŏng (foreign intelligence). After lunch, Kim Jong Il, accompanied by Ko Yong-hŭi, ordered everyone to gather at the center of the villa. When they arrived Jong Chul and Jong Un were already there, in military uniforms and standing at attention, despite being only ten and seven years old, respectively. Fujimoto, who at the time was attending to Kim Jong Il, saw the two boys for the first time. Kim Jong Il let all the attendees introduce themselves to his sons. It seemed that except for Chang Sŏng-t'aek, and the boys' uncle (Kyŏng-hŭi's husband), all the other secretaries were likewise seeing the boys in person for the first time. They referred

91 "Kim Jong-un's Aunt Fled to U.S." *Korea JoongAng Daily*, November 5, 2013, 3.
92 Fujimoto, *Pukhan*, 74.

to them as "princes" (Fujimoto later came to know that Yu-jŏng was called "princess"). They also nicknamed Jong Chul "Big General" and Jong Un "Little General," but when Jong Un expressed his dislike of the latter nickname they instead referred to him as "Comrade General" and Jong Chul as "Comrade Big General."[93]

As Fujimoto recalls, when he first outstretched his hand to Jong Chul, the boy warmly shook his hand. However, when he offered to shake hands with Jong Un, the boy "glared fiercely" at him, as if he were thinking, "You abhorrent Japanese!" It was only when Kim Jong Il introduced the chef that Jong Un weakly shook his hand. A week later, as the two "princes" tried to fly a kite with their mother in the villa's garden, Fujimoto lent the boys a hand. Seeing that the boys were pleased to get his help, Kim Jong Il instructed Fujimoto to become their play companion. According to Fujimoto:

> Jong Chul and Jong Un always played together. They especially loved playing basketball. Jong Un loved watching American basketball games on television. The eldest son of Ko Yong-hŭi's younger sister, who seemed to have been about Jong Un's age, frequently joined them. In addition, two pretty girls of similar age to the boys were assigned to Jong Chul and Jong Un.[94]

Regarding Kim Jong Un's love of basketball, Fujimoto further notes that the boy passed up no opportunity to play the game and would even defy his father's instructions to "rest for forty-five minutes after eating"—Kim Jong Un "couldn't even wait five minutes" before he would want to play again.[95]

Neither Jong Chul nor Jong Un were ever enrolled in elementary schools or junior high schools in the North. They were instead tutored by specially selected teachers at Kim Jong Il's Pyongyang home. They loved Japanese comics and movies; occasionally Fujimoto would teach them some Japanese. According to him, while Jong Chul had a gentle character and showed interest in music in general and popular guitar in particular, Jong Un tended to be hyper-competitive. Jong Un was assigned top-level instructors to teach him marksmanship and how to drive a car. (After Kim Jong Un became Kim Jong Il's successor, North Korean publications disseminated the legend that from the age of three he was able to hit any target with a gun. Fujimoto was dismissive: "I went shooting with Kim Jong Un when he was seventeen and he couldn't hit every mark."[96]) Chang Sŏng-t'aek was solely responsible for the boys' home-schooling. Since they lacked classmates, whenever they

93 O, "Fujimoto Kenji," 66–67.
94 Ibid., 68
95 Lee Young-jong and Jeong Yong-soo, "Kim's Sushi Chef Shares Memories of Jong Un," *Korea JoongAng Daily*, October 26, 2010, 3.
96 Lee and Jeong, "Kim's Sushi Chef Shares Memories."

wanted companions to play with, students their age were called in. Fujimoto recalled that Jong Un showed a strong disposition to be a leader: "Jong Un has also always been at the center of groups and he truly received Kim Jong Il's DNA."[97] With Jong Chul and Jong Un being raised in such a "royal" and completely secluded environment, we can only wonder how well Kim Il Sung knew his two grandsons. Yet a former KWP cadre once recalled a story "well known to every senior secretary" of the time Kim Il Sung praised Jong Chul by saying, "If Jong Il is a genius, Jong Chul is a super genius."[98]

In the 1990s, Kim Jong Il sent his two sons to Bern, Switzerland. First, Kim Jong Chul, under the pseudonym Pak Ch'ŏl (using the family name of the North Korean ambassador to Geneva, who was Ko Yong-hŭi's younger sister's husband), studied at the International School of Bern from September 1993 to August 1998. The school's K–12 tuition cumulatively amounted to more than $300,000 and "most students were the children of European royal families or ambassadors in developed countries."[99] Mun Kwang Tschol (Mun Kwang-ch'ŏl), a North Korean whose background has never been revealed, also attended this school. According to Cheong Seong-chang, who exhaustively investigated Jong Chul's school days in Bern, Mun—who was sturdily built—seemed to have been Jong Chul's bodyguard as well as his friend. Cheong continued,

> Unlike the eldest son, Kim Jong Nam, who had gone to an international school in Geneva all alone, Kim Jong Chul enjoyed his years in the company of a friend. . . . While Kim Jong Chul was enrolled in the school, rumors spread widely among his classmates that he was a son of a North Korean general and that Mun Kwang Tschol was his bodyguard.[100]

According to the school's principal at the time, Jong Chul was an ordinary hard-working schoolboy who, like others his age, had a sense of humor and enjoyed sports. He noted, "By the time he left school, Kim [Jong Chul] could speak English fluently. It must have been difficult for him to catch up with his class work because lessons were given in English, but Jong Chul always completed his assignments." In subjects other than English, the principal recollected, "He did above average. . . . He worked hard and focused particularly on math, which was his strength."[101] However, Ko Yong-suk, Ko Yong-hŭi's younger sister, remarked to U.S. officials after her defection to

97 Ibid.
98 Cheong Seong-chang, "Kim Jong Il's Illness and Prospects for Post-Kim Leadership," *East Asian Review* 20, no. 4 (Winter 2008): 22.
99 Ibid., 19.
100 Ibid.
101 Ibid.

the United States that Kim Jong Chul was "not very smart and liked to play rather than study."[102]

Jong Chul, unexpectedly, associated with and even befriended students from the United States and South Korea, at a time when there was much enmity between the two Koreas. Friends recalled that Jong Chul liked playing basketball and admired the NBA player Dennis Rodman. Whenever he played basketball, he "wore a Chicago Bulls shirt with Rodman's uniform number on the back." An American friend noted that "Jong Chul is not the type of guy who would do something to harm others. He is a nice guy who could never be a villain."[103] Later, Jong Chul would idolize Hollywood action star Jean-Claude Van Damme's physique. After returning to the North, Jong Chul was enrolled in a special class at the Kim Il Sung Comprehensive Military University from 2001 to 2006. It was said Ko Yong-hŭi urged Kim Jong Il to let Jong Chul (as well as Jong Un) "continue the tradition of military-first politics."[104]

Jong Un followed his elder brother's steps. In 1996, under the alias Pak Ŭn, he was also admitted to the International School of Bern. As a classmate recounted, "His English was bad at first. He had a strong accent and was given extra lessons. He also learned German. . . . His English got better but not his German. He was good in maths."[105] As Jong Un— despite an extravagant outlay of money—was unable to earn even the equivalent of a General Certificate of Secondary Education, Kim Jong Il allowed him to study at Liebefeld School, a public school, beginning August 1998. Wearing Nike trainers, a Chicago Bulls sweatshirt, and jeans, he was introduced to class 6A as the son of a North Korean diplomat. One of Kim Jong Un's former teachers, Peter Burri, said, "He worked enthusiastically on everything. He was good at mathematics, but his grades in English and German were also good."[106]

In contrast, his classmate Joao Micaelo, son of a Portuguese diplomat, recalled:

We weren't the dimmest kids in class but neither were we the cleverest. We were always in the second tier. He tried hard to express himself but he was not very good at German and became flustered when asked to give answers to a problem. The teachers would see him struggling ashamedly and then move on. They left him in peace. He left without getting any exam results at all. He was much more interested in football and basketball than lessons.

102 Ibid.
103 Ibid., 18–21.
104 Quoted in Cheong Seong-chang, "Kim Jong Eun's Early Life and Personality," *Vantage Point*, July 2009, 11.
105 Allan Hall, "Dim Jong Un; The Dictator's Son Who Came to Study in Europe," *The Sun* (London), November 24, 2010, 24–26
106 Cheong, "Kim Jong Eun's Early Life," 12.

Micaelo also spoke about Jong Un's private life: "He didn't live at the embassy but in a flat in a nice residential area near the school. He was surrounded by the best gadgets that the rest of us kids couldn't afford—TVs, video recorder, a Sony Play-Station. He had a cook, a driver, a private teacher."[107] Other students recalled that he was skilled in skiing and snowboarding. A former homeroom teacher, Simone Kuhn, related that he was "quiet, and appeared as if he were hidden in a veil of mystery."[108] In January 2001 Kim Jong Un left the school and returned to the North.

The depiction above of Kim Jong Un gives the superficial impression of a dull boy interested only in sports and luxurious living. There is some evidence, however, that he was maturing and thinking about more consequential things. During an August 2000 summer vacation spent in North Korea, Kim Jong Un had hours-long talks with Fujimoto, during which he raised serious issues about his country's situation. For example, he asked Fujimoto, "Why are goods so insufficient and rare in the DPRK's department stores and regular stores, in contrast to those in Western countries?" He observed, "North Korea, apart from uranium, lacks natural resources. It also suffers from a lack of electricity. Even in our special family villas, we sometimes experience power failures." Lamenting the underdevelopment of industrial technologies of the North, he asked Fujimoto, "Under such conditions, how are our people managing their lives?" Jong Un also mentioned the "economic success" of the People's Republic of China. He said, "I heard from my father that China is doing very well in many fields, including industry, commerce, hotels, and agriculture. In particular, I praise China's success in agriculture. While feeding its own 1.3 billion people, China is even exporting grains to foreign countries." He concluded, "After exhaustively examining our problems and China's methods, the DPRK should learn from China, and emulate it as our model." Kim Jong Un also revealed that he had secretly visited Japan with his mother. "Japan was defeated in the Second World War by the United States. But they have succeeded in rehabilitating their country and are living in material prosperity. What should North Korea do?" Fujimoto felt that the new and matured Jong Un had completely changed—but he was still strong-willed and overbearing.[109]

Between 2002 and December 2006, as his elder brother had done, Kim Jong Un studied in a special class at the Kim Il Sung Comprehensive Military University. This time, too, his mother was said to have strongly urged Kim Jong Il to have him study there. North Korean publications claimed that he

107 Hall, "Dim Jong Un," 25.
108 Quoted in Cheong, "Kim Jong Eun's Early Life," 11.
109 O, "Fujimoto Kenji," 78–79.

graduated summa cum laude from the three-year course for artillery commanders and its two-year graduate course. He supposedly submitted the dissertation, "A Simulation for the Improvement of Accuracy in the Operational Map by the Global Positioning System (GPS)," in fulfillment of the final graduation requirement. Major General Kim Yŏng-ch'ŏl allegedly helped him with the dissertation. More important to Kim Jong Un's career was that at this school he made friends with future North Korean military elites.[110]

On May 24, 2004, Ko Yong-hŭi died either of breast cancer or a cerebral embolism while in a Paris hospital. In contrast to Sung Hye-rim, a funeral service for Ko was held in Pyongyang, and she was buried there—although the two events were carried out in secrecy.[111] Two years after her death, Kim Ok, an intimate friend of Ko, became Kim Jong Il's new common-law wife. Born in 1964 and graduated from the Pyongyang University of Music and Dance, she worked first as Kim Jong Il's secretary, in charge of his medical schedule. It was she who accompanied Cho Myŏng-rok, KPA first vice marshal and NDC first vice-chairman, on his official visit to the White House in October 2000. She also accompanied Kim Jong Il on his unofficial visit to China in January 2006. On those two occasions, she was referred to as an NDC division director. Kim Jong Il even assigned her the secret task of carrying Ko Yong-hŭi's corpse from Paris to Pyongyang aboard his exclusive airplane.[112] In contrast to Ko, Kim Ok even appeared in the North Korean media a couple of times, although without her identity being revealed. Fujimoto recalled that she was "a cute and attractive woman who resembled Miyazawa Rie, a top Japanese movie actress in the 1980s." Denying a rumor that Kim Jong Un might have in fact been the son of Kim Jong Il and Kim Ok, Fujimoto asserted that the couple produced no children.[113] With the rise of Kim Ok to de facto First Lady, her father, Kim Hyo, also prospered. In 2009, he was elected to the Twelfth Supreme People's Assembly. For a KWP central party functionary to become a SPA delegate was indeed exceptional.

110 Cheong Seong-chang, "Kim Chŏng-ŭn ŭn nugu in'ga" [Who is Kim Jong Un], *Wŏlgan Chungang*, no. 420 (October 2010): 38; Hwang Il-do, "T'ŭkmyŏng: Pukhan yeja rŭl ch'achjare" [The special mission: Confirm the successor of North Korea], *Sindonga*, no. 615 (December 2010): 338–39.

111 *Chungang Ilbo*, September 2, 2004, 4.

112 Yi Yŏng-jong, "Sesŏp naejŏn" [Internecine struggle], *Wŏlgan Chunang*, no. 420 (November 2010): 48.

113 O Tong-ryong, "Fujimoto Kenji hoegyŏn" [Interview with Fujimoto Kenji], *Wŏlgan Chosun*, no. 368, November 2010, 72. See also Cheong Seong-chang, "Fujimoto Kenji hoegyŏn" [Interview with Fujimoto Kenji], *Sisa Journal*, no. 1,004 (January 14, 2009): 18–19.

6 Kim Jong Il's Designation of Kim Jong Un
   As His Successor, 2002–11

Wavering Between Kim Jong Chul and Kim Jong Un, 2002–04

Kim Jong Il's Initial Decision upon His Hwan'gap

The year 2002 was a significant one both for the DPRK and for Kim Jong Il. The DPRK's relations with the United States began a new phase on January 29 when President George W. Bush included it, along with Iran and Iraq, in his "axis of evil," the list of nations arming to threaten the peace of the world. In his State of the Union address, delivered before a joint session of Congress, Bush called the North a "regime arming with missiles and weapons of mass destruction, while starving its citizens."[1] The next day, the Center for Strategic and International Studies (CSIS) in Washington, DC, released a report showing America's strong and deep suspicion of the North's ballistic missiles as well as its nuclear, biological, and chemical warfare programs. The report included an ominous prediction by the Department of Defense that the "most likely large scale regional war scenario over the near term, which would involve the United States, would be on the Korean Peninsula."[2]

North Korea's reaction was immediate. On February 1 its foreign ministry spokesman said, "This is, in fact, little short of a declaration of war against the DPRK."[3] South Korea's Kim Dae Jung administration also criticized

1 "Text of President Bush's 2002 State of the Union Address," http://www.washingtonpost.com/wp-srv/onpolitics/transcripts/sou012902.htm.

2 Anthony H. Cordesman, *Proliferation in the "Axis of Evil": North Korea, Iran, and Iraq* (Washington, DC: The Center for Strategic and International Studies, 2002), 2–4, based on Department of Defense, "Proliferation and Response," January 2001, North Korea section.

3 *Rodong Sinmun*, February 2, 2002, 1. See also Seo Soo-min, "NK Likens Bush's Remarks to Declaration of War," *Korea Times*, February 2, 2002, 1.

Bush, arguing that his speech could destabilize the Korean Peninsula. In September Kim Jong Il succeeded in inviting Japanese prime minister Koizumi Junichiro to Pyongyang. At the first-ever summit between North Korea and Japan, Kim apologized for the "abduction of eleven Japanese citizens to serve as instructors for his terrorists, and [gave] assurances on the return of the four still living." In return, Koizumi apologized for Japan's colonial control of Korea. The surprise summit opened the way for the two countries to break the stalemate that characterized their earlier negotiations to normalize relations. It became clear that not only South Korea but also Japan, "the United States' two main allies in North Asia, [disagreed] with the uncompromising stance taken by Washington toward Pyongyang."[4]

As if to attempt to reverse this newly emerging trend in Northeast Asia, about one month later the Bush administration contended that the North had been, for the previous several years, conducting a major clandestine nuclear weapons development program using highly enriched uranium (HEU). The Bush administration claimed—based on statements that emerged during U.S.–North Korea talks held in Pyongyang on October 4— that "North Korea has a program to enrich uranium for nuclear weapons in violation of the Agreed Framework and other agreements."[5] The North denied the Bush administration's allegation. Soon after, the Bush administration stopped its supply of fuel oil to the North, which it had pledged to provide in the 1994 Agreed Framework; the North responded by reactivating its nuclear program at Yongbyon, which had been frozen under the accord. In early January 2003, the North went a major step further by declaring its withdrawal from the Treaty on the Non-Proliferation of Nuclear Weapons (NPT), the first member ever to do so. In this way, the so-called second nuclear crisis on the Korean Peninsula started.

Amid this increasing tension and friction with the Bush administration, Kim Jong Il on February 16 celebrated his *hwan'gap* (sixtieth birthday), an occasion generally regarded in Korea as a turning point in one's life. Three months later Sung Hye-rim, his common-law wife and Jong Nam's mother, died in a Paris hospital. In hindsight, we may guess that it was at this point that Kim Jong Il decided to start a campaign to prepare for succession. Ko

4 John Larkin, "Breakthrough: Japan-North Korea Ties," *Far Eastern Economic Review*, September 26, 2002, 24.

5 Yoichi Funabashi, *The Peninsula Question: A Chronicle of the Second Korean Nuclear Crisis* (Washington, DC: The Brookings Institution Press, 2007), 93–108; quote sourced from Richard Boucher's October 16, 2002, press statement for the U.S. Department of State.

Yong-hŭi was also pushing Kim Jong Il to designate their first son, Kim Jong Chul, as successor. Ko, who had been treated for mastitis in 1993 and for paralysis of her right hand in 2000, may have anticipated a premature death and wanted to see her eldest son designated as successor as early as possible.[6] To that end, Ko—according to testimony from defectors—had in the 1990s secured the support of Kim Yong-sun, KWPCC secretary for inter-Korean relations and someone well known in the West. Fujimoto recalled that Kim Yong-sun was an expert at magic tricks and occasionally entertained at parties hosted by Kim Jong Il. Ironically, it is said he died in October 2003 from injuries in a drunk-driving accident after attending Ko's June 16 birthday party.[7]

As we have discussed, Kim Jong Il had married informally five times and had fathered at least three sons and three daughters. Under a monarchy, the firstborn son is normally the successor. But the DPRK is not a monarchy, at least not constitutionally. Therefore, the designation of a successor by the incumbent power-holder, without any legal or institutional process, is itself unconstitutional in North Korea. Moreover, Kim Jong Il's designation of his son as his successor would extend the Kim regime's rule over quasi-Stalinist North Korea to a third generation. Anticipating that this move would spur intense criticism and even resistance—not to mention mockery—the North Korean ideologues further elaborated their so-called theories on succession from the 1980s and 1990s. These obscurantist theories were replete with abstract terminology and were virtually incomprehensible to outsiders living in democracies.[8]

At least four of the succession theories merit comment. The first suggested the primacy of "purity in blood" in the succession. The successor should have "purity of blood," meaning that he should descend from the anti-Japanese independence fighters of the colonial period. Since Kim Il Sung and his first wife Kim Jong Suk fought against the Japanese with Mount Paektu as their main military base, Kim Il Sung's successors were to be those who had inherited his "purity of blood imbued with the holy spirit of Mount Paektu." Already in March 1967, using this sort of twisted logic, Kim Jong Il had helped Kim Il Sung devise "ten principles in establishing

6 Cheong Seong-chang, "Kim Jong Eun's Early Life and Personality," *Vantage Point*, July 2009, 9.

7 Cheong, "Kim Jong Il's Illness," 23.

8 Summarized from the North Korean publications by Paik Hak-soon (Paek Hak-sun). See his *Pukhan kwŏllyŏk ŭi yŏksa: Sasang, chŏngch'esŏng, kujo* [The history of power in North Korea: Ideas, identities, and structures] (Seoul: Hanul Academy, 2011), 656–57.

the unitary ideology system of the KWP based on Kim Il Sung's thoughts," under which any thoughts other than those of Kim Il Sung were to be eradicated. Kim Jong Il went one step further. As explained earlier, he had argued that while Kim Il Sung's deceased first wife (Kim Jong Suk), who had participated in Kim Il Sung's anti-Japanese guerrilla movement, should be sanctified, his second wife (Kim Sŏng-ae), who had no connection with it, should be demoted in political status. And he argued that only the offspring of Kim Il Sung and Kim Jong Suk were regarded to have inherited Kim Il Sung's "pure blood imbued with the holy spirit of Mount Paektu."

A second theory maintained that the successor should be chosen not from the same generation as the present leader, but from the next generation—thus Kim Jong Il's successor should be chosen not from his peers, but from his son's generation. A third proposed that the successor should be chosen within the party by the party, thereby reconfirming the principle of the primacy of the party over the military. Finally, a fourth theory contended that only the Suryŏng was empowered to designate his successor—in short, only Kim Jong Il had that authority.

Based on these succession theories, the only eligible candidates for succession were Kim Jong Il's three sons: Kim Jong Nam, Kim Jong Chul, and Kim Jong Un. If Korean tradition and customs were to be observed, the first son, Jong Nam, should have become the successor. However, he had already become an exiled "prince" by the 1980s, living mainly in Moscow or Geneva, while visiting the North occasionally but in secret. Fujimoto Kenji testified that he had neither seen Kim Jong Nam nor heard of his name during his own thirteen-year stay in the North, and on that basis he predicted as early as 2001 that Jong Nam would never become the successor.[9]

Fujimoto's observation was correct in the sense that, from the beginning, Kim Jong Nam would not be considered for succession by Kim Jong Il. This was because he is an illegitimate child, and his mother, Sung Hye-rim, had already had a daughter in her first marriage before she gave birth to Jong Nam. Kim Kyŏng-hŭi is said to have once humiliated Sung by saying, "because you are older than my brother and you have your own daughter by your first marriage, I had better raise Jong Nam in your place."[10] On top of this, Sung Hye-rim belonged to a wealthy family with an intellectual background who had come to the north from the south—a triple jeopardy

9 Fujimoto Kenji, *Pukhan ŭi hugyeja, oe Kim Chŏng-ŭn in'ga?* [Why was Kim Jong Un chosen as North Korea's successor?], trans. Han Yu-hŭi (Seoul: Maxmedia, 2010), 60–62.

10 Yi Han-yŏng, *Taedong kang royal p'aemilli Sŏul chamhaeng sip-sa-nyŏn* [Fourteen years of secret lives in Seoul by a North Korean royal family] (Seoul: Dong-A Ilbosa, 1996), 27.

in North Korea. Pointing out these deficiencies, Hwang Chang-yŏp had on more than one occasion predicted that Jong Nam would never become the successor.[11]

Kim Jong Nam's political standing was further crippled when his aunt Sung Hye-rang (and perhaps his mother Sung Hye-rim, as well) attempted to take refuge in the West. In February 1996 Hye-rang succeeded in defecting to Paris from Moscow via Geneva. But Hye-rim is said to have given up the idea of defection out of concern for her son's safety. Also, according to a reliable North Korea watcher close to Chinese intelligence sources, Kim Jong Il became enraged when Jong Nam proposed policy reform and the opening up of the North. As a result, Kim Jong Nam was not allowed to settle in one place and was forced to roam around North Korea and China, in semi-exile.[12]

A year later, Hye-rang's son Il-nam, who had occasionally exposed the private lives of the "holy family" after his defection to South Korea, was assassinated in the suburbs of Seoul. The South Korean intelligence agency speculated that Jong Nam had sent his agents to kill his cousin in a bid to regain his father's confidence.[13] Such speculation lacks credibility since there is no persuasive evidence that Kim Jong Nam *had* such agents. Rather, North Korea's highest agency in charge of Southern operations may have been responsible.

Kim Jong Nam's failed attempt to visit Tokyo Disneyland hurt him even more. On May 1, 2001, Kim, along with two women and a boy, believed to be his wife, maid, and son, was detained upon arrival at Narita International Airport from Singapore. Japanese authorities leaked the fact that the four carried forged Dominican passports, whose holders did not require entry visas. They were deported to Beijing in view of about one hundred reporters and cameramen. Photographs of the group revealed a disheveled and unshaven Kim Jong Nam, as well as the women's expensive sunglasses, designer handbags, and other luxury goods. Enraged at the effect of the images on North Korea's international image, Kim Jong Il reportedly ordered his son to live outside the DPRK. In Seoul, there was speculation that Ko Yong-hŭi might have leaked his travel itinerary to Japanese authorities to expose him and thus hurt his internal standing.[14]

11 Kim Yŏn-gwang, "Hwang Chang-yŏp hŏegyŏn" [An interview with Hwang Chang-yŏp], *Wŏlgan Chosun*, March 2003, 111.

12 Paek Sŭng-gu, "Chungguk ttŏnonŭn Kim Chŏng Nam" [Kim Jong Nam who roams over China], *Wŏlgan Chosun*, October 2011, 217.

13 Ch'oe Yŏng-jae, "Kim Chŏng Nam Misŭt'eri" [The Kim Jong Nam mystery], *Sindonga*, July 2001, 131–33.

14 *Dong-A Ilbo*, May 7, 2001, A3.

A year later in May 2002 Sung Hye-rim died of a chronic disease in a Moscow hospital. With Jong Nam in attendance, a simple funeral service was held for her in secret; she was buried not in Pyongyang but in Moscow, without any formal announcement by the North Korean government, and not even under her own name, but under an alias, O Sun-hŭi.[15] As of this writing, Jong Nam lives in Singapore, sometimes visiting Hong Kong and Beijing, and giving occasional paid interviews to Japanese television.[16] On September 30, 2011, it was made public that he has one son (Kim Kŭm-sol, b. 1997) by his wife, and another son (Kim Han-sol, b. 1995) and a daughter (Kim Sol-hŭi, b. 1999) by a mistress.[17]

Superficially at least, Kim Jong Il's other two sons, Kim Jong Chul and Kim Jong Un, seem to be vulnerable to some of the same criticisms as Kim Jong Nam. Jong Chul and Jong Un are also illegitimate children. Their mother, Ko Yong-hŭi, and her parents were repatriated from Japan to North Korea in the early 1960s; in the North there are derogatory terms for such immigrants, so her background was a problem as well. To boot, their mother's younger sister defected to the United States with her husband and sons. However, there are considerable differences between the situation of Jong Nam and that of the brothers Kim Jong Chul and Kim Jong Un. Ko Yong-hŭi had never been married before becoming involved with Kim Jong Il; perhaps more important is that Kim Jong Il left Sung Hye-rim in favor of Ko Yong-hŭi, and then maintained their de facto married life for more than twenty-eight years until her death, whereupon she received a Pyongyang burial. As Hwang Chang-yŏp observed, "Once the king's love is transferred to another woman, it is natural that her son would become the crown prince."[18] Moreover, as Sung Hye-rang aptly pointed out, if Kim Jong Il were to declare Ko Yong-hŭi as his legitimate wife, Jong Chul and Jong Un would be recognized as their legitimate children.[19]

15 Chŏng Wi-yong, correspondent of *Dong-A Ilbo* to Moscow, was able to locate Sung Hye-rim's tomb in Moscow. In the list of those who were buried in the cemetery, she was recorded under the pseudonym, O Sun-hŭi. *Dong-A Ilbo*, July 28, 2009, A1.

16 Kim Jong Nam went to Singapore after fleeing Macau, supposedly in fear for his life. Julian Ryall, "Kim Jong-il's Son Reappears in Singapore," *The Telegraph*, November 15, 2012, http://www.telegraph.co.uk/news/worldnews/asia/northkorea/9680540/Kim-Jong -ils-son-reappears-in-Singapore.html.

17 Kim Han-sol was placed under police protection in France following the reported execution of Chang Sŏng-t'aek in December 2013. James Rothwell, "Kim Jong-un's Nephew 'Under Police Protection' at His Exclusive University in France," *The Independent*, December 18, 2013.

18 Kim, "Hwang Chang-yŏp hoegyŏn," 115.

19 Sung Hye-rang, *Tŭngnamu chip* [The wisteria house] (Seoul: Chisik Nara, 2000), 418.

There are indications that, between the two boys, Kim Jong Il had his eye on Kim Jong Un for the succession since the boy's childhood. Fujimoto had already predicted in 2003 that Jong Un would become the successor. He recalled that Jong Chul was a child who never got angry and had little ambition. As he observed Jong Chul's behavior, Kim Jong Il would note to Fujimoto that "Jong Chul cannot be the successor since he is effeminate."[20] (It has been noted in fact that Jong Chul favors his mother in appearance.) It was even rumored that Jong Chul had a "fatal disease"—"excessive female hormones, which makes him even bosomy."[21] Another strike against Jong Chul was that, as a high school student in Bern, he had composed a poem, "My Ideal World," in which he expressed a deep hatred of war and nuclear weapons.[22]

In contrast, Jong Un's young personality resembled that of his father; from boyhood, he demonstrated leadership skills and a strong desire to win. In short, while the young Jong Un showed *tokham* or "venomousness," which both Kim Il Sung and Kim Jong Il regarded as an important leadership attribute, Jong Chul did not. Kim Jong Il openly expressed his deep love for and trust of Jong Un, which were reflected even in the seating arrangements at family feasts.[23]

Fujimoto recalled a celebratory banquet for Kim Jong Un's ninth birthday held on January 8, 1992, at a villa in Wonsan. At Kim Jong Il's instructions, the band began playing a new song, "Footsteps":

> Following our General Kim's footsteps,
> Spreading the spirit of February,
> We, the people, march forward to a bright future.[24]

"The spirit of February" was a reference to Kim Jong Il, who was born in February. Thus, "our General Kim" was the person who would lead the country in the future, spreading the spirit of Kim Jong Il. In light of the fact that the song was dedicated to Kim Jong Un, Fujimoto immediately sensed it signaled Kim Jong Il's tacit designation of Kim Jong Un as the successor.[25]

20 Fujimoto, *Kim Jong Il's Chef*, 130.

21 *Shugan Kendai*, February 11, 2006, quoted in Seo Dong-shin, "Speculation Rekindled over NK Power Succession," *Korea Times*, February 18, 2006, 2.

22 An interview with his former classmate Steve Walaza broadcast on December 22, 2011, by the Korean Broadcasting System (KBS). For the first report on the poem in question, see Sin Chŏng-sŏn, "Kim Jong Chul ŭi Si" [Kim Jong Chul's poem], *Chosun Ilbo*, July 20, 2009, A4.

23 Fujimoto, *Kim Jong Il's Chef*, 227–28.

24 Quoted in Fujimoto, *Pukhan*, 125–26.

25 Ibid.

Kim Jong Il's Futile Attempts to Groom Kim Jong Chul, 2002–06

While there is evidence that Kim Jong Il long favored Kim Jong Un as his successor, the actual process of grooming was not so clear-cut. He seems to have taken initial steps to groom Jong Chul as his successor, evidenced in part by his positioning of Jong Chul "as a senior instructor in the central organ's division of the KWP Central Committee Organization and Guidance Department." When we recall that Kim Jong Il began his career in the same office as an instructor in 1964 and a senior instructor in 1966, it amounts to the son following his father's career path.[26] According to a North Korean defector, the slogan "Let's Establish Comrade Kim Jong Chul's Working System" could be found in the KWP Central Committee OGD around 2002 and there were "senior North Korean leaders who spoke highly of Kim Jong Chul's generosity and sharpness."[27]

In August 2002 Kim Jong Il initiated a campaign to prepare for the succession—but without mentioning the actual name of the successor—with the KPA's publication of the sixteen-page pamphlet, *Our Respected Mother Who Is Loyal to Our Beloved Supreme Commander Is the Loyalist among Loyalists.* Although the text did not explicitly state the name of the mother in question, most KWP and KPA cadres could identify her as Ko Yong-hŭi. She was elevated to the same status as Kim Jong Suk, Kim Jong Il's natural mother, who herself had been sanctified as one of the "Three Great Generals of Mount Paektu." Following publication of this pamphlet, North Korean authorities began to disseminate a number of songs in praise of "our respected mother."[28] A Japanese news agency and Hwang Chang-yŏp felt that the pamphlet and songs were aimed at elevating Ko's first son, Jong Chul, to Kim Jong Il's successor.[29]

Chang Sŏng-t'aek's Waning and the Rise of Kim Jong Chul

The North Korean succession issue inevitably triggered a series of debates in South Korea. Since Chang Sŏng-t'aek's visit to Seoul in October 2002 to consult on inter-Korean economic cooperation with the Kim Dae Jung administration, the international media sometimes reported rumors that Chang had become an object of suspicion and even surveillance by Kim Jong Il. The

26 Cheong, "Kim Jong Il's Illness," 21–22.

27 Ibid.

28 Cheong Seong-chang, "Kim Chŏng-il sidae ŭi Pukhan ŭi sŏnggye munje" [North Korea's succession issue in the times of Kim Jong Il], *Han'guk chŏngch'i hakhoebo* 39, no. 2 (Summer 2005): 350–53.

29 *Kyodo Tsushin*, February 15, 2003, quoted in *Dong-A Ilbo*, February 17, 2003, A2. See also Kim, "Hwang Chang-yŏp hoegyŏn," 115.

rumors seemed plausible; some outside observers even considered Chang Sŏng-t'aek an alternative to Kim Jong Il as part of an American plot seeking regime change in North Korea. At a public seminar in Seoul in July 2003, Hwang Chang-yŏp said, "In the event the Kim Jong Il regime collapses, there are many people who can succeed him. At that point, Chang Sŏng-t'aek would seem most likely to succeed because as Kim Kyŏng-hŭi's husband and first vice director of the KWPCCOGD, he has placed his supporters everywhere."[30]

Some background on Chang Sŏng-t'aek: he was born in Ch'ŏnnae, Kangwŏn Province, on February 6, 1946, while Kim Kyŏng-hŭi was born in Pyongyang on May 30, 1946. The two were classmates in the Faculty of Political Economy at Kim Il Sung University. Supposedly Kim Il Sung did not hold Chang in high regard, saying that he tended to pursue his own pleasures. According to Yi Il-nam's recollection, Kim Il Sung made Chang transfer to a college in Wŏnsan in the hope that the forced departure from Pyongyang would cool down the couple's love. But Kim Kyŏng-hŭi's courting was fervent and persistent and they were married in 1972. Chang would study at Moscow State University, but in the late 1970s Kim Il Sung, reprimanding his "negligence" of Kyŏng-hŭi, sent him to a local refinery. After receiving an "ideological education" there, he was allowed to return to Pyongyang. Following this belittlement, it was said that Kyŏng-hŭi would, even in public, haughtily call to her husband, "You, Chang Sŏng-t'aek!" This very unconventional behavior was regarded not only as impolite but even arrogant in Korea.[31]

Following Hwang's July 2003 remarks that suggested Chang was in the line of succession, two influential publications in Seoul reported that the George W. Bush administration was preparing a contingency plan to form an interim government led by Chang Sŏng-t'aek in the event of serious turmoil and drastic change in the North.[32] After these reports attracted much attention in the international media, Chang ceased appearing at public events in the North. A renowned North Korea watcher in Seoul observed:

> Ko Yong-hŭi, who wanted to promote Jong Chul as her husband's successor, must have taken Hwang's statement [and those reports] seriously. Subsequently, Chang was forced to stop all public activities beginning in July 2003 and his official duties were suspended in 2004. Apparently, Ko and her aides . . . incapacitated Chang.[33]

30 *Dong-A Ilbo*, July 5, 2003, A4.

31 Yi Han-yŏng, *Taedong kang royal p'aemilli Sŏul chamhaeng sip-sa-nyŏn* [Fourteen years of secret lives in Seoul by a North Korean royal family] (Seoul: Dong-A Ilbosa, 1996), 71–78.

32 *Dong-A Ilbo*, August 23, 2003, B7; Hwang Il-do, "Amerik'a ŏi Kim Chŏng-il chŏnggwŏn punggwae sinario" [America's scenario for the collapse of the Kim Jong Il regime], *Sindonga*, September 2003, 212–19.

33 Cheong, "Kim Jong Il's Illness," 23.

Some time probably in early 2004, Chang Sŏng-t'aek was intensively interrogated on suspicion of "factional behavior" and "misuse of power" by a team led by Ri Che-gang (first vice director for organizational life of central party staff members) and Ri Yong-ch'ŏl (first vice director for military affairs), key cadres of the powerful KWP Central Committee OGD. As top lieutenants loyal to Kim Jong Il and Ko Yong-hŭi, and supporters of succession by Jong Chul, they played a critical role in having Chang relieved of his duties. They also dismissed or demoted Chang's close allies in the KWP and KPA. Ch'oe Chun-hwang (first vice director of the KWP Propaganda and Agitation Department), Ri Kwang-gŏn (foreign trade minister), Chi Chae-ryong (vice director of the KWP International Department), and Pak Myŏng-ch'ŏl (chairman of the Physical Culture and Sports Guidance Commission) were all dismissed and sent for reeducation to the Kim Il Sung Higher Party School or banished to the countryside. Ch'oe Ryong-su, who had been newly appointed as People's Security minister in July 2003, was dismissed from his post after only a year. Ch'oe Chun-hwang allegedly died of carbon monoxide poisoning (from the burning of charcoal briquettes, used for heating in the North) not long after being transferred to the KWP South P'yŏngan Provincial Committee's secretary office, in charge of propaganda.[34]

There was also reportedly an intensive investigation of approximately eighty senior military officers close to Chang—including seven or eight generals. Among them was Vice Marshal Chang Sŏng-u, Chang's elder brother and the commander of the KPA Third Corps, a position that oversaw Pyongyang's defense.[35] He was reassigned to be chief of the KWP reserve forces department, probably as a precautionary move to prevent his involvement in a coup d'état.[36]

With Chang Sŏng-t'aek's disappearance in July 2003, Kim Jong Chul became vice director of the KWPCCOGD, which has responsibility "over personnel management and control over power elites in the party, the military, and the government."[37] Five months later, at a joint meeting among cadres working at the KWPCC and DPRKNDC, Kim Jong Il stressed the necessity of grooming Jong Chul as his successor.[38] Beginning around 2004

---

34 Cheong Seong-chang, "Kim Jong Il's Military-First Politics and a Change in the Power Elite," in *North Korea in Distress: Confronting Domestic and External Challenges*, ed. Paik Hak-soon and Cheong Seong-chang (Sŏngnam: The Sejong Institute, 2008), 53–54, 57.

35 Cheong, "Kim Jong Il's Illness," 30

36 Cheong, "Kim Jong Il's Military-First Politics," 56.

37 Cheong, "Kim Jong Il's Illness," 23–24.

38 Cheong Seong-chang, "Pukhan Kim Chŏng-ŭn sŏnggye ch'eje ŏi kongsik ch'ulbŏm" [The official inauguration of the Kim Jong Un succession regime in North Korea], *Wŏlgan Chosun*, November 2010, 89–90.

or 2005, according to a South Korean intelligence official, North Korean embassy staff members were seen at a North Korean restaurant in Beijing wearing Kim Jong Chul lapel pins.[39]

During the process of grooming Kim Jong Chul as the successor, the Eleventh SPA was elected on August 3, 2003, and convened on September 3, 2003. Expressing its strong support for Kim Jong Il's military-first politics, the SPA resolved that it was the honor of the republic to acclaim Kim Jong Il as chairman of its NDC again. The SPA re-elected Cho Myŏng-rok its first vice-chairman, and promoted Yŏn Hyŏng-muk from regular member to one of two vice-chairmen, while demoting Kim Il-ch'ŏl from vice-chairman to regular member. Ri Yong-mu maintained the vice-chairmanship. Why was Yŏn promoted? Five years earlier Yŏn had, as party chief of Chakang Province, initiated the Spirit of Kanggye campaign, which inspired workers to increase their production of military goods. Kim Jong Il had inspected factories and production facilities in January 1998 and was so excited that he called the movement the "Winds of Chakang Province" and awarded Yŏn Hyŏng-muk the Medal of Labor Hero.[40]

In contrast to these elections and promotions, the SPA excluded from the new NDC Ri Ŭl-sŏl, Paek Hak-rim, and Kim Ch'ŏl-man, all octogenarian members belonging to the Kim Il Sung generation. Instead, it recruited Ch'oe Ryong-su (People's Security minister and lieutenant general) and Paek Se-bong (SPA delegate), both part of the Kim Jong Il generation.[41] Paek Se-bong was a new face unknown to the outside world; he was probably fifty-seven years old and the youngest member. The new makeup of the SPA, nine members including Kim Jong Il, clearly indicated that the most powerful decision-making organ in North Korea was in the hands of Kim Jong Il.

The SPA re-elected Kim Yŏng-nam as chairman of the SPA Presidium, the ceremonial head of state position. Then the SPA appointed Pak Pong-ju, a former chemical industry minister, as prime minister, replacing the much older Hong Sŏng-nam. In his inaugural speech, the new premier, a typical pragmatic technocrat, stressed a "fundamental innovation in economic programs" as one of the cabinet's primary tasks. Accordingly, the DPRK economic team had five new members.[42] The North started radical price and wage reforms in July 2002. Only a year later, as it became clear that the "July measures" were badly planned and were resulting in escalating

---

39 *JoongAng Daily*, April 6, 2006, 4.

40 Suh Dae-sook, "New Political Leadership," in *The North Korean System in the Post-Cold War Era*, ed. Samuel S. Kim (New York: Palgrave, 2001), 78.

41 *Rodong Sinmun*, September 4, 2003, 1.

42 Park Kyung-ae, "North Korea in 2003: Pendulum Swing between Crisis and Diplomacy," *Asian Survey* 44, no. 1 (January-February 2004): 144.

inflation,[43] "for the first time since 1950, [the North] decided to sell government bonds . . . in an effort to mobilize hoarded capital circulating in unofficial markets and channel it into the official sector to finance [its] ambitious economic programs."[44]

In the spring of 2004, a North Korean incident made headlines. On April 22, two trains loaded with chemicals exploded at Ryongch'ŏn Station near Sinŭiju on the Sino–North Korean border. The explosion rocked the area with the force of a small nuclear bomb, raining debris over a radius of ten miles and sending acrid smoke over the nearby border with China.[45] The North Korean government announced that 154 persons had died, five were missing, and another 1,300 were injured. An international UN advance team in the city reported that 1,850 homes were destroyed and 8,000 people had had to evacuate the area.[46] Two days later, North Korean media announced that Kim Jong Il's exclusive train had passed through the area just eight hours before the tragedy, on Kim's way back from a trip to China. Eleven days after the incident, Kim Jong Il resurfaced in the Pyongyang media when he visited army troops.[47]

Western media speculated that the incident may not have been an accident "but instead an attempt by opponents of the regime to blow up the dictator and his entourage."[48] Soon it was rumored that Chang Sŏng-t'aek's followers had plotted the explosion to assassinate Kim. Later, North Korean specialists in the Bush administration placed Kim at the Ryongch'ŏn Station significantly closer to the time of the explosion than had been officially announced. According to them, Kim was saved from the explosion because he had disembarked from the train not far from the station and had returned to Pyongyang by automobile.[49] A month or so after the explosion,

43 On the contrary some analysts argued that the reforms had a positive and stabilizing effect on the North Korean economy. Dominique Dwor-Frecaut, "Korea: Long-term Decline in the North Korean Premium," Barclays Capital Research, Asian Rates and Credit Research, February 27, 2004, quoted in Peter M. Beck, "The Bush Administration's Failed North Korea Policy," in *The North Korean Crisis and Beyond*, ed. Stephen J. Epstein (Wellington: Asian Studies Institute, Victoria University of Wellington, 2004), 6.

44 Park, "North Korea in 2003," 145.

45 "Explosion Kills 150, Injures Thousands," *Korea Times*, April 24, 2004, 1; "Ryongchon 'Totally Flattened,'" *Korea Times*, April 26, 2004, 1.

46 *Dong-A Ilbo*, April 23, 2004, A1, A3 and April 24, A1–4. See also Hwang Il-do, "Ryongch'ŏn p'okp'al" [The Ryongch'ŏn explosion], *Sindonga*, October 2004, 120–27.

47 KCNA, May 3, 2004, quoted in *Dong-A Ilbo*, May 4, 2004, A8. See also "NK Leader Makes 1st Public Appearance Since Blast," *Korea Times*, May 4, 2004, 2.

48 Quoted in *Dong-A Ilbo*, September 20, 2004, A1, A4. See also "NK Defectors Say Blast Was a Plot Against Kim," *Korea Times*, April 30, 2004, 2.

49 *Dong-A Ilbo*, September 20, 2004, A1, A4. This daily also printed reports and comments by the *New York Times* and *International Herald Tribune* between April 24 and May 10, 2004.

Dong-A Ilbo in Seoul as well as Western media reported that Kim Jong Il had ordered the confiscation of all mobile phones in the country, including those belonging to officials. The same specialists noted that "there has been speculation that Kim gave the order after receiving word that the parties planning his assassination had contacted one another through their mobile phones regarding his whereabouts along the train route."[50]

The October issue of *Sindonga* (New East Asia), a leading Seoul monthly, reported that the South Korean NIS viewed the Ryongch'ŏn explosion as an "assassination attempt on Kim Jong Il." The monthly stated that around eight people—including Hŏ Ch'ang-sŏk, the nephew of the late Hŏ Tam, a former foreign minister, Fatherland Peaceful Unification Committee chairman, and KWPCC Politburo member—had been arrested and executed in early May on charges of attempted assassination. About twenty additional people had been imprisoned on the same charge.[51]

While it would be difficult to identify the particular triggering event for the attempt on Kim Jong Il's life—if indeed that is what the incident was—*Sindonga* alleged that the attempt was related to an internal power struggle centering on the issue of succession. The plotters, who were in their forties and supporters of Chinese-style reform, were said to have opposed hereditary succession from Kim Jong Il to one of his sons, and to have established contacts with high-ranking officials of the DPRK Central Committee. The monthly also said that Ri Che-gang,[52] vice director of the KWP Central Committee OGD, headed the group in favor of a succession to Kim Jong Chul.[53]

There were a number of rumors reported in the wake of the explosion. One version of the events alleged that Chang Sŏng-t'aek had been building up a faction of generals in hopes of one day installing his "son," Chang Hyŏn, now aged thirty-five, as leader.[54] Another version said that Chang Hyŏn had fired a shot at his younger rival, Kim Jong Chul,[55] although this claim is unsubstantiated.

50 *Dong-A Ilbo*, September 20, 2004, A1, A4.

51 Hwang, "Yongchŏn p'okp'al," 124.

52 Ri Che-gang was born in 1930. Upon graduating from Kim Il Sung University, he started his career as an instructor in the KWPCCOGD in 1973 and progressed up that organization. In 1978, he visited Gabon as Kim Il Sung's special envoy. Between then and 1983, he visited China, Pakistan, Somalia, and Thailand. Later he became a secretary in the powerful Kim Jong Il Secretariat, probably as successor to Mun Sŏng-sul, who was executed in 1999. See Cheong, "Kim Jong Il's Illness," 27.

53 Hwang, "Yongchŏn p'okp'al," 124.

54 There have been unsubstantiated rumors that Chang's children were in fact Kim Il Sung's illegitimate children.

55 *International Herald Tribune*, December 10, 2004, 1.

Yet another report concerned a purported high-level defection in May:

> Lieutenant General O Se-uk, a rising member of the military elite, left the
> North Korean port of Ch'ŏngjin by boat, met a Japanese boat in the Sea
> of Japan, and eventually made his way to the United States, according to [a
> November 4 report by] NHK television of Japan and Kazuhiro Araki, a pro-
> fessor of Korean politics at Takushoku University in Japan. The general's
> seventy-three-year-old father is O Kŭk-ryŏl, ranked second on the KWPCMC
> at the time, after Kim Jong Il. "The defection of such a [high-level] person was
> a great shock to the North Korean establishment," Professor Araki said.[56]

Some North Korea watchers discounted such reports and conjectures.
They said they thought that the U.S. Central Intelligence Agency was exag-
gerating or even fabricating stories about North Korea to sow suspicion
and distrust among the regime's ruling elite; these observers contended that
Chang Sŏng-t'aek was a victim of such a disinformation campaign. They
reasoned that the Western media, by publishing the "U.S.-planted story"
suggesting that Chang might succeed Kim if the latter were to be expelled
from power, had prompted some key personnel to gravitate to Chang, and
thus Kim had decided to send Chang to a reeducation camp.

While verifying these rumors and conjectures is impossible, it seems true
that Chang lost his position in the Kim hierarchy. The North Korean official
media did not mention his name again until early 2006. On November 24,
2004, the South's NIS reported to the National Assembly that it could confirm that Chang had been purged.[57]

Political Unrest?

The purge of Chang Sŏng-t'aek and his protégés did not cause political
unrest in North Korea. At least on the surface, there was no sign of turmoil inside the Kim Jong Il leadership. In late May 2004 Kim again received
Japanese prime minister Koizumi in Pyongyang, and they agreed to improve
their countries' relationship.[58] In *Time*'s June 21, 2004, Asia edition, Kim
appeared on the cover with the title, "Why Is This Man Smiling?" On July 8,
2004, the tenth anniversary of Kim Il Sung's death, North Koreans pledged
their loyalty to Kim Jong Il. While Kim Yŏng-nam, the titular head of state,
praised the younger Kim for his "scientific insight into the urgent demand
of the times and the acute situation," Kim Il-ch'ŏl, the PAFM minister

56 James Brooke, "Japanese Official Warns of Fissures in North Korea," *New York
Times*, November 22, 2004.

57 *Dong-A Ilbo*, November 25, 2004, A 1, A4.

58 Ryu Jin, "Seoul, US Welcome Kim–Koizumi Summit," *Korea Times*, May 24,
2004, A1.

with the rank of vice marshal, stressed the KPA's determination to "remain single-heartedly united around [him]."[59]

Notwithstanding the continuous litany of paeans to Kim, doubts about the stability of his regime did not abate. In early September, Western media reported that Bush administration officials had obtained information that "photographs and posters of Kim Jong Il in downtown Pyongyang have been defaced with spray paint, and that flyers containing messages of condemnation against Chairman Kim have been distributed."[60] On September 9, the fifty-sixth anniversary of North Korea's founding, two massive explosions rocked Kim Hyŏng-ik County (named after Kim Il Sung's father) in Ryanggang Province near the Chinese border. The blast was much bigger than that at Ryongch'ŏn Station six months earlier. The international press immediately raised the possibility that the North had conducted a nuclear test or suffered a massive armament accident.[61] The September 2004 issue of *Wŏlgan Chosun* speculated that an anti-Kim Jong Il conspiracy, led by Chang Sŏng-t'aek's protégés, might have had something to do with it. As speculation mounted, the North Korean foreign ministry issued a statement that the explosions had been controlled and were part of a hydroelectric power project. Doris Hertrampf, the German ambassador to Pyongyang, said she was told that the demolition had moved 150,000 cubic meters of earth and rock. Colin Powell, U.S. secretary of state, said, "The information North Korea gave is consistent with what we saw, that it might have been demolition work for a hydroelectric facility."[62]

In a September 2004 closed meeting on North Korea's internal dynamics during the period March to September, held at the American Embassy in Seoul, participants characterized the situation as "unsettling and dramatic." Fifteen participants—Bush administration officials, military personnel, and intelligence analysts—agreed, "There seems to be suspicious movements afoot inside North Korea, although we cannot go so far as to call them signs of an impending collapse or a military coup d'état."[63] Some eight weeks later, the U.S. media once repeated such suspicions. On November 8, the *New York Times* reprinted a *Der Spiegel* article outlining weaknesses in the Kim Jong Il regime:

> The people of North Korea are not as submissive as they appear to be. Unnoticed by the outside world, strong opposition to the regime of dictator Kim Jong Il is beginning to appear. Kim himself has now constructed a

59 Quoted in *Dong-A Ilbo*, July 9, 2004, 3.

60 *Dong-A Ilbo*, September 20, 2004, A2.

61 *Dong-A Ilbo*, September 13, 2004, A1, A2, A3 and September 14, 2004, A1, A4.

62 Reuben Stains, "NK's Blast Explanation Plausible, NIS Says," *Korea Times*, September 16, 2004, 1.

63 *Dong-A Ilbo*, September 20, 2004, A1, A4.

protective wall around himself. He constantly moves from one residence to another, and his houses in Pyongyang are connected by a system of tunnels. An elite unit of 100,000 soldiers dedicated to Kim exists solely to protect Kim against conspiracies.[64]

Six days later, the *Sunday Times* of London reported that diplomats in Pyongyang began to suspect trouble when their North Korean staff members (controlled by the government) were suddenly reassigned, telephones used by foreigners were cut off, and the secret police took over the country's mobile phone service. Agence France-Presse quoted Zhao Huji, a North Korea expert in China's elite Communist Party School in Beijing: "Not only generals are defecting to China, but many officials, such as cadres below the ministry level."[65]

Western reports on the removal of Kim Jong Il's photographs from public places can be read as part of the same script. Between November 17 and 19, a number of diplomats in Pyongyang and experts in Seoul said that Kim's portraits had been removed from some public places beginning as far back as August, in what may have been a bid to tone down the Kim Jong Il personality cult. The North Korean official response, however, was firm. A spokesman for North Korea's foreign ministry said, "It didn't happen before, and will never happen." He called the accounts a U.S. plot to overthrow the DPRK government, and concluded:

> General Kim Jong Il is the fate of the Korean people and the Democratic People's Republic of Korea's socialism. It is unimaginable that the Democratic People's Republic of Korea people and army can separate their fates from Kim Jong Il. It is nothing but stupid and ridiculous acts just like trying to remove the sun from the sky. The adoration for the leader originated from people's life. It will never change.[66]

On November 20, a pro-North daily published in Japan also denied that there was any change in North Korea's political landscape. The *Chosŏn Sinbo* (Korea news report) acknowledged the removal of Kim's portrait "from an international conference site" in North Korea, but stressed, "In ordinary homes and public places, the portraits of both Kim Il Sung and Kim Jong Il continue to be displayed. Speculation by the Western press that the absence of Chairman Kim Jong Il's portrait is due to internal power

64 Andreas Lorenz, "Joyful Dancing," *New York Times*, November 8, 2004.

65 Quoted in Agence France-Presse, "North Korean Generals, Officials Defecting, But Kim Jong-Il Still Strong," December 9, 2004, http://www.asiademocracy.org/content _view.php?section_id=1&content_id=170.

66 Martin Parry, "Kim Portraits Still Up, Irate North Korea Insists," *The Globe and Mail* [Toronto, Ont], November 20, 2004.

struggles is ridiculous." Three days later, South Korea's NIS briefed the press that the removal of Kim's portraits had been ordered by Kim himself beginning on July 8, the tenth anniversary of his father's death. They speculated that the removal was an attempt to improve Kim's international reputation, especially the Bush administration's view of him. Similarly, purportedly at Kim's urging, people stopped wearing badges bearing his image.[67]

There was some evidence to support this view. Since the re-election of George W. Bush in November 2004, administration officials and their neo-conservative supporters had spoken bluntly about the Kim Jong Il regime. Newly appointed presidential national security adviser Stephen J. Hadley said that the Bush administration would seek "regime transformation" in North Korea through managed pressure among countries concerned with the North Korean nuclear issue. Nicholas Eberstadt, a senior researcher at the American Enterprise Institute, called for the implementation of a six-point strategy aimed at ousting Kim Jong Il.[68] Facing such a new challenge, the North may indeed have been trying to moderate its image.

Ko Yŏng-gu, chief of South Korea's NIS, testified before the National Assembly on November 24 that his agency had found no evidence to support rumors of internal unrest in North Korea. He even denied the rumor of O Se-uk's defection to the United States. (Two years later, in the summer of 2004, American intelligence officials would confirm O's defection.[69]) The NIS could confirm, however, that in the previous spring the Kim Jong Il regime had revised the criminal code to increase the punishment for certain crimes. For instance, it had increased the penalty for "possessing or distributing broadcasts against the republic." It had also increased the punishment for armed rebellion against the state to life imprisonment with hard labor or execution. Previously, the maximum penalty had been ten years' confinement. Conversely, the new code reduced penalties for people caught crossing the border into China illegally, which presumably was intended to take into account the many North Koreans fleeing the country purely for reasons of economic hardship. These code revisions reflected concern with domestic unrest on the part of the ruling elite in the Kim regime.[70]

67 *Dong-A Ilbo*, November 4, 2004, A2. See also James Brooke, "Where Kim's Portrait Hung in Pyongyang, a Baffling Blankness," *New York Times*, November 17, 2004.

68 *The Weekly Standard*, November 29, 2004, 8–16.

69 Kim Sŏng-dong, "Pukhan esŏ sarajin O Kŏk-rdŏl adŏl ŏi haengbang" [The whereabouts of O Kŭk-ryŏl's son who disappeared from North Korea'], *Wŏlgan Chosun* (July 2006), 124–29.

70 Ha T'ae-won and Yi Sang-rok, "Puk, Hyŏngpop daep'ok kaep'yŏn" [The North revised the penal code drastically], *Dong-A Ilbo*, December 9, 2004, A8.

If the removal of Kim Jong Il's portraits and the revision of the penal code may have been internal measures in response to the Bush administration's stiffened stance, the North's announcement that it possessed a nuclear capability may be considered an external measure. On February 10, 2005, for the first time, the North Korean foreign ministry officially acknowledged having a nuclear arsenal.[71] The North also took a series of conciliatory steps toward the South, whose progressive government was criticized by some in the South and elsewhere as being pro–North Korean and anti-American. Kim Jong Il was rattling his saber at the Bush administration while cozying up toward the Roh Moo-hyun administration.

The October 2005 visit to Pyongyang by Hu Jintao, CCPCC general secretary and PRC president, was the first visit by a CCP head to the North since September 2001, and this also served to boost Kim Jong Il's position. In January 2006 Kim reciprocated with a visit to China—his fourth trip there since May 2000. On this occasion, Hu advised Kim to stimulate the North's business and trade through reforms and an opening-up policy. At the same time, Hu openly said, "The Chinese side is convinced that the DPRK side will, under Kim's leadership, make new achievements in building a strong and prosperous country with unity and arduous work." Those remarks were Hu's clear endorsement of Kim's leadership.[72] In response, Kim pledged that his country would pay more attention to business and trade.

Chang Sŏng-t'aek's Return and Kim Jong Chul's Fall

About ten days after Kim Jong Il's return to Pyongyang, in late January 2006, Chang Sŏng-t'aek made a public appearance as part of a group of officials accompanying Kim Jong Il at a lunar New Year ceremony. Chang was referred to as the first vice director of the KWP department for workers' organizations and construction of the capital. With his reappearance, some South Korean observers argued, "Kim needs someone like Chang to support his new policy, which would emulate China's economic policy." Others argued that "[t]here needs a person who is experienced in managing another hereditary power transition, and there is no other person who has ability to do so except Chang."[73] The death of Ko Yong-hŭi—who had been vigilant

71 *Rodong Sinmun*, February 11, 2005, 1. See also Ryu Jin, "North Korea Claims to Have Nuclear Weapons," *Korea Times*, February 11, 2005, 1.

72 Brian Lee and Chae Byung-gun, "China's Hope for 'Stability' in North Adds Twist to Visit," *JoongAng Daily*, January 19, 2006, 2. See also Lee Young-jong, "North Korea Seen as Ready to Focus on Business," *JoongAng Daily*, February 10, 2006, 1.

73 Han Ki-hŭng, "Chang Sŏng-t'aek," *Dong-A Ilbo*, January 31, 2006, X26; Kwon Dae-yŏl, "Puk Kwŏnryŏk yiinja Chang Sŏng-t'aek" [The North's second man Chang Sŏng-t'aek], *Chosun Ilbo*, January 31, 2006, A6.

against Chang—may have been a factor in Kim Jong Il allowing his return. With Chang's reappearance, some of the officials who had been purged or demoted due to their relationship with him were now reinstated. Ri Yong-bok, former chief secretary of the Namp'o City KWP Committee, who had been demoted to an office in a rural area, was reassigned to the KWPCC administration department; Ri Yong-su, a former vice director, returned to the department; and Chi Chae-ryong, a former vice director of the international department of the KWPCC, was also reinstated.[74]

In the months and years following his return to power, Chang Sŏng-t'aek would experience a number of personal misfortunes. His other elder brother, Chang Sŏng-gil, political commissar of a KPA corps with the rank of lieutenant general, died in July 2006. Chang's daughter, Chang Kŭm-song, died of an overdose of sleeping pills in August 2006 while studying in Paris;[75] it is believed that she committed suicide after refusing to be recalled to the DPRK. Following her death, there were reports in the media that her mother, Kim Kyŏng-hŭi, had descended into alcoholism and depression.[76] Chang himself was involved in a car accident in Pyongyang in broad daylight in September 2006. Some interpreted it as an assassination attempt, owing to the scarcity of cars on Pyongyang's streets.[77] His elder brother, Chang Sŏng-u, who commanded the October 1983 terrorist operation against ROK president Chun Doo-hwan (Chŏn Tu-hwan) and his entourage in Rangoon, would die in August 2009.[78]

In December 2005 Kim Jong Il reportedly ordered a crackdown on rampant discussion of the succession issue: "Our enemies are backbiting us by speculating about our [country's] future leadership and a father-to-son succession. I ask party and military leaders to strictly crack down on any public discussion on the [issue of our] next leader."[79] His remarks may have reflected his dissatisfaction with Kim Jong Chul's performance at the KWP Central Committee OGD. In the early months of 2006, Beijing sources told South Korean intelligence officials that Kim Jong Chul had failed to prove his ability as a leader. In June 2006 his reputation in the eyes of the North Korean leadership dropped another notch when Japan's Fuji TV aired footage of

74 Cheong, "Kim Jong Il's Military-First Politics," 56.

75 Cheong, "Kim Jong Il's Illness," 30.

76 Already on September 17, 2004, she was reported to have received medical treatment for alcoholism and depression in a Paris hospital. *Tokyo Shimbun*, September 17, 2004, quoted in *Dong-A Ilbo*, September 18, 2004, A8.

77 "Kim Jong Il's Kin Hurt," *Korea Times*, October 9, 2006, 2.

78 O, "Fujimoto Kenji hoekyŏn," 80.

79 "North Seen as Wary over Next 'Dear Leader,'" *JoongAng Daily*, December 11, 2005.

Kim Jong Chul attending an Eric Clapton concert in Frankfurt with a young woman. It was also reported that he had attended Clapton's other German shows in Stuttgart, Leipzig, and Berlin, travelling with the same woman, three bodyguards, and a maid. (In contrast to Kim Jong Nam, who often travels abroad alone, Kim Jong Chul is always accompanied by a group of bodyguards.)[80] Perhaps even worse, when reporters asked whether he had come from North Korea, he answered, "I came from Hong Kong."[81] In fervently patriotic North Korea, this response may have been perceived as borderline traitorous.

Kim Jong Il's Stroke and the Final Selection of Kim Jong Un As Successor, 2008–09

A Shortened and Compressed Process

On October 9, 2006, just one day before the sixty-first anniversary of the KWP'S founding, North Korea stunned the world again with its first nuclear test, in Kilju County, North Hamgyŏng Province. About two months later, in December, Kim Jong Il began to groom Kim Jong Un within the ruling circle as his successor. An important document that lends some support to this is *The Material in Teaching the Greatness of Respected Comrade General Kim Jung Un*, distributed by the KPA to every military unit between May and June 2009. The pamphlet highlighted Kim Jong Un's December 24, 2006, pledge at the Kim Il Sung Comprehensive Military University graduation ceremony to carry on revolutionary achievements based on *Juche*. The pamphlet noted that on that very day, Kim Jong Il gave high praise to his son's graduation thesis, commenting that it reflected the "great military strategy theories" developed by Kim Il Sung and Kim Jong Il. Soon Kim Jong Un, with his elder brother Kim Jong Chul, began joining Kim Jong Il on his inspections of military units and at his public appearances.[82]

About ten months after Kim Jong Un's graduation, North Korean authorities designated the house where he had been born in Ch'angsŏng County, North P'yŏng'an Province, as an historical site. Around the same time, in October 2007, Kim Jong Il had talks with visiting ROK president Roh Moo-hyun in Pyongyang and obtained Roh's pledge of massive economic assistance for the North. In return, Kim Jong Il agreed to work

80 Cheong, "Kim Jong Il's Illness," 24.

81 Ch'ŏn Kwang-am, "Puk Kim Jong Chul mimo yŏsŏngkwa tokyŏhaeng [Kim Jong Chul of the North travels to Germany with a beautiful woman," *Dong-A Ilbo*, June 16, 2006, A2.

82 Cheong, "Kim Jong Un," 167: Cheong, "Kim Jong Un's Early Life," 11.

with Roh to implement the Six-Party agreements on ending North Korea's nuclear weapons program.[83] The North's media emphasized that the agreement was the fruit of Kim Jong Il's unification policy.[84]

In October 2007 Chang Sŏng-t'aek, who had resurfaced in January 2006, was allowed to return to full power by Kim Jong Il:

> Chang was promoted to director of the KWPCC administration department and took over the responsibilities he had as the OGD first vice director for administration before his duties were suspended in 2004. The department, which was part of the OGD but became an independent organ upon Chang's appointment as its head, is responsible for providing administrative guidance to the State Security Agency [in charge of secret and political police], the Ministry of People's Security [in charge of regular police], the Central Persecutors' [sic] Office, and the Central Court.[85]

In the absence of his beloved wife, Kim Jong Il had finally assigned the crucial task of supervising the succession to his brother-in-law. About this time, Kim Man-bok, director of the NIS, told the press that Kim Jong Un might become Kim Jong Il's successor. [86]

The inauguration of the Lee Myung-bak (Yi Myŏng-bak) administration in February 2008 in Seoul strained the North's relations with the South, for the conservative president instituted a new policy based on reciprocity rather than on continuing to provide aid unconditionally to the North. While the North harshly denounced the Lee Myung-bak administration, at the same time it moved to improve its relations with the United States. The North's dramatic, televised destruction of the concrete cooling tower at its Yŏngbyŏn nuclear facility in South P'yŏngan Province on June 27, 2008, followed its submission, the day before, of "the long-delayed declaration covering its nuclear facilities, amount of plutonium produced and extracted, and how it would be used."[87] In October, the Bush administration reciprocated by removing North Korea from its list of state sponsors of terrorism. From Kim Jong Il's point of view, his successor would be relieved of at least that burden.

83 For the full text of "The Declaration on the Development of Inter-Korean Relations, Peace and Prosperity," see *Korea Times*, October 6, 2007, 1.

84 "Pukch'uk podo t'ŭkjing" [Characteristics of North Korea's reports], Ministry of Unification, *Wŏlgan Pukhan Tonghyang* [Monthly trends inside North Korea], October 2007, 9.

85 Cheong, "Kim Jong Il's Illness," 30–31.

86 *Yŏllin Pukhan T'ongsin* [Open news agency on North Korea], June 8, 2009.

87 Stephan Haggard and Marcus Noland, "North Korea in 2008: Twilight of the God?" *Asian Survey* 49, no. 1 (January–February 2009): 103.

On August 14, 2008, Kim Jong Il suffered a stroke. The details of the event remained unknown until after Kim's death in 2011, when French neurosurgeon François-Xavier Roux, chief of neurosurgery at Sainte-Anne Hospital in Paris, revealed he had been flown to Pyongyang in August 2008 with a team of French doctors to treat a mystery patient.[88] It was not the doctor's first encounter with the secretive DPRK. In 1993 he had been contacted by telephone and provided advice after Kim Jong Il suffered a head injury in a riding accident.

When the French team arrived in Pyongyang, they were taken to the Red Cross Society Hospital but did not initially get to see the patient. Instead, in a sort of blind test, Roux was asked to review and diagnose a number of anonymous cases. There was one patient whose details concerned Roux, yet even so it took hours before the staff would allow him and his team access to the patient. It turned out to be Kim Jong Il.

> "When I arrived, he was in intensive care, in a coma, in a bad way," Roux said.
> "My job was to try and save him from this critical state by talking with the other doctors, by giving medical advice, etc. He was in a life-threatening situation." [89]

Within two weeks Kim was able to speak and Roux would return to France:

> Roux said that as Kim began to gain awareness of his condition, he became concerned "as any of us would have been after a serious stroke." He wanted to know whether he would live normally again, "if he would walk normally again, work normally. He was asking very logical questions." [90]

Roux later theorized that the French team had been called in because the North Koreans needed physicians who were "not emotionally involved." He reported that the DPRK physicians "were. . . disturbed to be making decisions for their leader." Roux had the final say about the course of treatment for Kim. He noted that Kim Jong Un came to the hospital regularly but never spoke to him.[91]

Kim Jong Il's striking absence from the events celebrating the sixtieth anniversary of the founding of the DPRK on September 9, 2008, fueled

---

88 Jamey Keaten and Catherine Gaschka, "French Doctor Confirms Kim Had a Stroke in 2008," Associated Press, December 19, 2011. I have drawn liberally from this account.

89 Ibid.

90 Ibid.

91 Ibid. Roux said that Kim Jong Il communicated with the doctors in "a mix of French and English," that Kim was "profoundly Francophile," that he had a good knowledge of both French cinema and wines, and "wanted to establish political ties with France."

speculation about his health. A day later, NIS director Won Sei-hoon (Wŏn Se-hun) briefed the ROK National Assembly that "although Kim Jong Il has undergone rehabilitation since the operation and his condition has improved substantially, he still suffers from partial speech impairment and partial paralysis."[92] In September and late October, at Kim Jong Nam's request, Dr. Roux again visited Pyongyang to treat Kim Jong Il; in December, Dr. Roux told the press that Kim Jong Il's condition was improving.[93] Kim Jong Il's concern about his health may have spurred him to accelerate his original plan to officially declare Kim Jong Un as his successor in case of his sudden death or incapacitation.

On December 1, 2008, North Korea enacted the "December 1 Measure," which strictly limited traffic by South Koreans to the Kaesŏng Industrial Complex. The inter-Korean industrial park had been opened in October 2004 on the northern side of the Military Demarcation Line, only fifty miles from Seoul. The decision to limit access, which in retrospect seems related to the officialization of Kim Jong Un as successor, created new tensions in inter-Korean relations. At times the North seems intentionally to have raised tensions to bolster domestic solidarity, in this case to block potential opposition or resistance to a second hereditary succession. On January 8, 2009, Kim Jong Un's twenty-sixth birthday, Kim Jong Il officially notified the KWP Central Committee OGD and the KPAGPB of his final decision that Kim Jong Un would be his successor, marking the first step in the process of officializing the succession.[94] This process contrasted sharply with Kim Jong Il's own case; he had been designated as successor through the KWP congress, thus maintaining at least the appearance of a formal procedure. Kim Jong Un, however, was designated as successor merely by Kim Jong Il's notification of the fact.

Simultaneously with Kim Jong Il's notification, the reconstruction of Kim Jong Un's birth home as an historical site was completed. A special task force—consisting of top experts in the fields of politics, economics, culture and military affairs, in their forties and fifties—was formed to assist the successor-designate.[95] Kim Jong Il made his first post-stroke public appearance about two weeks later when he received a visiting Chinese delegation. Chinese delegates "insisted that he was in good health, although

92 *Dong-A Ilbo*, September 10, 2009, A2.

93 Yi Yŏng-jong, *Hugeja Kim Chŏng-ŭn* [Kim Jong Un, the successor] (Seoul: Nulp'um Plus, 2010), 100–03.

94 Cheong Seong-chang, "Kim Jong Un," 169–70.

95 Cheong, "Pukhan," 92–93.

photos in the North Korean media showed he had aged considerably and was not using his left arm."[96]

Following Kim Jong Il's notification of his decision about the successor, the most meaningful legal-institutional change in the North was the April 9, 2009, constitutional revision at the first session of the Twelfth SPA. This was the first constitutional revision since 1998, and there were some noteworthy changes regarding a possible succession. The new constitution put primary emphasis on the importance of the armed forces in North Korea; specifically, "soldiers" were added to the list of those to whom the DPRK's sovereignty belongs, a list that previously included only "workers, peasants, working intellectuals, and all working peoples." The revised constitution also made it the obligation of DPRK's "armed forces" to safeguard the "the core of the revolution," i.e., Kim Jong Il and Kim Jong Un, by accomplishing "the line of military-first revolution" suggested by Kim Jong Il beginning on January 1, 1995.

The constitutional revisions also extensively strengthened the authority of the NDC chairmanship. The NDC chairman was designated "the highest leader of the DPRK" and "the highest commander of the DPRK armed forces," with increased authority in "leading the country as a whole." For example, the NDC chair was now entitled to declare a national emergency, a state of war, and mobilization orders. NDC members also had their powers expanded in the new constitution.

On the same day as the revision, the SPA "decided to acclaim" Kim Jong Il as NDC chairman. Then the SPA expanded NDC membership from four to eight, and elected Chang Sŏng-t'aek as a new member. [97] The implications of these changes? Kim Jong Il would resort to the armed forces and the NDC to prevent and suppress any kind of organized resistance to the consolidation of the succession, and Chang would play a crucial role in the entire process.

Kim Jong Un's Assumption of Public Security Organs

After becoming the de facto successor, Kim Jong Un moved quickly to tighten his grip over both the KWP and KPA, aided by Chang Sŏng-t'aek, KWP administration department director and NDC member, and Ri Che-gang, KWPCCOGD first vice director.

96 Oh Kongdan and Ralph Hassig, "North Korea in 2009: The Song Remains the Same," *Asian Survey* 50, no.1 (January–February 2010): 95.

97 *Dong-A Ilbo*, April 10, 2010, A6. See also *Korea Times*, April 10, 2010, 5, and April 11–12, 2010, 2.

On the military side, Kim was assisted by Kim Chŏng-gak, KPAGPB first vice director, and Ri Yŏng-ho, the KPA chief of general staff. Kim Chŏng-gak was born in July 1941 in Chŭngsan County in South P'yong'an Province, entered the KPA in August 1959, and graduated from Kim Il Sung Comprehensive Military University. As vice minister with the rank of colonel general, he had commanded the military parade held in Kim Il Sung Square in October 2000 on the fifty-fifth anniversary of the KWP's founding. He was promoted to general in 2002 and named KPAGPB first vice director in March 2007; in 2009 he was elected to the NDC. Kim led the KPAGPB since the November 2010 death of Cho Myŏng-rok, vice marshal, NDC first vice-chairman, and KPAGPB general director. Some sources said that his prominent position in the North Korean power structure might be traced back to his being Kim Jong Un's tutor in military matters. A researcher in Seoul said, "We were tipped off that Kim Chŏng-gak taught the heir apparent Jong Un about how to control the military through the party."[98]

Ri Yŏng-ho was born in 1942, the same year as Kim Jong Il, in T'ongch'ŏn County, Kangwŏn Province, which was also the hometown of Chŏng Chu-yŏng, the late founder of the Hyundai Group. Ri's father Ri Pong-su was Kim Il Sung's personal physician during the anti-Japanese guerrilla campaigns, and his mother took care of Kim Jong Il and Kim Kyŏng-hŭi for some time after their mother's death. When Ri was lieutenant general, he was in charge of tightening security in Pyongyang, a critical job that Kim Jong Il would assign only to someone he absolutely trusted. Ri also commanded the military parade in 2007 that marked the KPA's seventy-sixth anniversary. Immediately after Kim Jong Il designated Kim Jong Un as his successor, he also promoted Ri to general and appointed him as KPA chief of general staff.

Thanks to the concerted efforts of Kim Chŏng-gak and Ri Yŏng-ho, the KPA is said to have changed as of February 2009 from the "Kim Jong Il armed forces" to the "Kim Jong Un armed forces."[99]

Sometime around March or April 2009, Kim Jong Il appointed Kim Jong Un as SSM minister.[100] This appointment was fraught with political meaning: recall that Kim Jong Il began his own career in the party apparatus. After serving as a North Korean *apparatchik* at various posts in the KWP Central Committee, Kim Jong Il was promoted to secretary for organizational affairs

98 Lee Young-jong and Kim Hee-jin, "General Whose Fortunes Rose with Kim Jong Eun," *Korea JoongAng Daily*, December 28, 2011, 3.

99 Cheong, "Pukhan," 92–93.

100 Pak Hyŏng-jung, "Pukhan kyŏngje chŏngch'aek ŏi kwŏllyŏk chŏngch'i" [Power politics of the North Korean economic policy], *Sindonga*, July 2010, 275.

and ideology; next he was allowed to enter the Politburo and acquire power to control the public security organs; and finally, at the end stage of his rise after his full-scale assumption of power over the KWP, he was allowed to exercise military power. In contrast, Kim Jong Il had Kim Jong Un *begin* his career by assuming power over the DPRK's core instrument for intelligence, state violence, and coercion. To assist his son, Kim Jong Il in September 2009 appointed Lieutenant General U Tong-ch'ŭk (b. 1942), someone whose career had matured within this apparatus, as SSM first vice director. General U was also a KWPCC Politburo candidate member and KWPCMC member.[101]

In early 2009, ostensibly because of the annual U.S.–ROK military exercises in March, the North cut all communications links between South Korea and Kaesŏng. Separately, the North Koreans arrested two American journalists, Laura Ling and Euna Lee, who had been reporting from the Sino-North Korean border area, and convicted them on the charge of "illegal border crossing." A South Korean worker at the Kaesŏng Industrial Complex was arrested as well, on unrelated charges. The North initiated two campaigns, the "150-day battle" and the subsequent "100-day battle," to mobilize all available North Korean human resources with the goal of increasing productivity.[102] On May 25 the DPRK conducted a second nuclear test. All of these actions can be seen in part as elements of a strategy of enhancing national solidarity by raising tensions. By the end of June 2009, Kim Jong Un's position as the successor-designate had become strong and stable enough for him to receive reports directly from the KPAGPB, SSM, and MPS.[103]

By the fall of 2009, with Kim Jong Un's position relatively secure, the North began to adopt a more conciliatory policy towards the United States and the South. In August 2009, the North freed the two American journalists in exchange for a visit to Pyongyang by former U.S. president Bill Clinton. (The team that accompanied Clinton included his personal physician, Roger A. Band of the University of Pennsylvania Medical School; at a dinner hosted by Kim Jong Il, Band was able to closely observe Kim and later briefed a U.S. intelligence agency on his physical condition.)[104] The North also freed the South Korean worker and allowed travel by the South Korean

101 Cheong Seong-chang, "Kim Jong Un," *Wŏlgan Chosun*, February 2010, 88–91.

102 As for the "150-day battle" and the "100-day battle," see Richard Lloyd Parry, "Extravagant Monuments Cannot Hide the Grim Reality of North Korea," *The Times*, October 7, 2009, 1.

103 Cheong Seong-chang, "Kim Jong Un," 89–90.

104 "Kim Opens Line to Washington," *Korea Times*, August 7, 2009, 5.

side to Kaesŏng after talks with Hyŏn Chŏng-ŭn (Hyun Jeong-Eun), head of the Hyundai-Asan Group, which had played a leading role among South Korean businesses in dealing with the North.

The DPRK notified its embassies abroad that Kim Jong Un was to be the successor, and the propaganda machine stepped up its efforts to promote him. The regime began to popularize the song "Footsteps" and disseminated leaflets and posters about him. A cult of personality began to be erected around Kim Jong Un. The regime described him as the "youth General who has inherited the holy spirit of Mount Paektu" and "the morning star shining over the whole nation," and extolled him as a "genius of geniuses, who has been endowed by nature with special abilities."[105]

On the night of April 14, 2009, Kim Jong Un held a massive fireworks exhibition in Pyongyang in commemoration of the late Kim Il Sung's ninety-seventh birthday, and pledged that the North would become a "strong and prosperous great country" by 2012, the year of Kim Il Sung's centennial.[106] A noteworthy aspect of the North's propaganda was its emphasis on the role of Kim Kyŏng-hŭi in Kim Jong Un's childhood. One book stressed that Kim Jong Un was in fact raised by his aunt—the sole daughter of Kim Il Sung and Kim Jong Suk and the younger sister of Kim Jong Il, i.e., the three Kims who constituted the holy trinity of the "Three Great Generals of Mount Paektu." In contrast, the book ignored Kim Jong Un's birth mother, Ko Yong-hŭi, who was ridiculed for her Japanese background.[107]

From the beginning of 2010, Kim Jong Un expanded his activities, especially those related to economic policies. The January 1, 2010, joint editorial of the party, the government, and the military primarily focused on the improvement of the peoples' livelihood. Three points stood out in the editorial. Rather than using the conventional term, *charyŏk kaengsaeng* (survival by self-reliance), it stressed that the present era was one of the "information industry" and the "knowledge-based economy." References to the "military-first" policy were drastically reduced. While only once mentioning the "defense economy"—previously peppered throughout New Year's editorials—the terms "light industry" and "agriculture" were used frequently.

105 Cheong Seong-chang, "Kim Jong Un," *Wŏlgan Chosun*, February 2010, 86–93; Cheong Seong-chang, "Kim Jong Un," *Wŏlgan Chosun*, November 2010, 85–97. See also Sin Chŏng-rok, "Kim Jong Un Taechang Tongchi" [Comrade General Kim Jong Un], *Chosun Ilbo*, October 6, 2009, A3.

106 Ha T'ae-gyŏng, "Kim Chŏng-il ŭi o-wŏl pang-Chung" [Kim Jong Il's visit to China in May], *Chugan Chosun*, July 12, 2010, 32–33.

107 Kang Chan-ho and Christine Kim, "Jong Un Never Met Chinese Bigwigs: Legislator," *Korea JoongAng Daily*, November 3, 2010, 1.

North Korea watchers in Seoul believed that these innovations originated with Kim Jong Un.[108]

The New Year's editorial gave hope that the North might take rational steps in steering the country; unfortunately, bloody purges and forced labor followed instead. The purges began with the dismissal of Pak Nam-gi from the directorship of the KWP planning and finance department after the failed currency reform of November–December 2009 brought about a sharp increase in the inflation rate, with a devastating effect on North Koreans. Pak's deputy, Kim T'ae-yŏng, was also dismissed on the same charge, and on March 12 both were publicly and brutally executed in Pyongyang.[109] About three months later, former railroad transportation minister Kim Yong-sam was also executed on the charge that he had revealed to "enemies" Kim Jong Il's return rail schedule from China to the North in April 2004—the occasion of that massive explosion at the railway station. Former finance minister Mun Il-bong was reportedly executed about the same time.[110] Amid these purges and executions, Kim Jong Un initiated the construction of one hundred thousand condominiums in Pyongyang, a five-year program that ran from September 2008 to 2012.[111] In all of these things, Kim reportedly was assisted by Chang Sŏng-t'aek. However, the construction program did not proceed well.

During Kim Jong Il's visit to China in May 2010, accompanied by Chang, some Western media reported that Kim Jong Un was acting in place of Kim Jong Il during his absence. It was around this time that he appeared for the first time in a North Korean newspaper photograph.[112] The sinking of the South Korean Navy corvette *Cheonan* (*Ch'ŏnan*) by a purported North Korean torpedo in March[113] and the bombardment of South Korea's Yŏnp'yŏng Island by North Korean artillery in November were both regarded in the South as shows of strength by the North at Kim Jong Un's direction.

In late August, Kim Jong Un accompanied Kim Jong Il on a sudden visit to China, including a meeting with Chinese president Hu Jintao in Changchun. Some media reports in Seoul and Tokyo asserted that Kim Jong Un was greeted by Chinese officials—suggesting China's acceptance of a

108 For a comprehensive analysis of the joint editorial, see *Hanbando Focus*, No. 11 (January–February 2011): 2–19. See also Cheong Seong-chang, "North Korea's Joint New Year's Editorial and Outlook of Change in Domestic and Foreign Policies," *Sejong Commentary*, no. 170 (January 5, 2010): 1–3.

109 *Daily NK* (internet), April 4, 2010, quoted in *Dong-A Ilbo*, April 5, 2010, A6.

110 *Chosun Ilbo*, April 4, 2011, A1.

111 *Chosun Sinbo*, January 18, 2008, 1. This Tokyo-based daily represented the KWP's official views.

112 *Dong-A Ilbo*, June 8, 2010, A2.

113 Choe Sang-hun, "Seoul Closer to Blaming Torpedo for Ship's Sinking," *International Herald Tribune*, April 26, 2010, 3.

third-generation succession in the North. A minority opinion was that "Kim Jong Il kept his son in the shadows deliberately because he felt the Chinese government was not too keen on a third-generation succession."[114] There is some evidence for this in a reported decision by Chinese officials regarding visits by the new DPRK leader. While the inconvenience of a Kim Jong Il visit to China was tolerated—these visits required extensive security measures and had a significant negative impact on traffic—officials expressed concern that Chinese citizens would no longer stand for the same sort of disruption from Kim Jong Un.[115] After returning to Pyongyang, it is known that Kim Jong Un played a principal role in preparing for the Third Conference of KWP Representatives. In light of such activities, Cheong Seong-chang concluded that "Kim Jong Un is exercising power on the same level with Kim Jong Il" and that the "present North Korean regime may be defined as a joint regime of Kim Jong Il and Kim Jong Un."[116]

As Kim Jong Un played major roles in initiating and executing important national tasks, Chang Sŏng-t'aek also rapidly expanded his role. On June 7, 2010, the third session of the Twelfth SPA elected Chang as NDC vice-chairman "at the recommendation of" Kim Jong Il. On the other hand, Ri Yong-ch'ŏl and Ri Che-gang—the two core first vice directors of the KWPCCOGD who had investigated the "wrongdoings" of Chang Sŏng-t'aek in 2003 and contributed to his being relieved from responsibilities in 2004—died in April and June, respectively. The official announcement that Ri Che-gang had died of a car accident in a Pyongyang street, just three days before Chang's elevation to the NDC vice-chairmanship, prompted speculation abroad that he might have been assassinated.[117] According to NIS sources, it was Chang who dismissed or demoted many military leaders who belonged to the "Ri Che-gang line." Among them was Kim Il-ch'ŏl, KPA vice marshal, NDC member, and PAFM first vice minister. He had been PAFM minister before Kim Jung Un's designation as the successor, but in May 2010 he was relieved of all posts.[118]

114 Kang and Kim, "Jong Un," *Korea JoongAng Daily*, November 3, 2010, 1.

115 *Dong-A Ilbo* reporters in charge of Sino–North Korean relations received this information from a couple of embassies in Seoul under conditions of anonymity around September 2010. I was chairman of *Dong-A Ilbo* at the time.

116 Cheong, "Pukhan," 92–94. See also Cheong Seong-chang, "Current State of Kim Jong Un Power Succession," *Vantage Point*, September 2011, 19.

117 Paek Sŭng-ju, "Ri Che-gang ŏn amsal twaendŏt" [Ri Che-gang Might Have Been Killed], *Chugan Dong-A*, No. 742 (June 29, 2010): 56–57. See also *Dong-A Ilbo*, June 8, A 1.

118 *Dong-A Ilbo*, May 15, 2010, A3; Paek Sŭng-ju, "Chang Sŏng-t'aek Rain kwa Ri Che-gang Rain" [The Chang Sŏng-t'aek line and the Ri Che-gang line]," *Wŏlgan JoongAng* (November 2010): 59–60.

Beyond the demotions and ousters, Chang Sŏng-t'aek also placed his own men in strategically important posts. Kim Yŏng-ch'un was appointed PAFM minister and O Kŭk-ryŏl was appointed NDC vice-chairman; Ri Yŏng-ho was appointed KPA chief of general staff, replacing Kim Kyŏk-sik. Kim Kyŏk-sik was sent to the western front to command the Fourth Army Corps. A Chinese specialist on North Korea commented:

> This was really an unexpected move, since Kim Jong Il deeply trusted Kim Kyŏk-sik. One explanation is that he was too powerful or capable to be entrusted with the task of assisting Kim Jong Un [to] take up the leadership. Another possible observation is that he is an ideal person to help Kim Jong Un secure his position as heir. Given the latter consideration, Kim Jong Il thought that Kim Kyŏk-sik should best stay out of Pyongyang. In case of a crisis against Kim Jong Un, he could command his troops to return to Pyongyang to suppress rebels.[119]

Ri Yŏng-ho continued to be rapidly promoted. In September 2010 he was promoted to KPA vice marshal and elected KWPCC Politburo member and CMC member. North Korea's armed forces maintain a single command system: the KPA chief of general staff directly commands and controls ground corps, tanks, infantry and artillery command, navy command, and air command. Why, then, did Chang Sŏng-t'aek and ultimately Kim Jong Il appoint this former Pyongyang garrison commander, a general with less power and in a relatively lower position in the military hierarchy, to such a strategically crucial post? A Chinese scholar suggested one answer:

> In comparison with other generals, Ri Yŏng-ho will have less ambition and power to challenge Kim Jong Un's leadership. More importantly, as a relatively inferior general, any action or behavior beyond the system's rules and traditional arrangement will easily lead to his defeat in a power struggle.[120]

With Chang's strong recommendation, NDC counselor Pak Myŏng-ch'ŏl was appointed to the newly inaugurated post of sports minister. It meant that the North Korean regime recognized the importance of "international sports diplomacy," an area in which South Korea has been strong. Pak is the son-in-law of the late Rikidōzan, the ring name of the Korean-Japanese godfather of professional wrestling in Japan. Kim Kyŏng-hŭi also reportedly exercised her influence and enabled the promotions of both Kim Rak-hŭi—chief secretary, responsible for the KWP Hwanghae provincial

119 Liu Ming, "Elite Cohesion: Probability of a Power Struggle among the Elite," a paper delivered at the conference on "The Viability of the North Korean Regime," hosted by the Asan Institute for Policy Studies, Seoul, September 8–9, 2011, 4.
120 Ibid.

committee—and Kang Nŭng-su, chairman of the (North) Korean Public Relations Committee, to the position of vice premier.[121]

The cabinet was reshuffled to give increased priority to the economy, finance, and industry. Ch'oe Yŏng-rim, former vice premier and state planning committee chairman, was promoted to premier, replacing Kim Yŏng-il. All of the newly appointed cabinet ministers were technocrats.

Kim Jong Il's Appointment of Kim Jong Un As Successor and Formation of a New Ruling Structure at the Third KWP Representatives Conference, 2010–11

On September 27, 2010, Kim Jong Il, in his capacity as KPA supreme commander, elevated Kim Jong Un to the rank of four-star general. The next day, the Third KWP Representatives Conference was held in Pyongyang—the first time this group met since 1966—and elected new Central Committee members, including Kim Jong Un. Immediately, the new Central Committee expanded its Politburo membership from nine to thirty-two. Five were elected to its Presidium or Standing Committee: Kim Jong Il (KWP general secretary and DPRKNDC chairman); Kim Yŏng-nam (head of state as chairman of the SPASC); Ch'oe Yŏng-rim (prime minister); Cho Myŏng-rok (NDC first vice-chairman); and Ri Yŏng-ho (KPA chief of general staff). While twelve were elected members, fifteen were elected as alternate members.[122] The expanded Politburo was a mixture of the senior group and the working-level group. It also reflected a considered balance among the KWP, KPA, cabinet, and social organizations, all under the primacy of the KWP.

We can make a few observations about the changes resulting from the conference. The transitional power structure was formed so that Kim Kyŏng-hŭi, Chang Sŏng-t'aek, Ri Yŏng-ho, and Kim Jong Un would have legal authority to control the country.[123] Kim Kyŏng-hŭi was admitted to the Politburo as a full member, while her husband was admitted as an alternate member. Kim Jong Il seemed to have decided to weaken the "second-in-command" image of Chang Sŏng-t'aek. Apart from Kim Kyŏng-hŭi and Chang Sŏng-t'aek, only Ri Yong-mu was related to the Kim family; the rest were

---

121 *Dong-A Ilbo*, June 8, 2010, A2.

122 Elected members were Kim Yŏng-ch'un, Chŏn Pyŏng-ho, Kim Kuk-t'ae, Kim Ki-nam, Ch'oe T'ae-bok, Yang Hyŏng-sŏp, Kang Sŏk-chu, Pyŏn Yŏng-rip, Ri Yong-mu, Chu Sang-sŏng, Hong Sŏk-hyŏng, Kim Kyŏng-hŭi; alternate members were Kim Yang-gŏn, Kim Yŏng-il, Pak To-ch'un, Ch'oe Ryong-hae, Chang Sŏng-t'aek, Chu Kyu-ch'ang, Ri T'ae-nam, Kim Rak-hŭi, T'ae Chong-su, Kim P'yŏng-hae, U Tong-ch'ŭk. Kim Chŏng-gak, Pak Chŏng-sun, Kim Ch'ang-sŏp, and Mun Kyŏng-dŏk.

123 Liu, "Elite Cohesion," 2.

people who had risen in their fields by demonstrating real expertise. Finally, Kang Sŏk-chu, who was promoted to vice premier from first vice foreign minister just four days earlier, was admitted to the Politburo as a full member. Kim Jong Il rewarded him with these double promotions for his active role in the North's "successful" negotiations with the United States beginning in June 1993. Kim Kye-gwan, who had assisted Kang Sŏk-chu as second vice foreign minister, became Kang's successor as first vice foreign minister. Since 1993, the professional diplomats Kang and Kim have been major players in both the bilateral DPRK-U.S. negotiations and the Six-Party Talks aimed at defusing the North Korean nuclear crisis.

Also on the first day of the Third KWP Representatives Conference, the representatives "acclaimed" Kim Jong Il as KWP general secretary and elected ten secretaries.[124] Each had demonstrated expertise in his field and none had family ties to Kim Jong Il. One of the newly elected secretaries was Kim Yŏng-Il (b. 1944), the premier from 2007 to 2010. Another, Hong Sŏk-hyŏng (b. 1936 in Seoul), was the grandson of the late Hong Myŏng-hŭi, a well-known anti-Japanese literary figure and author of the well-known novel *Im Kkŏk-chŏng*, a Korean version of Robin Hood.[125] In 2011 South Korean intelligence officers said that Hong Sŏk-hyŏng had apparently lost his membership in the Politburo and his position as secretary for planning and finance.[126]

The plenary session of the newly constituted Central Committee acclaimed Kim Jong Il as chairman of the KWP Central Military Committee and elected eighteen members.[127] Among these eighteen new KWPCMC

124 They were Kim Ki-nam (propaganda and agitation), Ch'oe T'ae-bok (international affairs and education), Ch'oe Ryong-hae (social organizations), Mun Kyŏng-dŏk (Pyongyang Special City), Pak To-ch'un (military supply), Kim Yŏng-il (China affairs), Kim Yang-gŏn (South Korea), Kim P'yŏng-hae (cadres), T'ae Chong-su (general affairs), and Hong Sŏk-hyŏng (planning and finance).

125 Hong Myŏng-hŭi, together with his family, had gone to the North in 1948 and would become DPRK vice premier. His two sons, Hong Ki-mun and Hong Ki-mu, also played important roles in the North.

126 *Choson Ilbo*, October 6, 2011, 2.

127 The elected members were Kim Jong Un (general and SSM minister); Ri Yŏng-ho (vice marshal, KWPCC Politburo Presidium member, and KPA chief of general staff); Kim Yŏng-ch'un (vice marshal, KWPCC Politburo member, NDC vice-chairman, and PAFM minister); Kim Chŏng-gak (general, KWPCC Politburo alternate member, NDC member, and first vice director of the KPAGPB); Kim Myŏng-guk (general and director of the KPAGPB operations bureau); Kim Kyŏng-ok (general and first vice director of the KWPCCOGD); Kim Wŏn-hong (general and vice director for organization of the KPAGPB); Chŏng Myŏng-do (general and navy commander); Ri Pyŏng-ch'ŏl (general and air force commander); Ch'oe Pu-il (general and KPA vice chief of general staff); Kim

members, Ri Yŏng-ho, Kim Chŏng-gak, and Kim Yŏng-ch'ol were regarded as the most important generals in both that body and the KPA. But it was noteworthy that three *lieutenant* generals—Kim Yŏng-ch'ŏl, Ch'oe Sang-ryŏ, and Ch'oe Kyŏng-sŏng—were included in the KWPCMC, an organ into which most full generals were unable to gain admission. How could these lieutenant generals be included in this most powerful elite organ in the North? The answer may lie in the fact that they were all involved in the North's military and espionage operations against the South.

Kim Yŏng-ch'ŏl, (b. 1946 in Ryanggang Province) was educated at Man'gyŏngdae Revolutionary School and Kim Il Sung Comprehensive Military University. As a KPA major, he worked with North Korean delegates to P'anmunjŏm to negotiate with the United States on the USS Pueblo issue in 1968. He also led the North Korean delegation in inter-Korean military meetings in 1992 and 2006–07. In early 2009, the North consolidated three organs—the KPA's espionage operation department, the KPA's Thirty-Fifth Office (Office 35, in charge of espionage against the South), and the PAFM's reconnaissance bureau—to form the Reconnaissance General Bureau. Formally it existed as an organ under the KPA general staff, but in reality it was controlled by Kim Jong Il personally. Kim Jong Il appointed Kim Yŏng-ch'ŏl—who had taught Kim Jong Un at Kim Il Sung Comprehensive Military University—to direct this combined organ. South Korean intelligence officers maintain that it was this "very arrogant and pompous" general who planned the sinking of the *Cheonan* in 2010.[128]

Information on Ch'oe Sang-ryŏ is largely unavailable. In 1992, 1997, and 2010, he received promotions successively to brigadier general, major general, and lieutenant general. He apparently earned the full confidence of Kim Jong Il, as he was placed in charge of the country's critically important missile development project. Ch'oe Kyŏng-sŏng commanded the so-called Storm Corps, an elite special warfare corps based in Tŏkch'ŏn County, South P'yongan Province, which reportedly consisted of ten brigades, with between forty and eighty thousand men.[129]

Yŏng-ch'ŏl (lieutenant general and KPA general director of reconnaissance); Yun Chŏng-rim (general and KPA safeguard headquarters commander); Chu Kyu-ch'ang (KWPCC Politburo alternate member); Ch'oe Sang-ryŏ (lieutenant general and KPA director for missile); Ch'oe Kyŏng-sŏng (lieutenant general and KPA eleventh corps commander); U Tong-ch'ŭk; Ch'oe Ryong-hae; and Chang Sŏng-t'aek.

128 *JoongAng Ilbo*, December 28, 2011, 10. See also Jeong Yong-soo and Kim Hee-jin, "A Pair of Former Spy Bosses Lurk in the Shadows," *Korea JoongAng Daily*, January 3, 2012, 3.

129 *Chosun Ilbo*, December 14, 2011, A6.

A noteworthy individual in the new lineup was Ch'oe Ryong-hae. Ch'oe, who had been censured and sent to the countryside in 1998, secured concurrent membership in the Politburo, secretariat, and Central Military Committee with the rank of four-star general. Born in 1950 as the second son of Ch'oe Hyŏn, Kim Il Sung's partisan comrade and PAFM minister, and reared in a special residential compound reserved for the top elite, including Kim Il Sung, he befriended Kim Jong Il from boyhood. He helped Kim Jong Un in the field of social organization after his return to Pyongyang in the early 2000s. But even more noteworthy than Choe's rise was that the KWPCMC's power expanded sharply with the participation of all core military commanders, overshadowing the NDC. The KWPCMC had been a loose and irregular forum; now it became a tightly constituted standing committee.[130]

The newly composed Central Committee created vice-chairmen positions within the KWP Central Military Committee, and Kim Jong Il, in his capacity as KWP chairman, appointed Kim Jong Un along with Ri Yŏng-ho to the new posts. On October 10, as the sixty-fifth anniversary of the founding of the KWP was being celebrated, Kim Jong Un made his public debut at a military parade and also appeared at an evening celebration in Pyongyang. These were broadcast live on state television, and most North Koreans were reportedly struck by his resemblance to the young Kim Il Sung. Yang Hyŏng-sŏp, a KWPCC Politburo member and vice president of the SPA Presidium, declared, "Our people are honored to serve the great chairman Kim Il Sung and the great leader Kim Jong Il. Now we also have the honor of serving young General Kim Jong Un."[131] On the very day that Kim Jong Un made his public debut in Pyongyang, Hwang Chang-yŏp's death from natural causes, at the age of eighty-seven, was publicly announced in Seoul. The North Korean media regarded the defector's death as a good omen for the new leader.[132]

On November 10, when the members of the state funeral committee for the late Cho Myŏng-rok were announced, Kim Jong Un was listed second, after Kim Jong Il and just before Kim Yŏng-nam, the ceremonial head of state.[133] The death of Cho Myŏng-rok meant the conclusive dissolution of the Cho Myŏng-rok–Kim Il-ch'ŏl–Kim Yŏng-ch'un triumvirate in the

130 Cheong Seong-chang, *Hyŏndae Pukhan ŭi chŏngch'i: Yŏksa, inyom, kwŏnllyŏk ch'egye* [Contemporary North Korean politics: History, ideology, and power system] (Seoul: Hanul Academy, 2011), 288–322.

131 *Rodong Sinmun*, September 28, 2010, 1, and September 29, 2010, 1. See also Associated Press, "Top Official Confirms Son Will Be Kim's Successor," *International Herald Tribune*, October 9–10, 2010, 3.

132 Quoted in *Dong-A Ilbo*, October 14, 2010, 2.

133 *Rodong Sinmun*, November 11, 2010, 1.

North Korean military establishment. (Recall that Kim Il-ch'ol was relieved from all posts in May 2010.) Although Kim Yŏng-ch'un remained a KWP Central Committee Politburo member and PAFM minister, he had to follow the orders of Ri Yŏng-ho, KWPCC Politburo's Standing Committee member and KPA chief of general staff.

Kim Jong Un's status as Kim Jong Il's successor was confirmed in yet another way. On January 5, 2011, three days before his son's twenty-seventh birthday, Kim Jong Il enacted an unpublicized regulation[134] that prohibited the North Korean people from having "Jong Un" as a given name. The pamphlet containing that the regulation, which was made public in the South in December 2014, made clear that those already having "Jong Un" as their given name should adopt different names.[135] Just as with Kim Il Sung and Kim Jong Il, the North Korean people were prohibited from using the "sacred" names of their leaders.

The "Jasmine Revolution," during which dictatorial regimes in Tunisia, Egypt, and Libya all toppled between December 2010 and June 2011, may have been a strain on the KWP leadership. In January 2011 the regime, which strictly controlled mobile phone use by ordinary citizens, publicly executed a certain Mr. Chŏng, an ordinary worker, in Hamhŏng, South Hamgyŏng Province, on the charge that he used his mobile phone to reveal information on the price of rice to a North Korean defector in the South.[136] There was also a high-level defection during this period: a grandson of the late Paek Nam-un, a Marxist economist who had gone to the north in 1947 and had occupied many higher posts, including that of SPA chairman, defected to the South with his family. He said, "I saw no hope in the North. For the future of my sons, I decided to defect to the South."[137]

An even more serious matter was the secret execution of Lieutenant General Ryu Kyŏng, a powerful SSM vice minister, in early January. As commander of fifty thousand officers and soldiers, Ryu wielded great power, although his name and photograph never appeared in the North's media. It is known that one of Ryu's assignments was the surveillance of Chang Sŏng-t'aek and his followers. When Kim Jong Un realized that the SSM was under Ryu's full control, he apparently decided to eliminate him. According

134 The pamphlet was distributed only to Party functionaries.

135 KBS television network showed the pamphlet during its regular 9:00 p.m. news broadcast on December 3, 2014. See also Lee Ji-son, "Puk, Chumindŭlaekae 'Kim Jong Un' Yirŭm Sayongkŭmji," [The North prohibits the use of "Jong Un" in a citizen's given name], *Kyŏnghyang Sinmun*, December 4, 2014, 4.

136 Yun Chŏng-a, "Puk" [The North], *Munhwa Ilbo*, May 12, 2011, 2.

137 Cho Sung-ho, "Nan Paek Nam-un sonja" [I am Paek Nam-un's grandson], *Dong-A Ilbo*, October 6, 2011, 2.

to NIS sources, realizing that it would be practically impossible to arrest Ryu by normal means, Kim Jong Il, Kim Jong Un, and Chang Sŏng-t'aek invited him to a feast at Kim Jong Il's residence, where they disarmed and arrested him. Within a few days, they executed Ryu in the compound of Kim Jong Il's residence.[138] All of Ryu's family members were banished to one of the notorious concentration camps in the barren backcountry.

Conditions for prisoners, who are believed to number in the millions, are extremely miserable in these camps. A reliable report released in October 2003 drawing on interviews conducted with thirty camp survivors and former guards revealed that "[i]n a network of prison camps hidden in isolated valleys and mountains of North Korea, hundreds of thousands of prisoners work, often to their deaths, in conditions of starvation food rations, routine torture, and imprisonment of entire families."[139] The report continued, "All the prison facilities are characterized by very large numbers of deaths in detention from forced, hard labor accompanied by deliberate starvation-level food rations." According to the report, "former prisoners . . . [explained] that many of their fellow captives did not expect to survive long enough to complete their sentences—and that thousands of them did not survive."[140]

Anne Applebaum, author of *Gulag: A History*, writes in an introduction to the report:

> . . . the North Korean camps were built according to a Stalinist model, and. . . they continue to be run that way. . . . [A]s in Stalin's time, North Korea's leadership doesn't want anyone to know any of these details, since such revelations not only will damage their foreign reputations, but put their own regime at risk.[141]

In March 2011 Chu Sang-sŏng was relieved as MPS minister, a position responsible for the regular police, on the charge that he was ineffective in controlling border-crossings. This meant that the regime would tighten the border and that hungry North Koreans would find it much more difficult to defect to China. On April 7, 2011, the fourth session of the Twelfth SPA relieved the aged Chŏn Pyŏng-ho (in his mid-eighties) from NDC membership and elected Pak To-ch'un to that post. It also appointed Ri Myŏng-su as MPS minister.[142] Relatively young military leaders were promoted to the

138 Kang Ch'ŏl-hwan and Ahn Yong-hyŏn, "Ryu Kyŏng" [Ryu Kyŏng], *Chosun Ilbo*, May 20, 2011, A1.

139 James Brook, "North Korea's Gulag: Torture, Starvation, Prisoners Worked to Death," *International Herald Tribune*, October 23, 2003.

140 David Hawk, *The Hidden Gulag: Exposing North Korea's Prison Camps* (Washington, DC: The Committee for Human Rights in North Korea, 2003), 15–20.

141 Brooke, "North Korea's Gulag."

142 *Dong-A Ilbo*, April 8, 2011, A1.

ranks of general, lieutenant general, and major general. North Korea watchers in Seoul conjectured that Kim Jong Un was replacing old cadres with new cadres in state agencies in charge of intelligence and state violence and coercion.[143]

Beginning in the middle of October 2011, the North Korean media began to report more on Kim Jong Un and to use the phrase, "Respected Comrade General Kim Jong Un." These practices reminded North Korea watchers in Seoul of the summer of 1984, when the North Korean media began to focus more seriously on Kim Jong Il than on Kim Il Sung. On October 25, 2011, four days after the news of the execution of Muammar Gaddafi was broadcast worldwide, all North Korean media referred to Kim Jong Un as "Respected Comrade General" when they reported his visit, along with his father and Chang Sŏng-t'aek, to the KPA Safeguard Headquarters, which is responsible for the physical protection of the Kim family.

143 Han Pyŏng-gwan, "Kim Chŏng-ŭn tŏngjang ku-gaewŏl" [Nine months after the advent of Kim Jong Un], *Pukhan Sosik*, July 6, 2011, 6.

7 The Death of Kim Jong Il and Advent of Kim Jong Un's Leadership, 2011–14

The Prepared Transition from Kim Jong Il to Kim Jong Un

In a special broadcast at noon on December 19, 2011, an anchorwoman on the North's Korean Central Television tearfully announced that Kim Jong Il had died of heart failure while traveling by train. According to a KCNA report:

> Due to accumulated physical and mental fatigue, the Leader suffered from acute myocardial infarction, followed by severe heart shocks. All emergency medical actions were taken immediately, but the Leader died at 8:30 a.m. on [December 17].

The report added that an autopsy was performed on December 18 to confirm the cause of death—which turned out to be exactly the same as Kim Il Sung's. A joint statement announcing Kim's death—termed "a message to all party members, soldiers, and the people"—was issued by the KWP Central Committee and Central Military Committee, the National Defense Commission, the Supreme People's Assembly Presidium, and the cabinet. They declared that a period of national mourning would begin on December 19 and continue until December 29 and that the North would not receive delegates from foreign countries for the commemorative events.[1] On December 22 *Rodong Sinmun*, like KCNA, reported that Kim had died during a field trip on a train running to the "northern side."[2]

1 *Rodong Sinmun*, December 20, 2011, 1–2.
2 Chŏng Sŏng-il, "Widaehan nunbora Han Saeng" [Great turbulent life], *Rodong Sinmun*, December 22, 2011, 5.

South Korean journalist Ser Myo-ja summarized the North's reporting of the leader's passing:

> The announcements of Kim's death glorified the North Korean leader's achievements, calling him a great revolutionary who has wisely led the Workers' Party, military, and the people for a long time. His efforts to uphold the North's founding ideology of *Juche*, or self-reliance, to build a strong country with a "military first" policy were highlighted in the announcements. Kim was also praised for having made the North an "untouchable nuclear power."[3]

Citing these merits, the Standing Committee of the Supreme People's Assembly conferred upon Kim the title of "Hero of the Republic," making him the only person apart from Kim Il Sung to have thrice received this highest of titles. On December 20, state-run television showed Kim Jong Il's body—covered with a red blanket with his head resting on a white pillow—installed inside a glass coffin at the Kumsusan Memorial Palace in Pyongyang. The coffin was surrounded by white chrysanthemums and *Kimjongilia*, a variety of begonia named after the deceased leader.[4]

The North's official broadcast made it clear that Kim Jong Un was now the DPRK's top leader. Korean Central Television announced:

> At the forefront of our revolution, there is our comrade Kim Jong Un standing as the great successor to our *Juche* ideology and the leader of our party, army, and people. Under the guidance of Comrade Kim Jong Un, we should fight more aggressively for a new, great victory of *Juche* revolution, changing our sadness into power and courage.[5]

North Korean media emphasized that the new top leader would be guided by his father's *yuhun*—testaments left behind by Kim Jong Il. The essence of Kim Jong Il's *yuhun* was the observance of military-first politics. Thus the *Rodong Sinmun* editorialized on December 22, "We should walk our own path of the self-reliant, military-first revolution by keeping the *yuhun* of Comrade Kim Jong Il. . . . We are now full of passion to revere the military-first leadership of Comrade Kim Jong Un."[6] In sum, this editorial used the term "military-first" twenty-one times. While stressing that Kim Jong Un would respect his father's testament, the North Korean media slightly modified a trademark term that Kim Jong Il had used since January

3 Ser Myo-ja, "Kim Jong Il Dies at 69," *Korea JoongAng Daily*, December 20, 2011.

4 *Rodong Sinmun*, December 21, 2011, 2.

5 Quoted in Kim Hee-jin, "All Eyes Are Now on Kim Jong Un," *Korea JoongAng Daily*, December 20, 2011.

6 Quoted in *Korea JoongAng Daily*, December 23, 2011. See also Lee Tae-hoon, "North Korea Declares Era of Kim Jong Un," *Korea Times*, December 23, 2011.

1999. Recognizing that it would be almost impossible to become a *kangsŏng taeguk* (literally, a great country that is strong and prosperous, sometimes also translated as "rich nation, strong army") by the target year of 2012, the media officially downgraded the goal to *kangsŏng kukka* (powerful and prosperous state).[7]

A number of observations can be made based on the official reports. First, contrary to how most media depicted Kim's death as having been "sudden" or "abrupt," it had been expected and even predicted. On February 3, 2010, about eighteen months after Kim Jong Il had a stroke, Kurt M. Campbell, the American assistant secretary of state for East Asian and Pacific affairs, said in a closed-door meeting with South Korean opinion leaders at the U.S. embassy in Seoul that "based on all medical information, his life span would not continue for more than three years."[8] On September 9, 2010, *Forbes* predicted in its "News from the Future" that Kim would die by the end of 2011.[9]

Suspicions lingered about the official announcement that he died at 8:30 A.M. aboard a moving train. ROK NIS director Won Sei-hun briefed the National Assembly on December 21 that Kim Jong Il's personal train had been at Pyongyang's No 1. Station in Yongsŏng at the time in question. He implied that Kim might actually have died at his residence.[10] In contrast, South Korean military intelligence officials leaked to the press that Kim's personal train had been moving and headed toward a particular destination.[11] On December 22, quoting "White House sources," lawmaker Pak Sŏn-yŏng contended that Kim died around 1:30 A.M. on December 16 in his exclusive villa at Jamosan, not far from Pyongyang. This villa was known to have its own hospital and to be linked with Kim's office in Pyongyang by an underground tunnel. Another lawmaker, Song Yŏng-sŏn, followed suit with a similar claim.[12] On the same day, Tokyo's TV Asahi reported that Kim had died around one o'clock in the morning of December 17 in his resort office

7 For example, see the December 22, 2011, *Rodong Sinmun* editorial, p. 1.

8 Campbell's remarks were belatedly reported in the Seoul media. For example, see Lee Tae-hoon, "Kim Jong Il Has Only 3 Years Left to Live," *Korea Times*, March 18, 2010.

9 Lee Woo-young, "Forbes Predicts Death of Kim Next Year," *Korea Herald*, September 14, 2010.

10 Park Si-soo, "Suspicious Linger over Dictator's Death," *Korea Times*, December 22, 2011.

11 Ch'oe Kyŏng-un and Cho ŭi-jun, "Kun, umjikyotta" [The military answered the trains moved], *Chosun Ilbo*, December 21, 2011.

12 Chung Min-uck, "Lawmaker Raises Suspicion over Time of Kim's Death," *Korea Times*, December 23, 2011, 2.

near Pyongyang. His last words to his bodyguard were said to have been, "Give me water."[13] TV Asahi added the comments of Yi Yun-kŏl, a defector who had worked in the Safeguard Command for Kim Jong Il. Quoting a few high-ranking Chinese sources, Yi said that Kim had died around eight o'clock at his residence on the evening of December 16.

A year later, Seoul's *Choson Ilbo* claimed it could confirm the authenticity of the original official announcement. Quoting North Korean sources and South Korean NIS sources, the daily said that Kim had indeed been aboard a train heading for Huich'ŏn County, Chakang Province, where a huge power plant that would be symbolic of his achievements was being constructed. Kim reportedly was infuriated on receiving a confidential report that the construction was delayed due to a lack of raw materials, and en route he suffered a heart attack and died instantly. His attending medical team had no chance to treat him.[14]

In any event, it seems probable that the North Korean official version, whether completely factual or not, was intended to give the people of North Korea the impression that Kim had worked himself to death for them, including on guidance trips by rail such as this.[15]

Fifty-one hours and thirty minutes elapsed between the time of Kim's death and its announcement, compared to thirty-four hours in the case of Kim Il Sung. Since Kim Jong Il was already the de facto supreme leader at the time of Kim Il Sung's death, his position was strong enough to proceed with a quick funeral. In contrast, Kim Jong Un needed time to consult about the funeral with a few core elites of the North Korean power structure, during which his own position was probably consolidated. The national funeral committee list (see table 7.1) was certainly also decided or at least finalized in this process, as the list of the 232 committee members was released simultaneously with the announcement of Kim's death.[16]

The list did not reveal a hidden pecking order—instead it showed that the order of the funeral committee was according to each person's official KWP position. That is why Chang Sŏng-t'aek, alternate member of the KWP

13 Quoted in Chang In-sŏ, "Kim Jong Il, pyŏljangaesŏ samanghaetta" [Kim Jong Il died at the villa], *Asia Kyŏngje* [Asian economy], December 24, 2011. On December 22, 2011, KBS and MBC, major South Korean TV networks, also relayed TV Asahi's story on their evening news broadcasts.

14 Yi Yong-su, "Kim Jong Il hyŏngchang ch'ajakada jŭksa [Kim Jong Il died instantly]" *Chosun Ilbo*, December 25, 2012.

15 Park Si-soo, "Suspicions Linger over Dictator's Death," *Korea Times*, December 22, 2011; Chung Mun-uck, "Lawmaker Raises Suspicion over Time of Kim's Death," *Korea Times*, December 23, 2011.

16 For the list, see *Rodong Sinmun*, December 20, 2011, 4–5.

TABLE 7.1

The first ten names on Kim Jong Il's national funeral committee list

Name	Position
Kim Jong Un	
Kim Yŏng-nam	Nominal head of state as the SPASC chairman
Ch'oe Yŏng-rim	Premier
Ri Yŏng-ho	Vice-chairman of the KWPCMC and chief of KPA general staff
Kim Yŏng-ch'un	PAFM minister
Chŏn Pyŏng-ho	Political Bureau director of the cabinet
Kim Kuk-t'ae	KWP Control Committee chairman
Kim Ki-nam	KWPCC secretary for propaganda
Ch'oe T'ae-bok	KWPCC secretary for international affairs and education
Yang Hyŏng-sŏp	Vice-chairman of the SPASC

Politburo, was listed nineteenth, while his wife, Kim Kyŏng-hŭi, a member of the KWP Politburo, was listed before him at fourteenth. Kim Ok, the de facto widow of Kim Jong Il, was not included in the committee using the same logic—she had no official title in either the party or the cabinet.[17]

The funeral committee list also showed a balance between KWP cadres and KPA generals, who together far outnumbered the cabinet members on the list. The average age of a member of the funeral committee (based on the ones whose ages were available) was around seventy-three. There was not a single person on the list under the age of fifty, with the exception of Kim Jong Un himself. One individual's absence from the list was conspicuous: former PAFM minister and incumbent General Kim Kyŏk-sik. South Korean authorities suspected that Kim directed the sinking of the South Korean Navy corvette *Ch'ŏnan* and the shelling of the South Korea's Yŏnp'yŏng Island in 2010. Some analysts speculated the omission might amount to a signal by the North of its willingness to negotiate with the South, while others contended that Kim Kyŏk-sik had actually been ousted from the power structure.[18] However, as we shall see, Kim Kyŏk-sik maintained major positions within the KPA, including as chief of the KPA General Staff and PAFM minister.

In the days following the official announcement of Kim Jong Il's death, the North Korean media produced a number of apocrypha. According to the December 20 *Rodong Sinmun*, a few days before Kim Jong Il's death medical doctors had recommended "in tears" that he should get some rest.

17 Pak Su-sŏng and Ko Su-sŏk, "Kim Ok changŭiwiwon pajida" [Kim Ok was deleted from the funeral committee], *JoongAng Ilbo*, December 22, 2011, 5.
18 Ibid.

He refused, replying, "In order to take care of my soldiers, workers, and people, I am sorry that I must disobey you, medical doctors. Now it is your turn to obey me."[19] Another *Rodong Sinmun* story professed that, two days before his death, Kim Jong Il had instructed that all the musical recordings he had preserved for many decades should be given to a music library in Pyongyang for all the people to use.[20] On December 22 the KCNA claimed that on the very day of Kim's death, all the ice blocks in Ch'ŏnji Lake at the top of Mt. Paektu cracked simultaneously, making a thundering noise, and that "on December 20, near Mt. Paektu, a snowstorm ended suddenly and a mysterious red-colored light began shining over a rock that bears the words 'the sacred revolutionary Mt. Paektu,' engraved by Kim Jong Il himself." It added that a flock of white cranes had appeared around Mt. Paektu.[21] From December 23 to 26, North Korean television broadcast showed flocks of magpies flying from local towns to Pyongyang "to express their condolences for the deceased Kim Jong Il."[22] On December 25, North Korean media lavished praise on the late Kim Jong Suk—the biological mother of late Kim Jong Il, sanctified as one of "Three Great Generals of Mt. Paektu"—on the occasion of her ninety-third birthday. The media emphasized that supporting Kim Jong Un would be tantamount to upholding his grandmother's legacies.[23] In contrast, the media never mentioned Kim Jong Un's biological mother. South Korean observers contended that this was done to avoid reminding North Koreans of Ko Yong-hŭi's status as a "Japo"—a derogatory term for those who came to the North from Japan—and someone unrelated to the "holy blood-lineage of Mt. Paektu."[24] While the North's media occasionally reported on Kim Jong Suk's contributions to the anti-Japanese movement and the establishment of the DPRK,[25] it never mentioned Ko Yong-hŭi.

What the National Funeral Revealed

The eleven-day national funeral period, from December 19 to 29, gave some indications of the newly formed hierarchical order among the North

19 "Chŏngron: Yŏngwondan Wuriŭi Kim Jong Il Tongji" [Editorial: Our eternal comrade Kim Jong Il], *Rodong Sinmun*, December 20, 2011, 5.

20 Ibid.

21 *Rodong Sinmun*, December 22, 2011, 6. See also Yun Wan-jun, "Paektusan ŏlŭm" [Ice of Mt. Paektu], *Dong-A Ilbo*, December 23, 2011, A 2.

22 Kim Su-kyŏng, "Puk Teabi Kach'idea Pammadamoyŏ Kim Jong Il Aeto" [The North's TV: "Magpies mourn the death of Kim Jong Il"], dongA.com, December 26, 2011.

23 Yi Yong-su, "Puk, Kim Jong Un Halmŏni Usanghwa" [The North's personality cult of Kim Jong Un's grandmother], *Chosun Ilbo*, December 26, 2011, A 5.

24 Ibid.

25 For example, see *Rodong Sinmun*, September 1, 2013, 2, and September 20, 3013, 1.

Korean power elite and hinted at the future of the regime under Kim Jong Un. Above all, it indisputably showed that Kim Jong Un was the top leader. On December 19, just a few hours before the announcement of Kim Jong Il's death, Kim Jong Un had issued "General's Order No. 1" to the KPA under the authority of the KWP Central Military Committee, commanding all officers and soldiers to return to their military units. Kim was appointed as a KPA general on September 27, 2010, and the issuance of this order meant that he was already in charge of the KWP Central Military Committee.[26] It also indicated that the KWPCMC would be the central and most powerful organ of decision-making in Kim Jong Un's North Korea.

On December 20, *Rodong Sinmun* called Kim Jong Un "the successor of the Kim Il Sung Nation and the Kim Jong Il *Chosŏn*";[27] on December 22, it called him "the successor of the revolutionary achievements and the leader of the people."[28] Two days later, the North's media went a step further. Calling Kim "our supreme commander" and "our heart," they urged him to accept the top military post: "Comrade Kim Jong Un, please assume the supreme commandership, as wished by the people." Meanwhile, KCNA addressed him as "our highest leader of the revolutionary armed forces, as well as our parent who takes care of our people." When top military generals visited Kumsusan mausoleum on December 24, they flanked Kim Jong Un and vowed their allegiance to him. According to KCNA, all of them also prayed for the deceased Kim Jong Il's "immortality." KCNA stressed, "Let the whole army remain true to the leadership of Kim Jong Un over the army," a call that some noted echoed Kim Jong Il's own words when he was elevated to supreme commander.[29] As Choe Sang-Hun reported, "That official plea, along with television footage of the generals, signaled that the military was spearheading Kim Jong Un's succession."[30]

On December 25, *Rodong Sinmun* called Kim Jong Un "the sun of the twenty-first century." Finally, on December 26, *Rodong Sinmun* referred to him as the head of the KWP and the KWPCMC. It declared, "All party organizations across the country are upholding Great Comrade Kim Jong Un's ideology and leadership with one mind." The implication was that the

26 *Dong-A Ilbo*, December 23, 2011, 1.

27 Quoted in Kim Su-jŏng, "Kim Jong Un," *Dong-A Ilbo*, December 21, 2011, 2. *Chosŏn* is a traditional name of Korea. North Korea uses it as part of its official name, unlike the South, which uses "Hanguk."

28 Quoted in *Munhwa Ilbo*, December 22, 2011, 3.

29 "Jang Song-thaek [Chang Sŏng-t'aek] Puts on Uniform," *Korea JoongAng Daily*, December 26, 2011, 3.

30 Choe Sang-Hun, "Military Signals Its Support for Kim's Son," *International Herald Tribune*, December 26, 2011.

North's core ruling elites had also consented to give the son the highest titles that Kim Jong Il had possessed—KWP general secretary and KPA supreme commander—thus ensuring that Kim Jong Un was in charge of the country.[31] But it was not until December 30 that the KWPCC Politburo officially acclaimed Kim as the "Supreme Commander of the KPA."

Choe Sang-Hun reported on the funeral held at Kim Il Sung Square in Pyongyang on December 28, where Kim Yŏng-nam, the titular head of state, addressed the crowd of a hundred thousand:

> "Respected Comrade Kim Jong Un is now supreme leader of our party, military, and people. . . . He inherits the ideology, leadership, character, courage, and audacity of Comrade Kim Jong Il". . . [H]e also called on North Koreans to "solidify the monolithic leadership" of Kim Jong Un and called the fact that the son had resolved the issue of succession his "most noble achievement."[32]

A one-day memorial service was held in all cities and counties on December 29, thereby officially bringing the mourning period to a close. With Kim Jong Un hailed as the new supreme leader of the North, many observers commented that the occasion seemed less like a funeral and more like a ceremony for Kim Jong Un's accession to the throne—public confirmation that Kim Jong Un's era had begun.

A second observation about the funeral is that all the members of the so-called side-branches of the Kim Il Sung–Kim Jong Il family tree were absent from it. These included Kim Jong Il's stepmother, Kim Sŏng-ae; his uncle, Kim Yŏng-ju; his half brother, Kim P'yong-il; Kim Jong Il's legal wife, Kim Yŏng-suk, as well as her daughters; and Kim Jong Nam, Kim Jong Il's son by Sŏng Hye-rim, along with Kim Jong Nam's sons. Even Kim Jong Chul—Kim Jong Il's first son by Ko Yong-hŭi—was not to be found at the funeral. All were excluded from the national funeral committee. Only Kim Kyŏng-hŭi (Kim Jong Il's biological younger sister), Kim Yŏ-jŏng (Kim Jong Il's daughter by Ko Yong-hŭi), and Kim Ok (Kim Jong Il's last common-law wife) were permitted to attend the funeral. Kim Ok, in tears, turned toward Kim Jong Un and bowed deeply. Kim nodded in return.[33] Kim P'yŏng-il, Kim Jong Il's younger half brother and then ambassador to Poland, did not return to the DPRK for the funeral; Western TV footage showed him in tears

---

31 "North's Paper Calls Kim by Father's Titles," *Korea JoongAng Daily*, December 27, 2011.

32 Choe Sang-Hun, "North Korea Ushers in the Era of Kim Jong Un," *International Herald Tribune*, December 30, 2011.

33 Choe Sang-Hun, "Family Intrigue Throws Shadows on Future of Kim Dynasty," *International Herald Tribune*, December 23, 2011.

receiving condolences from Poles.[34] Kim Jong Nam was only allowed to visit Pyongyang in secret and to pay last respects to his father briefly while reportedly under Chinese protection—neither the media nor anyone else saw him.[35]

The state funeral provided the first clues about the men who would gather around new leader Kim Jong Un. As reported by Choe Sang-Hun:

> Leading the funeral alongside and behind Kim Jong Un were a familiar mix of military generals and party secretaries, including both octogenarian stalwarts from the days of Kim Jong Il and his father . . . Kim Il Sung, and those younger who expanded their influence while playing crucial roles in grooming the son as successor under the father's tutelage.[36]

In the procession, behind Kim on the right side were KWP secretaries Chang Sŏng-t'aek, Kim Ki-nam, and Ch'oe T'ae-bok; on the left were KPA generals Ri Yŏng-ho, Kim Yŏng-ch'un, Kim Chŏng-gak, and U Tong-ch'ŭk. Outside observers took note that Chang, reputed to be a regent of sorts for Kim Jong Un, walked immediately behind his twenty-something nephew. Four days earlier, Chang had appeared in military uniform wearing a four-star general's insignia for the first time.[37]

News of Kim Jong Il's death had reached the PRC government on December 17, and reportedly "Chinese officials [began] moving quickly to deepen their influence over the next generation of leaders in North Korea." After the announcement of Kim Jong Il's death, a Chinese Foreign Ministry spokesman declared that Kim had been a "great leader" and that "China and North Korea will strive together to continue making positive contributions to consolidating and developing the traditional friendship between our two parties, governments, and peoples. . . ."[38] The CCP Central Committee and other key organs expressed condolences as well, adding that China wanted to see the North maintain stability under the "leadership of Comrade Kim Jong Un."[39] From December 20 to 21, all of the top nine Chinese leaders, including Hu Jintao, PRC president and general secretary of the CCP Central Committee, as well as Prime Minister Wen Jiabao, visited the

34 *Choson Ilbo*, December 24, 2011, A 6.

35 "Kim Jong Il's Eldest Son Secretly Pays Last Respects," *Korean Times*, January 2, 2012, 1.

36 Choe Sang-Hun, "Glimpse of Possible Korean Power Elites," *International Herald Tribune*, December 29, 2011.

37 Ahn Yong-hyŏn, "Chang Sŏng-t'aek Daejang [General Chang Sŏng-t'aek]," *Chosun Ilbo*, December 26, 2011.

38 Edward Wong, "Beijing Anxiously Seeks Stability in its Neighbor and Often Erratic Ally," *International Herald Tribune*, December 20, 2011.

39 *JoongAng Ilbo*, December 21, 2011, 1.

North Korean embassy in Beijing to pay condolences.[40] On December 31 President Hu sent a telegram to Kim Jong Un congratulating him on becoming the KPA supreme commander.[41]

Finally, apart from the possible shifts in power revealed by the funeral, some observers claimed that the North Korean people were behaving differently than they had after Kim Il Sung's 1994 death. According to a defector living in Seoul:

> After the hearse passed by, mourners standing in the front row were crying but those behind didn't show any reaction. I saw a person putting his hands in his pockets. Those standing at the back of the crowd were dispersing after the cars left. Although the weather was bad, that kind of response was unimaginable for the founder's 1994 funeral.[42]

However, there were no signs indicating any sort of political and social unrest; evidently most North Koreans accepted Kim Jong Un as their new leader.

The Reign of the "Group of Seven"?

The composition of the national funeral committee and the funeral itself provided clues to whose stars were rising or falling as a new leadership emerged in the world's most secretive regime. They also suggested which institutions would play leading roles in sustaining Kim Jong Un's leadership. In fact, however, there was little change in the ruling structure, which had been formed by Kim Jong Il in late September 2010 in anticipation of his death, as discussed earlier. The only change in the ruling structure was that Kim Jong Un now stood at its head.

Most observers paid serious attention to the "group of seven" who walked with Kim Jong Un alongside Kim Jong Il's hearse and who were expected to rule over the North with the young new leader. Chang Sŏng-t'aek and Ri Yŏng-ho were clearly the most prominent. Chang, husband of Kim Kyŏng-hŭi, Kim Jong Il's younger sister, walked behind Kim Jong Un in his position as vice-chairman of the NDC with the rank of general. Reporting on the funeral, Choe Sang-Hun noted that Chang's "influence as power broker expanded after Kim Jong Il . . . suffered a stroke in 2008. He appeared committed to extending the Kim family's dynastic

40 *Rodong Sinmun*, December 21, 2011, 2.
41 *Rodong Sinmun*, January 1, 2012, 4.
42 Kim Hee-jin, "Snowy Weather Delays Funeral of 'Dear Leader,'" *Korea JoongAng Daily*, December 29, 2011.

rule to the third generation, but his own ambition remained shrouded in mystery."[43] Some speculated that Chang was interested in pursuing economic reform:

Analysts say that he may have more interest in liberalizing North Korea's economy. In October 2002, at the heyday of South Korea's "Sunshine Policy" toward the North, he was part of a delegation that spent nine days in Seoul observing its economy.

As first vice director of the KWP Organization and Guidance Department, he visited the offices of Samsung Electronics, COEX Mall, local factories, rode the subways, and even indulged himself at a "room salon," or hostess bar. South Korean officials said he expressed a deep interest in the market economy, even asking the South Korean government to appoint former Daewoo Chairman Kim U-jung to be director-in-charge of their special economic zone in Sinŭiju.[44]

There were rumors alleging that Chang was in charge of the Kim family's secret fund, which was stashed abroad. It was also alleged that Chang, a heavy drinker and womanizer, had to seek medical treatment a couple of times in Tianjin, China, beginning in 2007. Kim Kyŏng-hŭi herself reportedly suffered from chronic illness.

Chang Sŏng-t'aek built up his career in connection with the Socialist Labor Youth League, the KWP's youth organization. (Since 1996 it has been called the Kim Il Sung Socialist Youth League of Chosun.) Its membership numbers have never been officially released, but as of 2012 it was assumed to have five million members, about two million more than the KWP membership.[45] Since 1982, when Chang was appointed vice director of the KWP's youth and boys department, he maintained close relations with cadres of the Socialist Labor Youth League. Chang led this massive organization primarily with the assistance of Ch'oe Ryong-hae, Mun Kyŏng-dŏk, Ri Myŏng-su, and Chi Chae-ryong, termed the "group of four."[46] Mun Kyŏng-dŏk was born in 1957 in Pyongyang into an ordinary family without any revolutionary background, and graduated from the Faculty of Political Economy at Kim Il Sung Comprehensive University. He accompanied Chang on his visit

43 Choe Sang-Hun, "Glimpse of Possible Korean Power Elites; At Kim Jong Il's Funeral, Procession is Scrutinized for Hints of Heir's Circle," *International Herald Tribune*, December 29, 2011.

44 Kim Su-jeong and Kim Hee-jin, "Kim's Aunt and Uncle are North's Power Couple," *Korea JoongAng Daily*, December 29, 2011.

45 Ahn Yong-hyŏn, "Saroch'ŏng" [The Socialist Youth League], *Chosun Ilbo*, December 25, 2011.

46 Ibid.

to Seoul in October 2002. At the time of the national funeral, Mun was chief secretary of the KWP Pyongyang Municipal Chapter as well as a secretary of the KWP Central Committee, and Ri Myŏng-su was vice director of the KWP administrative department, while Chi Chae-ryong was ambassador to China.[47] Although Ch'oe Ryong-hae might be regarded as Chang's protégé, recall that Kim Jong Il reportedly promoted him to prominent posts to prevent Chang from becoming too powerful, as discussed earlier.

Vice Marshal Ri Yŏng-ho, chief of KPA general staff and co-vice-chairman of the KWP Central Military Committee along with Kim Jong Un, was speculated to have assumed the "role of a guardian protecting the new, young leader." According to *Korea Joongang Daily*:

> "Ri seems to have taken the role played by O Chin-u, the late PAFM minister, in the 1970's," said An Ch'an-il, a defector-turned-researcher in Seoul. "In his suit, Ri physically resembles Kim Ch'aek, an anti-Japanese guerrilla close to Kim Il Sung and deputy premier in the Kim Il Sung cabinet, which helps Kim Jong Un remind people of his grandfather."

> South Korean analysts say Ri's political stance is hardline, given the fact that the purported sinking of the ROKS *Ch'ŏnan* and the artillery attack on Yŏnp'yŏng Island occurred after he became KWP chief of general staff. But some say Ri could be moderate.[48]

Kim Ki-nam, the man just behind Chang Sŏng-t'aek in the funeral procession, was born in August 1929 in Kŭmya County, South Hamgyŏng Province, and educated at the Man'gyŏngdae Revolutionary School, Kim Il Sung University, and Moscow University for International Studies. He began working in the field of propaganda and agitation in the KWP in 1966. He served as editor-in-chief of *Kŭlloja* and then *Rodong Sinmun* (1972–86), and from 1985 to 2010 he was either director of the KWP propaganda-agitation department or the KWP Central Committee secretary for propaganda-agitation. In August 2009 he participated in former ROK president Kim Dae Jung's funeral, and took the opportunity to meet then ROK president Lee Myong-bak. Kim is a typical symbol-manipulator of the North who led the personality cults around Kim Il Sung and Kim Jong Il.[49]

Ch'oe T'ae-bok, the last man on the right side of the hearse, was born in December 1920 in Namp'o, South P'yong'an Province, and educated at

---

47 Ibid.

48 Hoh Kui-seek and Kim Hee-jin, "The North's Most Important General," *Korea JoongAng Daily*, December 26, 2011, 3.

49 *Pukhan inmyŏng sajŏn* [Who's who in North Korea] (Seoul: Seoul Sinmunsa, 2004), 118–122. See also Chŏng Yong-kwan, "Kim Jong Il insamal" [Kim Jong Il's message of greeting], *Dong-A Ilbo*, August 25, 6.

Man'gyŏngdae Revolutionary School, Kim Il Sung University, and an engineering school in Leipzig, East Germany. After serving as a researcher or professor at various institutions, he was elected to the KWP Central Committee in 1986. Since then he has occupied a number of important posts, including service as the KWP Central Committee secretary for education, science, and cultural exchanges, and finally the SPA chairman. He is seen as someone with little ambition for power.[50]

Kim Yŏng-ch'un, the general just behind Ri Yŏng-ho, was born in March 1936 in Hoeryŏng County, North Hamgyŏng Province, and educated at Man'gyŏngdae Revolutionary School, Kim Il Sung University, and Frunze Military Academy in Moscow. In the 1970s and 1980s, he fervently supported Kim Jong Il as successor and was rewarded with promotion to full general in 1992 and assigned to be Sixth Corps commander in 1994. As discussed earlier, he was well known for his prevention of an attempted coup d'état within his corps in June 1995. After foiling the coup, Kim was immediately promoted to vice marshal and PAFM minister, and in 1998 he was elected to the National Defense Commission, at the time the most powerful organ in the DPRK. During 2005–2009 he was promoted and served as NDC vice-chairman and was reappointed as PAFM minister. With the death of his patron, vice marshal Cho Myŏng-rok, in November 2010, Kim's political backing weakened.[51] Kim Chŏng-gak was located just behind Kim Yŏng-ch'un. We examined his career in detail earlier, and will return to his role shortly.

U Tong-ch'ŭk, the fourth general on the left side of the hearse, was the first vice director of the SSM, the national security affairs agency—North Korea's powerful and dreaded secret police. He was born in 1942, the same year officially cited as the year of Kim Jong Il's birth, and the two men attended Kim Il Sung University together. When Kim Jong Il entered politics in 1964 as a member of the KWP Organization and Guidance Department, U was appointed to the same post as Kim. In 2009, he became the first vice director of the national security affairs agency. In April 2009, he was named a NDC vice-chairman with Kim Jong Un. It was the first time a national security affairs agency official was named to the NDC. After the execution of Ryu Kyŏng (discussed earlier), he completely controlled the SSM with the support of Kim Jong Un and Chang Sŏng-t'aek.[52]

50 *Pukhan yinmyŏng sajŏn*, 968–74.

51 *Pukhan yinmyŏng sajŏn*, 218–23; See also Sin Sŏk-ho, "Kim Yŏng-ch'un," *Dong-A Ilbo*, December 3, 2009, 2.

52 Ko Soo-suk and Kim Hee-jin, "Pyongyang's Pair of Powerful Wingmen," *Korea JoongAng Daily*, January 2, 2012.

As we shall see below, however, five among the "group of seven" would be excluded or expelled from the ruling structure by demotion, forced retirement, or even execution. Only two civilians, both in their mid-eighties, would survive.

Efforts to Change Personal Leadership to Collective Leadership

Soon after the funeral, Kim Jong Un began consolidating his power via the above-mentioned institutions and individuals. One strategy to ensure a successful transition was to "[groom] the twenty-something to look and act more like [Kim Il Sung]," with the North Korean media attempting to make Kim Jong Un his grandfather's "avatar."[53] As one writer put it, "the state has attempted to transfer Kim Il Sung's charisma to his grandson by accentuating their physical resemblance."[54] Rumors even had it that Kim Jong Un had undergone cosmetic surgery to resemble Kim Il Sung. Indeed, video footage of Kim Jong Un revealed a striking resemblance to his grandfather. Soon, the Kim Jong Il and Kim Jong Un personality cults were reinitiated. On January 12, 2012, the KWPCC Politburo released a special public message. Declaring that Kim Jong Il's body would be embalmed like that of his father had been, it reiterated that both Kim Il Sung and Kim Jong Il were "immortal." In this spirit, the Politburo also decided to erect towers in commemoration of Kim Jong Il in Pyongyang and other major cities and to designate his birthday as a national holiday. While Kim Il Sung's birthday was known as the "Festival Day of the Sun," Kim Jong Il's birthday would be called the "Festival Day of the Bright Star."[55]

In anticipation of the centennial birthday of the late Kim Il Sung (April 15, 2012), the North held two conventions in Pyongyang to officialize Kim Jung Un's assumption of the top posts both in the KWP and the DPRK state. On April 11, the Fourth KWP Representatives Conference was convened. Its first step was to revise its regulations; these included creating the title of "Eternal General Secretary" and the post of "First Secretary." Simultaneously, while retaining *Juche* thought, the revised regulations used a new term, Kimilsung-Kimjongiljuŭi (Kim Il Sung–Kim Jong Il-ism), to characterize the KWP's guiding ideology.

While declaring the late Kim Jong Il "Eternal General Secretary of the KWP," the conference acclaimed Kim Jong Un as the "First Secretary of the KWP." It also declared him a member of the standing committee of the

53 Ko Tae-young, "Avatar of Grandfather?" *Korea Times*, January 7, 2012, 2.

54 Lim Jae-cheon, "North Korea's Hereditary Succession: Comparing Two Key Transitions in the DPRK," *Asian Survey* 52, no. 3 (May–June 2012): 563.

55 *Rodong Sinmun*, January 12, 2012, 1.

TABLE 7.2

Positions gained by the "group of seven" at the
Fourth KWP Representatives Conference

Name	Elected position
Chang Sŏng-t'aek	Politburo and CMC member
Ri Yŏng-ho	Politburo standing committee member and CMC vice-chairman
Kim Yŏng-ch'un	CMC member
Kim Ki-nam	Politburo and secretariat member
Ch'oe T'ae-bok	Politburo and secretariat member
Kim Chŏng-gak	Politburo and CMC member
U Tong-ch'ŭk	CMC member

Source: Rodong Sinmun, April 12, 2012, 1–2.

Politburo and chairman of the CMC of the KWP.[56] This meant that Kim Jong Un had become the leader of the Politburo, the secretariat, and the CMC—all three of the KWP's major organs. A week later, before the cadres of the newly composed KWP Central Committee, Kim Jong Un would stress again that "the ideology guiding the KWP is Kim Il Sung-Kim Jong Il-ism."[57]

The conference elected members of the three major KWP organs. Observers did not miss the fact that each member of the "group of seven" would gain entry into at least one of these organs (see table 7.2).

While Ri Yŏng-ho retained his title as chief of the KPA General Staff concurrently with membership in two major organs, PAFM minister Kim Yŏng-ch'un, who had held positions above Ri Yŏng-ho for many years, became merely a CMC member—one of nineteen on that committee.[58]

Two other career progressions merit note. One was the spectacular rise of Ch'oe Ryong-hae, who entered all three organs. He secured membership in the Politburo's standing committee as well as the powerful directorship of the KPA General Political Bureau with the rank of vice marshal, although he completely lacked a military career. The other was the ascendancy of Kim Kyŏng-hui, who secured membership in both the Politburo and the secretariat. Following the death of Kim Jong Il, the Western media called her and

56 *Rodong Sinmun*, April 12, 2012, 1–2.
57 "Kim Jong Un Tongjiŭi Chosonrodongdang Chungangwiwonhoe Ch'aekimilgund-ŭlkwaui Tamhwa [Comrade Kim Jong Un's speech before the cadres of the KWPCC]," *Rodong Sinmun*, April 19, 2012, 1.
58 *Rodong Sinmun*, April 12, 2012, 2.

Chang Sŏng-t'aek the "North's power couple."[59] Now her powerful status was official.

Two days later, on April 13, the Supreme People's Assembly was held. It revised the constitution to make the late Kim Jong Il the "Eternal Chairman of the NDC" and Kim Jong Un the "First Chairman of the NDC." In addition, the SPA adopted a resolution that termed "Comrade Kim Jong Un, the First Chairman of the NDC," as "the highest head of the DPRK."[60] Ch'oe Yŏng-rim, a typical technocrat in his early eighties, retained the premiership, while Kang Sŏk-ju, first vice minister of the Foreign Ministry responsible for nuclear negotiations with the United States, was promoted to deputy prime minister. Chang Sŏng-t'aek was promoted to NDC co-vice-chairman, second to vice-chairman Ri Yŏng-ho. Chang's close aide Ri Myŏng-su was appointed to PSM minister, the position in control of the national police.[61] Replacing Kim Yŏng-ch'un, Kim Chŏng-gak was promoted to PAFM minister. But U Tong-ch'ŭk failed to win promotion to SSM minister. While Kim Won-hong occupied that position, U barely retained his position as the first vice director of the SSM, losing a seat in the NDC.[62]

On April 15, 2012, a massive military parade was held in Pyongyang's Kim Il Sung Square to commemorate the centennial of Kim Il Sung's birthday. In his debut public speech, Kim Jong Un pledged he would faithfully follow the teachings of Kim Il Sung and Kim Jong Il.[63] Other leaders urged the people to be prepared to "die" for Kim Jong Un in case of a national emergency. With the new composition of the three KWP organs and the cabinet—as well as the new composition of the NDC—the military parade marked the official start of Kim Jong Un's regime. At least one analyst would remark, "North Korea thus far successfully managed the initial phase of power transition to Kim Jong Un."[64]

From the beginning, Kim Jong Un's governance of North Korea marked a significant departure from the past in a number of ways. Cheong Seong-chang's keen observations merit repeating at some length:

> When visiting units of the KPA, Kim Jong Un would hold the hands of military officers and walk with them or inspect the accommodations and cafeterias of soldiers to communicate the image of a "friendly and warm leader." This was very

59 Kim Su-jeong and Kim Hee-jin, "Kim's Aunt, Uncle Are North's Power Couple," *Korea JoongAng Daily*, December 29, 2011, 3.

60 *Rodong Sinmun*, April 14, 2012, 1.

61 Chang T'aek-tong, "Kim Jong Un," *Dong-A Ilbo*, April 13, 2012, A 14.

62 *Rodong Sinmun*, April 14, 2–3.

63 *Rodong Sinmun*, April 16, 2012, 1.

64 Lee Hong Yung, "North Korea in 2012: Kim Jong Un's Succession," *Asian Survey* 53, no. 1 (January/February 2013): 178.

different from Kim Jong Il, who projected a mystical, distant image, avoiding physical contact with the public for security reasons. Kim Jong Un's more affable approach immediately provoked comparisons with his grandfather, Kim Il Sung.

At the military parade held in Kim Il Sung Square on April 15, 2012, Kim Jong Un once again revealed himself to be different from his father, who never addressed the public through speeches on such occasions. Like his grandfather, he presented the KWP's thinking directly to the public in order to gain their support. After Kim Il Sung's death in 1994, Kim Jong Il chose not to deliver a New Year's address, instead presenting the party's thinking in editorials that appeared in the official newspapers of the KWP, the Army and the Youth League. In contrast, following in the footsteps of Kim Il Sung, Kim Jong Un personally delivered the New Year's address in 2013 and 2014, once again deepening the impression that North Korean politics was returning to the time of Kim Il Sung.[65]

More importantly, unlike his father, whose personal leadership style was based on a cult of personality and the support of the military, Kim Jong Un has depended upon formal ruling institutions, especially the party and the cabinet.[66]

In the case of the party, Kim Jong Un has frequently convened meetings of the Politburo—which was moribund under Kim Jong Il—and the Central Military Committee, as well as the Central Committee. With the benefit of hindsight, one may assert that Kim Jong Un's speech before KWPCC cadres, delivered on April 6, 2012, marked an important turning point.[67] On the one hand, Kim Jong Un urged the "exhaustive and extensive erection of the party's unitary leadership system." (He would repeat the same theme on July 19, 2013, and August 25, 2013.) Before the cadres of the KWP, the KPA, and the cabinet, he would stress that the "party's unitary leadership system should be firmly established more exhaustively" and that "only the party makes the decision in which direction the military aims a gun." On the other hand, he also stressed the importance of the cabinet in economic affairs, calling it "the general headquarters of the state economy."[68] He even used the term "the cabinet-centered system, under which the cabinet should

65 Cheong Seong-chang, "The Anatomy of Kim Jong Un's Power," *Global Asia* 9 no. 1 (Spring 2014): 11–12.

66 Cheong Seong-chang, "Kim Jong Un ch'eje yinyŏn p'yongka" [An assessment: the Kim Jong Un regime in two years], *Chŏngsewa Chŏngch'aek* [Political situation and policy], December 2012, 23. See also Lee Ki-tong, "Kim Jong Un ui kwŏnryŏk sŭngkyae kwajŏng kwa kwŏnryŏkkujo" [The process leading to Kim Jong Un's power succession and his power structure], *Pukhanyŏnkuhakhoepo* [The journal of North Korean studies] 16, no. 2 (2012): 1–21.

67 Kim's speech was belatedly reported in *Rodong Sinmun*, April 19, 2012, 1.

68 Ibid.

be responsible for state economic management," and added that the party and all other state organs should devote themselves to helping the cabinet. A year later, he would replace Premier Ch'oe Yŏng-rim with Pak Pong-ju, a former premier in his seventies who was well known for his devotion to the "recovery" and "reform" of the North's economy.[69] Younger technocrats in their forties and fifties would be recruited to ministries related to industry, trade, and the economy.

A more important decision was made in September 2012, when the KWP Central Committee and Central Military Committee, the NDC, and the KPA supreme command in unison revised "detailed rules that would be applied in wartime"—originally stipulated in 2004—to the effect of stressing the role of the party. Henceforth, a "declaration of war" would be decided not by the supreme commander alone but by joint agreement among the KWP Central Committee and Central Military Committee, the NDC, and the KPA supreme command. This meant that under Kim Jong Un, North Korean policymaking was evolving from personal leadership to collective leadership. This trend was reinforced in June 2013, when Kim Jong Un revised the Ten-point Program for the Establishment of Unitary Thoughts System, which had been promulgated in 1967 and elaborated in 1974. The revised system stressed the unitary leadership of the party rather than the unitary thought of Kim Il Sung, although it still paid the highest tribute to Kim Il Sung and Kim Jong Il.[70] An interesting addition was the inclusion of a vague phrase warning against "those who have different dreams within the KWP." The revised program stressed that "the KWP should fight resolutely against them."

The Fall of the "Group of Seven"

Kim Jong Un's new policy of stressing the party's primacy over the military created tension between the KWP and the KPA. When Chang Sŏng-t'aek and Ch'oe Ryong-hae, representing the KWP, pressed Vice Marshal Ri Yŏng-ho, then the most powerful KPA general, to follow KWP guidance, he resisted. Ri had walked on the left side of Kim Jong Il's hearse in his

---

69 Chu Sŏng-ha and Cho Sung-ho, "Pak Pong-ju," *Dong-A Ilbo*, April 2, 2013, 2; see also Kim Hee-jin, "North Replaces Its Economic Team," *Korea JoongAng Daily*, April 3, 2013, 2.

70 Pak Hyŏng-jung, "Kim Jong Un sidae pukhanŭi chŏngch'iwa kyŏngjeui tonghak: Chang Sŏng-t'aek sukch'ŏngui kujojŏk paekyŏng" [Dynamics of North Korea's politics and economy in the era of Kim Jong Un: structural background of the purge of Chang Sŏng-t'aek], *Hankuk kwa kukjechŏngch'i* [Korea and international politics] 30, no. 1 (Spring 2014): 17.

capacity as a Politburo standing committee member, KWPCMC vice-chairman, and chief of the KPA General Staff. Ri's resistance would result in his being purged; on July 15, 2012, by a decision of the KWPCC Politburo, he was relieved of all his posts. Although the Politburo attributed its decision to his "illness,"[71] the move was seen as the result of a power struggle between the party and the military. Cheong Seong-chang, a senior fellow at Seoul's Sejong Institute, elaborated:

> This was a warning to the military that anyone refusing to follow guidance and instructions from the party could be removed from power at any moment no matter how close they are to Kim Jong Un.[72]

Park Hyŏng-jung, a senior fellow at the state-run Unification Research Institute in Seoul, argued that the struggle between the party and the military stemmed from conflicts of interest. According to Park, both the party and the military had operated their own international trade firms to earn foreign currency since the 1990s. Foreign currency was used to maintain and subsidize party organizations at the central and local levels, and a source of political funds to be sent to Kim Il Sung and Kim Jong Il. Under Kim Jong Il's "military-first politics," the military had expanded its business and trading activities. It had accumulated a huge amount of money, which could be used for political purposes. Kim Jong Un regarded this massive fund as a threat and thus had Ch'oe Ryong-hae and Chang Sŏng-t'aek force the transfer of some of the military's businesses to the party. Ri's resistance resulted not just in himself being purged but also seventeen generals close to him.[73] Some South Korean intelligence sources believe that Ri was shot to death in front of top-level cadres of both the KWP and the KPA; other sources claim that he was incarcerated in a camp for political prisoners.

Ri's successor was Hyŏn Yŏng-ch'ŏl, a four-star general who was immediately promoted to vice marshal. Hyŏn, sixty-five, was born in North Hamkyong Province and was commander of the KPA's Eighth Corps, in charge of security in the northwestern border region with China.[74] Three days after Ri Yŏng-ho was purged, the KWP Central Committee and Central Military Committee, the National Defense Commission, along with the

---

71 Quoted in Kim Young-jin, "N. Korean Military Chief Relieved," *Korea Times*, July 16, 2012, 2.

72 Ibid.

73 Pak, "Kim Jong Un Sidae," 4–24. See also Ha Ŏ-yŏng, "Pukhan Kwon ryŏk Saedaekyoch'e [A generational change in the North Korean power structure], *Hankyoreh*, December 5, 2013, 4.

74 Kim Hee-jin, "North Taps Newest Defense Minister," *Korea JoongAng Daily*, June 26, 2014, 2.

SPA Standing Committee, decided in unison to confer the title of Marshal (*wonsu*) of the DPRK on Kim Jong Un.[75]

Ri Yŏng-ho's dismissal was followed by that of Kim Chŏng-gak, who had also accompanied Kim Jong Il's hearse on the left side. Kim Chŏng-kak was removed from his post as PAFM minister and in November 2012 assigned to be president of Kim Il Sung Military University, a sinecure. About this time, U Tong-ch'ŭk was said to have been relieved as SSM first vice director—recall that Kim Yŏng-ch'un had already been removed as PAFM minister in mid-April and assigned to a sinecure in the KWPCC. Thus, the four military men (Ri Yŏng-ho, Kim Yŏng-ch'un, Kim Chŏng-kak, and U Tong-ch'uk) who had walked alongside the hearse on the left were excluded from the ruling circle;[76] their removal spelled the end of the era of Kim Jong Il's top-level military leaders.

Kim Chŏng-gak's successor was Kim Kyŏk-sik, but his tenure would be short. In May 2013 he was replaced by Chang Chŏng-nam, who would in turn be replaced by Hyŏn Yŏng-ch'ŏl in June 2014. The fate of the chief of the KPA General Staff was similar: Hyŏn Yŏng-ch'ŏl was replaced by Kim Kyŏk-sik in May 2013, and Kim was replaced by Ri Yŏng-kil in August 2013.[77] It was the same with the director of KPA military operations: with the inauguration of Kim Jong Un's leadership in April 2012, Kim Myŏng-kuk was replaced by Ch'oe Pu-il, who had taught Kim Jong Un how to play basketball; in March 2013, Ch'oe was replaced by Ri Yŏng-kil, and five months later Ri was replaced by Pyon In-sŏn.[78] Kim Jong Un seemed to be attempting to cultivate personal loyalty in the military through frequent replacements and dismissals, forcing Kim Jong Il–era military cadres to retire and filling the vacant posts with his own men. South Korean intelligence sources said:

> Kim Jong Un appears to be weeding out his father's generation of loyalists, forcibly retiring military officials aged sixty-five years old or above. In fact, as of December 2013 44 percent of all the full and three-star generals in the KPA were replaced by individuals in their fifties loyal to Kim Jong Un.[79]

75 *Rodong Sinmun*, July 19, 2012, 1.

76 Chŏng Yong-su, "Unkuch'a ch'ilin" [Seven men who walked alongside the hearse], *JoongAng Ilbo*, December 4, 2013, 2.

77 Ibid. See also Choe Sang-Hun, "North Korean Leader Tightens Grip With Removal of His Top General," *New York Times*, October 10, 2013, http://www.nytimes.com/2013/10/11/world/asia/north-korean-leader-tightens-grip-with-removal-of-top-general.html.

78 Ahn Chun-ho, "Kim Jong Un chipkwon yihu" [After the capture of power by Kim Jong Un], *Chosun Ilbo*, November 11, 2013, A3.

79 Sa Chŏng-won, "Kim Jong Un ch'eje yinyŏn" [Two years of the Kim Jong Un regime], *Hankuk Ilbo*, December 10, 2013, 4. See also Jeong Yong-soo, "Old Soldiers are Purged in North," *Korea JoongAng Daily*, December 11, 2013, 1.

This trend would continue in years to follow, resulting in a generational shift in the military that transformed the "Kim Jong Il military" into the "Kim Jong Un military."

The Execution of Chang Sŏng-T'aek

The fall of the "Group of Seven," dubbed the "curse of the hearse,"[80] climaxed with the execution of Chang Sŏng-t'aek in December 2013. The drama began in August 2013 with the reported defection of a DPRK bureaucrat and his family from China to Seoul.[81] A ROK NIS official leaked to the media that the defector had delivered an "enormously huge" amount of foreign currency to South Korean authorities. The defector's position was not revealed, but later it was learned that he had been a colonel general assigned to the KWP administrative department directed by Chang Sŏng-t'aek. Perhaps sensing that Chang's position was perilous, he had sought refuge in the South.[82]

Based on information gleaned from the defector, the NIS focused its attention on Chang Sŏng-taek and was eventually able to confirm that Chang was being closely surveilled by his competitors in general and the SSM in particular. In early November 2013 Chang held a dinner party for twenty-five close aides. According to another defector, Ri Yong-ha and Chang Su-kil (first vice director and vice director of the KWP administrative department, respectively) shouted something like "Long live Comrade Chang Sŏng-t'aek" or "Hurrah, Comrade Chang Sŏng-t'aek" at the party. These careless remarks were immediately reported to Kim Jong Un through Kim Won-hong, SSM minister. Despite Chang Sŏng-t'aek's repeated appeals for clemency for them, the two were arrested by a military detachment sent by the General Bureau for the Protection of Kim Jong Un—nothing less would do for men as powerful as Ri and Chang. In late November, both men were tried by a military tribunal and sentenced to death on charges of crimes against the party. They were summarily executed before the cadres of the KWP, KPA, cabinet, and SSM.[83] Some Seoul intelligence sources reported that antiaircraft guns were used for the execution. They added that Chang Sŏng-t'aek, who was forced to observe the scene, collapsed on the spot.[84]

80 Jeong Yong-su, "Wunkuch'aŭi chŏju" [The curse of the hearse], *JoongAng Ilbo*, December 17, 2013, 4.

81 Pak Min-hyŏk, "Puk Kwanryo Hankuk Mangmyŏng" [A North Korean bureaucrat defected to the South], *Dong-A Ilbo*, December 24, 2013, A5.

82 Ibid.

83 Ha Sŏn-yŏng, "Kukchŏngwon" [The National Intelligence Service], *JoongAng Ilbo*, December 4, 2013, 4.

84 Pang Sŭng-bae, "Sukch'ŏng paekyŏng" [The background of the purge], *Munhwa Ilbo*, December 10, 2013, 3.

At this critical juncture, two significant meetings were held. On November 20, the KPA held a meeting of its anti-espionage agents (PoAnWon) in Pyongyang for the first time since 1993. On the following day, the meeting made headline news in *Rodong Sinmun*. Since the primary aim of anti-espionage agents is the surveillance of the military, the six leaders on the podium attracted much attention (see table 7.3).

One outcome of the meeting was to step up surveillance of enemies within the KPA. Soon these men in charge were dubbed the "Group of Six," a new pillar of support inside the KPA for Kim Jong Un's leadership.[85]

The second meeting was a secret conclave on November 29 held in Samjiyŏn County, Ryangkang Province, near Mt. Paektu, attended by only eight of Kim Jong Un's confidants (see table 7.4).

Note that Kim Won-hong and Hwang Pyŏng-sŏ participated in *both* meetings. These vice directors (Hwang, Kim, Ma, Pak, Hong) have been called the "Group of Five," or "Group of Samjiyŏn," symbolizing the "new elites" of Kim Jong Un's post–Chang Sŏng-t'aek era. At the meeting it was finally decided to execute Chang and, as a preparatory measure, to place him under house arrest.[86] Kim Kyŏng-hui, Chang's wife, reportedly reluctantly consented to her nephew's decision and divorced Chang.[87] However, South Korean intelligence sources recently leaked to Seoul media that in fact, she did not know at that time of Kim Jong Un's decision to execute her husband.

After this decision, the North's media began to signal Chang's imminent purge. On December 4 *Rodong Sinmun* editorialized that Kim Jong Un required "100 percent loyalty," because someone with only "99 percent loyalty" could still become a turncoat at any moment. Some thought this sounded like an ominous warning to Chang Sŏng-t'aek.[88] On December 7 all scenes showing Chang Sŏng-t'aek were deleted from a state-produced documentary on Kim Jong Un's "field guidance trips."[89] The next day, an

85 Yi Yŏng-chong, "Yukinpang" [The group of six], *JoongAng Ilbo*, December 14, 2013, 5.

86 Kim Ch'ŏl-jung and Yun Sang-ho, "Samjiyŏn hoiŭi" [A meeting at Samjiyŏn], *Dong-A Ilbo*, December 6, 2013, A4.

87 Chŏng Won-yŏp, "Namp'yŏn Ilŭn Kim Kyŏng-hui" [Kim Kyŏng-hui without her husband], *Joongang Ilbo*, December 14, 2013, 3. See also Sarah Kim and Lee Young-jong, "Aunt of Jong Un Appears Spared," *Korea JoongAng Daily*, December 16, 2013, 1. According to this article, Kim Kyŏng-hui divorced Chang Sŏng-t'aek on December 11 on Kim Jong Un's order.

88 Yi Yŏng-jong, "Kim Jong Un, Chang Sŏng-t'aek chekŏ" [Kim Jong Un purged Chang Sŏng-t'aek]," *JoongAng Ilbo*, December 4, 2013, 1.

89 Kim Hee-jin, "Jang Deleted from Footage in Regime's Documentary," *Korea JoongAng Daily*, December 9, 2013, 1.

TABLE 7.3

The "Group of Six"

Ch'oe Ryong-hae	KPA chief of political bureau
Kim Won-hong	SSM minister
Yŏm Ch'ŏl-sŏng	KPA colonel general
Cho Kyŏng-ch'ŏl	KPA colonel general
Kim Su-kil	KPA lieutenant general
Hwang Pyŏng-sŏ	KPA vice director of the OGD

TABLE 7.4

Attendees, including the "Group of Five," at the secret meeting on November 29, 2013

Name	Role
Kim Won-hong	SSM minister
Kim Yang-kŏn	KWPCC secretary for united front department
Hwang Pyŏng-sŏ	KWPCC vice director of the OGD
Kim Pyŏng-ho	KWPCC vice director of the OGD
Ma Won-ch'un	KWPCC vice director
Pak T'ae-sŏng	KWPCC vice director
Hong Yŏng-ch'il	KWPCC vice director for machine industry

extended meeting of the KWPCC Politburo decided to relieve Chang of all titles, posts, and duties, and expel him from the party.[90] On December 9, Colonel General Yŏm Ch'il-sŏng, one of the "Group of Six," contributed to a front page *Rodong Sinmun* article, demanding that the KPA execute Chang Sŏng-t'aek.[91] The same day, *Rodong Sinmun* introduced a new musical paean to Kim Jong Un, "We Know Only Comrade Kim Jong Un."[92]

Three days later, on December 12, a special military tribunal under the SSM tried Chang Sŏng-t'aek and sentenced him to death under Article 60 of the criminal code, stipulating his crime as treason against the party and the state. The court asserted that Chang "had different dreams within the KWP," in violation of the Ten-Point Program; Chang was accused of being "one who dreamt of becoming cabinet premier and overthrowing the present

90 For the full text of the decision, see *Rodong Sinmun*, December 9, 2103, 1.

91 Quoted in Yi Yŏng-jong, "Pyongyang kwŏnryŏk" [Power in Pyongyang], *JoongAng Ilbo*, December 14, 2013, 5.

92 *Rodong Sinmun*, December 9, 2013, 1.

socialist system." He had "committed anti-party, anti-revolutionary sectarianism, which damaged the unity of the KWP and hinders a unitary supreme leadership."[93] The KCNA dispatch attributed a litany of crimes to Chang and his associates. It said they did "enormous harm" by "throwing the state financial management system into confusion and committing such acts of treachery as selling off precious resources of the country at cheap prices."[94]

Rodong Sinmun released an image of Chang at court; some thought it was obvious he had been severely tortured. On the same day as his sentencing, Chang Sŏng-t'aek was executed using antiaircraft guns, along with seven of his subordinates.[95] The North Korean regime filmed the execution and distributed the video to the cadres of the KWP, the KPA and the cabinet.[96] As horrible, even grotesque rumors about the method of execution circulated in the West, the North Korean ambassador to London, Hyŏn Hak-pong, would tell British Skynews TV more than a month later only that Chang had been executed by a "gun."[97] Clearly, as some have suggested, "Kim Jong Un was planting the fear that anyone reluctant to show blind allegiance will be inexorably removed from power."[98]

Two points should be noted about this event. First, it was unusual for the North's official media to go into such detail about a case of treason. The full texts of the decisions of the extended meeting of the Politburo and the special military tribunal were released immediately. Second, the removal of Chang Sŏng-t'aek meant that Kim Jong Un had disregarded part of his father's testament of October 8, 2011. That document was revealed on April 12, 2012, by Yi Yun-kŏl, a high-level defector from the North, and was accepted as authentic by most North Korea watchers in South Korea and Japan. In the lengthy testament, left in the hands of his younger sister Kim Kyŏng-hui, Kim

93 The KCNA press release was paraphrased and examined in Lee Chŏng-ŭn, "Puk, Chang Sŏng-t'aek ch'ŏhyŏng" [The North executed Chang Sŏng-t'aek], *Dong-A Ilbo*, December 14, 2013, 1.

94 Ibid.

95 Jeong Yong-soo, "North Executed Seven Subordinates with Jang," *Korea JoongAng Daily*, December 30, 2013, 2.

96 Kim Hyun-ki and Kim Hee-jin, "Jong Un Drunk When He Ordered Some Purges," *Korea JoongAng Daily*, December 23, 2013, 2. See also the report of Pak T'ae-kŭn, reporter of *Channel A*, a South Korean television network, on December 13, 2014. See also Kwon Ho, "Chang Sŏng-t'aek ch'oehu" [The last of Chang Sŏng-t'aek], *JoongAng Ilbo*, December 14, 2013, 3. See also Chŏng Sŏng-t'aek, "Chang Sŏng-t'aek," *Dong-A Ilbo*, December 14, 2014, A6.

97 Chŏn Sŭng-hun, "Yŏngjuje Pukdaesa" [The North's ambassador to United Kingdom], *Dong-A Ilbo*, February 3, A6.

98 "Editorials: Jong Un Consolidates His Power," *Korea JoongAng Daily*, December 10, 2013, 8.

Jong Il instructed Kim Jong Un to trust and allow Kim Kyŏng-hui, Chang Sŏng-t'aek, Ri Yŏng-ho, and Kim Chŏng-gak to help him.[99] As we have seen, however, all of these people ended up either demoted, purged, or executed. [100]

Four days after Chang's execution, a meeting to commemorate the second anniversary of Kim Jong Il's death was held in Pyongyang, with Kim Jong Un in attendance. Participants vowed to unite behind Kim Jong Un, shouting, "We know only Comrade Kim Jong Il. We don't know anybody except Comrade Kim Jong Il. Without you, we cannot live any longer."[101] Ch'oe Ryong-hae, who seemed to have risen to the number two position in the regime, delivered a speech emphasizing that the KPA would follow "the ever-victorious leadership of our supreme commander, Great Leader Kim Jong Un."[102] It was the first instance that Kim Jong Un was referred to as the "Great Leader."[103]

Meanwhile, the absence of Chang's widow Kim Kyŏng-hui was noteworthy. Soon intelligence sources in Seoul suggested that she had already died or "was in a vegetative state after undergoing brain surgery."[104] However, she did appear in a documentary rerun by state media between April and October 2014.[105]

Two basic explanations have been suggested as the cause of Chang's downfall; they supplement rather than contradict each other. One centers on conflicts of interest between Chang Sŏng-t'aek, as KWP administrative department director and National Defense Commission vice-chairman, and the KPA and the KWPCCOGD. NIS director Nam Jae-joon briefed lawmakers in a closed-door hearing at the National Assembly on December 23, 2013, that Chang's downfall was "not because of a power struggle between

99 Kim Hee-jin, "Before His Death, Kim Jong Il Wrote Instructions," *Korea Joong-Ang Daily*, April 13–15, 2012, 1.

100 Kim Jong Un's "betrayal of his father's testament" was elaborated in Pak Hŏn-ok, "Pukhan, Kim Jong Un ch'ejeŭi tang kun kwankae Punsŏk" [An analysis of the party-military relations in the Kim Jong Un regime of North Korea]," *Kunsa Nondan* [Military forum], no. 78 (Summer 2014): 39.

101 Hwang Tae-chin, "Kim Jong Il yijuki" [The second anniversary of Kim Jong Il's death], *Chosun Ilbo*, December 18, 2013, 1. See also *Rodong Sinmun*, December 21, 2013, 1.

102 "North Korea Presents a Unified Front After Purge," *International New York Times*, December 18, 2013, 3.

103 Ch'oe Hyŏn-jun, "Widaehan Yŏngdoja" [Great Leader], *Hankyŏreh*, December 11, 2014, 5.

104 Park Seung-hee and Jeong Yong-soo, "Kim Kyong-hui in Coma," *Korea JoongAng Daily*, January 9, 2014, 1.

105 "NK Leader's Aunt Shown Again on TV," *Yonhap News* (Seoul), quoted in *Korea Times*, October 13, 2014, 2.

him and other officials, but because of some internal conflicts over profitable businesses of North Korea."[106] After Kim Jong Il's stroke in August 2008, Chang, with Kim's blessing, had expanded the KWP administrative department at the expense of the powerful KWPCCOGD; he had the NDC's Fifty-Fourth Bureau practically monopolize the North's most profitable exports to China, including coal, clams, and crabs. When rival forces based inside the KPA attempted "to retake control of one of the sources of those exports,"[107] suggesting that they were acting on Kim Jong Un's orders, Chang's lieutenants reportedly not only insisted that they must first report to Chang Sŏng-t'aek, but they also physically beat them. According to Choe Sang-Hun and David E. Sanger of the New York Times, Kim Jong Un regarded the incident as a challenge to his authority. Infuriated, he ordered the KPA to overcome the resistance with additional military forces.[108]

The second theory is that Chang's downfall was an act of revenge by the KPA and especially the KWPCCOGD. According to the state-run Unification Research Institute in Seoul, the KPA resisted Chang's policy of favoring the party over the military, suspecting that Chang's ultimate aim was the "civilianization of the North Korean political system."[109] In the case of the KWPCCOGD, cadres wanted to restore the department's power and authority, which had been reduced by Chang's administrative department. Some of them even assumed that the death of KWPCCOGD first vice director Ri Che-gang in an automobile accident in June 2010 had actually been an assassination ordered by Chang Sŏng-t'aek. As noted earlier, Chang, taking advantage of Ri's death, had dismissed or demoted many party and military leaders who belonged to the "Ri Che-gang line." When KWPCCOGD cadres found confirmation of Chang's corruption, his accumulated wealth from profitable businesses, his arrogant behavior—even towards Kim Jong Un—and even his ignoring of Kim's orders, they pressed Kim Jong Un to remove him. Southern intelligence sources leaked to the media that Cho Yŏn-jun, the first vice director of the KWP OGD, played a major role in Chang's expulsion. In early September 2013, they said, Cho presented a file detailing Chang's accumulation of

106 Kim Hee-jin, "Mysteries Surrounding Jang's Death Uncovered," Korea JoongAng Daily, December 24, 2013, 1.

107 Choe Sang-Hun and David E. Sanger, "Korea Execution Is Tied to Clash over Businesses," International New York Times (Asia Pacific), December 23, 2013.

108 Ibid. See also Choe Sang-Hun, "Killing of Kim's Uncle Blamed on Business," International New York Times, December 24–25, 2013, 3. See also Ch'oe Sŭng-hyŏn and Kim Myŏng-sŏng, "Chang sukch'ŏng" [The purge of Chang], Chosun Ilbo, December 12, 2013, A3.

109 Hwang Tae-chin, "T'ongilyŏnkuwon Punsŏk" [An analysis of the Unification Research Institute], Chosun Ilbo, December 30, 2013, 1.

wealth, his misdeeds including lascivious behavior with a host of women, and "anti-party activities." Also pointed out as an example of disregarding Kim Jong Un's orders was Chang's failure to say a single word about the nuclear weapons program during talks with high-ranking Chinese officials, including President Hu Jintao, in August 2012 in Beijing. The SSM demanded that Kim Jong Un eliminate Chang before he was able to accumulate more influence within the KWP and the KPA.[110]

Did Kim Jong Un play an active or a passive role in his uncle's purge? Some North Korea watchers in Seoul suggest that he and his family were a driving force. They argue that Kim Sŏl-song, Kim Jong Un's half sister, and her husband, Sin Pong-nam, initiated the purge with Kim Jong Un's encouragement. The Kims' major concern was the $40 billion in secret funds managed by Chang and deposited in banks abroad, funds crucial for Kim Jong Un's effective control of the ruling elites.[111] Other observers felt that Kim Jong Un's role was more passive. Thomas Schaeffer, German ambassador to Pyongyang from 2007 to 2010, suggested at a December 2013 forum in Berlin that Kim Jong Un had been forced to purge and subsequently execute his uncle under pressure from KPA and KWPCCOOGD hardliners. Schaeffer said that Kim Jong Un's power was not as strong and extensive as many outsiders believed.[112]

Kim Jong Un's New Lineup

The purge of Chang Sŏng-taek and his associates provided Kim Jong Un with an opportunity to fill the ranks with his own chosen personnel. According to an NIS report, as of December 18, 2013, "a total of thirty-one high-ranking officials in the KWP, the cabinet, and the KPA were purged, demoted, or retired, while fifty-two new figures arose."[113] In the election to the Thirteenth Supreme People's Assembly on March 9, 2014—the first after Kim Jong Un's assumption of power—376 of the 687 delegates (55 percent) were new.[114] On April 8, 2014, the KWPCC Politburo convened and appointed vice premier Kang Sŏk-ju as the Central Committee's secretary

110 Yi Yŏng-jong, "Cho Yŏn-jun," *JoongAng Ilbo*, December 12, 2013, 3; Lee Young-jong, "Jang's Downfall Started in 2012," *Korea JoongAng Daily*, February 11, 2014, 1.

111 Yi, "Cho Yŏn-jun," 3.

112 Sŏk Nam-jun "Schaeffer Taesa" [Ambassador Schaeffer], *Chosun Ilbo*, December 12, 2013, A3.

113 *Rodong Sinmun*, March 12, 2014, 4; Lee Young-jong, "Report Details North Korea's Rising, Falling 'Stars,'" *Korea JoongAng Daily*, December 19, 2013, 1.

114 Chŏng Ch'ang-hyŏn, "Kim Jong Un chajun insa" [Kim Jong Un's frequent personnel shifts], *JoongAng Sunday*, May 4–5, 2014, 11.

for international affairs. As noted, Kang was a career diplomat who had participated in the North Korea–U.S. nuclear negotiations. The following day, the Supreme People's Assembly reacclaimed Kim Jong Un as First Chairman of the NDC and elected PAFM minister Chang Chŏng-nam and Cho Ch'un-ryong, a member of the cabinet's economic committee, to the NDC. On the other hand, Kim Yŏk-ch'un, Kim Kyŏk-sik, Chu Kyu-ch'ang and Paek Se-bong, all regarded as Kim Jong Il's men, were removed.[115] The retirement of Chu and Paek, coupled with the death of Chŏn Pyŏng-ho in July 2014, all three key figures in military supply and missile development, marked generational change in those fields.[116]

The Supreme People's Assembly also re-elected Kim Yŏng-nam as chairman of its Standing Committee and reappointed Pak Pong-ju and Ro Tu-ch'ŏl as premier and vice premier, respectively. In cooperation with Kwak Pŏm-ki, a KWPCC secretary for economic affairs, Pak and Ro have been enthusiastically pursuing a policy of expanding the North's external business activities.[117] The assembly also appointed as foreign minister Ri Su-yong, a career diplomat experienced in Western Europe, the Middle East, and the inducement of foreign capital. As ambassador to Switzerland, he is said to have managed the slush fund for the Kim family. In cooperation with Kang Sŏk-ju, Ri was expected to focus on the West, including the United States.[118]

The most meaningful change after the execution of Chang Sŏng-t'aek and his associates might be the absorption of the KWP administrative department into the KWPCCOGD; this was tantamount to the administrative department's dissolution.[119] As the OGD expanded, its cadres occupied the strategically most crucial KWP and KPA posts. While vacating the OGD directorship, Kim Jong Un decided to lead this powerful organ in his capacity as the KWPCC first secretary. In other words, he became its de facto director. Cho Yŏn-jun, Kim Kyong-ok, and Ri Pyŏng-ch'ŏl were chosen to the posts of OGD first vice directors.[120] In the KPA, replacing Ch'oe

115 *Rodong Sinmun*, April 10, 2014, 1–3. See also Kim Hee-jin, "Inner Circle in Regime Mostly Stays Intact," *Korea JoongAng Daily*, April 11, 2014, 2.

116 *Rodong* Sinmun, July 9, 2014, 4; Hwang Tae-chin, "Chŏn Pyŏng-ho samang" [The death of Chŏn Pyŏng-ho], *Chosun Ilbo*, July 10, 2014, 1.

117 Chŏng Ch'ang-hyŏn, "Kim Jong Un chajun insa" [Kim Jong Un's frequent personnel shifts], *JoongAng Sunday*, May 4–5, 2014, 11.

118 Ibid.

119 Chŏng Yong-su and Chŏng Yong-kyo, "Cho Yŏn-jun," *JoongAng Ilbo*, December 12, 2013, 3

120 My interview with a noted North Korean watcher in Seoul under conditions of anonymity on March 9, 2015.

Ryong-hae,[121] Hwang Pyŏng-so, the first vice director of the OGD, was appointed to chief of the General Political Bureau with the rank of vice marshal in late April 2014.[122] Hwang is in a position to control the KPA General Staff, the PAFM, the SSM, and the PSM. The interpretation of his appointment to such a crucial position is that Kim Jong Un has prioritized the KWP over the KPA and that he has in fact decided to control the KPA through the KWP.[123]

Kim Kyŏng-ok, OGD first vice director, concurrently secured membership in the KWPCMC. In the KWPCC, Cho Yŏn-jun, the first vice director of the OGD, was concurrently admitted to the Politburo as an alternate member, and Kim P'yong-hae, an OGD cadre, was admitted to the secretariat as a secretary. Ri Che-il, an OGD cadre, was chosen to be the first vice director of the propaganda-agitation department. In the KWP Audit Committee, Chŏng Myŏng-hak, an OGD cadre, was elected as its first vice chairman. At the provincial and local levels, too, the South Korean media has claimed, men from the OGD have occupied most of the important posts,[124] thereby opening the "era of the OGD." Relying on intelligence sources in Seoul, Yun Wan-jun of *Dong-A Ilbo* even claimed that Kim Jong Un's power and authority are limited by the OGD.[125]

*   *   *   *   *

Despite our knowledge of many of the leading people of North Korea and of their machinations, we are still left with the question: who rules North Korea? Undeniably, Kim Jong Un is the single most powerful person in the country, ruling it with an iron fist. In addition to him, however, he has

121 Ch'oe Ryong-hae was transferred to a KWPCC secretary. Yun Wan-jun, "Ch'oe Ryong-hae chowach'ŏn" [Ch'oe Ryong-hae's demotion], *Dong-A Ilbo*, May 6, 2014, 8; see also Lee Kyung-min, "NK's Choe Ryong-hae Losing Ground," *Korea Times*, January 30–February 2, 2014, 14.

122 Pak Pyong-su, "Puk Hwang Pyŏng-sŏ" [The North's Hwang Pyŏng-sŏ], *Hankyoreh*, May 2, 2014, 10. It seems he was appointed on April 26, 2014. See also Jeong Young-soo and Kim Hee-jin, "Pyongyang's Star Shines Even Brighter," *Korea JoongAng Daily*, April 29, 2014, 6.

123 Hwang's curriculum vitae is not clear. However, he seems to have been born in 1949 and made a career in the KWPCCOGD. In 2010, he was promoted to lieutenant general while vice director of the OGD. In March 2010, he was promoted to first vice director of the OGD with the rank of general. Chinese intelligence sources said that he played the crucial role in the purge of Chang Sŏng-t'aek. Chŏng Yong-su, "Hwang Pyŏng-sŏ," *JoongAng Ilbo*, May 3, 2014, 10.

124 Yun Wan-jun, "Puk Nodongdang Chojikchidopu Haepu" [An anatomy of the North's KWP Organizational Guidance Department], *Dong-A Ilbo*, June 26, 2014, A8

125 Yun Wan-jun, "Puken Chopia" [In the North, OGD prevails], *Dong-A Ilbo*, June 26, 2014. 1.

TABLE 7.5

Fifteen "lieutenants" and the six groups they represent

Group	Name	Role/title
Kim family	Kim Yŏ-jŏng	Younger sister of Kim Jong Un, vice director of the KWP propaganda-agitation department and chief of the secretariat belonging to the office of the KWP First Secretary, in charge of all political funds in general and the foreign currency slush fund in particular
Revolutionary tradition	Ch'oe Ryong-hae	Son of the late Ch'oe Hyŏn, an anti-Japanese guerilla warrior and PAFM minister; currently member of the KWP Politburo standing committee and secretary of the KWPCC in charge of the KWPOGD
	O Il-jŏng	Son of the late O Chin-u, an anti-Japanese guerrilla warrior and PAFM minister; currently vice director of the KWP military department
KWP	Cho Yŏn-jun	KWPOGD first vice director
	Kim Yang-Kŏn	KWPCC secretary for united front strategy
	Han Kwang-sang	Director, KWP finance and accounting department
KPA	Hwang Pyŏng-sŏ	NDC vice president and chief of the KPA General Political Bureau
	Kim Yŏng-ch'ŏl	Chief of the KPA General Inspection Bureau
	Ri Yŏng-kil	Chief of the KPA General Staff
	Hyŏn Yŏng-ch'ŏl	PAFM minister
State coercive agencies	Kim Wŏn-hong	SSM minister (represents the secret police)
	Ch'oe Pu-il	PSM minister (represents the regular police)
Regular state organs	Kim Yŏng-nam	Titular head of state as president of the SPA standing committee
	Pak Pong-ju	Premier
	Ri Su-yong	Foreign minister

fifteen lieutenants in six groups: the Kim family itself, descendants of the revolutionary leaders, the KWP, the KPA, the state's coercive agencies, and the regular state organs (see table 7.5).

Among these, Cho Yŏn-jun deserves particular attention as the one who led the purge and, ultimately, the execution of Chang Sŏng-t'aek, in collaboration with Kim Wŏn-hong. A typical undistinguished party *apparatchik*, it is believed that he came from a poor farming family in South Hamkyong Province and is around seventy-five years old. Chu Sŏng-ha, a Kim Il Sung Comprehensive University graduate who defected to the South and works as a reporter at *Dong-A Ilbo*, terms him "the modern version of the chief eunuch in the Kim Jong Un palace."[126] Based on reliable North Korean

126 Chu Sŏng-ha, "Kim Jong Unŭi 'Munkori Kwŏnryŏk' Cho Yŏn-jun" [A eunuch close to Kim Jong Un], *Dong-A Ilbo*, October 2, 2014, A33.

sources, Chu says that Cho, who established a strong alliance with Hwang Pyŏng-sŏ after Chang's execution, reports daily to Kim Jong Un on state, party, and military affairs, including foreign affairs, and that Kim Jong Un automatically consents to his recommendations.

An analysis of eighty-eight personnel who have occupied high-level posts at the National Defense Commission, the KWP, the KPA, the Supreme People's Assembly, and the cabinet provides interesting data on how power has shifted under Kim Jong Un's regime. The average age is 68.4 years, which is fourteen months younger compared to the eighty-eight personnel in the same posts in the Kim Jong Il era. Most personnel (45.6 percent) were born in either North Hamkyŏng Province or South Hamkyŏng Province, an increase from 26 percent under Kim Jong Il; this means that the proportion of personnel born in Pyong'an Province and Pyongyang has decreased. Finally, the percentage of personnel who have graduated from Kim Il Sung Comprehensive University has slightly increased under Kim Jong Un (from 31.2 percent to 34.6 percent).[127]

The DPRK's External Relations and Its Nuclear Project under Kim Jong Un

When Kim Jong Un succeeded his father in December 2011, some Western observers expressed cautious hope that he might govern in a different style and show more openness and moderation. They noted that as a youth Kim Jong Un had been educated in Switzerland and thus had had more exposure to the West than his father. His remarks in April 2012—"We should catch up with international trends"[128]—seemed to suggest that such hopes might be justified. When, on April 13, 2012, a satellite launched in celebration of Kim Il Sung's birth centennial exploded 134 seconds after liftoff, Kim Jong Un reportedly ordered that the fact be announced in the North's media. This was a degree of transparency about a state failure that was rare if not unprecedented in the history of North Korea.[129] Similarly, the frequent appearances of Ri Sŏl-ju, Kim Jong Un's wife, in the DPRK media during his "field guidance trips" beginning in July 2012 were also seen as a sign of change, even if minor.[130] In the Kim Jong Il era, the First Lady had never appeared at public events and was never seen in the media.

127 JoonAng Ilbo's Unification Research Center performed the analysis based on data prepared by the South Korean Unification Ministry. *JoongAng Ilbo*, January 27, 2015, 8.

128 Quoted in An Yong-hyŏn, "Puk chŏnraeŏpnŭn pŏstleidi marketing" [The North's unprecedented "First Lady marketing"], *Chosun Ilbo*, September 7, 2012, A8.

129 Yu Yong-won, "Kongjung p'okp'al" [The explosion in the sky], *Chosun Ilbo*, April 14, 2012, 1.

130 An Yong-hyŏn, "Puk chŏnraeŏpnŭn pŏstleidi marketing" [The North's unprecedented "First Lady marketing"], *Chosun Ilbo*, September 7, 2012, A8.

But Kim Jong Un's record in his first three years of rule has been mixed. On issues of national security and internal control, he has been far from moderate. He tightened control along the border with China, ordering that would-be defectors should be shot. Not surprisingly, the number of defectors has declined drastically since 2012.[131] The execution of Chang Sŏng-t'aek marked Kim internationally as a merciless despot. Kim has been steadfast in continuing the development of a nuclear capability. On December 12, 2012, the North successfully launched the Kwangmyŏngsŏng 3 satellite, signaling that it has made "significant progress in its intercontinental ballistic missile capability."[132] On February 12, 2013, the North successfully conducted its third nuclear test at an underground site at P'unggye-ri in the northeast, over the strong objections and threat of sanctions by the United Nations, including the United States and China.[133] On March 26, 2014, the North would launch two mid-range missiles, again demonstrating its growing ballistic missile capabilities.[134]

When China expressed strong objections to the North's nuclear test and called for denuclearization of the Korean Peninsula, Kim Jong Un sent vice marshal Choe Ryong-hae, director of the KPA's General Political Bureau, as his special envoy to Beijing on May 22, 2013.[135] But Chinese president Xi Jinping only met him on the last day of his three-day trip—in sharp contrast to Xi's numerous meetings with ROK president Park Geun-hye in both Seoul and Beijing—and urged the North to cease its pursuit of nuclear weapons.[136] In addition, Xi did not give a clear response to Kim's request that he be allowed to make a state visit to Beijing.[137] Four days later, a *Rodong Sinmun* editorial stated that the North would not give up its nuclear weapons program, terming it "a shield" against American nuclear threats.[138] However, in a conciliatory gesture, on June 14 the North proposed high-level talks with the United States "to ease tensions on the

131 Kim Chŏl-jung, "Kim Jong Un kongp'o chŏngch'i" [Kim Jong Un's politics of terror], *Dong-A Ilbo*, December 25, 2013, A2.

132 Kim Young-jin, "Will NK Get Away With It?" *Korea Times*, December 13, 2012, 1.

133 Chung Mun-uck, "NK Presses on with Nuke Test," *Korea Times*, February 13, 2013. 1.

134 Choe Sang-Hun, "North Korea Launches 2 Midrange Missiles," *International New York Times*, March 27, 2014, 4.

135 Kim Hee-jin and Ser Myo-ja, "North Korea Dispatches Special Envoy to China," *Korea JoongAng Daily*, May 23, 2013, 1.

136 Kim Hee-jin, "North Envoy Meets Xi in China," *Korea JoongAng Daily*, May 25–26, 2013, 1.

137 Kim Hee-jin, "Jong Un Highly Eager to Visit Beijing," *Korea JoongAng Daily*, May 28, 2013, 2.

138 Quoted in Kim Hee-jin, "North Reiterates Will Keep Nukes," *Korea JoongAng Daily*, May 29, 2013, 3.

Korean Peninsula and establish regional peace and security." In what he called an "important statement," a DPRK NDC spokesman said that the two countries could meet at "any time and at any place the United States wants." He reaffirmed that "the denuclearization of the Korean Peninsula was an unchanged will and resolution of our military and the people."[139] The United States rejected the offer, arguing that the North first needed to demonstrate that it was prepared to negotiate in good faith. In the meantime, Kim Jong Un invited Dennis Rodman, the former NBA star player whom Kim had admired from his boyhood days in Switzerland, to Pyongyang four times between February 2013 and January 2014.[140] North Korean officials may have hoped that their leader's association with Rodman, who called Kim a "friend for life," would improve the West's image of both Kim Jong Un and his country.[141]

With the brutal execution of his uncle Chang Sŏng-t'aek in December 2013, however, Kim Jong Un's image only worsened, as evidenced by the fact that a significant portion of UN member states in October 2014 adopted a strongly worded resolution condemning North Korea for human rights abuses. Under increasing pressure, Kim Jong Un sent his special envoy, Ch'oe Ryong-hae, to Moscow. On November 18, 2014, Ch'oe met with Russian president Vladimir Putin and delivered a letter from Kim. Two days later, Ch'oe met foreign minister Sergei Lavrov. After the talks, Lavrov raised "the possibility of a summit" between Putin and Kim. Lavrov also made clear Russia's objection to the UN resolution, because it had raised "a possibility of international prosecution of the North's leaders, including Kim Jong Un, at the International Criminal Court."[142]

On the domestic front, at the March 2013 KWP Central Committee plenum Kim Jong Un proposed "a new strategic line on carrying out economic construction and building nuclear armed forces simultaneously."[143] His suggestion of specific goals such as "an increase in productivity in basic

139 Quoted in Choe Sang-Hun, "North Korea Proposes High-Level Talks with U.S.," *International New York Times* (Asia Pacific), June 15, 2013, 1.

140 Gerry Mullany, "Return to Pyongyang for 'a basketball diplomacy,'" *International New York Times*, September 4, 2013, 3; Rick Gladstone, "Betting on a North Korean Draw," *International New York Times*, December, 20, 2013, 15; *Rodong Sinmun*, January 9, 2014, 1.

141 "Rodman Names Players for Game in Pyongyang," *Korea JoongAng Daily*, January 6, 2014, 2.

142 Ser Myo-ja, "Jong Un's Envoy Ends Russia Trip," *Korea JoongAng Daily*, November 25, 2014, 2.

143 March 31, 2013, KCNA press release, quoted in Kim Hee-jin, "Pyongyang Adopts Two-Track Strategy," *Korea JoongAng Daily*, April 2, 2013, 2.

industries [and stabilization of] the livelihood of people through boosting the agriculture and light industry"[144] seemed to distinguish his policies from his father's "military-first" policy. Yet Kim Jong Un's economic policies in general have not been effective. Rather, as seen in the collapse of a twenty-three-story apartment building under construction in Pyongyang on May 13, 2014, in which perhaps four or five hundred people died, pursuing economic campaigns with Stakhanovite "speed battle" strategies has significant pitfalls. Yet it was noteworthy that the North's official media made the accident public, and that the scene of the PSM minister officially tendering his apology, head bowed, was widely broadcasted.[145] A similar case occurred again in late October 2014, when an apartment building under construction near the National Defense Commission in Pyongyang collapsed. South Korean intelligence officials tacitly confirmed that about eighty workers and soldiers were killed in that building's collapse. This time, however, the regime did not publicize the incident.[146]

Toward South Korea, the Kim Jong Un regime has acted as if it has a split personality. At times it has increased its bellicose rhetoric, as when it threatened to attack the presidential Blue House in Seoul.[147] Yet it also sent its athletes to the seventeenth Asian Games, held in September and October 2014 in Inch'ŏn, South Korea. Kim Jong Un publicly stated that his decision to do so was "a symbol of dialogue and reconciliation between the two Koreas."[148] He went one step further by sending a high-level delegation—Hwang Pyŏng-so, Ch'oe Ryong-hae, and Kim Yang-Kŏn—to the Asian Games' closing ceremony on October 4, 2014. On this occasion, the delegation delivered Kim Jong Un's "warm greetings" to ROK president Park Geun-hye.[149] Even after this dramatic gesture, however, the North persisted in raising tensions along the maritime and land demarcation lines with the South.

144 Ibid.
145 Ch'a Hak-bong, "Pyongyang apat pungkwe" [The collapse of the apartment building in Pyongyang], *Chosun Ilbo*, May 26, 2014, A8.
146 Kim Myŏng-sŏng, "Puk Kukpangwich'ŏngsa chŭngchŭk" [Collapse of the North's National Defense Commission office complex], *Chosun Ilbo*, December 10, 2014, A6.
147 Kang Seung-woo, "NK Threatens to Attack Cheong Wa Dae," *Korea Times*, August 2–3, 2014, 2.
148 Sarah Kim, "North is Already Playing its Games," *Korea JoongAng Daily*, July 21, 2014, 1.
149 Ser Myo-ja, "North Korean Delegation Makes a Rare Visit," *Korea JoongAng Daily*, October 6, 2014, 1.

8 What Does the Future Hold for Kim Jong Un?

A review of the first three years of Kim Jung Un's rule—from December 2011 to December 2014—shows that the initial personnel lineup prearranged by Kim Jong Il in 2010 had been entirely changed by the end of 2013. The "Group of Seven" who walked alongside Kim Jong Il's hearse were all removed, beginning with the purge of the most powerful KPA general, Ri Yŏng-ho, in July 2012. By the end of 2012, three other military leaders—Kim Yŏng-ch'un, Kim Chŏng-gak, and U Tong-ch'ŭk—had been demoted or purged. The final stroke was the December 2013 execution of Chang Sŏng-t'aek, Kim Jong Un's uncle and the one-time "Grand Duke." Kim Jong Il's testament, discussed previously, would end up being ignored or even betrayed. The individuals whom Kim Jong Il had highly recommended to Kim Jong Un as aides—Chang Sŏng-t'aek, Ri Yŏng-ho, and Kim Chŏng-gak—were progressively purged or demoted. Kim Kyŏng-hui, Chang Sŏng-t'aek's wife, was effectively incapacitated. The only people recommended by Kim Jong Il who remained in Kim Jong Un's lineup were Ch'oe Ryong-hae, Kim Kyŏng-ok, and Hyŏn Ch'ŏl-hae. Ch'oe Yŏng-rim also remains, in the honorary post of the SPA standing committee, but he is in his eighties. Kim Jong Un has thus built up his own personnel roster with KWPCCOGD cadres as its core, while removing or eradicating most of the Kim Jong Il old guard.

What does the future hold for Kim Jong Un? Let us start with his physical health. He is approximately 5'7" tall and weighed about 220 pounds only a few years ago. But a Chinese source claimed that as of May 2014 Kim's weight had ballooned to 265 pounds. The Chinese source claimed that "after Chang Sŏng-t'aek was executed, Kim Jong Un experienced anxiety and depression, which led to overeating, and revealed a facial paralysis syndrome."[1] In the past Kim was reported to have suffered from hypertension and symptoms of diabetes. In July 2014 North Korean television networks broadcast a scene in which Kim walked with a noticeable limp.[2] Then, from September 4 to October 13, 2014, he completely disappeared from the public eye; he did not appear even for the October 10 national ceremony commemorating the sixty-ninth anniversary of the KWP's founding. This extended disappearance from public view sparked in media worldwide "a wild run of speculation ranging from a coup against him to his untimely death."[3] When Kim Jong Un ended his forty-day absence on October 14, shown leaning on a cane, the NIS leaked to the Seoul media that he had only undergone surgery to remove a cyst on his right ankle. Since then, Kim has in fact resumed a brisk schedule of public activities.[4] Cheong Seong-chang's October 2010 appraisal may be still valid, when he commented that "Kim Jong Un's health is not so bad as to endanger his leadership position."[5] However, there are other assessments—including an unconfirmed report that a U.S. intelligence source recently conveyed to the NIS that Kim Jong Un would not last beyond the end of 2017 due to hypertension, complications from diabetes, and mental stress.[6] If such a predication proves accurate, the North will face serious political turmoil.

Dynastic Family Discord?

Could an internecine struggle among "princes" take place during Kim Jong Un's reign? Korea's distant past contains a number of precedents. In the last stage of the Koguryŏ Kingdom (37 BCE–668 CE), struggles among a deceased dictator's three sons and brother contributed to the kingdom's collapse. A similar development occurred at the end of the Later Paekche Kingdom (892–936). When King Kyŏnhwŏn designated as his successor the first son from his second marriage, the three sons from his first marriage revolted in unison, confining the king in a temple and killing their half brother.

1 Yun Wan-jun, "Puk Kim Jong Un" [The North's Kim Jong Un], *Dong-A Ilbo*, May 8, 2014, A2.

2 "Kim Jong Un Reported to Have a Limp," *Korea JoongAng Daily*, July 10, 2014, 2.

3 Yi Whan-woo, "He's Back," *Korea Times*, October 15, 2014, 1.

4 Kang Seung-woo, "'Kim Recovering from Surgery,'" *Korea Times*, October 25, 2014, 1.

5 Cheong Seong-chang, "Kim Jong Un's Early Life and Personality," *Vantage Point*, July 2009, 12.

6 Kim Sŏng-tong and Paek Sŭng-ku, "Kim Jong Un Kŏnkang Yisangsŏl," *Wolgan Chosun*, November 2014, 62–83.

Enraged, Kyŏnhwŏn escaped and surrendered to King Wang Kŏn of the Koryŏ dynasty, who then subdued the sons. Such scenarios recurred in the initial period of the Chosŏn dynasty (1392–1910). When its founder, Yi Sŏng-gye, made his second son by his second wife the crown prince, his six sons by his first wife revolted and killed their two half brothers. This is known as the "first revolt among princes." Soon, however, the succession struggle resumed, this time among the six brothers born of the same mother, ending in victory for the fifth son, Yi Pang-wŏn, which is called the "second revolt among princes."

Could such struggles among brothers take place in modern-day North Korea? There have been occasional reports of attempts by Kim Jong Un to assassinate his half brother Kim Jong Nam. Some reports alleged that in mid-November 2004, the Austrian state intelligence agency prevented North Korean secret agents from killing Kim Jong Nam, who was visiting Vienna at the time. Others claimed that in April 2009 Kim Jong Un's secret agents attempted to kill Kim Jong Nam when he was visiting the North and staying at his Uam villa in Pyongyang.[7] Song Yŏng-sŏn, a member of the ROK National Assembly at the time, told the press, "In 2009, Kim Jong Un attempted to kill Kim Jong Nam in Macao, but failed." She further alleged that "in retaliation, Kim Jong Nam spread the rumor that Kim Jong Un is not Ko Yong-hŭi's son, but Kim Ok's."[8] Such reports of assassination attempts continued. Relying on information from Chinese North Korea watchers, a Seoul monthly reported that in June 2010 Northern SSM agents planned to kill Kim Jong Un in Beijing, but Chinese public security authorities thwarted the plot.[9]

With such reports and speculation rife, remarks by Kim Jong Un's half-brother Kim Jong Nam openly opposing a third-generation succession naturally received intense attention. One day before Kim Jong Un's public debut as successor, Kim Jong Nam said on Tokyo's TV Asahi, "I am against the third-generation succession." Was this a challenge to his younger brother's rise to power? Not necessarily. In the same interview, he backpedaled with remarks such as: "I believe there must have been some reasons, and if those reasons exist, I think they should be followed." He added, "I hope my brother will do his best for the people and their material lives. I am

---

7 Ibid., June 16, 2009, A2; Yi Yŏng-jong, "Sesŭpnaejŏn" [Internecine war for succession], *Wolgan JoongAng*, November 2010, 43.

8 Pak Sŏng-hyŏn, "Song Yŏng-sŏn ŭiwon interview" [Interview with lawmaker Song Yŏng-sŏn]," *Wŏlgan JoongAng*, November 2010, 81.

9 Paek Sŭng-ku, "Chungguk ttŏdonŭn Kim Chŏng-nam" [Kim Jong Nam who roams over China], *Wŏlgan Chosun*, October 2011, 220.

willing to help my brother even if I am abroad. I will help him whenever."[10] Most analysts viewed his remarks as self-serving; one wrote, "He is calculating very closely, showing his half brother and cronies that he is not a threat but an asset to the regime outside the country."[11] Andrei Lankov, a Russian North Korea specialist, suggested that Kim Jong Nam might be wise enough not to want to try to become the successor of a totally bankrupt country, since the ruler would inevitably become the scapegoat in case of a military coup or mass revolt.[12] About a hundred days after Kim Jong Nam's comments about the succession, he clarified his stance. In a January 2011 interview with *Tokyo Shimbun*, he asserted, "I have no intention to challenge or criticize my younger brother." Noting that Kim Jong Il himself had also originally opposed a third-generation succession but had changed his mind, Kim Jong Nam said that the succession was inevitable for the stability of the nation. He denied being aware of any attempts on his life and said he would never exile himself in the West.[13]

But only five days after Kim Jong Il's funeral, in an email to *Tokyo Shimbun*, Kim Jong Nam said that rational thinkers could not accept a third generation of hereditary succession. He pointed out the shortness of the period during which Kim Jong Un was groomed to be the new leader, and even questioned whether the young successor would be able to maintain his status.[14]

Kim Jong Il himself apparently did not regard Kim Jong Nam as a threat; in October 2011, exactly two months before his death, in a note to his younger sister, Kim Kyŏng-hŭi, he wrote, "Be nice to Jong Nam. He is not a bad boy."[15] Members of Kim Jong Un's regime may have felt differently, however. According to diplomatic sources in Beijing, Kim Yŏng-il, KWPCC secretary for international affairs, visited the Chinese capital and asked for Kim Jong Nam to be repatriated from Macao to Pyongyang. In

10 Christine Kim, "Kim's Eldest Son Breaks Silence on Brother's Climb," *Korea JoongAng Daily*, October 13, 2010, 1

11 Ibid.

12 Andrei Lankov, "Kim Chŏng-nam ch'unggyŏk chŏk parŏn e sumŭn ttŭt" [A meaning hidden in Kim Jong Nam's shocking comment], *Chosun Ilbo*, October 21, 2010, A39.

13 Quoted in *Dong-A Ilbo*, January 29, 2011, A2. See also Ahn Sung-kyoo, "North Leader's Son Denies Asylum Rumors," *JoongAng Daily*, June 7, 2010, 1.

14 "Eldest Brother Casts Doubts on New NK Leader," *Korea Times*, January 13, 2012, 4.

15 The full text of Kim Jong Il's testament was released on November 23, 2012, in Seoul. See the summary, Kim Hee-jin, "Before His Death, Kim Jong Il Wrote Instructions," *Korea JoongAng Daily*, April 13–15, 2012, 1.

talks with Kim Yŏng-il on April 22, 2012, Dai Bingguo, the PRC state minister in charge of international affairs, reportedly rejected the request.[16]

Is there any possibility that Kim Jong Nam would assume leadership of the North if an unforeseen internal conflict or other event were to remove Kim Jong Un from the picture? Japanese and South Korean media have occasionally suggested scenarios in which an emergency in the North would prompt the CCP to install Kim Jong Nam as the North Korean leader.[17] In an unconfirmed report, diplomatic sources in Seoul likewise claimed that around the end of 2012, South Korean and U.S. intelligence agencies prepared a contingency plan to have Kim Jong Nam take refuge in the United States and establish a provisional government with him as head. Ultimately, however, they reportedly abandoned the plan to avoid infuriating the North.[18]

Despite such reports and speculation, it is very unlikely that Kim Jong Nam will ever find himself in charge of North Korea, due to his political and personal weaknesses discussed earlier. Son Kwang-ju, a long-time researcher on the Kim family, predicted that "Kim Jong Nam will have to spend the rest of his life abroad."[19] Kim was spotted in Jakarta on May 4, 2014, at an Italian restaurant with the chef;[20] on September 29, 2014, he was seen touring Paris with a young lady.[21] His son, Kim Han-sol, is a student at the Le Havre campus of the Paris Institute of Political Studies (Sciences Po).[22]

If Kim Jong Nam is out of the picture, what about Kim Jong Chul? Could he ever challenge his younger brother? Most observers speculate that due to his gentle character he would never oppose his younger brother's power. Fujimoto says he is certain that "Jong Chul is kind and he will support Jong

16 *Munhwa Ilbo*, April 24, 2012, 8.

17 This scenario was criticized as unlikely in Cheong Seong-chang, "Pukhan hugye munje wa kwŏnlyŏk ch'ekte mit p'awŏ elllit'ŭ pyŏndong" [The North Korean succession issue, the power system, and the change in power elite], a paper prepared for a lecture at the Japanese Research Association of World Politics and Economy, July 22, 2011, 34. Paek Sŭng-gu also suggested this scenario. See Paek, "Chungguk dŏdonŭn Kim Chŏng-nam," 214–23.

18 Cho Sung-ho and Kim Chŏng-an, "Kim Jong Nam Mi Mangmyŏng Ch'ukinsŏl" [Rumors of Kim Jong Nam's exile to the United States], *Dong-A Ilbo*, December 20, 2013, A4.

19 Quoted in Choe, "Family Intrigue," 3.

20 Kim Myŏng-sŏng, "Jakartae Nat'anan Kim Jong Nam [Kim Jong Nam appeared in Jakarta], *Chosun Ilbo*, May 21, 2014, A8.

21 Yi Se-hyŏng, "Puk Kim Jong Nam Paris-ae" [Kim Jong Nam of the North appeared in Paris], *Dong-A Ilbo*, October 1, 2014, 1.

22 Kang Hae-ran, "Kim Han Sol," *JoongAng Ilbo*, December 18, 2013, 4.

Un, not attack him."²³ Relying on intelligence sources in Seoul, a Seoul daily reported that Jong Chul, along with his younger sister, Yŏ-jong, are both hard at work assisting Jong Un.²⁴ South Korean intelligence sources recently asserted that Kim Jong Un ordered his lieutenants to look after his uncles and aunts from Kim Il Sung's second marriage to Kim Sŏng-ae. Based on all available information, a North Korea watcher in Seoul has predicted that there will be no "internecine struggle among the princes" in the North.²⁵

A Coup?

What about the possibility of a military coup against the regime? As we saw in earlier chapters, the third KWP Representatives Conference reorganized the KWPCMC, granting it the power to "guide overall defense operations." With this increased authority of the KWPCMC and a corresponding reduction in the role of the NDC, North Korea's military power has been concentrated in the party's Central Military Commission.

Moreover, in the reorganized KWPCMC, power has been centered on First Chairman Kim Jong Un. The sixteen other committee members, including eleven key military leaders of the PAFM and KPA from the army, navy, and air force, four key KWP cadres, and one key cadre of the SSM,²⁶ have all been loyal to Kim Jong Un. In addition, the Third Conference of KWP Representatives revised KWP regulations to increase the party's power over the military. One of the new rules states that "all military activities of the KPA are to be executed under the leadership of the KWP." Another stipulates, "All political members placed in each military unit lead and command the unit's general operations as representatives of the party with full responsibility."²⁷ With the KWPCMC holding so much military power, and, in turn, Kim Jong Un having so much power over the KWPCMC, most

23 Quoted in Lee Young-jong and Jeong Yong-soo, "Kim's Sushi Chef Shares Memories of Jong Un," *Korea JoongAng Daily*, October 26, 2010, 3

24 Kim Myŏng-sŏng, "Kim Jong Un Puk t'ongch'i" [Kim Jong Un's rule of the North], *Chosun Ilbo*, July 1, 2014, A6.

25 Kim T'ae-wan, "Wangja ŭi nan ŭn ŏpsŭl kŏt" [There will be no revolt among the princes], *Wolgan Chosun*, October 2010, 119.

26 Lee Gee-dong, "Chosun rodongdang che samch'a taep'yoja taehoe ihu Pukhan kwollyŏk kujo ŭi konggohoi issŏsŏ ŭi chaengjŏmk wa kwaje" [Issues and tasks in the consolidation of the North Korean power structure since the third KWP representatives conference], *Han'guk kwa kukje chŏngch'i* [Korea and international politics], no. 71 (Winter 2010): 224–26.

27 Lee Young-jong and Christine Kim, "Rules Tweaked to Block Challenges to Jong Un," *Korea JoongAng Daily*, January 8–9, 2011, 2.

North Korea watchers in Seoul see little possibility of a military coup in the foreseeable future.

But the minority opinion may warrant attention. For example, Kim Jin, a seasoned Seoul journalist who has observed the North Korean political scene for three decades, warns that the North may experience a chain of dramatic events, including bloody clashes among competing North Korean military leaders and even the assassination of Kim Jong Un in 2015 or 2016. He cites the intense psychological tension caused by the brutal execution of Chang Sŏng-t'aek, the competition for loyalty, and the conflicts of interest among top military leaders.[28] Kim Jin recalls a report by a Chinese daily in Beijing on April 8, 2014. The *Huanqiu Shibao* reported that on March 15, 2014, the North Korean regime held a secret military exercise in Pyongyang to subdue "enemy forces and the terrorists against Kim Jong Un"; he added that core KPA and SSM cadres observed the drill.[29] A *Dong-A Ilbo* report of December 4, 2014, may be read in a similar light; it reported on a rumor spreading in Pyongyang that Kim Kyŏng-ok, first vice director of the KWPOGD in charge of Kim Jong Un's physical protection, was executed in early October 2014 on the charge that he was involved in a plot to assassinate Kim Jong Un.[30]

An Uprising?

Could the DPRK experience a popular revolt? North Korea watchers believe there have been signs of discontent among North Koreans in Pyongyang. On November 2, 2010, Tokyo's *Asahi Shimbun* quoted Chinese sources who reported on a new song going around Pyongyang by word of mouth. "Three Bears"—an obvious references to Kim Il Sung, Kim Jong Il, and Kim Jong Un—included lyrics such as, "When three bears gain weight, we the people become thin and hungry."[31] On December 27, 2010, Open Radio for North Korea, an American NGO based in Washington, DC, and broadcasting from South Korea, reported that on December 11 a train carrying a birthday present for Kim Jong Un was derailed by a group of people opposed to the succession scheme.[32] In December 2010 ROK president Lee

---

28 Kim Jin, *Yich'ŏnsiponyŏn Kim Jong Un Kŭpbyŏn T'ŏjilkŏtinka?* [In 2015, will there be drastic change in Kim Jong Un's North Korea?] (Seoul: Nŭlp'um P'ŭllŏsŭ, 2015), 80–93.

29 Ibid., 103. See also *Dong-A Ilbo*, April 9, 2014, A5.

30 Chu Sŏng-ha, "Puk silsae Kim Kyŏng-ok ch'ŏhyŏngsŏl" [The rumor that the North's powerful man Kim Kyŏng-ok was executed]," *Dong-A Ilbo*, December 4, 2014, A6.

31 Quoted in *Dong-A Ilbo*, November 2, 2010, A21.

32 *Korea JoongAng Daily*, December 28, 2010, 2.

Myung-bak noted on more than one occasion that there were "some serious signs indicating instability in the North."[33] Several North Korea watchers in Seoul have stressed the sharply increasing influence of street markets, active in about eight cities or counties throughout the nation; despite intermittent intervention by authorities, these street markets are slowly mitigating the regime's power,[34] in part by expanding the prevalence of bribery of government officials by market participants.[35] Watchers also point out a series of defections by North Koreans from the country's elite social strata and note that "information on the South is rapidly circulating in the North thanks to the dissemination of mobile phones."[36] Brian R. Myers was alluding to this when he wrote, "Most dangerous to the [North Korean] regime is the inevitable spread of public awareness that for all their anti-Americanism, the South Koreans are happy with their own republic and do not want to live under Pyongyang's rule."[37]

However, most North Korea watchers still agree that in light of the extreme nature of North Korean society, which excludes most outside information and exerts near-total control through brainwashing, coercion, and outright force, a mass revolt in the near future is quite improbable. Hungarian scholar Balázs Szalontai aptly points out the essence of the regime's power:

> What keeps the regime in power is not so much the population's satisfaction with its performance or its unawareness of the country's problems but rather the people's acute awareness of the regime's capability and willingness to use brute force. . . . As Machiavelli said, it is far safer to be feared than loved if you cannot be both.[38]

Regime Collapse?

Could North Korea's economic decline, even ruin, since the mid-1990s—nationwide poverty, hunger, malnutrition, and, for a time, even starvation, along with energy shortages and, since late 2009, a high inflation rate—spell the end of Kim Jong Un's rule? As Andrei Lankov pointed out:

33 *Munhwa Ilbo*, December 28, 2010, 4.

34 For example, see remarks by Kim Yŏng-su, professor at Sŏgang University in Seoul, quoted in *Munhwa Ilbo*, December 28, 2010, 1.

35 Kim Byung-yeon, "Markets, Bribery, and Regime Stability in North Korea" (*EAI Asia Security Initiative Working Paper*, no. 4, Seoul, April 2010), 2.

36 Ibid.

37 Brian R. Myers, *The Cleanest Race: How North Koreans See Themselves, and Why It Matters* (Brooklyn: Melville House, 2010), 168–69.

38 Quoted from an email exchange in Bradley K. Martin, "Undercurrents of Dissent up North," *Korea JoongAng Daily*, December 17, 2010, 8.

The North Korean *nomenklatura* has demonstrated an indifference to the suf-ferings of the common people that has few parallels even in the blood-stained history of other Stalinist and Maoist regimes. . . . After the tragedy of the great famine it is clear that the death of commoners is merely seen as a price, per-haps a regrettable one, to be paid for the regime's survival.[39]

The implication is that, as long as the regime feeds the residents of the major cities, including Pyongyang, along with KPA cadres in strategically important corps, divisions, regiments and battalions, famine and even star-vation among the common people will not trigger mass revolts leading to a regime collapse. CNN's Wolf Blitzer, who visited North Korea in late December 2010, summed it up, "Outsiders have been predicting its demise for sixty years, but I didn't get the impression this country was on the verge of crumbling."[40]

While North Korea's neighbors would not object to change in the nation, China, Japan, Russia, and South Korea all want to avoid a North Korean collapse, an event that would flood those countries with starving refugees.[41] Dartmouth College professor Jennifer Lind contends that the North's "great-est deterrent lies not in its power but in its weakness." She says that "the grim specter of the potential chaos associated with the collapse of the Kim regime in the event of war has led neighboring countries to treat it with kid gloves." Lind adds that fears of civil war and a refugee crisis, and loss of control over the North's nuclear weapons, have restrained neighboring countries from unilaterally intervening in the DPRK.[42]

With dynastic family discord, a coup, a popular uprising, and regime collapse all unlikely in the short term, does it mean that the initial years of Kim Jong Un's reign are likely to be trouble-free? Not necessarily. Unfore-seen factors involving North Korean palace politics could make the con-solidation process "bumpy," in the words of Charles L. Pritchard, former special envoy for North Korea under George W. Bush.[43] At a seminar on Kim Jong Un's future, most South Korean panelists also expressed pessimistic views, pointing to the young leader's inexperience in politics and even his

39 Andrei Lankov, "Soft Landing: Opportunity or Illusion?" in *The North Korean Crisis and Beyond*, ed. Stephen J. Epstein (Wellington: Asia Studies Institute, Victoria University of Wellington, 2004), 20–21.

40 Quoted in *Dong-A Ilbo*, December 24, A 19. The quoted part was broadcast on December 22, 2010, in English.

41 Ian Bremmer, "Dangerous Insecurity: North Korea," *International Herald Tri-bune*, May 26, 2010, 6.

42 Jennifer Lind, "The Once and Future Kim: Succession and Stasis in North Ko-rea," *Foreign Affairs*, October 25, 2010, 4.

43 Quoted in *Chosun Ilbo*, January 1, 2012, A8.

lack of understanding of his own country.[44] Some Western scholars, such as John Hamre, director of the Center for Strategic and International Studies, have even asserted that Kim Jong Un's survival probability is almost zero.[45]

These views tend, however, to disregard the unique durability of the North Korean political system. Andrei Lankov aptly sums up that durability as being a product of "intense police surveillance; harsh oppression of even the slightest dissent; and maintaining a strict information blockade." However, Lankov notes, the effectiveness of these strategies have weakened in recent years—partly due to the government's lack of funds—and that "sooner or later the gradual disintegration of the police and security apparatus, and increasing access to unauthorized information, along with manifold social changes, will bring it down, probably, in a chain of dramatic, even cataclysmic events."[46]

Hopes for Reform

Will Kim Jong Un, likely to be able to remain in power for some time to come but facing a great long-term risk, choose to pursue even a limited reform policy? It certainly did not happen at the beginning of his rule, as some observers had hoped. Chinese analyst Liu Ming has argued that reform depends on a number of variables, including the effect of Chinese policy on Kim Jong Un, but in general Liu argues against too much optimism. In the end, he feels, the logic of the cult of personality will dominate; "system inertia [and] the embedded autocracy will automatically prevent [North Korea] from self-reforming."[47]

Victor Cha, a noted American North Korea watcher, writes that one reason North Korea cannot reform is that the system has eliminated any apparent domestic opposition:

> There is no symbolic figure in North Korea who is lionized . . . as a champion of democracy, through whom a reformist government could credibly signal its genuine reformist intentions. The regime in Pyongyang has deliberately and effectively rendered nameless and faceless any political dissidents or antiregime activists. If there is no individual face who can personalize the resistance, such as Aung San Suu Kyi in Burma or Kim Dae Jung in authoritarian South Korea, then there can be no magnet for international support.[48]

44 *Munhwa Ilbo*, October 13, 2010, 4.
45 Quoted in *Chosun Ilbo,* January 1, 2011, A14.
46 Ibid., 22.
47 Ibid.
48 Victor Cha, "Can North Korea Be Like Burma," *Korea JoongAng Daily*, December 13, 2011, 9.

Jean Jacques Grauhar, chairman of the EU Chamber of Commerce and Industry in Seoul, has asserted that there is little probability of a "spring in Pyongyang." Grauhar lived in Pyongyang from 1986 to 1992 as a consultant to European businesses interested in investing in North Korea and has since remained a regular visitor to the North. He sees North Korea proceeding "in accordance with the scenario [the] late Kim Jong Il prepared." While unwilling to predict Kim Jong Un's future policy direction, Grauhar is confident there will not be "big change in the North."[49] Karen Wolstenholme, the British ambassador to North Korea, is of a similar mind. In an interview in Seoul on January 18, 2012, she noted, "Kim Jong Un seems to be very confident. The transition certainly appears smooth and I think having had almost eighteen months' preparation has made it easier for Kim Jong Un."[50] Others, like Vasily Miheyev, vice director of the Moscow-based Institute of World Economy and International Relations, believe that Kim Jong Un is a "provisional leader" and his regime will not last "more than three or five years."[51]

Will Kim Jong Un forgo the North's nuclear program? Lee Soo-hyuk (Yi Su-hyŏk), South Korea's chief delegate to the Six-Party Talks from 2003 to 2005, believes that the North will never give up its nuclear ambitions, even after the dust of the succession process has completely settled. Rather than being a "bargaining chip" for economic assistance, Lee says that "possession of nuclear weapons is a matter of national security and survival for North Korea" and that the only approach that will result in the North giving up the weapons would be "to reassure North Korea that we won't demolish its national security."[52]

In the earlier-mentioned memo sent to Kim Kyŏng-hŭi, Kim Jong Il instructed that North Korea should continue developing nuclear weapons: "Retaining and developing nuclear power, long-range missiles, and biochemical weapons is the way to maintain peace on the Korean Peninsula. . . . If we are lax in national defense, we will be slaves of superpowers."[53] In February 2013, a year after Kim Jong Il's death, the North carried out its third underground nuclear test. Some North Korea watchers in the West say that the country "appears to have had success in developing a miniature,

49 *Chosun Ilbo*, December 22, 2011, A2.

50 Lee Chŏng-ŭn, "Kim Jong Un kŏnryŏk changak sunt'anhalkŏt" [Kim Jong Un's power maintenance will be smooth], *Dong-A Ilbo*, January 19, 2012, A6.

51 Yi Yong-su, "Kim Jong Un Chŏngkwon Sam-O Nyŏn Mot Kalkŏt" [The longevity of the Kim Jong Un regime will be three to five years], *Chosun Ilbo*, January 19, 2012, A4.

52 Kim Hee-jin, "Interview: Economic Aid Won't Tempt North to Disarm Nukes," *Korea JoongAng Daily*, December 28, 2011, 9.

53 Kim Hee-jin, "Before His Death."

light nuclear bomb capable of being loaded on top of a long-range ballistic missile."[54]

Immediately after the death of Kim Jong Il, there were a number of diplomats and scholars in the United States who recommended a new, positive approach to the North. For example, Paul B. Stares of the Council on Foreign Relations wrote that the United States should "seize the moment in North Korea."[55] Whether or not there was or is in fact any moment to be seized, remains to be determined—we still do not know to what degree son Kim Jong Un will follow in father Kim Jong Il's footsteps or strike out on a new and better road.

Initially, many hoped that Kim Jong Un's Swiss education had provided him with a different perspective than that of his father. But analyst Liu Ming has noted that simply because Kim Jong Un was educated in Switzerland may not mean that he is "genuinely imbued with Western thoughts." Instead, he may be like other dictator's children who have been educated abroad, yet once back home and in power are preoccupied with their own "regime interest and one-ruler culture."[56]

If the son does emulate the father, foreign hopes that North Korea may take a "positive approach" in its foreign policy are likely to be unrealized. Kim Jong Il's reign was characterized by extreme ruthlessness and cruelty (tokham). He did not hesitate to purge party and military cadres whom he suspected of disloyalty, even those who were former anti-Japanese guerrilla fighters or Kim Il Sung's own lieutenants, not to mention the vast number of ordinary North Koreans who he sent with their families to concentration camps or executed without trial. According to Hwang Chang-yŏp, "Kim Jong Il used to say to his lieutenants and party as well as military leaders that when any of them were to lose his confidence, he or she would become a mere lump of meat."[57]

One wonders if the execution of Chang Sŏng-t'aek means that Kim Jong Un intends on matching his father's tokham. We will have to wait and see how the history of North Korea unfolds.

54 Kim Hee-jin, "Kim's New Year's Speech Is Heated," *Korea JoongAng Daily,* January 2, 2014, 2.

55 Paul B. Stares, "Seize the Moment in North Korea," *International Herald Tribune,* December 23, 2011, 6; Robert L. Gallucci, "What to Do, and Not Do, about North Korea," *International Herald Tribune,* December 22, 2011, 8.

56 Liu, "Elite Cohesion," 5–6.

57 Hwang Chang-yŏp, *Na nŭn yŏksa ŭi chilli rŭl po'atta: Hwang Chang-yŏp hoegorok* [I saw the truth in history: Memoirs by Hwang Chang-yŏp] (Seoul: Hanul Publishing Co., 1999), 284.

Index

The authorized representative in the EU for product safety and compliance is:
Mare Nostrum Group
B.V Doelen 72
4831 GR Breda
The Netherlands

www.ingramcontent.com/pod-product-compliance
Lightning Source LLC
Chambersburg PA
CBHW020339270326
41926CB00007B/248

*9 7 8 1 9 3 1 3 6 8 3 0 8 *